D1055589

PERCY'S RELIQUES.

RELIQUES OF

Ancient English Poetry,

CONSISTING OF

OLD HEROIC BALLADS, SONGS, AND OTHER

PIECES OF OUR EARLIER POETS,

TOGETHER WITH SOME FEW

OF LATER DATE,

BY THOMAS PERCY, D.D.,

BISHOP OF DROMORE,

EDITED, WITH A GENERAL INTRODUCTION, ADDITIONAL

PREFACES, NOTES, GLOSSARY, ETC., BY

HENRY B. WHEATLEY, F.S.A.

IN THREE VOLUMES.

VOL. II.

NEW YORK

DOVER PUBLICATIONS, INC.

This Dover edition, first published in 1966, is an unabridged and unaltered republication of the work originally published by Swan Sonneschein, Lebas, & Lowrey in 1886.

The publisher is grateful to the Columbia University Libraries for making a copy of this work available for purpose of reproduction.

Library of Congress Catalog Card Number: 66-20326

Manufactured in the United States of America
Dover Publications, Inc.
180 Varick Street
New York, N. Y. 10014

CONTENTS OF VOLUME THE SECOND.

BOOK THE FIRST.

BOOK THE SECOND.

BOOK THE THIRD.

APPENDIX.

INDEX.

RELIQUES OF ANCIENT POETRY, ETC

SERIES THE SECOND.

BOOK I.

"Though some make slight of Libels, yet you may see by them how the wind sits: As, take a straw and throw it up into the air, you may see by that which way the wind is, which you shall not do by casting up a stone. More solid things do not shew the complexion of the times so well as Ballads and Libels."—Selden's *Table-Talk*.

I.

RICHARD OF ALMAIGNE,

"BALLAD made by one of the adherents to Simon de Montfort, Earl of Leicester, soon after the battle of Lewes, which was fought May 14, 1264,"
— affords a curious specimen of ancient satire, and shews that the liberty, assumed by the good people of this realm, of abusing their kings and princes at pleasure, is a privilege of very long standing.

To render this antique libel intelligible, the reader is to understand that just before the battle of Lewes, which proved so fatal to the interests of Henry III., the barons had offered his brother Richard, King of the Romans, 30,000*l.* to procure a peace upon such terms, as would have divested Henry of all his regal power, and therefore the treaty proved abortive. The consequences of that battle are well-known: the king, prince Edward his son, his brother Richard, and many of his friends, fell into the hands of their enemies: while two great barons of the king's party, John, Earl of Warren, and Hugh Bigot, the king's justiciary, had been glad to escape into France.

In the first stanza the aforesaid sum of thirty thousand pounds is alluded to, but with the usual misrepresentation of party malevolence, is asserted to have been the exorbitant demand of the king's brother.

With regard to the second stanza the reader is to note that Richard, along with the earldom of Cornwall, had the honours of Walingford and Eyre confirmed to him on his marriage with Sanchia, daughter of the Count of Provence, in 1243. Windsor Castle was the chief fortress belonging to the king, and had been garrisoned by foreigners : a circumstance which furnishes out the burthen of each stanza.

The third stanza alludes to a remarkable circumstance which happened on the day of the battle of Lewes. After the battle was lost, Richard, king of the Romans, took refuge in a windmill, which he barricaded, and maintained for some time against the barons, but in the evening was obliged to surrender. See a very full account of this in the *Chronicle of Mailros,* Oxon. 1684, p. 229.*

The fourth stanza is of obvious interpretation : Richard, who had been elected king of the Romans in 1256, and had afterwards gone over to take possession of his dignity, was in the year 1259 about to return into England, when the barons raised a popular clamour, that he was bringing with him foreigners to over-run the kingdom : upon which he was forced to dismiss almost all his followers, otherwise the barons would have opposed his landing.

In the fifth stanza the writer regrets the escape of the Earl of Warren, and in the sixth and seventh stanzas insinuates that if he and Sir Hugh Bigot once fell into the hands of their adversaries, they should never more return home ; a circumstance which fixes the date of this ballad, for, in the year 1265, both these noblemen landed in South Wales, and the royal party soon after gained the ascendant. See Holinshed, Rapin, &c.

The following is copied from a very ancient MS. in the British Museum. (Harl. MSS. 2253, fol. 58 v°.) This MS. is judged, from the peculiarities of the writing, to be not later than the time of Richard II.; *th* being everywhere expressed by the character þ ; the *y* is pointed after the Saxon manner, and the *i* hath an oblique stroke over it.

[The date of the MS. in which this ballad occurs is usually placed at an earlier period than that fixed upon by Percy. Mr. Thomas Wright, who prints it in his volume of *Political Songs of England* (Camden Society), with several other poems in French, Anglo-Norman, and Latin, on Simon de Montfort and the Barons' Wars, assigns it to the reign of Edward II. It will be seen from Percy's note to verse 44, that the last stanza was printed for the first time in the fourth edition of the *Reliques.* This is explained by the fact that these lines are written on a new folio of the MS., and must therefore have been overlooked by the original copyist.

This little poem is without rival as an early exhibition of English popular feeling in the vernacular ; and it also stands alone as the first dated English historical ballad in existence. It was probably

---

[* Robert of Gloucester wrote :
"The king of Alemaigne was in a windmulle income."]

written during the first flush of enthusiasm after the memorable battle of Lewes, because, before a year had gone by, victory had passed to the other side, and at the battle of Evesham, fought on the 4th of August, 1265, Simon, his eldest son Henry, and a host of distinguished men, fell on the fatal field. As Drayton sang :

" Great Lester here expired with Henry his brave sonne,
When many a high exploit they in that day had done."

Prince Edward, who had passed his boyhood in Henry's company and was much attached to him, personally attended his funeral.

Richard, Earl of Cornwall, brother of Henry III., was elected King of the Romans on the 13th of January, 1256-7, at Frankfort, and is styled in Latin documents *Rex Alemanniæ*. In earlier times Richard had been a leader of malecontents, and " all from the child to the old man heaped frequent blessings upon him," but Montfort (then a courtier) gained him over to the King's side, and the insurgents were in consequence dispersed.

Richard was probably not so base a man as the writer of the ballad would wish us to believe, and a good action is recorded of him which was very ill returned. He interceded for the life of De Montfort's second son Simon, when that youth surrendered to the royal party at Northampton in 1266, and he was successful in his suit. In 1271, Simon and his brother Guy assassinated Henry, Richard's son, then in the suite of Philip of France, on his return from the Holy Land, while he was at mass in the church of St. Lawrence, at Viterbo. Richard himself died in this same year at Berkhampstead, and his estates descended to his son Edmond, Earl of Cornwall.

The uncertain manner in which biographic honours are apportioned is noteworthy, and a writer in the *Quarterly Review* (vol. cxix. p. 26) very justly points out a deficiency in English literature, when he writes that Simon de Montfort V., second Earl of Leicester, " the founder of the English House of Commons, has had no biographer."[1] Mr. Freeman, however, promises to do full honour to his memory in a forthcoming volume of his history.

This is not the place to give any detailed account of De Montfort, but a few words on the great leader may be allowable, more particularly as Percy's introduction does injustice to the anti-royalist party.

Simon de Montfort, fourth son of Simon de Montfort IV., fourth

---

[1 A German has taken upon himself the duty of an Englishman, but Dr. Pauli's life of the hero has not yet been translated out of the German language.]

Comte de Montfort,[1] married Eleanor, Countess of Pembroke, the daughter of King John. She had made a vow of widowhood, and although her brother Henry III. gave her away when she was married, by one of the royal chaplains, in the king's private chapel at Westminster, 6th January, 1238, Edmund, Archbishop of Canterbury, remonstrated strongly against the marriage. It is said that when the prelate left England, he stood on a hill which commanded a view of London, and, extending his hands towards the city, pronounced a parting blessing on his country, and a curse on the countess and the offspring of her unholy union.

Events so came about that the courtier and alien became the representative leader of Englishmen, with the famous war-cry of " England for the English." The battle of Lewes placed everything in the power of Simon de Montfort, but in his prosperity many of his followers fell away from him. The last scene of the great man's life is truly pathetic. He lay at Evesham awaiting the troops which his son was to bring from Kenilworth. He did not know, however, that the garrison of that town had been surprised by Prince Edward, who had escaped from confinement. The army that marched upon Evesham bore the banners of Simon's son, but they were flying in the van of an enemy. Simon's first words, when he saw the force approach, were those of soldierly pride: " By the arm of St. James they come on well ; they learnt that order from me." Before he spoke again, however, he had realized his position, and he cried out: " May God have mercy on our souls, for our bodies are Prince Edward's." When he died liberty seemed to have been crushed out of existence, but it was not so, for his spirit lived though his body died, and the real victory was with him.

The fate of Simon de Montfort was a subject of general lamentation, but none of the songs upon it that have come down to us are in English. In an Anglo-Norman lament he is likened to Thomas of Canterbury, and described as " a precious flower." Priest and layman united in his praise, and he was revered as a saint and martyr. Prayers were said in his honour, and a hymn was sung at his shrine, beginning :

> " Salve Symon Montis-Fortis
> Totius flos militiæ
> Duras pœnas passus mortis,
> *Protector gentis Angliæ.*"

Miracles were supposed · to be worked by the power of his name,[2]

---

[1] Montfort is a small town between Paris and Chartres.
[2] See *Miracula Simonis de Montfort.* MS. Cotton. Vespas. A.

and the character of these miracles may be judged by the following samples. The "old Countess of Gloucester" had a palfrey, which was asthmatic for two years, until one day in journeying from Tewkesbury to Evesham, it drank from the earl's well and was restored to perfect health. The next instance of miraculous healing is still more remarkable. A chick, which belonged to Agnes of Selgrave, fell into a pond and was drowned. Its mistress pulled it out and commended it to "blessed Simon," whereupon it got up and walked as usual.

Simon had six children by his wife Eleanor, viz., Henry, Simon, Guy, Amauri, Richard, and Eleanor. Henry was slain with his father, but the countess and the other children escaped out of England. Simon and Guy went to Tuscany; Amauri accompanied his mother to France, was taken prisoner in 1276, and kept in confinement by Edward for a time, but set at liberty in 1280; Richard went to Bigorre, but nothing certain is known of his after career, and it is said that he settled in England under the assumed name of Wellysborne, an assertion founded on two or three deeds of doubtful authenticity.[1] Eleanor was married to Llewellyn, Prince of Wales, in 1279, Edward I. paying all the expenses of the ceremony, which was performed with great pomp.]

SITTETH alle stille, ant herkneth to me;
The kyn[g] of Alemaigne,[2] bi mi leaute,[3]
Thritti thousent pound askede he
For te make the pees[4] in the countre,
Ant so he dude more.   5
Richard, thah[5] thou be ever trichard,[6]
Tricthen[7] shalt thou never more.

---

vi., annexed to Mr. Halliwell's edition of William de Rishanger's *Chronicle of the Barons' Wars* (Camden Society), 1840.

[1] This tradition is possibly connected with the one to be found in the *Beggar's Daughter of Bethnal Green*, where the Blind Beggar is said to be Henry de Montfort, who was taken off the battlefield, blind but not dead.

[2] Germany.   [3] loyalty.   [4] peace.   [5] though.
[6] treacherous.   [7] deceive (should be *trichen*).]

Richard of Alemaigne, whil that he wes kyng,
He spende al is tresour opon swyvyng,[1]
Haveth he nout of Walingford o ferlyng,[2]   10
Let him habbe,[3] ase he brew, bale to dryng,[4]
    Maugre[5] Wyndesore.
    Richard, thah thou be ever, &c.

The kyng of Alemaigne wende do[6] ful wel,
He saisede the mulne[7] for a castel,   15
With hare[8] sharpe swerdes he grounde the stel,[9]
He wende that the sayles were mangonel[10]
    To helpe Wyndesore.
    Richard, thah thou be ever, &c.

The kyng of Alemaigne gederede ys host,   20
Makede him a castel of a mulne post,
Wende with is prude,[11] ant is muchele bost,[12]
Brohte[13] from Alemayne mony sori gost
    To store Wyndesore.
    Richard, thah thou be ever, &c.   25

By God, that is aboven ous, he dude muche synne,
That lette passen over see the erl of Warynne:
He hath robbed Engelond, the mores,[14] ant th[e] fenne,
The gold, ant the selver, and y-boren henne,[15]
    For love of Wyndesore.   30
    Richard, thah thou be ever, &c.

[[1] lechery.
[2] He has not of Wallingford one furlong. The MS. reads *oferlyng*, and Percy and Warton explain that word to mean *superior*, in opposition to underling, but it has not been met with elsewhere. Mr. Wright's reading of " one furlong " is much more in accordance with the context.
  [3] have.   [4] evil to drink.   [5] in spite of.   [6] thought to do.
  [7] he seized the mill.   [8] their.   [9] steel.
  [10] a military engine for throwing great stones.   [11] pride.
  [12] great boast.   [13] brought.   [14] moors.
  [15] bore them away hence.]

Sire Simond de Mountfort hath suore bi ẏs chẏn,
Hevede[1] he nou here the erl of Warẏn,
Shulde he never more come to is ẏn,[2]
Ne with sheld, ne with spere, ne with other gẏn,[3]   35
      To help of Wyndesore.
   Richard, thah thou be ever, &c.

Sire Simond de Montfort hath suore bi ys cop,[4]
Hevede he nou here Sire Hue de Bigot :[5]
Al[6] he shulde quite here twelfmòneth scot[7]   40
Shulde he never more with his fot pot[8]
      To helpe Wyndesore.
   Richard, thah thou be ever, &c.

Be the luef, be the loht,[9] sire Edward,
Thou shalt ride sporeles o thy lyard[10]   45
Al the ryhte way to Dovere-ward,
Shalt thou never more breke foreward ;
     Ant that reweth sore
     Edward, thou dudest as a shreward,[11]
     Forsoke thyn emes lore[12]   50
   Richard, &c.

*** This ballad will rise in its importance with the reader, when he finds that it is even believed to have occasioned a law in our statute book, viz. " Against slanderous reports or tales, to cause discord betwixt king and people." (*Westm. Primer*, c. 34, anno 3 Edw. I.)   That it had this effect is the opinion of an

---

Ver. 44. This stanza was omitted in the former editions.

[Ver. 40. Percy prints *grante here* (*i.e.* grant their), but the MS. reads *qte here* (*i.e.* quite or pay here).
  [1] had.   [2] house.   [3] engine.   [4] sworn by his head.
  [5] The Hugh Bigod here mentioned, was the cousin of Hugh Bigod, who took part with the barons, and was slain at Lewes.
  [6] although.   [7] tax or revenue.
  [8] with his foot push on. Percy prints this *sot pot*, but it is undoubtedly *fot* in the MS.   [9] whether you like it or loathe it.
  [10] ride spurless on thy grey horse.   [11] male shrew.
  [12] forsookest thy uncle's teaching. De Montfort was Prince Edward's uncle.]

eminent writer [the Hon. Daines Barrington], see *Observations upon the Statutes,* &c. 4to. 2nd edit. 1766, p. 71.

However, in the Harl. Collection may be found other satirical and defamatory rhymes of the same age, that might have their share in contributing to this first law against libels.

II.

ON THE DEATH OF K. EDWARD THE FIRST.

E have here an early attempt at elegy. Edward I. died July 7, 1307, in the 35th year of his reign, and 69th of his age. This poem appears to have been composed soon after his death. According to the modes of thinking peculiar to those times, the writer dwells more upon his devotion than his skill in government, and pays less attention to the martial and political abilities of this great monarch, in which he had no equal, than to some little weaknesses of superstition, which he had in common with all his contemporaries. The king had in the decline of life vowed an expedition to the Holy Land, but finding his end approach, he dedicated the sum of £32,000 to the maintenance of a large body of knights (140 say historians, eighty says our poet), who were to carry his heart with them into Palestine. This dying command of the king was never performed. Our poet, with the honest prejudices of an Englishman, attributes this failure to the advice of the king of France, whose daughter Isabel, the young monarch, who succeeded, immediately married. But the truth is, Edward and his destructive favourite, Piers Gaveston, spent the money upon their pleasures. To do the greater honour to the memory of his heroe, our poet puts his eloge in the mouth of the Pope, with the same poetic licence as a more modern bard would have introduced Britannia or the Genius of Europe pouring forth his praises.

This antique elegy is extracted from the same MS. volume as he preceding article; is found with the same peculiarities of writing and orthography; and tho' written at near the distance of half a century contains little or no variation of idiom : whereas the next following poem by Chaucer, which was probably written not more than fifty or sixty years after this, exhibits almost a new

language. This seems to countenance the opinion of some antiquaries, that this great poet made considerable innovations in his
mother tongue, and introduced many terms, and new modes of
speech from other languages.

[When Henry III. died, highly laudatory songs were sung in
honour of the new king, but when Edward I. died the people
were too grieved at their loss to sing the praise of his successor.
The present song is printed by Mr. Thomas Wright in his *Political
Songs of England* (Camden Society, 1839, p. 246), where he also
prints a French version, and points out that the one is clearly
translated from the other, adding that the French song was probably the original. In verse 27, Percy printed hue (*i.e.* she) with
a capital H, under the impression that it was "the name of the
person who was to preside over the business."]

ALLE, that beoth of huerte trewe,[1]
 A stounde herkneth[2] to my song
Of duel,[3] that Deth hath diht[4] us newe,
 That maketh me syke, ant sorewe among;
Of a knyht, that wes so strong,   5
 Of wham God hath don ys wille;
Me-thuncheth[5] that deth hath don us wrong,
 That he so sone shall ligge stille.[6]

Al Englond ahte[7] for te knowe
 Of wham that song is, that y synge; 10
Of Edward kyng, that lith[8] so lowe,
 Yent[9] al this world is nome con springe:[10]
Trewest mon of alle thinge,
 Ant in werre war ant wys,[11]
For him we ahte oure honden wrynge,[12] 15
 Of Christendome he ber the prys.

[[1] are of true heart. [2] for a while hearken ye. [3] grief.
[4] wrought. [5] methinketh. [6] lie still. [7] ought.
[8] lieth. [9] through. [10] his name spread abroad.
[11] in war wary and wise. [12] hands wring.]

Byfore that oure kyng was ded,
　He spek ase[1] mon that wes in care,
" Clerkes, knyhtes, barons, he sayde,
　" Y charge ou by oure sware[2],　　　　　　20
" That ye to Engelonde be trewe.
　" Y deye, y ne may lyven na more ;[3]
" Helpeth mi sone, ant crouneth him newe,
　" For he is nest to buen y-core.[4]

" Ich biqueth myn herte aryht,[5]　　　　　25
　" That hit be write at mi devys,[6]
" Over the see that hue be diht,[7]
　" With fourscore knyhtes al of prys,
" In werre that buen war ant wys,
　" Ayein the hethene for te fyhte,　　　　30
" To wynne the croiz[8] that lowe lys,
　" Myself y cholde yef[9] that y myhte."

Kyng of Fraunce, thou hevedest[10] ' sinne,'
That thou the counsail woldest fonde,[11]
To latte[12] the wille of ' Edward kyng '　　35
To wende to the holy londe :
That oure kyng hede take on honde
All Engelond to yeme ant wysse,[13]
To wenden in to the holy londe
To wynnen us heve[n]riche[14] blisse.　　　40

The messager to the pope com,
And seyde that our kynge was ded :
Ys oune hond the lettre he nom,[15]
Ywis[16] his herte was full gret :[17]

Ver. 33. sunne, MS.　Ver. 35. kyng Edward, MS.　Ver. 43. *ys*
is probably a contraction of *in hys* or *yn his*.

[[1] as.　[2] I charge you by your oath.　[3] I die, I may not
live more.　[4] next to be chosen.　[5] rightly.　[6] devise.
[7] she be sent (see Glossary).　[8] cross.　[9] I would if.
[10] hadst.　[11] try.　[12] hinder.　[13] govern and teach.
[14] heavenly.　[15] took.　[16] verily.　[17] grieved.]

The Pope him self the lettre redde,   45
  Ant spec[1] a word of gret honour.
"Alas! he seid, is Edward ded?
  "Of Christendome he ber the flour."

The Pope to is chaumbre wende,
  For dol[2] ne mihte he speke na more;   50
Ant after cardinals he sende,
  That muche couthen[3] of Cristes lore,
Bothe the lasse,[4] ant eke the more,
  Bed hem bothe rede ant synge:
Gret deol me myhte se thore,[5]   55
  Mony mon is honde wrynge.

The Pope of Peyters[6] stod at is masse
  With ful gret solempnetè,
Ther me con[7] the soule blesse:
  "Kyng Edward honoured thou be: 60
"God lene[8] thi sone come after the,
  "Bringe to ende that thou hast bygonne,
"The holy crois y-mad of tre,[9]
  "So fain thou woldest hit hav y-wonne.

"Jerusalem, thou hast i-lore[10]   65
  "The flour of al chivalrie
"Now kyng Edward liveth na more:
  "Alas! that he yet shulde deye!
"He wolde ha rered up ful heyye[11]
  "Oure banners, that bueth broht[12] to grounde;
"Wel longe we mowe clepe[13] and crie   71
  "Er we a such kyng han y-founde."

Ver. 55, 59. *Me, i.e.* Men, so in Robert of Gloucester, *passim.*

[[1] spake.   [2] grief.   [3] knew.   [4] less.
[5] great grief might be seen there.   [6] Peter's.
[7] there they began.   [8] give.   [9] cross made of wood.
[10] lost.   [11] high.   [12] are brought.
[13] very long we may call. Percy printed this incorrectly, Wel!
longe.]

Nou is Edward of Carnarvan
　King of Engelond al aplyht,[1]
God lete him ner be worse man　　　　　　　75
　Then his fader, ne lasse of myht,
To holden is pore men to ryht,
　And understonde good counsail,
Al Engelond for to wysse ant dyht ;[2]
　Of gode knyhtes darh[3] him nout fail.　　80

Thah[4] mi tonge were mad of stel,
　Ant min herte y-yote[5] of bras,
The godness myht y never telle,
　That with kyng Edward was :
Kyng, as thou art cleped[6] conquerour,　　85
　In uch[7] bataille thou hadest prys ;
God bringe thi soule to the honour,
　That ever wes, ant ever ys.

* Here follow in the original three lines more, which, as seemingly redundant, we chuse to throw to the bottom of the page, viz. :

　"That lasteth ay withouten ende,
　　Bidde we God, ant oure Ledy to thilke blisse
　Jesus us sende.　Amen."

III.

AN ORIGINAL BALLAD BY CHAUCER.

HIS little sonnet, which hath escaped all the editors of Chaucer's works, is now printed for the first time from an ancient MS. in the Pepysian Library, that contains many other poems of its venerable author. The versification is of that species, which the French call *rondeau*, very naturally Englished by our honest countrymen *round O.* Tho' so

[¹ entirely.　² to govern and order.　³ need.　⁴ though.
⁵ cast.　⁶ called.　⁷ each.]

early adopted by them, our ancestors had not the honour of
inventing it : Chaucer picked it up, along with other better things,
among the neighbouring nations. A fondness for laborious trifles
hath always prevailed in the dark ages of literature. The Greek
poets have had their wings and axes : the great father of English
poesy may therefore be pardoned one poor solitary *rondeau*.—
Geofrey Chaucer died Oct. 25, 1400.

[These verses are printed in Morris's *Aldine Edition of Chaucer*
(vol. vi. pp. 304-5), but there is no conclusive evidence that they
are really by Chaucer. Mr. Furnivall writes (*Trial Forewords*,
Chaucer Society, 1871, p. 32) :—"With the *Pity* I should like
much to class the *Roundel* . . . as one of the poet's genuine
works, though it is not assigned to him (so far as I know), by any
MS. of authority. It exactly suits the *Compleynte of Pite;* there
is nothing in it (so far as I can see), to make it not Chaucer's, and
it is of the same form as his Roundel in the *Parliament of Foules*."
Mr. Hales suggests to me that the poem may have been written by
one of Chaucer's followers, and refers to verse 260 of the *Knight's
Tale:*

"The freissche beauté sleeth me sodeynly,"

as having probably given the hint to the writer of this *rondeau*.]

I. 1.

OURE two eyn will sle me sodenly,
I may the beaute of them not sustene,
So wendeth it thorowout my herte kene.

2.

And but your words will helen hastely
My hertis wound, while that it is grene,
Youre two eyn will sle me sodenly.

3.

Upon my trouth I sey yow feithfully,
That ye ben of my liffe and deth the quene;
For with my deth the trouth shal be sene.
Youre two eyn, &c.

II. 1.

So hath youre beauty fro your herte chased
Pitee, that me n' availeth not to pleyn ;[1]
For daunger halt[2] your mercy in his cheyne.

2.

Giltless my deth thus have ye purchased ;
I sey yow soth,[3] me nedeth not to fayn :
So hath your beaute fro your herte chased.

3.

Alas, that nature hath in yow compassed
So grete beaute, that no man may atteyn
To mercy, though he sterve for the peyn.
So hath youre beaute, &c.

III. 1.

Syn I fro love escaped am so fat,
I nere thinke to ben in his prison lene ;
Syn I am fre, I counte hym not a bene.[4]

2.

He may answere, and sey this and that,
I do no fors,[5] I speak ryght as I mene :
Syn I fro love escaped am so fat.

3.

Love hath my name i-strike out of his sclat,
And he is strike out of my bokes clene :
For ever mo 'ther'* is non other mene.
Syn I fro love escaped, &c.

---

* This, MS.

[1 complain.   2 holdeth.   3 I tell you truth.
4 bean, a term of contempt.   5 I do not care.]

IV.

THE TURNAMENT OF TOTTENHAM:

OR, THE WOOEING, WINNING, AND WEDDING OF

TIBBE, THE REEV'S DAUGHTER THERE.

T does honour to the good sense of this nation, that while all Europe was captivated with the bewitching charms of chivalry and romance, two of our writers in the rudest times could see thro' the false glare that surrounded them, and discover whatever was absurd in them both. Chaucer wrote his *Rhyme of Sir Thopas* in ridicule of the latter; and in the following poem we have a humorous burlesque of the former. Without pretending to decide, whether the institution of chivalry was upon the whole useful or pernicious in the rude ages, a question that has lately employed many good writers,* it evidently encouraged a vindictive spirit, and gave such force to the custom of duelling, that there is little hope of its being abolished. This, together with the fatal consequences which often attended the diversion of the turnament, was sufficient to render it obnoxious to the graver part of mankind. Accordingly the Church early denounced its censures against it, and the State was often prevailed on to attempt its suppression. But fashion and opinion are superior to authority: and the proclamations against tilting were as little regarded in those times, as the laws against duelling are in these. This did not escape the discernment of our poet, who easily perceived that inveterate opinions must be attacked by other weapons, besides proclamations and censures: he accordingly made use of the keen one of ridicule. With this view he has here introduced, with admirable humour, a parcel of clowns, imitating all the solemnities of the tourney. Here we have the regular challenge—the appointed day—the lady for the prize—the formal preparations—the display of armour—the scucheons and devices—the oaths taken on entering the lists—the various acci-

---

* See (Mr. Hurd's) *Letters on Chivalry*, 8vo. 1762, *Memoires de la Chevalerie, par M. de la Curne de Sainte-Palaye*, 1759, 2 tom. 12mo. &c.

dents of the encounter—the victor leading off the prize—and the magnificent feasting—with all the other solemn fopperies that usually attended the pompous turnament. And how acutely the sharpness of the author's humour must have been felt in those days, we may learn from what we can perceive of its keenness now, when time has so much blunted the edge of his ridicule.

The *Turnament of Tottenham* was first printed from an ancient MS. in 1631, 4to., by the Rev. William Bedwell, rector of Tottenham, who was one of the translators of the Bible. He tells us, it was written by Gilbert Pilkington, thought to have been some time parson of the same parish, and author of another piece, intitled, *Passio Domini Jesu Christi*. Bedwell, who was eminently skilled in the Oriental and other languages, appears to have been but little conversant with the ancient writers in his own, and he so little entered into the spirit of the poem he was publishing, that he contends for its being a serious narrative of a real event, and thinks it must have been written before the time of Edward III. because turnaments were prohibited in that reign. "I do verily beleeve," says he, "that this turnament was acted before this proclamation of K. Edward. For how durst any to attempt to do that, although in sport, which was so straightly forbidden, both by the civill and ecclesiasticall power? For although they fought not with lances, yet, as our authour sayth, 'It was no childrens game.' And what would have become of him, thinke you, which should have slayne another in this manner of jeasting? Would he not, trow you, have been *hang'd for it in earnest? yea, and have bene buried like a dogge?*" It is, however, well known that turnaments were in use down to the reign of Elizabeth.

In the first editions of this work, Bedwell's copy was reprinted here, with some few conjectural emendations; but as Bedwell seemed to have reduced the orthography at least, if not the phraseology, to the standard of his own time, it was with great pleasure that the Editor was informed of an ancient MS. copy preserved in the Museum (Harl. MSS. 5396), which appeared to have been transcribed in the reign of K. Hen. VI. about 1456. This obliging information the Editor owed to the friendship of Tho. Tyrwhitt, Esq., and he has chiefly followed that more authentic transcript, improved however by some readings from Bedwell's book.

[A writer in the *Gentleman's Magazine* (July, 1794, p. 613), calls attention to the fact that this ballad is "a burlesque upon the feudal custom of marrying an heiress to the knight who should vanquish all his opponents at a solemn assembly holden for the purpose."

Bedwell's MS. is now in the Cambridge public library (Ff. 5, 48), and Mr. Thomas Wright, who has printed it in a miniature volume, believes it to have been written as early as the reign of Edward II.

Bedwell was chaplain to Sir Henry Wotton in his embassy to Venice, where he is said to have assisted the celebrated Father Paul in the composition of his *History of the Council of Trent.* The following is a copy of the inscription on Bedwell's monument in the chancel of Tottenham church :—" Here lyes interred in this chancel Mr. William Bedwell, sometime vicar of this church and one of King James's translators of the Bible, and for the Easterne tongues as learned a man as most lived in these moderne times. Aged 70. Dyed May the 5th, 1632."]

F all thes kene conquerours to carpe[1] it
 were kynde;
Of fele feyytyng[2] folk ferly[3] we fynde;
The Turnament of Totenham have we in
 mynde;
It were harme sych hardynes were holden byhynde,
 In story as we rede   5
  Of Hawkyn, of Herry,
  Of Tomkyn, of Terry,
  Of them that were dughty[4]
   And stalworth[5] in dede.

It befel in Totenham on a dere[6] day,   10
Ther was mad a shurtyng[7] be the hy-way:
Theder com al the men of the contray,
Of Hyssylton,[8] of Hy-gate, and of Hakenay,
 And all the swete swynkers.[9]
  Ther hopped Hawkyn,   15
  Ther daunsed Dawkyn,
  Ther trumped Tomkyn,
   And all were trewe drynkers.

[¹ talk.   ² fierce fighting.   ³ wonder.   ⁴ doughty.
⁵ stout.   ⁶ dire or sad.   ⁷ sport.   ⁸ Islington.
⁹ labourers.]

Tyl the day was gon and evyn-song past,
That thay schuld reckyn ther scot and ther counts
      cast;   20
Perkyn the potter into the press past,
And sayd Randol the refe,[1] a doyter[2] thou hast,
    Tyb the dere:
        Therfor faine wyt wold I,[3]
        Whych of all thys bachelery   25
        Were best worthye
            To wed hur to hys fere.[4]

Upstyrt thos gadelyngys[5] wyth ther lang staves,
And sayd, Randol the refe, lo! thys lad raves;
Boldely amang us thy doyter he craves;   30
We er rycher men then he, and mor gode haves
    Of cattell and corn;
        Then sayd Perkyn, To Tybbe I have
            hyyt[6]
        That I schal be alway redy in my ryyt,
        If that it schuld be thys day sevenyyt,   35
            Or elles yet to morn.[7]

Then sayd Randolfe the refe, Ever be he waryd,[8]
That about thys carpyng lenger wold be taryd:
I wold not my doyter, that scho[9] were miscaryd,
But at hur most worschip I wold scho were maryd, 40
    Therfor a Turnament schal begynne
        Thys day sevenyyt,—
        Wyth a flayl for to fyyt:
        And 'he,' that is most of myght
            Schal brouke hur wyth wynne.[10]   45

Ver. 20.   It is not very clear in the MS. whether it should be
conts, or *conters*.

[1] bailiff.   [2] daughter.   [3] know would I.
[4] to wed her for his mate.   [5] idle fellows.
[6] promised.   [7] it be to-morrow.   [8] accursed.
[9] she.   [10] shall have possession of her with joy.]

Whoso berys¹ hym best in the turnament,
Hym schal be granted the gre² be the comon assent,
For to wynne my doyter wyth 'dughtynesse' of dent,³
And 'coppell' my brode-henne 'that' was broyt out
    of Kent :
      And my dunnyd kowe   50
          For no spens⁴ wyl I spare,
          For no cattell wyl I care,
          He schal have my gray mare,
          And my spottyd sowe.

Ther was many 'a' bold lad ther bodyes to bede :⁵ 55
Than thay toke thayr leve, and homward they yede ;⁶
And all the weke afterward graythed ther wede,⁷
Tyll it come to the day, that thay suld do ther dede.
      They armed ham⁸ in matts ;
          Thay set on ther nollys,⁹   60
          For to kepe ther pollys,¹⁰
          Gode blake bollys,¹¹
          For batryng of bats.¹²

Thay sowed tham in schepeskynnes, for thay schuld
    not brest :¹³
Ilk-on¹⁴ toke a blak hat, insted of a crest :   65
'A basket or a panyer before on ther brest,'
And a flayle in ther hande ; for to fyght prest,¹⁵
      Furth gon thay fare :¹⁶
          Ther was kyd¹⁷ mekyl fors,¹⁸
          Who schuld best fend hys cors :¹⁹   70
          He that had no gode hors,
          He gat hym a mare.

Ver. 48. Dozty, MS. V. 49. coppeld. We still use the phrase
"a copple-crowned hen." V. 57. gayed, *PC.* V. 66 is wanting
in MS. and supplied from *PC.* V. 72. He borrowed him, *PC.*

[¹ beareth.   ² prize.   ³ blow.   ⁴ expense.   ⁵ bid or offer.
⁶ went.   ⁷ made ready their clothing.   ⁸ them.   ⁹ heads.
¹⁰ polls.   ¹¹ bowls.   ¹² cudgels.   ¹³ burst.   ¹⁴ each one.
¹⁵ ready.   ¹⁶ they began to go forth.   ¹⁷ shown.
¹⁸ much strength.   ¹⁹ best defend his body.]

Sych another gadryng[1] have I not sene oft,
When all the gret company com rydand to the croft :[2]
Tyb on a gray mare was set up on loft　　　　75
On a sek ful of fedyrs,[3] for scho schuld syt soft,
　　　And led 'till the gap.'
　　　　　　For cryeng of the men
　　　　　　Forther wold not Tyb then,
　　　　　　Tyl scho had hur brode hen　　　80
　　　　　　Set in hur Lap.

A gay gyrdyl Tyb had on, borowed for the nonys,[4]
And a garland on hur hed ful of rounde bonys,[5]
And a broche on hur brest ful of 'sapphyre' stonys,
Wyth the holy-rode tokenyng,[6] was wrotyn[7] for the
　　　nonys ;　　　　85
　　　For no 'spendings' thay had spared.
　　　　　　When joly Gyb saw hur thare,
　　　　　　He gyrd so hys gray mare,
　　　　　　'That scho lete a fowkin'[8] fare
　　　　　　At the rereward.　　　90

I wow to God, quoth Herry, I schal not lefe behynde,
May I mete wyth Bernard on Bayard the blynde,
Ich man kepe hym out of my wynde,
For whatsoever that he be, before me I fynde,

Ver. 76. The MS. had once *sedys*, *i.e.* seeds, which appears to
have been altered to *fedyrs*, or feathers.　　Bedwell's copy has
Senvy, *i.e.* Mustard-seed.　V. 77. and led hur to cap, MS.　V. 83.
Bedwell's *PC.* has "Ruel-Bones."　V. 84. safer stones, MS.　V.
85. *wrotyn*, *i.e.* wrought.　*PC.* reads, written.　V. 86. No catel
(perhaps chatel) they had spared, MS.　V. 89. Then . . .
faucon, MS.

[[1] gathering.　　　　　　[2] riding to the inclosure.
[3] sackfull of feathers.　　[4] nonce or occasion.
[5] Chaucer uses the expression "rowel boon" in his *Tale of
Sir Thopas*, which is explained as *round bone*.　　[6] token.
[7] wrought.　　　　　　[8] *crepitus ventris*.]

I wot I schall hym greve. 95
    Wele sayd, quoth Hawkyn.
    And I wow, quoth Dawkyn,
    May I mete wyth Tomkyn,
      Hys flayle I schal hym reve.[1]

I make a vow, quoth Hud, Tyb, son schal thou se, 100
Whych of all thys bachelery 'granted' is the gre :
I schal scomfet[2] thaym all, for the love of the ;
In what place so I come thay schal have dout[3] of me,
    Myn armes ar so clere :
      I bere a reddyl,[4] and a rake, 105
      Poudred wyth a brenand drake,[5]
      And three cantells[6] of a cake
        In ycha[7] cornere.

I vow to God, quoth Hawkyn, yf ' I ' have the gowt,[8]
Al that I fynde in the felde 'thrustand' here aboute, 110
Have I twyes or thryes redyn thurgh the route,
In ycha stede ther thay[9] me se, of me thay schal have
    doute,
    When I begyn to play.
      I make avowe that I ne schall,
      But yf Tybbe wyl me call,[10] 115
      Or I be thryes don fall,[11]
        Ryyt onys[12] com away.

Then sayd Terry, and swore be hys crede ;
Saw thou never yong boy forther hys body bede,[13]
For when thay fyyt fastest and most ar in drede, 120
I schall take Tyb by the hand, and hur away lede :

Ver. 101. grant, MS. V. 109. yf he have, MS. V. 110. the
MS. literally has *th*^r. *sand*, here.

[[1] deprive.   [2] discomfit.   [3] fear.   [4] riddle or sieve.
[5] sprinkled over with firebrands.   [6] pieces.   [7] each.
[8] though I have the gout.   [9] in each place where they.
[10] unless Tib will call me.   [11] ere I be thrice made to
[12] even once.   [13] engage.]

I am armed at the full ;
 In myn armys I bere wele
 A doy trogh,[1] and a pele,[2]
 A sadyll wythout a panell,   125
  Wyth a fles of woll.[3]

I make a vow, quoth Dudman, and swor be the stra,
Whyls me ys left my ' mare,' thou gets hurr not swa ;[4]
For scho ys wele schapen, and liyt as the rae,[5]
Ther is no capul[6] in thys myle befor hur schal ga ;[7] 130
 Sche wul ne noyt begyle :
  Sche wyl me bere, I dar say,
  On a lang somerys day,
  Fro Hyssylton to Hakenay,
   Noyt other half myle.   135

I make a vow, quoth Perkyn, thow speks of cold rost,
I schal wyrch ' wyselyer '[8] withouten any bost :
Five of the best capulys, that ar in thys ost,
I wot I schal thaym wynne, and bryng thaym to my
 cost,
 And here I grant thaym Tybbe.   140
  Wele boyes here ys he,
  That wyl fyyt, and not fle,
  For I am in my jolyte,
   Wyth so forth, Gybbe.

When thay had ther vowes made, furth can thay
 hie,   145
Wyth flayles, and hornes, and trumpes mad of tre :
Ther were all the bachelerys of that contre ;
Thay were dyyt[9] in aray, as thaymselfes wold be :

Ver. 137. fwyselier, MS. V. 128. merth, MS. V. 146. flailes
and harnisse, *PC*.

[[1] dough trough. [2] a baker's long-handled shovel.
[3] fleece of wool. [4] so. [5] roe. [6] horse.
[7] go. [8] work more wisely. [9] dressed.]

Thayr baners were ful bryyt
  Of an old rotten fell ;[1]   150
  The cheveron of a plow-mell ;[2]
  And the schadow of a bell,
    Poudred wyth the mone lyyt.[3]

I wot yt 'was' no chylder[4] game, whan thay togedyr
    met,
When icha freke[5] in the feld on hys feloy[6] bet,   155
And layd on styfly, for nothyng wold thay let,
And foght ferly[7] fast, tyll ther horses swet,
    And few wordys spoken.
      Ther were flayles al to slatred,[8]
      Ther were scheldys al to flatred,   160
      Bollys and dysches al to schatred,
        And many hedys brokyn

There was clynkyng of cart-sadellys, & clatteryng of
    cannes ;
Of fele frekys[9] in the feld brokyn were their fannes ;
Of sum were the hedys brokyn, of sum the brayn-
    pannes,[10]   165
And yll were thay besene,[11] or thay went thanns,
  Wyth swyppyng of swepyls :[12]
      Thay were so wery for-foght,[13]
      Thay myyt not fyyt mare oloft,[14]
      But creped about in the 'croft,'   170
        As thay were croked crepyls.

Ver. 151. The chiefe, *PC.* V. 154. yt ys, MS. V. 163. The
boyes were, MS. V. 170. creped then about in the croft, MS.

[[1] hide.
[2] a small wooden hammer occasionally fixed to the plough.
[3] moonlight.   [4] child's.   [5] man.   [6] fellow.
[7] wonderfully.   [8] splintered.   [9] many men.   [10] skulls.
[11] dressed.   [12] striking fast of the staffs of the flails.
[13] over-fought.   [14] on horseback.]

Perkyn was so wery, that he began to loute ;[1]
Help, Hud, I am ded in thys ylk rowte :
An hors for forty pens, a gode and a stoute!
That I may lyytly come of my noye[2] oute,   175
  For no cost wyl I spare.
        He styrt up as a snayle,
        And hent[3] a capul be the tayle,
        And 'reft' Dawkin hys flayle,
          And wan there a mare.   180

Perkyn wan five, and Hud wan twa :
Glad and blythe thay ware, that they had done sa ;
Thay wold have tham to Tyb, and present hur with
  tha :[4]
The Capulls were so wery, that thay myyt not ga,
  But styl gon thay stond.   185
        Alas! quoth Hudde, my joye I lese ;[5]
        Mee had lever then a ston of chese,
        That dere Tyb had al these,
          And wyst it were my sond.[6]

Perkyn turnyd hym about in that ych thrang,   190
Among thos wery boyes he wrest and he wrang ;
He threw tham doun to the erth, and thrast tham
  amang,
When he saw Tyrry away wyth Tyb fang,[7]
  And after hym ran ;
        Off his horse he hym drogh,[8]   195
        And gaf hym of hys flayl inogh :
        We te he! quoth Tyb, and lugh,
          Ye er a dughty man.

Ver. 179. razt, MS.   V. 185. stand, MS.   V. 189. sand, MS.
V. 190. the *PC*. reads, ilk throng.

[[1] stoop.   [2] hurt.   [3] laid hold of.   [4] them.
[5] lose.   [6] knew it were my sending.   [7] make off.
[8] drew.]

' Thus' thay tugged, and rugged, tyl yt was nere nyyt:
All the wyves of Tottenham came to se that syyt 200
Wyth wyspes, and kexis,[1] and ryschys[2] there lyyt,
To fetch hom ther husbandes, that were tham trouth
     plyyt;
    And sum bróyt gret harwos,[3]
      Ther husbandes hom to fetch,
      Sum on dores, and sum on hech,[4]   205
      Sum on hyrdyllys, and som on crech,[5]
      And sum on whele-barows.

Thay gaderyd Perkyn about, ' on ' everych syde,
And grant hym ther ' the gre,' the more was hys
     pryde :
Tyb and he, wyth gret 'mirth,' homward con thay ryde,
And were al nyyt togedyr, tyl the morn tyde ; 211
    And thay ' to church went : '
      So wele hys nedys he has sped,
      That dere Tyb he ' hath ' wed ;
      The prayse-folk,[6] that hur led,   215
      Were of the Turnament.

To that ylk fest com many for the nones ;
Some come hyphalte,[7] and some trippand 'thither'
    on the stonys ;
Sum a staf in hys hand, and sum two at onys ;
Of sum where the hedes broken, of some the schulder
    bonys :   220

Ver. 199. Thys, MS. V. 204. hom for to fetch, MS. V. 208.
about everych side, MS. V. 209. the gre, is wanting in MS.
V. 210. mothe, MS. V. 212. and thay ifere assent, MS. V. 214.
had wed, MS. V. 215. The cheefemen, *PC.* V. 218. trippand
on, MS.

[[1] elder sticks used for candles.   [2] rushes.   [3] harrows.
[4] half door of a cottage.   [5] crutch.   [6] singing men and
women.   [7] lame in the hip.]

With sorrow come thay thedyr.
    Wo was Hawkyn, wo was Herry,
    Wo was Tomkyn, wo was Terry,
    And so was all the bachelary,
       When thay met togedyr.   225

*At that fest thay wer servyd with a ryche aray,
Every fyve & fyve had a cokenay;[1]
And so thay sat in jolyte al the lung day;
And at the last thay went to bed with ful gret deray :[2]
    Mekyl myrth was them among ;   230
      In every corner of the hous
      Was melody delycyous
      For to here precyus
        Of six menys song.†

---

* In the former impressions this concluding stanza was only given from Bedwell's printed edition, but it is here copied from the old MS. wherein it has been since found separated from the rest of the poem, by several pages of a money account, and other heterogeneous matter.

† Six-men's song, *i.e.* a song for six voices. So Shakespeare uses three-man song-men, in his *Winter's Tale,* act iii. sc. 3, to denote men that could sing catches composed for three voices. Of this sort are Weelkes's madrigals mentioned below, book ii. song 9. So again Shakespeare has three-men beetle ; *i.e.* a beetle or rammer worked by three men, 2 *Hen. IV.* act i. sc. 3.

[1 a lean chicken.   2 confusion.]

V.

FOR THE VICTORY AT AGINCOURT.

THAT our plain and martial ancestors could wield their swords much better than their pens, will appear from the following homely rhymes, which were drawn up by some poet laureat of those days to celebrate the immortal victory gained at Agincourt, Oct. 25, 1415. This song or hymn is given meerly as a curiosity, and is printed from a MS. copy in the Pepys collection, vol. i. folio. It is there accompanied with the musical notes, which are copied on the opposite page.

[When the news of this great victory arrived in England, the people "were literally mad with joy and triumph," and although Henry V. on his entrance into London after the battle, commanded that no " ditties should be made and sung by minstrels or others" in praise of Agincourt, " for that he would whollie have the praise and thankes altogether given to God," several songs have come down to us on this soul-inspiring theme. Besides the present ballad there are, 1. *Agincourte Battell*, beginning—

"A councell brave our King did hold,"

in the Percy Folio MS. (see Hales and Furnivall's edition, vol. ii. p. 166).

2. *Agincourt, or the English Bowman's Glory*, a spirited ballad quoted in Heywood's *King Edward IV.*, the first stanza of which is as follows—

" Agincourt, Agincourt !
Know ye not Agincourt?
Where English slue and hurt
    All their French foemen?
With our pikes and bills brown,
How the French were beat downe,
    Shot by our bowman."

3. *King Henry V., his Conquest of France*, commencing—

"As our King lay musing on his bed."

4. *The Cambro-Briton's Ballad of Agincourt*, by Michael Drayton.

Besides these ballads there are a poem attributed to Lydgate, and Drayton's *Battaile of Agincourt.* For further information on the subject the reader should see Sir Nicholas Harris Nicolas's *History* of the Battle, and Hales and Furnivall's edition of the Percy Folio MS. (vol. ii. pp. 158, 595).

Dr. Rimbault describes the music attached to the present ballad " as the first English regular composition of which we have any remains."]

Deo gratias Anglia redde pro victoria!

WRE kynge went forth to Normandy,
With grace and myyt of chivalry;
The God for hym wrouyt marvelously,
Wherefore Englonde may calle, and cry　5
　　　Deo gratias:
Deo gratias Anglia redde pro victoria.

He sette a sege, the sothe for to say,
To Harflue[1] toune with ryal aray;
That toune he wan, and made a fray,　　　10
That Fraunce shall rywe tyl domes day.
　　　Deo gratias, &c.

Then went owre kynge, with alle his oste,
Thorowe Fraunce for all the Frenshe boste;
He spared 'for' drede of leste, ne most,　15
Tyl he come to Agincourt coste.[2]
　　　Deo gratias, &c.

Than for sothe that knyyt comely
In Agincourt feld he fauyt manly,
Thorow grace of God most myyty　　　20
He had bothe the felde, and the victory.
　　　Deo gratias, &c.

[1 Harfleur.　　　　　2 region.]

Ther dukys, and erlys, lorde and barone,
Were take, and slayne, and that wel sone,
And some were ledde in to Lundone   25
With joye, and merthe, and grete renone.
             Deo gratias, &c.

Now gracious God he save owre kynge,
His peple, and all his wel wyllynge,
Gef him gode lyfe, and gode endynge,   30
That we with merth mowe savely synge
             Deo gratias :
Deo gratias Anglia redde pro victoria.

VI.

THE NOT-BROWNE MAYD.

THE sentimental beauties of this ancient ballad have always recommended it to readers of taste, notwithstanding the rust of antiquity which obscures the style and expression. Indeed if it had no other merit than the having afforded the groundwork to Prior's *Henry and Emma*, this ought to preserve it from oblivion. That we are able to give it in so correct a manner, is owing to the great care and exactness of the accurate editor of the *Prolusions*, 8vo. 1760 ; who has formed the text from two copies found in two different editions of Arnolde's *Chronicle*, a book supposed to be first printed about 1521. From the copy in the *Prolusions* the following is printed, with a few additional improvements gathered from another edition of Arnolde's book* preserved in the public library at Cambridge. All the various readings of this copy will be found here, either

---

* This (which my friend Mr. Farmer supposes to be the first edition) is in folio ; the folios are numbered at the bottom of the leaf, the song begins at folio 75. The poem has since been collated with a very fine copy that was in the collection of the late James West, Esq. ; the readings extracted thence are denoted thus, " Mr. W."

received into the text, or noted in the margin.   The references to
the *Prolusions* will shew where they occur.   In our ancient folio
MS.* described in the preface, is a very corrupt and defective copy
of this ballad, which yet afforded a great improvement in one
passage. See v. 310.

It has been a much easier task to settle the text of this poem,
than to ascertain its date.   The ballad of the *Nutbrowne Mayd*
was first revived in *The Muses Mercury* for June, 1707, 4to. being
prefaced with a little *Essay on the old English Poets and Poetry;*
in which this poem is concluded to be "near 300 years old," upon
reasons which, though they appear inconclusive to us now, were
sufficient to determine Prior, who there first met with it.   However, this opinion had the approbation of the learned Wanley, an
excellent judge of ancient books.   For that whatever related to
the reprinting of this old piece was referred to Wanley, appears
from two letters of Prior's preserved in the British Museum (Harl.
MSS. No. 3777).   The editor of the *Prolusions* thinks it cannot
be older than the year 1500, because, in Sir Thomas More's tale
of *The Serjeant*, &c., which was written about that time, there
appears a sameness of rhythmus and orthography, and a very near
affinity of words and phrases with those of this ballad.   But this
reasoning is not conclusive, for if Sir Thomas More made this
ballad his model, as is very likely, that will account for the sameness of measure, and in some respect for that of words and phrases,
even tho' this had been written long before ; and as for the orthography, it is well known that the old printers reduced that of
most books to the standard of their own times.   Indeed it is
hardly probable that an antiquary like Arnolde would have inserted it among his historical collections, if it had been then a
modern piece ; at least he would have been apt to have named its
author.   But to shew how little can be inferred from a resemblance
of rhythmus or style, the Editor of these volumes has in his ancient
folio MS. a poem on the victory of Flodden-field, written in the
same numbers, with the same alliterations, and in orthography,
phraseology, and style nearly resembling the *Visions of Pierce
Plowman*, which are yet known to have been composed above 160
years before that battle.   As this poem is a great curiosity, we
shall give a few of the introductory lines :

> "Grant gracious God, grant me this time,
> That I may say, or I cease, thy selven to please ;
> And Mary his mother, that maketh all this world ;
> And all the seemlie saints, that sitten in heaven ;

[* Hales and Furnivall's edition, vol. iii. p. 174.]

> I will carpe of kings, that conquered full wide,
> That dwelled in this land, that was alyes noble;
> Henry the seaventh, that soveraigne lord," &c.*

With regard to the date of the following ballad, we have taken a middle course, neither placed it so high as Wanley and Prior, nor quite so low as the editor of the *Prolusions;* we should have followed the latter in dividing every other line into two, but that the whole would then have taken up more room than could be allowed it in this volume.

[The edition of Richard Arnold's *Chronicle* (1521) mentioned above, is the second; and the first, which is undated, was printed at Antwerp in 1502. This edition is described in Brydges' *Censura Literaria* (vol. vi. p. 114), where the *Nut-Brown Maid* is printed. A copy from the Balliol MS. 354, of about the same date, is printed in Percy's folio manuscript, ed. Hales and Furnivall, vol. iii. p. 174. Warton will not allow that the poem was written before the beginning of the sixteenth century, but as Percy says, it is highly improbable that an antiquary would insert a modern piece in his miscellany of curiosities.

Percy has inserted the following note in his folio MS.: "From the concluding words of this last stanza—

> ['but men wold that men shold
> be kind to them eche one,
> yett I had rather, god to obay
> and serve but him alone']

it should seem that the author was a woman."

Mr. Skeat remarks that the part of the fourth stanza before the woman speaks, and the first two verses, are still more conclusive on this point. On the other side it is noticeable that the author speaks as a man at line 353:

> ". . . that we may
> To them be comfortable ; '

but this may only be a blind.

Few readers will agree with Percy's estimate of Prior's poem, and *Henry and Emma* is now only remembered because of its connection with the *Nut-Brown Maid.*

Warton justly points out how the simplicity of the original is decorated, dilated, and consequently spoilt by Prior, who crowds his verses with zephyrs, Chloe, Mars, the Cyprian deity, &c. Such lay figures as these are quite out of keeping with the realities of this most exquisite poem.

[* Folio Manuscript, ed. Hales and Furnivall, vol. i. p. 212.]

One instance of Prior's inability to appreciate the beauties of his original will be sufficient.   The tender allusion at v. 232-3 :

> " O my swete mother, before all other
> For you I have most drede,"

followed by the reflection :

> " But nowe adue !   I must ensue
> Where fortune doth me lede,"

is entirely omitted by the later poet, who changes

> " To shorte my here, a bowe to bere,
> To shote in tyme of nede,"

into

> " Wanting the scissors, with these hands I'll tear
> (If that obstructs my flight) this load of hair."

The *Nut-Brown Maid* has always been highly popular (a proof of the good taste of the people), and in consequence it figures in Captain Cox's collection described by Laneham.   Another proof of its popularity is the existence of various parodies, one of which is of very early date.

It was a common practice in the sixteenth century to turn ordinary ballads into religious songs.   *The New Nutbrowne Maid*, printed by John Skot about 1520, reprinted by George Isted in 1820 for the Roxburghe Club, and again reprinted by Dr. Rimbault for the Percy Society (vol. iv.), 1842, is an instance of this practice.   It is a close parody of the original, and purports to be "upon the passion of Cryste."   The *he* and *she* are changed to *Maria the mayde* and *Jesus*.

Another version is given in the Percy folio MS. (ed. Hales and Furnivall, vol. ii. p. 334), which is entitled *A Jigge*.

The incidents are vulgarized, "but," Mr. Hales observes, " the beauty of the original is too great to be altogether destroyed, however rude the hands that handle it.   Something of the charm of the *Nut Brown Maid* lingers around this *Jig*."]

BE it ryght, or wrong, these men among[1]
   On women do complayne; *
Affyrmynge this, how that it is
   A labour spent in vayne,
To love them wele; for never a dele[2]   5
   They love a man agayne:
For late a man do what he can,
   Theyr favour to attayne,
Yet, yf a newe do them persue,
   Theyr first true lover than   10
Laboureth for nought; for from her[3] thought
   He is a banyshed man.

I say nat nay, but that all day
   It is bothe writ and sayd
That womans faith is, as who sayth,   15
   All utterly decayd;
But, neverthelesse, ryght good wytnèsse
   In this case might be layd,
That they love true, and continùe:
   Recorde the Not-browne Mayde: 20
Which, when her love came, her to prove,
   To her to make his mone,
Wolde nat depart; for in her hart
   She loved but hym alone.

---

* My friend Mr. Farmer proposes to read the first lines thus as a Latinism:
> "Be it right or wrong, 'tis men among,
>   On women to complayne."

Ver. 2. Woman, *Prolusions* and Mr. West's copy. V. 11. her, *i.e.* their.

[1 at intervals, sometimes.   2 not a bit.   3 their.]

Than betwaine us late us dyscus   25
  What was all the manere
Betwayne them two : we wyll also
  Tell all the payne, and fere,[1]
That she was in.   Nowe I begyn,
  So that ye me answère ;   30
Wherfore, all ye, that present be
  I pray you, gyve an ere.
" I am the knyght ; I come by nyght,
  As secret as I can ;
Sayinge, Alas ! thus standeth the case, 35
  I am a banyshed man."

And I your wyll for to fulfyll
  In this wyll nat refuse ;
Trustyng to shewe, in wordès fewe,
  That men have an yll use   40
(To theyr own shame) women to blame,
  And causelesse them accuse :
Therfore to you I answere nowe,
  All women to excuse,—

                SHE.*

Myne owne hart dere, with you what chere ? 45
  I pray you, tell anone ;
For, in my mynde, of all mankynde
  I love but you alone.

                HE.

It standeth so ; a dede is do[2]
  Wherof grete harme shall growe :   50
My destiny is for to dy
  A shamefull deth, I trowe ;

[* Percy printed the " She " at the beginning of this stanza.
[1] pain and fear.   In the Balliol MS. 354, the reading is *in-fere*
(or in company with her lover).   [2] done.]

Or elles to fle : the one must be.
    None other way I knowe,
But to withdrawe as an outlawe,   55
    And take me to my bowe.
Wherfore, adue, my owne hart true!
    None other rede I can :[1]
For I must to the grene wode go,
    Alone, a banyshed man.   60

She.

O lord, what is thys worldys blysse,
    That changeth as the mone!
My somers day in lusty may
    Is derked[2] before the none.
I here you say, farewell : Nay, nay,   65
    We dèpart[3] nat so sone.
Why say ye so ? wheder[4] wyll ye go ?
    Alas ! what have ye done ?
All my welfâre to sorrowe and care
    Sholde chaunge, yf ye were gone ;   70
For, in my mynde, of all mankynde
    I love but you alone.

He.

I can beleve, it shall you greve,
    And somewhat you dystrayne ;[5]
But, aftyrwarde, your paynes harde   75
    Within a day or twayne
Shall sone aslake ;[6] and ye shall take
    Comfort to you agayne.
Why sholde ye ought ? for, to make thought,
    Your labour were in vayne.   80

Ver. 63. The somers, *Prol.*

[[1] advice I know.   [2] darkened.   [3] separate.
[4] whither.   [5] afflict.   [6] abate.]

And thus I do; and pray you to,
  As hartely,[1] as I can;
For I must to the grene wode go,
  Alone, a banyshed man.

SHE.

Now, syth that ye have shewed to me   85
  The secret of your mynde,
I shall be playne to you agayne,
  Lyke as ye shall me fynde.
Syth it is so, that ye wyll go,
  I wolle not leve[2] behynde;   90
Shall never be sayd, the Not-browne Mayd
  Was to her love unkynde:
Make you redy, for so am I,
  Allthough it were anone;
For, in my mynde, of all mankynde   95
  I love but you alone.

HE.

Yet I you rede[3] to take good hede
  What men wyll thynke, and say:
Of yonge, and olde it shall be tolde,
  That ye be gone away,   100
Your wanton wyll for to fulfill,
  In grene wode you to play;
And that ye myght from your delyght
  No lenger make delay.
Rather than ye sholde thus for me   105
  Be called an yll womàn,
Yet wolde I to the grene wode go,
  Alone, a banyshed man.

Ver. 91. Shall it never, *Prol.* and Mr. W.   V. 94. Althought,
Mr. W.

[[1] earnestly.   [2] remain.   [3] advise.]

SHE.

Though it be songe of old and yonge,
  That I sholde be to blame,   110
Theyrs be the charge, that speke so large
  In hurtynge of my name:
For I wyll prove, that faythfulle love
  It is devoyd of shame;
In your dystresse, and hevynesse,   115
  To part with you, the same:
And sure all tho,[1] that do not so,
  True lovers are they none;
For, in my mynde, of all mankynde
  I love but you alone.   120

HE.

I counceyle you, remember howe,
  It is no maydens lawe,
Nothynge to dout, but to renne[2] out
  To wode with an outlàwe:
For ye must there in your hand bere   125
  A bowe, redy to drawe;
And, as a thefe, thus must you lyve,
  Ever in drede and awe;
Wherby to you grete harme myght growe:
  Yet had I lever than,[3]   130
That I had to the grene wode go,
  Alone, a banyshed man.

SHE.

I thinke nat nay, but as ye say,
  It is no maydens lore:
But love may make me for your sake,   135
  As I have sayd before

Ver. 117. To shewe all, *Prol.* and Mr. W. V. 133. I say **nat,**
Prol. and Mr. W.

[[1] those.   [2] run.   [3] rather then.]

To come on fote, to hunt, and shote
    To gete us mete in store;
For so that I your company
    May have, I aske no more: 140
From which to part, it maketh my hart
    As colde as ony stone;
For, in my mynde, of all mankynde
    I love but you alone.

HE.

For an outlawe this is the lawe,   145
    That men hym take and bynde;
Without pytè, hanged to be,
    And waver with the wynde.
If I had nede, (as God forbede!)
    What rescous[1] coude ye fynde?   150
Forsoth, I trowe, ye and your bowe
    For fere wolde drawe behynde:
And no mervayle; for lytell avayle
    Were in your counceyle than:
Wherfore I wyll to the grene wode go,   155
    Alone, a banyshed man.

SHE.

Ryght wele knowe ye, that women be
    But feble for to fyght;
No womanhede it is indede
    To be bolde as a knyght: 160
Yet, in such fere yf that ye were
    With enemyes day or nyght,
I wolde withstande, with bowe in hande,
    To greve them as I myght,

Ver. 138. and store, Camb. copy.   V. 150. succours, *Prol.*
and Mr. W.   V. 162. and night, Camb. copy.   V. 164. to helpe
ye with my myght, *Prol.* and Mr. W.

[1 rescue.]

And you to save; as women have   165
   From deth 'men' many one :
For, in my mynde, of all mankynde
   I love but you alone.

HE.

Yet take good hede; for ever I drede
   That ye coude nat sustayne   170
The thornie wayes, the depe valèies,
   The snowe, the frost, the rayne,
The colde, the hete : for dry, or wete,
   We must lodge on the playne;
And, us above, none other rofe   175
   But a brake bush, or twayne :
Which sone sholde greve you, I beleve;
   And ye wolde gladly than
That I had to the grene wode go,
   Alone, a banyshed man.   180

SHE.

Syth I have here bene partynère
   With you of joy and blysse,
I must also parte of your wo
   Endure, as reson is :
Yet am I sure of one plesùre ;   185
   And, shortely, it is this:
That, where ye be, me semeth, pardè,
   I coude nat fare amysse.
Without more speche, I you beseche
   That we were sone agone ;   190
For, in my mynde, of all mankynde
   I love but you alone.

Ver. 172. frost and rayne, Mr. W.   V. 174. Ye must, *Prol.*
V. 190. shortley gone, *Prol.* and Mr. W.

He.

If ye go thyder, ye must consyder,
  Whan ye have lust to dyne,
There shall no mete be for you gete,   195
  Nor drinke, bere, ale, ne wyne.
No shetés clene, to lye betwene,
  Made of threde and twyne;
None other house, but leves and bowes,
  To cover your hed and myne,   200
O myne harte swete, this evyll dyéte
  Sholde make you pale and wan;
Wherfore I wyll to the grene wode go,
  Alone, a banyshed man.

She.

Amonge the wylde dere, such an archère,   205
  As men say that ye be,
Ne may nat fayle of good vitayle,
  Where is so grete plentè:
And water clere of the ryvére
  Shall be full swete to me;   210
With which in hele[1] I shall ryght wele
  Endure, as ye shall see;
And, or we go, a bedde or two
  I can provyde anone;
For, in my mynde, of all mankynde   215
  I love but you alone.

He.

Lo yet, before, ye must do more,
  Yf ye wyll go with me:
As cut your here up by your ere,[2]
  Your kyrtel by the kne;   220

Ver. 196. Neyther bere, *Prol.* and Mr. W. V. 201. Lo myn,
Mr. W. V. 207. May ye nat fayle, *Prol.* *Ib.* May nat fayle, Mr.
W. V. 219. above your ere, *Prol.* V. 220. above the kne, *Prol.*
and Mr. W.

    [1 health.   2 hair up by your ear.]

With bowe in hande, for to withstande
　Your enemyes, yf nede be :
And this same nyght before day-lyght,
　To wode-warde wyll I fle.
Yf that ye wyll all this fulfill,   225
　Do it shortely as ye can ;
Els wyll I to the grene wode go,
　Alone, a banyshed man.

SHE.

I shall as nowe do more for you
　Than longeth to womanhede ;   230
To shorte my here,[1] a bowe to bere,
　To shote in tyme of nede.
O my swete mother, before all other
　For you I have most drede :
But nowe, adue ! I must ensue,[2]   235
　Where fortune doth me lede.
All this make ye : Now let us fle ;
　The day cometh fast upon ;
For, in my mynde, of all mankynde
　I love but you alone.   240

HE.

Nay, nay, nat so ; ye shall nat go,
　And I shall tell ye why,—
Your appetyght is to be lyght
　Of love, I wele espy :
For, lyke as ye have sayed to me,   245
　In lyke wyse hardely
Ye wolde answére whosoever it were,
　In way of company.

Ver. 223. the same, *Prol.* and Mr. W.

[[1] shorten my hair.   [2] follow.]

It is sayd of olde, Sone hote, sone colde;
  And so is a womàn.   250
Wherfore I to the wode wyll go,
  Alone, a banyshed man.

SHE.

Yf ye take hede, it is no nede
  Such wordes to say by me;
For oft ye prayed, and longe assayed,   255
  Or[1] I you loved, pardè :[2]
And though that I of auncestry
  A barons daughter be,
Yet have you proved howe I you loved
  A squyer of lowe degrè;   260
And ever shall, whatso befall;
  To dy therfore* anone;
For, in my mynde, of all mankynde
  I love but you alone.

HE.

A barons chylde to be begylde!   265
  It were a cursed dede;
To be felàwe with an outlawe!
  Almighty God forbede!
Yet beter were, the pore squyère
  Alone to forest yede,[3]   270
Than ye sholde say another day,
  That, by my cursed dede,
Ye were betray'd : Wherfore, good mayd,
  The best rede[4] that I can,
Is, that I to the grene wode go,   275
  Alone, a banyshed man.

Ver. 251. For I must to the grene wode go, *Prol.* and Mr. W.
V. 253. yet is, Camb. copy. Perhaps for yt is. V. 262. dy with
him, Editor's MS.

   * *i. e.* for this cause ; tho' I were to die for having loved you.

  [[1] ere.   [2] *par Dieu.*   [3] went.   [4] advice.]

SHE.

Whatever befall, I never shall
　Of this thyng you upbrayd :
But yf ye go, and leve me so,
　Than have ye me betrayd.　　　　　　　280
Remember you wele, howe that ye dele ;
　For, yf ye, as ye sayd,
Be so unkynde, to leve behynde,
　Your love, the Not-browne Mayd,
Trust me truly, that I shall dy　　　　　　285
　Sone after ye be gone ;
For, in my mynde, of all mankynde
　I love but you alone.

HE.

Yf that ye went, ye sholde repent ;
　For in the forest nowe　　　　　　　　290
I have purvayed[1] me of a mayd,
　Whom I love more than you ;
Another fayrère, than ever ye were,
　I dare it wele avowe ;
And of you bothe eche sholde be wrothe　295
　With other, as I trowe :
It were myne ese, to lyve in pese ;
　So wyll I, yf I can ;
Wherfore I to the wode wyll go,
　Alone, a banyshed man.　　　　　　　300

SHE.

Though in the wode I undyrstode
　Ye had a paramour,
All this may nought remove my thought,
　But that I wyll be your :

Ver. 278. outbrayd, *Prol.* and Mr. W.　V. 282. ye be as,
Prol. and Mr. W.　V. 283. Ye were unkynde to leve me **behynde,**
Prol. and Mr. W.

[1 provided.]

And she shall fynde me soft, and kynde,   305
 And courteys every hour;
Glad to fulfyll all that she wyll
 Commaunde me to my power :
For had ye, lo, an hundred mo,
 ' Of them I wolde be one ; '   310
For, in my mynde, of all mankynde
 I love but you alone.

HE.

Myne owne dere love, I se the prove
 That ye be kynde, and true ;
Of mayde, and wyfe, in all my lyfe,   315
 The best that ever I knewe.
Be mery and glad, be no more sad,
 The case is chaunged newe ;
For it were ruthe, that, for your truthe,
 Ye sholde have cause to rewe.   320
Be nat dismayed ; whatsoever I sayd
 To you, whan I began ;
I wyll nat to the grene wode go,
 I am no banyshed man.

SHE.

These tydings be more gladd to me,   325
 Than to be made a quene,
Yf I were sure they sholde endure :
 But it is often sene,
Whan men wyll breke promyse, they speke
 The wordés on the splene.[1]   330
Ye shape some wyle me to begyle,
 And stele from me, I wene :

Ver. 310. So the Editor's MS. All the printed copies read,
Yet wold I be that one. V. 315. of all, *Prol.* and Mr. W.
V. 325. gladder, *Prol.* and Mr. W.

[1 in haste.]

Than, were the case worse than it was,
  And I more wo-begone :
For, in my mynde, of all mankynde   335
  I love but you alone.

HE.

Ye shall nat nede further to drede ;
  I wyll nat dysparàge
You, (God defend)! syth ye descend
  Of so grete a lynàge.   340
Nowe undyrstande ; to Westmarlande,
  Which is myne herytage,
I wyll you brynge ; and with a rynge,
  By way of maryage
I wyll you take, and lady make,   345
  As shortely as I can :
Thus have you won an erlys son,
  And not a banyshed man.

AUTHOR.

Here may ye se, that women be
  In love, meke, kynde, and stable ;   350
Late[1] never man reprove them than,
  Or call them variable ;
But, rather, pray God, that we may
  To them be comfortable ;
Which sometyme proveth such, as he loveth, 355
  Yf they be charytable.
For syth men wolde that women sholde
  Be meke to them each one ;
Moche more ought they to God obey,
  And serve but hym alone.   360

Ver. 340. grete lynyage, *Prol.* and Mr. W. V. 347. Then have,
Prol. V. 348. And no banyshed, *Prol.* and Mr. W. V. 352.
This line wanting in *Prol.* and Mr. W. V. 355. proved—loved,
Prol. and Mr. W. *Ib.* as loveth, Camb. V. 357. Forsoth, *Prol.*
and Mr. W.

[1 let.]

VII.

A BALET BY THE EARL RIVERS.

HE amiable light in which the character of Anthony Widville, the gallant Earl Rivers, has been placed by the elegant author of the *Catal. of Noble Writers* [Horace Walpole], interests us in whatever fell from his pen. It is presumed, therefore, that the insertion of this little sonnet will be pardoned, tho' it should not be found to have much poetical merit. It is the only original poem known of that nobleman's ; his more voluminous works being only translations. And if we consider that it was written during his cruel confinement in Pomfret castle a short time before his execution in 1483, it gives us a fine picture of the composure and steadiness with which this stout earl beheld his approaching fate.

This ballad we owe to Rouse, a contemporary historian, who seems to have copied it from the earl's own handwriting. " In tempore," says this writer, " incarcerationis apud Pontem-fractum edidit unum *balet* in anglicis, ut mihi monstratum est, quod subsequitur sub his verbis : *Sum what musyng*, &c." Rossi, *Hist.* 8vo. 2 ed. p. 213. In Rouse the second stanza, &c. is imperfect, but the defects are here supplied from a more perfect copy printed in *Ancient Songs, from the time of King Henry III. to the Revolution,* p. 87 [by Joseph Ritson].

This little piece, which perhaps ought rather to have been printed in stanzas of eight short lines, is written in imitation of a poem of Chaucer's, that will be found in Urry's ed. 1721, p. 555, beginning thus :

> " Alone walkyng, In thought plainyng,
>   And sore sighying, All desolate.
> My remembrying Of my livyng
>   My death wishyng Bothe erly and late.
> Infortunate Is so my fate
>   That wote ye what, Out of mesure
> My life I hate ; Thus desperate
>   In such pore estate, Doe I endure," &c.*

[* See Aldine edition of *Chaucer's Poetical Works*, ed. Morris, vol. vi. p. 305. We ought, perhaps, to read " attributed to Chaucer."]

[This gallant and learned nobleman (brother of Edward
IV.'s queen), who was murdered in the forty-first year of his
age, figures as a character in Shakspere's *Richard III.*, and as a
ghost appears to warn the tyrant on the eve of the battle of Bos-
worth:

" Let me sit heavy on thy soul to-morrow,
Rivers that died at Pomfret! despair and die."]

UMWHAT musyng, And more mornyng,
    In remembring The unstydfastnes;
This world being Of such whelyng,
    Me contrarieng, What may I gesse?

I fere dowtles, Remediles,   5
    Is now to sese My wofull chaunce.
[For unkyndness, Withouten less,
    And no redress, Me doth avaunce,

With displesaunce, To my grevaunce,
    And no suraunce Of remedy.]   10
Lo in this traunce, Now in substaunce,
    Such is my dawnce, Wyllyng to dye.

Me thynkys truly, Bowndyn am I,
    And that gretly, To be content:
Seyng playnly, Fortune doth wry[1]   15
    All contrary From myn entent.

My lyff was lent Me to on intent,
    Hytt is ny[2] spent. Welcome fortune!
But I ne went Thus to be shent,[3]
    But sho[4] hit ment; Such is hur won.[5]   20

Ver. 15. That fortune, Rossi, *Hist.*   V. 19. went, *i.e.* weened.

[1 turn aside.   2 it is near.   3 abashed.
4 she.   5 wont or custom.]

VIII.

CUPID'S ASSAULT : BY LORD VAUX.

THE reader will think that infant poetry grew apace between the times of Rivers and Vaux, tho' nearly contemporaries; if the following song is the composition of that Sir Nicholas (afterwards Lord) Vaux, who was the shining ornament of the court of Henry VII., and died in the year 1523 [1524, see below].

And yet to this lord it is attributed by Puttenham in his *Art of Eng. Poesie*, 1589, 4to., a writer commonly well informed. Take the passage at large : " In this figure [Counterfait Action] the Lord Nicholas Vaux, a noble gentleman and much delighted in vulgar making, and a man otherwise of no great learning, but having herein a marvelous facilitie, made a dittie representing the Battayle and Assault of Cupide, so excellently well, as for the gallant and propre application of his fiction in every part, I cannot choose but set downe the greatest part of his ditty, for in truth it cannot be amended. *When Cupid Scaled,*" &c. p. 200. For a farther account of Nicholas, Lord Vaux, see Mr. Walpole's *Noble Authors*, vol. i.

Since this song was first printed off, reasons have occurred which incline me to believe that Lord Vaux, the poet, was not the Lord Nicholas Vaux who died in 1523, but rather a successor of his in the title. For, in the first place, it is remarkable that all the old writers mention Lord Vaux, the poet, as contemporary, or rather posterior, to Sir Thomas Wyat and the E. of Surrey, neither of which made any figure till long after the death of the first Lord Nicholas Vaux. Thus Puttenham, in his *Art of English Poesie*, 1589, in p. 48, having named Skelton, adds : "In the latter end of the same kings raigne [Henry VIII.] sprong up a new company of courtly Makers [Poets], of whom Sir Thomas Wyat th' elder, and Henry Earl of Surrey were the two chieftaines, who having travailed into Italie, and there tasted the sweet and stately measures and stile of the Italian poesie . . . greatly polished our rude and homely manner of vulgar poesie . . . In the same time, or not long after, was the Lord Nicholas Vaux, a man of much facilitie in vulgar makings."* Webbe, in his *Discourse of English*

---

* *i.e.* Compositions in English.

Poetrie, 1586, ranges them in the following order: "The E. of Surrey, the Lord Vaux, Norton, Bristow." And Gascoigne, in the place quoted in the first volume of this work [B. ii. No. 2.] mentions Lord Vaux after Surrey. Again, the stile and measure of Lord Vaux's pieces seem too refined and polished for the age of Henry VII., and rather resemble the smoothness and harmony of Surrey and Wyat, than the rude metre of Skelton and Hawes. But what puts the matter out of all doubt, in the British Museum is a copy of his poem, *I lothe that I did love* [vid. vol. i. *ubi supra*], with this title, " A dyttye or sonet made by the Lord Vaus, in the time of the noble Quene Marye, representing the image of Death." Harl. MSS. No. 1703, sec. 25.

It is evident then that Lord Vaux, the poet, was not he that flourished in the reign of Henry VII., but either his son or grandson; and yet, according to Dugdale's *Baronage*, the former was named Thomas and the latter William : but this difficulty is not great, for none of the old writers mention the Christian name of the poetic Lord Vaux,* except Puttenham; and it is more likely that he might be mistaken in that lord's name, than in the time in which he lived, who was so nearly his contemporary.

Thomas, Lord Vaux, of Harrowden, in Northamptonshire, was summoned to parliament in 1531. When he died does not appear, but he probably lived till the latter end of Queen Mary's reign, since his son William was not summoned to parliament till the last year of that reign, in 1558. This lord died in 1595. See Dugdale, vol. ii. p. 304. Upon the whole I am inclined to believe that Lord Thomas was the poet.

The following copy is printed from the first edition of Surrey's *Poems*, 1557, 4to. See another song of Lord Vaux's in the preceding volume, B. ii. No. 2.

[Percy is correct in his supposition that the poet was Thomas, second Lord Vaux, and not his father Nicholas, who died May 14th, 1524, only seventeen days after he was advanced to the peerage.]

---

* In the *Paradise of Dainty Devises*, 1596, he is called simply " Lord Vaux the elder."

HEN Cupide scaled first the fort,
    Wherein my hart lay wounded sore ;
The batry was of such a sort,
    That I must yelde or die therfore.

There sawe I Love upon the wall,   5
    How he his banner did display ;
Alarme, alarme, he gan to call :
    And bad his souldiours kepe aray.

The armes, the which that Cupide bare,
    Were pearced hartes with teares besprent,[1]   10
In silver and sable to declare
    The stedfast love, he alwayes ment.

There might you se his band all drest
    In colours like to white and blacke,
With powder and with pelletes prest   15
    To bring the fort to spoile and sacke.

Good-wyll, the maister of the shot,
    Stode in the rampire[2] brave and proude,
For spence[3] of pouder he spared not
    Assault! assault! to crye aloude.   20

There might you heare the cannons rore ;
    Eche pece discharged a lovers loke ;
Which had the power to rent, and tore
    In any place whereas they toke.

And even with the trumpettes sowne[4]   25
    The scaling ladders were up set,
And Beautie walked up and downe,
    With bow in hand, and arrowes whet.

[[1] besprinkled.   [2] rampart.   [3] expense.   [4] sound.]

Then first Desire began to scale,
　And shrouded him under ' his' targe ;[1]　　30
As one the worthiest of them all,
　And aptest for to geve the charge.

Then pushed souldiers with their pikes,
　And halberdes with handy strokes ;
The argabushe[2] in fleshe it lightes,　　35
　And duns the ayre with misty smokes.

And, as it is the souldiers use
　When shot and powder gins to want,
I hanged up my flagge of truce,
　And pleaded up for my livès grant.　　40

When Fansy thus had made her breche,
　And Beauty entred with her band,
With bagge and baggage, sely[3] wretch,
　I yelded into Beauties hand.

Then Beautie bad to blow retrete,　　45
　And every souldier to retire,
And mercy wyll'd with spede to set
　Me captive bound as prisoner.

Madame, quoth I, sith that this day
　Hath served you at all assayes,　　50
I yeld to you without delay
　Here of the fortresse all the kayes.

And sith that I have ben the marke,
　At whom you shot at with your eye ;
Nedes must you with your handy warke,　　55
　Or salve my sore, or let me die.

Ver. 30. her, ed. 1557, so ed. 1585.

[[1] shield.　[2] harquebuss, or old-fashioned musket.　[3] simple.]

IX.

SIR ALDINGAR.

HIS old fabulous legend is given from the Editor's folio MS. with conjectural emendations, and the insertion of some additional stanzas to supply and compleat the story.

It has been suggested to the Editor that the author of this poem seems to have had in his eye the story of Gunhilda, who is sometimes called Eleanor, and was married to the Emperor (here called King) Henry.

[Percy's MS. note in his folio is as follows: "Without some corrections this will not do for my *Reliques.*" Readers will be able to judge for themselves as to the relative beauties of the two, now that the original is printed at the end of Percy's amended copy. To make the interpolations more apparent, Percy's added verses are placed between brackets, and it will be seen that these contain much of the phraseology and many of the stock prettinesses of the polite ballad-monger; some of the most vivid bits of the old ballad being passed over. Percy keeps tolerably to the story, except that he makes the second messenger one of the queen's damsels instead of a man. Sir Walter Scott supposes *Sir Aldingar* to be founded upon the kindred ballad of *Sir Hugh le Blond,* but, as Professor Child says, without any reason. The story occurs in most of the literatures of Europe.]

UR king he kept a false stewàrde,
    Sir Aldingar they him call;
    [A falser steward than he was one,
        Servde not in bower nor hall.]

He wolde have layne by our comelye queene,   5
    Her deere worshippe to betraye:
Our queene she was a good womàn,
    And evermore said him naye.

Sir Aldingar was wrothe in his mind,
    With her hee was never content,   10
[Till traiterous meanes he colde devyse,]
    In a fyer to have her brent.[1]

There came a lazar[2] to the kings gate,
    A lazar both blinde and lame :
He tooke the lazar upon his backe,   15
    Him on the queenes bed has layne.

" Lye still, lazàr, wheras thou lyest,
    Looke thou goe not hence away ;
Ile make thee a whole man and a sound
    In two howers of the day." *   20

Then went him forth sir Aldingar,
    [And hyed him to our king :]
" If I might have grace, as I have space,
    [" Sad tydings I could bring."]

Say on, say on, sir Aldingar,   25
    Saye on the soothe[3] to mee.
" Our queene hath chosen a new new love,
    And shee will have none of thee.

" If shee had chosen a right good knight,
    The lesse had beene her shame ;   30
But she hath chose her a lazar man,
    A lazar both blinde and lame."

If this be true, thou Aldingar,
    The tyding thou tellest to me,
Then will I make the a rich rich knight,   35
    Rich both of golde and fee.

---

* He probably insinuates that the king should heal him by his power of touching for the king's evil.

[1 burnt.   2 leper.   3 truth.]

But if it be false, sir Aldingar,
  [As God nowe grant it bee!
Thy body, I sweare by the holye rood,]
  Shall hang on the gallows tree.   40

[He brought our king to the queenes chambèr,
  And opend to him the dore.]
A lodlye[1] love, king Harry says,
  For our queene dame Elinore !

If thou were a man, as thou art none,   45
  [Here on my sword thoust dye ;]
But a payre of new gallowes shall be built,
  And there shalt thou hang on hye.

[Forth then hyed our king, I wysse,
  And an angry man was hee ;   50
And soone he found queene Elinore,
  That bride so bright of blee.[2]]

Now God you save, our queene, madame,
  And Christ you save and see;
Heere you have chosen a newe newe love,   55
  And you will have none of mee.

If you had chosen a right good knight,
  The lesse had been your shame :
But you have chose you a lazar man,
  A lazar both blinde and lame.   60

[Therfore a fyer there shall be built,
  And brent all shalt thou bee.——]
" Now out alacke !" said our comly queene,
  "Sir Aldingar's false to mee.

Now out alacke !" sayd our comlye queene,   65
  [My heart with griefe will brast.[3]]
I had thought swevens[4] had never been true ;
  I have proved them true at last.

[[1] loathsome.   [2] complexion.   [3] burst.   [4] dreams.]

I dreamt in my sweven on thursday eve,
   In my bed wheras I laye,   70
I dreamt a grype[1] and a grimlie beast
   Had carryed my crowne awaye ;

My gorgett[2] and my kirtle[3] of golde,
   And all my faire head-geere :
And he wold worrye me with his tush[4]   75
   And to his nest y-beare :

Saving there came a litle 'gray' hawke,
   A merlin him they call,
Which untill the grounde did strike the grype,
   That dead he downe did fall.   80

Giffe[5] I were a man, as now I am none,
   A battell wold I prove,
To fight with that traitor Aldingar ;
   Att him I cast my glove.

But seeing Ime able noe battell to make,   85
   My liege, grant me a knight
To fight with that traitor sir Aldingar,
   To maintaine me in my right."

" Now forty dayes I will give thee
   To seeke thee a knight therin :   90
If thou find not a knight in forty dayes
   Thy bodye it must brenn."

[Then shee sent east, and shee sent west,
   By north and south bedeene :[6]
But never a champion colde she find,]   95
   Wolde fight with that knight soe keene.

Ver. 77. see below, v. 137.

[[1] griffin.   [2] neckerchief.   [3] petticoat.
[4] tooth.   [5] if.   [6] immediately.]

[Now twenty dayes were spent and gone,
    Noe helpe there might be had ;
Many a teare shed our comelye queene
    And aye her hart was sad.   100

Then came one of the queenes damsèlles,
    And knelt upon her knee,
" Cheare up, cheare up, my gracious dame,
    I trust yet helpe may be :

" And here I will make mine avowe,[1]   105
    And with the same me binde ;
That never will I return to thee,
    Till I some helpe may finde."

Then forth she rode on a faire palfràye
    Oer hill and dale about :   110
But never a champion colde she finde,
    Wolde fighte with that knight so stout.

And nowe the daye drewe on a pace,
    When our good queene must dye ;
All woe-begone was that faire damsèlle,   115
    When she found no helpe was nye.

All woe-begone was that faire damsèlle,
    And the salt teares fell from her eye :]
When lo ! as she rode by a rivers side,
    She met with a tinye boye.   120

[A tinye boye she mette, God wot,
    All clad in mantle of golde ;]
He seemed noe more in mans likenèsse,
    Then a childe of four yeere olde.

[Why grieve you, damselle faire, he sayd,   125
    And what doth cause you moane ?
The damsell scant wolde deigne a looke,
    But fast she pricked on.]

[[1] vow or oath.]

Yet turn againe, thou faïre damsèlle,
   And greete thy queene from mee :   130
When bale[1] is att hyest, boote[2] is nyest,
   Nowe helpe enoughe may bee.

Bid her remember what she dreamt
   In her bedd, wheras shee laye ;
How when the grype and the grimly beast   135
   Wolde have carried her crowne awaye,

Even then there came the litle gray hawke,
   And saved her from his clawes :
Then bidd the queene be merry at hart,
   [For heaven will fende[3] her cause.]   140

Back then rode that faire damsèlle,
   And her hart it lept for glee :
And when she told her gracious dame
   A gladd woman then was shee.

[But when the appointed day was come,   145
   No helpe appeared nye :
Then woeful, woeful was her hart,
   And the teares stood in her eye.

And nowe a fyer was built of wood ;
   And a stake was made of tree ;   150
And now queene Elinor forth was led,
   A sorrowful sight to see.

Three times the herault he waved his hand,
   And three times spake on hye :
Giff any good knight will fende this dame,   155
   Come forth, or she must dye.

No knight stood forth, no knight there came,
   No helpe appeared nye :
And now the fyer was lighted up,
   Queen Elinor she must dye.   160

[[1] evil.   [2] help.   [3] defend.]

And now the fyer was lighted up,
    As hot as hot might bee;]
When riding upon a little white steed,
    The tinye boy they see.

"Away with that stake, away with those brands, 165
    And loose our comelye queene :
I am come to fight with sir Aldingar,
    And prove him a traitor keene."

Forthe then stood sir Aldingar,
    But when he saw the chylde, 170
He laughed, and scoffed, and turned his backe,
    And weened[1] he had been beguylde.

" Now turne, now turne thee, Aldingar,
    And eyther fighte or flee ;
I trust that I shall avenge the wronge, 175
    Thoughe I am so small to see."

The boye pulld forth a well good sworde
    So gilt it dazzled the ee ;
The first stroke stricken at Aldingar
    Smote off his leggs by the knee. 180

" Stand up, stand up, thou false traitòr,
    And fight upon thy feete,
For and thou thrive, as thou begin'st,
    Of height wee shall be meete."

A priest, a priest, sayes Aldingàr, 185
    While I am a man alive.
A priest, a priest, sayes Aldingàr,
    Me for to houzle and shrive.[2]

I wolde have laine by our comlie queene,
    Bot shee wolde never consent; 190
Then I thought to betraye her unto our kinge
    In a fyer to have her brent.

[¹ supposed.   ² to give the sacrament and to confess.]

There came a lazar to the kings gates,
  A lazar both blind and lame :
I tooke the lazar upon my backe,   195
  And on her bedd had him layne.

[Then ranne I to our comlye king,
  These tidings sore to tell.]
But ever alacke ! sayes Aldingar,
  Falsing never doth well.   200

Forgive, forgive me, queene, madame,
  The short time I must live.
" Nowe Christ forgive thee, Aldingar,
  As freely I forgive."

Here take thy queene, our king Harryè,   205
  And love her as thy life,
[For never had a king in Christentye,
  A truer and fairer wife.

King Henrye ran to claspe his queene,
  And loosèd her full sone :   210
Then turnd to look for the tinye boye ;
  ——The boye was vanisht and gone.

But first he had touchd the lazar man,
  And stroakt him with his hand :
The lazar under the gallowes tree   215
  All whole and sounde did stand.]

The lazar under the gallowes tree
  Was comelye, straight and tall ;
King Henrye made him his head stewàrde
  To wayte withinn his hall.   220

***

[THE following is the original version from the folio MS.
 reprinted from Hales and Furnivall's ed. vol. i. p. 166:

  Our king he kept a ffalse steward,
  men called him Sir Aldingar

he wold haue layen by our comely queene,
   her deere worshipp to haue betraide.   4
our queene shee was a good woman,
   & euer more said him nay.

Aldingar was offended in his mind,
   with her hee was neuer content,   8
but he sought what meanes he cold find out,
   in a fyer to haue her brent.

There came a lame lazer to the Kings gates,
   a lazer was [b]lind & lame ;   12
he tooke the lazer vpon his backe,
   vpon the queenes bed he did him lay :

he said, "lye still, lazer, wheras thou lyest,
   looke thou goe not away,   16
Ile make thee a whole man & a sound
   in 2 howres of a day."

& then went forth Sir Aldingar
   our Queene for to betray,   20
and then he mett with our comlye King,
   saies, "god you saue & see !

"If I had space as I haue grace,
   A message I wold say to thee."   24
"Say on, say on, Sir Aldingar,
   say thou on and vnto me."

"I can let you now see one of [the] greiuos[est] sights
   that euer Christen King did see :   28
Our Queene hath chosen a New New loue,
   She will haue none of thee ;

"If shee had chosen a right good Knight,
   the lesse had beene her shame,   32
but she hath chosen a Lazar man
   which is both blinde & lame."

"If this be true, thou Aldingar,
   that thou dost tell to me,   36
then will I make thee a rich Knight
   both of gold and fee ;

"But if it be false, Sir Aldingar,
   that thou doest tell to me,   40
then looke for noe other death
   but to be hangd on a tree.

goe with me," saide our comly king,
   " this Lazar for to see." 44

When the King he came into the queenes chamber,
   standing her bed befor,
"there is a lodly lome," says Harry King
   "for our dame Queene Elinor ! 48

" If thou were a man, as thou art none,
   here thou sholdest be slaine ;
but a paire of new gallowes shall be biil[t]
   thoust hang on them soe hye ; 52

"and fayre fyer there shalbe bett,
   and brent our Queene shal bee."
fforth then walked our comlye King,
   & mett with our comly Queene, 56

saies, " God you saue, our Queene, Madam,
   and Christ you saue & see !
heere you [haue] chosen a new new loue,
   and you will haue none of mee. 60

" If you had chosen a right good Knight
   the lesse he beene your shame,
but you haue chosen a lazar man
   that is both blind & lame." 64

" Euer alacke !" said our comly Queene,
   " Sir Aldingar is false to mee ;
but euer alacke !" said our comly Queene,
   " Euer alas, & woe is mee ! 68

" I had thought sweuens had neuer been true ;
   I haue prooued them true at the last ;
I dreamed in my sweauen on thursday at eueninge
   in my bed wheras I lay, 72

" I dreamed the grype & a grimlie beast
   had carryed my crowne away,
my gorgett & my kirtle of golde,
   and all my faire heade geere ; 76

"How he wold haue worryed me with his tush
   & borne me into his nest,
saving there came a litle hawk
   flying out of the East, 80

" saving there came a litle Hawke
    which men call a Merlion,
vntill the ground he stroke him downe,
    that dead he did fall downe.   84

" giffe I were a man, as I am none,
    a battell I would proue,
I wold fight with that false traitor;
    att him I cast my gloue !   88

" Seing I am able noe battell to make,
    you must grant me, my leege, a Knight
to fight with that traitor, Sir Aldingar,
    to maintaine me in my right."   92

" Ile giue thee 40 dayes," said our King,
    " to seeke thee a man therin ;
if thou find not a man in 40 dayes,
    in a hott fyer thou shall brenn."   96

Our Queene sent forth a Messenger,
    he rode fast into the south,
he rode the countryes through & through,
    soe ffar vnto Portsmouth ;   100

he cold find never a man in the south country
    that wold fight with the knight soe keene.

the second messenger the Queen forth sent,
    rode far into the east,   104
but—blessed be God made sunn and moone !—
    he sped then all of the best :

as he rode then by one riuer side,
    there he mett with a litle child,   108
he seemed noe more in a mans likenesse
    then a child of 4 yeeres old ;

He askt the Queenes Messenger how far he rode :
    loth he was him to tell ;   112
the litle one was offended att him,
    bid him adew, farwell !

Said, " turne thou againe, thou messenger,
    greete our Queene well from me ;   116
when Bale is att hyest, boote is att next,
    helpe enough there may bee !

" bid our queene remember what she did dreame
 in her bedd wheras shee lay;   120
shee dreamed the grype & the grimly beast
 had carryed her crowne away,

" her gorgett & her kirt[l]e of gold,
 alsoe her faire head geere,   124
he wold have werryed her with his tushe
 & borne her into her nest,

" Saving there came a litle hawke—
 men call him a merlyon—   128
vntill the ground he did strike him downe,
 that dead he did ffall downe.

" bidd the queene be merry att her hart,
 euermore light & glad,   132
when bale is att hyest, boote is at next,
 helpe enoughe there shalbe [had."]

then the Queenes Messenger rode backe,
 a gladed man then was hee;   136
when he came before our Queene,
 a gladd woman then was shee;

shee gaue the Messenger 20ͫ:
 O lord, in gold & ffee,   140
saies, " spend & spare not while this doth last,
 then feitch thou more of me."

Our Queene was put in a tunne to burne,
 She thought no thing but death;   144
thé were ware of the litle one
 came ryding forth of the East

with a Mu (*line cut away*) . . .
 a louelie child was hee: 148
when he came to that fier,
 he light the Queene full nigh;

said, " draw away these brands of fire
 lie burning before our Queene,   152
& feitch me hither Sir Aldingar
 that is a knight soe keene."

When Aldingar see that litle one,
 ffull litle of him hee thought,   156
if there had beene halfe a 100 such,
 of them he wold not haue wrought.

hee sayd, "come hither Sir Aldingar,
 thou see-must as bigge as a ffooder !   160
I trust to god, ere I haue done with thee,
 God will send to vs anger."

saies, "the first stroke thats giuen, Sir Aldingar,
 I will giue vnto thee,   164
& if the second giue thou may,
 looke then thou spare not mee."

the litle one pulld forth a well good sword,
 I-wis itt was all of guilt,   163
it cast light there over that feild,
 it shone soe all of guilt :

he stroke the first stroke att Aldingar,
 he stroke away his leggs by his knee,   172

sayes, "stand vp, stand vp, thou false traitor,
 & fight vpon thy feete !
"for & thou thriue as thou begins,
 of a height wee shalbe meete."   176

"A preist, a preist !" sayes Aldingar,
 "me for to houzle & shriue !
A preist, a preist," sayes Aldingar,
 "while I am a man liuing a-liue !   180

"I wold haue laine by our comlie Queene ;
 to it shee wold neuer consent ;
I thought to haue betrayed her to our King,
 in a fyer to haue had her brent ;   184

"there came a lame lazer to the Kings gates,
 a lazar both blind & lame ;

"I tooke the lazar vpon my backe,
 in the Queenes bed I did him lay,   188
I bad him 'lie still, Lazar, where he lay,
 looke he went not away,
I wold make him a whole man & a sound
 in 2 houres of a day.'   192

"euer alacke !" sayes Sir Aldingar,
 "falsing neuer doth well ;

"forgiue, forgiue me, Queene, Madam !
 for Christs loue forgiue me !"   196
"God forgaue his death, Aldingar,
 & freely I forgiue thee."

"Now take thy wife, thou K[ing] Harry,
   & loue her as thou shold;   200
thy wiffe shee is a[s] true to thee
   as stone that lies on the castle wall."

the Lazar vnder the gallow tree
   was a pretty man & small,   204
the Lazar vnder the gallow tree
   was made steward in King Henerys hall.

                                   ffins.]

X.

THE GABERLUNYIE MAN.

A Scottish Song.

TRADITION informs us that the author of this song was King James V. of Scotland. This prince (whose character for wit and libertinism bears a great resemblance to that of his gay successor, Charles II.) was noted for strolling about his dominions in disguise,* and for his frequent gallantries with country girls. Two adventures of this kind he hath celebrated with his own pen, viz. in this ballad of *The Gaberlunyie Man;* and in another intitled *The Jolly Beggar*, beginning thus:

" Thair was a jollie beggar, and a begging he was boun,
And he tuik up his quarters into a land'art toun.
                        Fa, la, la," &c.

It seems to be the latter of these ballads (which was too licentious to be admitted into this collection) that is meant in the *Catalogue of Royal and Noble Authors*,† where the ingenious writer remarks, that "there is something very ludicrous in the young woman's distress when she thought her first favour had been thrown away upon a beggar."

Bishop Tanner has attributed to James V. the celebrated ballad of *Christ's Kirk on the Green*, which is ascribed to King James I. in Bannatyne's MS. written in 1568: and, notwithstanding that

---

* Sc. of a tinker, beggar, &c.   Thus he used to visit a smith's daughter at Niddry, near Edinburgh.   † Vol. ii. p. 203.

authority, the editor of this book is of opinion that Bishop Tanner
was right.

King James V. died Dec. 13th, 1542, aged 33.

[James V. was called the *King of the Commons*, from his popular
manners and vagrant habits, and many stories are told of his adventures when in disguise.   One of these is worth relating here.
On a certain occasion he heard himself abused by a country lad
as a tyrant and a man odious in every respect, until, unable to re-
strain himself, he threw off his disguise, and told his accuser that
he was the king.   " Are you really the king ? " said the lad, retain-
ing his self-possession; " weel, ye'll maybe hae heard o' my father :
he gaed daft three days regularly every year, and in a' that time
spoke naething but lies and nonsense : now I'm exactly the same
way, and this is *one of my three days.*"   There is no authority for
attributing the present song to James V., except ancient and
universal tradition.   The word *gaberlunyie* is compounded of *gaber*,
a wallet, and *lunyie*, the loins : hence a travelling tinker or beggar
carrying a wallet by his side, was called a " gaberlunyie man."
Scott has sketched a vivid portrait of one of these privileged beggars in his *Antiquary*, Edie Ochiltree, to wit.   The *Jolly Beggar* is
printed in Herd's *Scottish Songs*, ii. 164, and in Ritson's *Scottish
Songs*, i. 168.   Competent authorities are not willing to take the
credit of the authorship of *Christ's Kirk on the Green* from
James I. and give it to James V.]

HE pauky auld Carle[1] came ovir the lee
  Wi' mony good-eens and days to mee,
  Saying, Goodwife, for your courtesie,
    Will ye lodge a silly[2] poor man ?
The night was cauld, the carle was wat,   5
And down ayont the ingle[3] he sat ;
My dochters shoulders he gan to clap,
  And cadgily[4] ranted and sang.

O wow ![5] quo he, were I as free,
As first when I saw this countrie,   10
How blyth and merry wad I bee !
  And I wad nevir think lang.

[¹ sly old man.   ² simple or poor.   ³ beyond the fire.
⁴ merrily.   ⁵ exclamation of admiration or surprise.]

He grew canty,[1] and she grew fain ;[2]
But little did her auld minny ken[3]
What thir slee twa[4] togither were say'n,   15
    When wooing they were sa thrang.[5]

And O ! quo he, ann ye were as black,
As evir the crown of your dadyes hat,
Tis I wad lay thee by my back,
    And awa wi' me thou sould gang.   20
And O ! quoth she, ann I were as white,
As evir the snaw lay on the dike,
Ild clead me braw,[6] and lady-like,
    And awa with thee Ild gang.

Between the twa was made a plot ;   25
They raise a wee before the cock,
And wyliely they shot the lock,
    And fast to the bent are they gane.
Up the morn the auld wife raise,
And at her leisure put on her claiths,   30
Syne to the servants bed she gaes
    To speir for the silly poor man.

She gaed to the bed, whair the beggar lay,
The strae was cauld, he was away,
She clapt her hands, cryd, Dulefu' day !   35
    For some of our geir will be gane.
Some ran to coffer, and some to kist,[7]
But nought was stown[8] that could be mist.
She dancid her lane,[9] cryd, Praise be blest,
    I have lodgd a leal poor man.   40

Ver. 29. The carline, other copies.

[1 merry.   2 fond.   3 mother know.
4 these sly two.   5 so close.   6 clad me handsomely.
7 chest.   8 stolen.   9 alone by herself.]

Since naithings awa, as we can learn,
The kirns to kirn,[1] and milk to earn,
Gae butt the house,[2] lass, and waken my bairn,
    And bid her come quickly ben.[3]
The servant gaed where the dochter lay,   45
The sheets was cauld, she was away,
And fast to her goodwife can say,
    Shes aff with the gaberlunyie-man.

O fy gar ride, and fy gar rin,
And hast ye, find these traitors agen;   50
For shees be burnt, and hees be slein,
    The wearyfou[4] gaberlunyie-man.
Some rade upo horse, some ran a fit,
The wife was wood,[5] and out o' her wit;
She could na gang, nor yet could she sit,   55
    But ay did curse and did ban.

Mean time far hind out owre the lee,
For snug in a glen, where nane could see,
The twa, with kindlie sport and glee,
    Cut frae a new cheese a whang.[6]   60
The priving[7] was gude, it pleas'd them baith,
To lo'e her for ay, he gae her his aith.
Quo she, to leave thee, I will be laith,
    My winsome gaberlunyie-man.

O kend my minny I were wi' you,   65
Illfardly[8] wad she crook her mou,[9]
Sic a poor man sheld nevir trow,
    Aftir the gaberlunyie-mon.

[1 churns to churn.   2 go to the outer apartment.
3 in.   4 troublesome.   5 mad.
6 slice.   7 proof.   8 ill-favouredly.
9 mouth.

My dear, quo he, yee're yet owre yonge;
And hae na learnt the beggars tonge, 70
To follow me frae toun to toun,
    And carrie the gaberlunyie on.

Wi' kauk and keel,[1] Ill win your bread,
And spindles and whorles[2] for them wha need,
Whilk is a gentil trade indeed 75
    The gaberlunyie to carrie—o.
Ill bow my leg and crook my knee,
And draw a black clout owre my ee,
A criple or blind they will cau me :
    While we sall sing and be merrie—o. 80

XI.

ON THOMAS LORD CROMWELL.

T is ever the fate of a disgraced minister to be forsaken by his friends, and insulted by his enemies, always reckoning among the latter the giddy inconstant multitude. We have here a spurn at fallen greatness from one of the angry partisans of declining popery, who could never forgive the downfall of their Diana and loss of their craft. The ballad seems to have been composed between the time of Cromwell's commitment to the Tower, June 10th, 1540, and that of his being beheaded, July 28 following. A short interval ! but Henry's passion for Catharine Howard would admit of no delay. Notwithstanding our libeller, Cromwell had many excellent qualities ; his great fault was too much obsequiousness to the arbitrary will of his master ; but let it be considered that this master had raised him from obscurity, and that the high-born nobility had shewn him the way in every kind of mean and servile compliance. The original copy, printed at London in 1540, is intitled, *A newe*

[1 chalk and ruddle.
2 instruments used for spinning in Scotland.]

ballade made of Thomas Crumwel, called " *Trolle on away.*"   **To it**
is prefixed this distich by way of burthen :

> " Trolle on away, trolle on awaye.
> Synge heave and howe rombelowe trolle on away."

The following piece gave rise to a poetic controversy, which
was carried on thro' a succession of seven or eight ballads, written
for and against Lord Cromwell.   These are all preserved in the
archives of the Antiquarian Society, in a large folio collection of
proclamations, &c., made in the reigns of King Henry VIII., King
Edward VI., Queen Mary, Queen Elizabeth, King James I., &c.

[Thomas Cromwell, called *Malleus Monachorum*, came of a
good old Lincolnshire family.   He was born about the year 1490
at Putney, where his father carried on the business of an iron-
founder, which his enemies reduced to that of a blacksmith.   His
father died early, and in consequence of the re-marriage of his
mother, he became a wanderer.

The author of the poor play, entitled *The Life and Death of
Thomas Lord Cromwell*, which has been absurdly attributed to
Shakspere, makes " old Cromwell, a blacksmith, of Putney," live to
see his son " made lord keeper."

There is a fragment of a ballad on Cromwell without any beginning in the Folio MS. (ed. Hales and Furnivall, vol. i. p. 127),
which ends as follows :

> " How now?   How now? the king did say,
>   Thomas how is it with thee ?
> Hanging and drawing O King ! he saide ;
>   You shall never gett more from me."

Mr. Hales points out a coincidence not mentioned by Mr.
Froude, viz. that the minister was beheaded and the king married
to Catherine Howard on one and the same day.   In 1525 Cromwell undertook for Wolsey the work of visiting and breaking up
the small monasteries which the Pope had granted for the foundation of Wolsey's new colleges, thus commencing the work which
gained him the enmity of the adherents of the old faith.   He was
the first to cause Bibles in the English language to be deposited in
all the churches, and to him we owe the institution of parish registers.]

OTH man and chylde is glad to here tell
Of that false traytoure Thomas Crumwell,
Now that he is set to learne to spell.
                    Synge trolle on away.

When fortune lokyd the in thy face,
Thou haddyst fayre tyme, but thou lackydyst grace ; 5
Thy cofers with golde thou fyllydst a pace.
                    Synge, &c.

Both plate and chalys came to thy fyst,
Thou lockydst them vp where no man wyst,
Tyll in the kynges treasoure suche thinges were myst.
                    Synge, &c.

Both crust and crumme came thorowe thy handes, 10
Thy marchaundyse sayled over the sandes,
Therfore nowe thou art layde fast in bandes.
                    Synge, &c.

Fyrste when kynge Henry, God saue his grace!
Perceyud myschefe kyndlyd in thy face,
Then it was tyme to purchase the a place.   15
                    Synge, &c.

Hys grace was euer of gentyll nature,
Mouyd with petye, and made the hys seruyture ;
But thou, as a wretche, suche thinges dyd procure.
                    Synge, &c.

Thou dyd not remembre, false heretyke,
One God, one fayth, and one kynge catholyke,   20
For thou hast bene so long a scysmatyke.
                    Synge, &c.

Thou woldyst not learne to knowe these thre ;
But euer was full of iniquite :
Wherfore all this lande hathe ben troubled with the.
                    Synge, &c.

All they, that were of the new trycke,   25
Agaynst the churche thou baddest them stycke;
Wherfore nowe thou haste touchyd the quycke.
                              Synge, &c.

Bothe sacramentes and sacramentalles
Thou woldyst not suffre within thy walles;
Nor let vs praye for all chrysten soules.   30
                              Synge, &c.

Of what generacyon thou were no tonge can tell,
Whyther of Chayme, or Syschemell,
Or else sent vs frome the deuyll of hell.
                              Synge, &c.

Thou woldest neuer to vertue applye,
But couetyd euer to clymme to hye,   35
And nowe haste thou trodden thy shoo awrye.
                              Synge, &c.

Who-so-euer dyd winne thou wolde not lose;
Wherfore all Englande doth hate the, as I suppose,
Bycause thou wast false to the redolent rose.
                              Synge, &c.

Thou myghtest have learned thy cloth to flocke   40
Upon thy gresy fullers stocke;
Wherfore lay downe thy heade vpon this blocke.
                              Synge, &c.

Yet saue that soule, that God hath bought,
And for thy carcas care thou nought,
Let it suffre payne, as it hath wrought.   45
                              Synge, &c.

Ver. 32. *i.e.* Cain, or Ishmael. See below, the note, book ii.
No. III. stanza 3rd.   V. 41. Cromwell's father is generally said
to have been a blacksmith at Putney: but the author of this
ballad would insinuate that either he himself or some of his ancestors were fullers by trade.

God saue kyng Henry with all his power,
And prynce Edwarde that goodly flowre,
With al hys lordes of great honoure.
   Synge trolle on awaye, syng trolle on away.
   Hevye and how rombelowe[1] trolle on awaye. 50

XII.

HARPALUS.

An Ancient English Pastoral.

THIS beautiful poem, which is perhaps the first attempt at pastoral writing in our language, is preserved among the *Songs and Sonnettes* of the Earl of Surrey, &c., 4to. in that part of the collection which consists of pieces by *uncertain auctours*. These poems were first published in 1557, ten years after that accomplished nobleman fell a victim to the tyranny of Henry VIII.; but it is presumed most of them were composed before the death of Sir Thomas Wyatt in 1541. See Surrey's Poems, 4to. fol. 19, 49.

Tho' written perhaps near half a century before the *Shepherd's Calendar*,* this will be found far superior to any of those eclogues, in natural unaffected sentiments, in simplicity of style, in easy flow of versification, and all other beauties of pastoral poetry. Spenser ought to have profited more by so excellent a model.

[Warton describes this poem as "perhaps the first example in our language now remaining of the pure and unmixed pastoral, and in the erotic species for ease of numbers, elegance of rural allusion excelling everything of the kind in Spenser, who is erroneously ranked as our earliest English bucolic." He did not, however, take into account *Robin and Makine*, which follows *Harpalus* in this book, but was written more than half a century before it. Spenser-lovers also are not likely to agree with Percy's and Warton's summary judgments upon the *Shepherd's Calendar*.]

---

* First published in 1579.
[1 The burden of an old song.]

HYLIDA was a faire mayde,
As fresh as any flowre;
Whom Harpalus the herdman **prayde**
To be his paramour.

Harpalus, and eke Corin,   5
Were herdmen both yfere :[1]
And Phylida could twist and spinne,
And thereto sing full clere.

But Phylida was all tò coye,
For Harpalus to winne :   10
For Corin was her onely joye,
Who forst[2] her not a pinne.

How often would she flowers twine?
How often garlandes make
Of couslips and of colombine?   15
And al for Corin's sake.

But Corin, he had haukes to lure,
And forced more the field :[3]
Of lovers lawe he toke no cure;
For once he was begilde.   20

Harpalus prevailed nought,
His labour all was lost;
For he was fardest from her **thought,**
And yet he loved her most.

Therefore waxt he both pale and leane, 25
And drye as clot of clay:
His fleshe it was consumed cleane;
His colour gone away.

[[1] together.   [2] regarded.   [3] cared more for field sports.]

His beard it had not long be shave;
　His heare hong all unkempt:　　　　30
A man most fit even for the grave,
　Whom spitefull love had spent.

His eyes were red and all 'forewacht;'[1]
　His face besprent with teares:
It semde unhap had him long 'hatcht,'　35
　In mids of his dispaires.

His clothes were blacke, and also bare;
　As one forlorne was he;
Upon his head alwayes he ware
　A wreath of wyllow tree.　　　　40

His beastes he kept upon the hyll,
　And he sate in the dale;
And thus with sighes and sorrowes shril,
　He gan to tell his tale.

Oh Harpalus! (thus would he say)　45
　Unhappiest under sunne!
The cause of thine unhappy day,
　By love was first begunne.

For thou wentest first by sute to seeke
　A tigre to make tame,　　　　50
That settes not by thy love a leeke;
　But makes thy griefe her game.

As easy it were for to convert
　The frost into 'a' flame;
As for to turne a frowarde hert,　　55
　Whom thou so faine wouldst frame.

Ver. 33, &c. The corrections are from ed. 1574.

[1 overwakeful.]

Corin he liveth carèlesse :
　He leapes among the leaves :
He eates the frutes of thy redresse :[1]
　Thou ' reapst,' he takes the sheaves.　　　60

My beastes, a whyle your foode refraine,
　And harke your herdmans sounde :
Whom spitefull love, alas ! hath slaine,
　Through-girt[2] with many a wounde.

O happy be ye, beastès wilde,　　　　65
　That here your pasture takes :
I se that ye be not begilde
　Of these your faithfull makes.[3]

The hart he feedeth by the hinde :
　The bucke harde by the do :　　　70
The turtle dove is not unkinde
　To him that loves her so.

The ewe she hath by her the ramme :
　The yong cow hath the bull :
The calfe with many a lusty lambe　　75
　Do fede their hunger full.

But, wel-away ! that nature wrought
　The, Phylida, so faire :
For I may say that I have bought
　Thy beauty all tò deare.　　　　80

What reason is that crueltie
　With beautie should have part ?
Or els that such great tyranny
　Should dwell in womans hart ?

I see therefore to shape my death　　85
　She cruelly is prest ;[4]
To th'ende that I may want my breath :
　My dayes been at the best.

[[1] care.　　[2] pierced through.　　[3] mates.　　[4] ready.]

O Cupide, graunt this my request,
 And do not stoppe thine eares ;   90
That she may feele within her brest
 The paines of my dispaires :

Of Corin 'who' ïs carèlesse,
 That she may crave her fee :
As I have done in great distresse,   95
 That loved her faithfully.

But since that I shal die her slave ;
 Her slave, and eke her thrall :[1]
Write you, my frendes, upon my grave
 This chaunce that is befall.   100

" Here lieth unhappy Harpalus
 By cruell love now slaine :
Whom Phylida unjustly thus
 Hath murdred with disdaine."

XIII.

ROBIN AND MAKYNE.

An Ancient Scottish Pastoral.

HE palm of pastoral poesy is here contested by a co-
temporary writer with the author of the foregoing.
The critics will judge of their respective merits; but
must make some allowance for the preceding ballad,
which is given simply as it stands in the old editions ; whereas this,
which follows, has been revised and amended throughout by
Allan Ramsay, from whose *Evergreen,* vol. i. it is here chiefly
printed. The curious reader may, however, compare it with the
more original copy, printed among *Ancient Scottish Poems,* from the

---

[¹ captive.]

MS. of George Bannatyne, 1568, Edinburgh, 1770, 12mo. Mr. Robert Henryson (to whom we are indebted for this poem) ap-pears to so much advantage among the writers of eclogue, that we are sorry we can give little other account of him besides what is contained in the following eloge, written by W. Dunbar, a Scottish poet, who lived about the middle of the sixteenth century:

> " In Dunfermline he [Death] hes done roun
> Gud Maister Robert Henrisoun."

Indeed, some little further insight into the history of this Scot-tish bard is gained from the title prefixed to some of his poems preserved in the British Museum, viz. *The morall Fabillis of Esop*, compylit be Maister Robert Henrisoun, scolmaister of Dum-fermling, 1571. Harl. MSS. 3865, § 1.

In Ramsay's *Evergreen*, vol. i. are preserved two other little Doric pieces by Henryson : the one intitled *The Lyon and the Mouse*, the other *The garment of gude Ladyis*. Some other of his poems may be seen in the *Ancient Scottish Poems*, printed from Bannatyne's MS. above referred to.

[This remarkable poem is peculiarly interesting as being the earliest specimen of pastoral poetry in the language. Campbell calls it "the first known pastoral, and one of the best in a dialect rich with the favours of the pastoral muse." Langhorne writes justly :

> " In gentle Henryson's unlaboured strain
> Sweet Arethusa's shepherd breath'd again."

Percy errs in describing Henryson as a contemporary of Surrey, as the Scottish poet lived half a century before the English one. The dates of his birth and death are not known, but he flourished in the reign of James III. (1460-1488). "On the 10th of Septem-ber, 1462, the venerable master Robert Henrysone, Licentiate in Arts and Bachelor in Degrees, was incorporated or admitted a member of the newly founded University of Glasgow." He was a notary public, and probably the master of the grammar school at-tached to the Abbey of Dunfermline, not as might be supposed a mere parish schoolmaster. According to the tradition of the last century, our poet was the representative of the family of Henryson or Henderson, of Fordell, in the county of Fife ; but Mr. David Laing thinks that it is a gratuitous assumption to suppose that he or his predecessors ever possessed a single acre of the lands of Fordell.

Percy has used the version given in Ramsay's *Evergreen*, which is slightly altered in diction from the original in the Bannatyne MS. ; for instance, the last stanza occurs in the latter as follows :

" Makyne went hame blyth anneuche,
  Attour the holltis hair ;
Robene murnit, and Makyne leuche ;
  Scho sang, he sichit sair
And so left him, bayth wo and wreuch,
  In dolour and in cair,
Kepand his hird under a huche
  Amangis the holtis hair."

In the *Evergreen* version, the last verse is altered to " Amang the rushy gair," either because the words " holtis hair " occur in verse two of the stanza, or that the Editor saw an impropriety in the close vicinity of the similar words *holt* and *heuch*. The two words " holtis hair " are explained as hoary hills or hoary woods, but Finlay (*Scottish Historical and Romantic Ballads*, 1808, vol. ii. p. 193) holds that " hair " really means high, and derives it from Isl. har = altus. He says that a high rock in some of the northern counties of Scotland, where the dialect is strongly tinctured with Danish, is called " hair craig," and that the same word lingers on in the Hare-stone of the Borough Moor, Edinburgh, which obtained its name in the following manner : The laird of Pennycuik held certain lands by a strange tenure. He was obliged to mount a large stone or rock, and salute the king with three blasts of a horn whenever he passed that way. This rock or eminence was called the " Hare-stone," and still exists near Morningside Church. Hoary, however, is to be understood as grey and not as white with snow, so that the hare-stone is probably the grey stone. The word holt may also mean a heath, and Cædmon uses the phrase " har hæð " = hoar or grey heath.

The date (1571) attached to Henryson's version of *Æsop's Fables* is that of transcription. It is not known when the Fables were first printed, but they were reprinted by Robert Lekpreuik for Henry Charteris in 1570. They are supposed to have been written between 1470 and 1480.

Henryson wrote several other short poems, as well as the *Testament of Cresseid*, written as a continuation or supplement to Chaucer's *Troilus and Cresseide*, all of which have been collected for the first time into an elegant volume by David Laing, who has added notes and a memoir of the poet (Edinburgh, 1865).

This *Testament* has a particular interest for us, because Shakspere referred to it when he wrote " Cressida was a beggar " (*Twelfth Night*, act iii. sc. 1). The lines in Henryson's poem which illustrate this passage, are as follows :

" Thair was na buit [help], bot furth with thame scho yeid
  Fra place to place, quhill cauld and houngir sair
Compellit hir to be ane rank beggair."   Ll. 481-3.]

ROBIN sat on the gude grene hill,
    Keipand a flock of fie,[1]
Quhen mirry[2] Makyne said him till,[3]
    " O Robin rew[4] on me :
I haif thee luivt baith loud and still,[5]   5
    Thir towmonds[6] twa or thre ;
My dule in dern bot gif thou dill,[7]
    Doubtless but dreid Ill die."

Robin replied, Now by the rude,
    Naithing of love I knaw,   10
But keip my sheip undir yon wod :
    Lo quhair they raik on raw.[8]
Quhat can have mart[9] thee in thy mude,[10]
    Thou Makyne to me schaw ;
Or quhat is luve, or to be lude ?[11]   15
    Fain wald I leir[12] that law.

" The law of luve gin thou wald leir,
    Tak thair an A, B, C ;
Be heynd,[13] courtas, and fair of feir,[14]
    Wyse, hardy, kind and frie,   20
Sae that nae danger do the deir,[15]
    Quhat dule in dern thou drie ;[16]
Press ay to pleis,[17] and blyth appeir,
    Be patient and privie."

Ver. 19. Bannatyne's MS. reads as above, *heynd*, not *keynd*, as
in the Edinb. ed. 1770.   V. 21. So that no danger, Bannatyne's
MS.

[[1] keeping a flock of sheep.   [2] when merry.   [3] unto.
[4] take pity.   [5] openly and secretly.   [6] these twelvemonths.
[7] unless thou share my secret woe.   [8] they extend themselves in a row.   [9] marred.   [10] mood.   [11] loved.
[12] learn.   [13] gentle.   [14] fair of countenance.
[15] do thee hurt.   [16] whatever sorrow you may endure in secret.
[17] be eager to please.]

Robin, he answert her againe,
   I wat not quhat is luve; 25
But I haif marvel in certaine
   Quhat makes thee thus wanrufe.[1]
The wedder is fair, and I am fain ;[2]
   My sheep gais hail abuve ;[3] 30
And sould we pley us on the plain,
   They wald us baith repruve.

" Robin, tak tent[4] unto my tale,
   And wirk[5] all as I reid ;[6]
And thou sall haif my heart all hale, 35
   Eik and my maiden-heid :
Sen God, he sendis bute for bale,[7]
   And for murning remeid,[8]
I'dern with thee bot gif I dale,[9]
   Doubtless I am but deid." 40

Makyne, to-morn be this ilk tyde,
   Gif ye will meit me heir,
Maybe my sheip may gang besyde,
   Quhyle we have liggd full neir ;
But maugre haif I, gif I byde,[10] 45
   Frae thay begin to steir,
Quhat lyes on heart I will nocht hyd,
   Then Makyne mak gude cheir.

" Robin, thou reivs[11] me of my rest ;
   I luve bot thee alane." 50
Makyne, adieu ! the sun goes west,
   The day is neir-hand gane.

[1 uneasy.   2 glad.   3 go healthful in the uplands.
4 heed.   5 do.   6 advise.
7 since God sends good for evil.   8 for mourning remedy.
9 in secret with thee, unless I share thy favour.
10 But ill will may I have if I stay.   11 bereavest.]

" Robin, in dule[1] I am so drest,
　　That luve will be my bane."
Makyn, gae luve quhair-eir ye list,　　　　55
　　For leman I luid nane.

" Robin, I stand in sic a style,
　　I sich[2] and that full sair."
Makyne, I have bene here this quyle ;
　　At hame I wish I were.　　　　　　60
" Robin, my hinny, talk and smyle,
　　Gif thou will do nae mair."
Makyne, som other man beguyle,
　　For hameward I will fare.

Syne Robin on his ways he went,　　　　65
　　As light as leif on tree ;
But Makyne murnt and made lament,
　　Scho[3] trow'd him neir to see.
Robin he brayd attowre the bent :[4]
　　Then Makyne cried on hie,　　　　70
" Now may thou sing, for I am shent ![5]
　　Quhat ailis luve at me ?"

Makyne went hame withouten fail,
　　And weirylie could weip ;
Then Robin in a full fair dale　　　　75
　　Assemblit all his sheip.
Be that some part of Makyne's ail,
　　Out-throw his heart could creip ;
Hir fast he followt to assail,
　　And till her tuke gude keip.[6]　　　80

Abyd, abyd, thou fair Makyne,
　　A word for ony thing ;
For all my luve, it sall be thyne,
　　Withouten departing.[7]

[1 sorrow.　　　　　　2 sigh.　　　　3 she.
4 he hastened over the field.　　　　5 confounded.
6 and took good watch of her.　　　　7 dividing.]

All hale thy heart for till have myne,   85
　　Is all my coveting ;
My sheip to morn quhyle houris nyne,
　　Will need of nae keiping.

" Robin, thou hast heard sung and say,
　　In gests and storys auld,   90
The man that will not when he may,
　　Sall have nocht when he wald.
I pray to heaven baith nicht and day,
　　Be eiked[1] their cares sae cauld,
That presses first with thee to play   95
　　Be forrest, firth, or fauld."[2]

Makyne, the nicht is soft and dry,
　　The wether warm and fair,
And the grene wod richt neir-hand by,
　　To walk attowre all where :   100
There may nae janglers[3] us espy,
　　That is in luve contrair ;
Therin, Makyne, baith you and I
　　Unseen may mak repair.

" Robin, that warld is now away,   105
　　And quyt brocht till an end :
And nevir again thereto, perfay,
　　Sall it be as thou wend ;
For of my pain thou made but play ;
　　I words in vain did spend :   110
As thou hast done, sae sall I say,
　　Murn on, I think to mend."

Makyne, the hope of all my heil,[4]
　　My heart on thee is set ;
I'll evermair to thee be leil,[5]   115
　　Quhyle I may live but lett,[6]

Ver. 99. Bannatyne's MS. has *woid*, not *woud*, as in ed. 1770.
[[1] enlarged.　　　[2] by forest, copse, or field.　　　[3] tell-tales.
[4] health or happiness.　　[5] true.　　[6] live without hindrance.]

Never to fail as uthers feill,
   Quhat grace so eir I get.
" Robin, with thee I will not deill;
   Adieu, for thus we met."   120

Makyne went hameward blyth enough,
   Attowre the holtis hair ;[1]
Pure Robin murnd, and Makyne leugh;[2]
   Scho sang, and he sicht sair :[3]
And so left him bayth wo and wreuch,[4]   125
   In dolor and in care,
Keipand his herd under a heuch,[5]
   Amang the rushy gair.[6]

XIV.

GENTLE HERDSMAN, TELL TO ME.

DIALOGUE BETWEEN A PILGRIM AND HERDSMAN.

THE scene of this beautiful old ballad is laid near Walsingham, in Norfolk, where was anciently an image of the Virgin Mary, famous over all Europe for the numerous pilgrimages made to it, and the great riches it possessed. Erasmus has given a very exact and humorous description of the superstitions practised there in his time. See his account of the *Virgo parathalassia*, in his colloquy, intitled, *Peregrinatio religionis ergo.* He tells us, the rich offerings in silver, gold, and precious stones, that were there shewn him, were incredible, there being scarce a person of any note in England, but what some time or other paid a visit, or sent a present to *our lady*

Ver. 117. Bannatyne's MS. reads as above feill, not faill, as in ed. 1770.

[[1] over the grey woods (see p. 81).   [2] laughed.   [3] sighed sore.
[4] wretchedness.   [5] height or hill.   [6] rushy strip of land.]

*of Walsingham.** At the dissolution of the monasteries in 1538, this splendid image, with another from Ipswich, was carried to Chelsea, and there burnt in the presence of commissioners; who, we trust, did not burn the jewels and the finery.

This poem is printed from a copy in the Editor's folio MS. which had greatly suffered by the hand of time; but vestiges of several of the lines remaining, some conjectural supplements have been attempted, which, for greater exactness, are in this one ballad distinguished by italicks.†

[The shrine of the Virgin ɔt Walsingham was the favourite English resort of pilgrims for nearly four hundred years, and the people of Norfolk were in great distress when their image was taken away from them, and the stream of votaries was suddenly stopped. In a copy of the *Reliques* in the library of the British Museum, there is a MS. note by William Cole to the following effect: " I was lately informed that the identical image of our lady of Walsingham being mured up in an old wall, and there discovered on pulling it down, was presented by the Earl of Leicester (Coke) to a relative of his of the Roman Catholic religion."

The shrine was connected with a Priory of Augustinian Canons, which was founded during the episcopate of William Turbus, Bishop of Norwich (1146-1174). When Henry III. made his pilgrimage to the shrine in the year 1241, it had long been famous, and was probably more frequented even than the tomb of St. Thomas a Becket at Canterbury. Foreigners of all nations came hither on pilgrimage, and in number and quality the devotees appear to have equalled those who toiled to the Lady of Loretto in Italy. Several of our kings visited the shrine after Henry III. had set the example. Edward I. was there in 1280 and in 1296, Edward II. in 1315, and Edward IV. and his queen in 1469. Henry VII. offered his prayers in " our Lady's Church" at Christmas time 1486-7, and in the following summer, after the battle of Stoke, "he sent his banner to be offered to our Lady of Walsingham, where before he made his vows." Spelman gives on hearsay evidence the report that Henry VIII., in the second year of his reign, walked barefoot to Walsingham from a neighbouring village, and then presented a valuable necklace to the image. Bartholo-

---

* See at the end of this ballad an account of the annual offerings of the Earls of Northumberland.

[† In the Folio MS. is the following note by Percy:—" Since I first transcribed this song for the press part of the leaf has been worne away. It was once exactly as I have represented it in my book." Ed. Hales and Furnivall, vol. iii. p. 526.]

mew, Lord Burghersh, K.G., by his will made in 1369, ordered a statue of himself on horseback to be made in silver, and offered to our Lady of Walsingham ; and Henry VII., in his lifetime, gave a kneeling figure of himself.   There are numerous references to Walsingham in the *Paston Letters*, and in 1443 we find Margaret Paston writing to her husband to tell him that her mother had vowed another image of wax of his own weight, to " our Lady of Walsingham," and that she herself had vowed to go on pilgrimage there for him.   (Ed. Fenn, iii. 22.)

The total income of the place (including the offerings) was reported to be £650 in the twenty-sixth year of Henry VIII.'s reign, and Roger Ascham, when visiting Cologne in 1550, makes this remark: " The Three Kings be not so rich, I believe, as was the Lady of Walsingham."   Now the treasures at Cologne are said to have been worth six millions of francs (£240,000).

The road to Walsingham was a well-frequented one, and a cross was set up in every town it passed through.   An old track running by Newmarket, Brandon, and Castle Acre, which was used by the pilgrims, was known as the "Palmer's Way" or "Walsingham Green Way."

The Milky Way ("the Watling-street of the heavens," as Chaucer has it) has been associated with pilgrimages in several countries. In Norfolk, the long streaming path of light was supposed to point the pilgrim on his road to Walsingham, and was in consequence called the "Walsingham Way."   In Italy, in France, and in the north of Europe it has been called "St. Jago's Way," "Jacobsstrasse," &c., as pointing the way to Compostella, and one of its Turkish names is "The Hadji's Way," as indicating the road to Mecca.[1]

Among the Rawlinson MSS. in the Bodleian Library is *A Lament for Walsingham*, in the handwriting of Philip, Earl of Arundel, the third stanza of which is as follows:

"Bitter, bitter, oh! to behould
   the grasse to growe
Where the walles of Walsingam
   So statly did sheue.
Such were the workes of Walsingam
   While shee did stand!
Such are the wrackes as now do shewe
   of that holy land!
Levell, Levell with the ground
   the towres doe lye."

[1] R. J. King's *Sketches and Studies*, 1874, p. 262.

The whole poem is printed in the Folio MS. ed. Hales and
Furnivall, vol. iii. p. 470.

The late Mr. John Gough Nichols published in 1849 a very interesting volume, containing a translation of the *Colloquy of Erasmus*, with valuable notes in illustration of it, under the following
title: " Pilgrimages to Saint Mary of Walsingham and Saint
Thomas of Canterbury, by Desiderius Erasmus, newly translated
. . . and illustrated by J. G. Nichols. Westminster. 1849."
sm. 8vo. This work has lately been reprinted.

An excellent description of Walsingham Priory, with an account
of the excavations made on its site in 1853, will be found in
Henry Harrod's *Gleanings among the Castles and Convents of Norfolk*, 8vo. Norwich, 1857, pp. 155-197.]

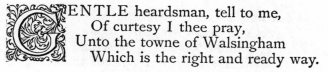

ENTLE heardsman, tell to me,
   Of curtesy I thee pray,
Unto the towne of Walsingham
   Which is the right and ready way.

" Unto the towne of Walsingham   5
   The way is hard for to be gon ;
And verry crooked are those pathes
   For you to find out all alone."

Weere the miles doubled thrise,
   And the way never soe ill,   10
Itt were not enough for mine offence ;
   Itt is soe grievous and soe ill.

" Thy yeeares are young, thy face is faire,
   Thy witts are weake, thy thoughts are greene ;
Time hath not given thee leave, as yett,   15
   For to committ so great a sinne."

Yes, heardsman, yes, soe woldest thou say,
   If thou knewest soe much as I ;
My witts, and thoughts, and all the rest,
   Have well deserved for to dye.   20

I am not what I seeme to bee,
  My clothes and sexe doe differ farr :
I am a woman, woe is me !
  Born[1] to greeffe and irksome care.

For my beloved, and well-beloved,   25
  My wayward cruelty could kill :
And though my teares will nought avail,
  Most dearely I bewail him still.

*He was the flower of n*oble wights,
  None ever more sincere colde bee ;   30
Of comely mien and shape hee was,
  And tenderlye hee loved mee.

*When thus I saw he lo*ved me well,
  *I grewe so proud his pa*ine to see,
That I, who did not know myselfe,   35
  Thought scorne of such a youth as hee.

*And grew soe coy and nice to please,
  As women's lookes are often soe,

---

* Three of the following stanzas have been finely paraphrased
by Dr. *Goldsmith*, in his charming ballad of *Edwin and Emma ;*
the reader of taste will have a pleasure in comparing them with the
original.

" ' And ' still I try'd each fickle art,
    Importunate and vain ;
And while his passion touch'd my heart,
    I triumph'd in his pain.

" 'Till quite dejected with my scorn,
    He left me to my pride ,
And sought a solitude forlorn,
    In secret, where he dy'd.

" But mine the sorrow, mine the fault,
    And well my life shall pay ;

[¹ Mr. Furnivall suggests *a prey.*]

He might not kisse, nor hand forsooth,
　　Unlesse I willed him soe to doe. 4·

Thus being wearyed with delayes
　　To see I pittyed not his greeffe,
He gott him to a secrett place,
　　And there he dyed without releeffe.

And for his sake these weeds I weare, 45
　　And sacriffice my tender age;
And every day Ile begg my bread,
　　To undergoe this pilgrimage.

Thus every day I fast and pray,
　　And ever will doe till I dye; 50
And gett me to some secrett place,
　　For soe did hee, and soe will I.

Now, gentle heardsman, aske no more,
　　But keepe my secretts I thee pray;
Unto the towne of Walsingam 55
　　Show me the right and readye way.

" Now goe thy wayes, and God before!
　　For he must ever guide thee still:
Turne downe that dale, the right hand path,
　　And soe, faire pilgrim, fare thee well!" 6·

*** To shew what constant tribute was paid to *Our Lady of Walsingham*, I shall give a few extracts from the "*Houshold-Book of Henry Algernon Percy*, 5th Earl of Northumberland." Printed 1770, 8vo.

I'll seek the solitude he sought,
　　And stretch me where he lay.

" And there forlorn despairing hid,
　　I'll lay me down and die:
'Twas so for me that Edwin did
　　And so for him will I."

[Goldsmith did not follow the last two verses, but made his ending much more sentimental than that of the old ballad.]

Sect. xliii. p. 337, &c.

Item, My Lorde usith yerly to send afor Michaelmas for his Lord-schip's Offerynge to our Lady of Walsyngeham.—*iiij* d.

Item, My Lorde usith ande accustumyth to sende yerely for the upholdynge of the Light of Wax which his Lordschip fyndith birnynge yerly befor our Lady of Walsyngham, contenynge *xj* lb. of Wax in it after *vij* d. ob. for the fyndynge of every lb. redy wrought by a covenaunt maid with the Channon by great, for the hole yere, for the fyndinge of the said Lyght byrnning,— *vi* s. *viiij* d.

Item, My Lord useth and accustomith to syende yerely to the Channon that kepith the Light before our Lady of Walsyngham, for his reward for the hole yere, for kepynge of the said Light, lightynge of it at all service tymes dayly thorowt the yere,— *xij* d.

Item, My Lord usith and accustomyth yerely to send to the Prest that kepith the Light, lyghtynge of it at all service tymes daily thorowt the yere,—*iij* s. *iiij* d.

XV.

K. EDWARD IV. AND TANNER OF
TAMWORTH

WAS a story of great fame among our ancestors. The author of the *Art of English poesie*, 1589, 4to, seems to speak of it as a real fact.—Describing that vicious mode of speech, which the Greeks called *Acyron, i. e.* "When we use a dark and obscure word, utterly repugnant to that we should express ;" he adds, "Such manner of uncouth speech did the Tanner of Tamworth use to king Edward the fourth ; which Tanner, having a great while mistaken him, and used very broad talke with him, at length perceiving by his traine that it was the king, was afraide he should be punished for it, [and] said thus, with a certain rude repentance,

'*I hope I shall be hanged to-morrow,*'

for [*I feare me*] *I shall be hanged;* whereat the king laughed a good,* not only to see the Tanner's vaine feare, but also to heare

---

[* for good deal.]

his illshapen terme: and gave him for recompence of his good sport, the inheritance of Plumpton-parke. *I am afraid,"* concludes this sagacious writer, *" the poets of our times that speake more finely and correctedly, will come too short of such a reward,"* p. 214.— The phrase, here referred to, is not found in this ballad at present,* but occurs with some variation in another old poem, intitled *John the Reeve,* described in the following volume (see the Preface to *the King and the Miller*),† viz.

> " Nay, sayd John, by Gods grace,
> And Edward wer in this place,
> Hee shold not touch this tonne:
> He wold be wroth with John *I hope,*
> Thereffore I beshrew the soupe,
> That in his mouth shold come." Pt. ii. st. 24.

The following text is selected (with such other corrections as occurred) from two copies in black-letter. The one in the Bodleyan library, intitled, " A merrie, pleasant, and delectable historie betweene K. Edward the Fourth, and a Tanner of Tamworth, &c. printed at London, by John Danter, 1596." This copy, ancient as it now is, appears to have been modernized and altered at the time it was published; and many vestiges of the more ancient readings were recovered from another copy, (though more recently printed,) in one sheet folio, without date, in the Pepys collection.

But these are both very inferior in point of antiquity to the old ballad of *The King and the Barker,* reprinted with other " Pieces of Ancient Popular Poetry from Authentic Manuscripts and old Printed Copies, &c." Lond. 1791, 8vo. As that very antique Poem had never occurred to the Editor of the Reliques, till he saw it in the above collection, he now refers the curious reader to it, as an imperfect and incorrect copy of the old original ballad.

[This ballad was a great favourite with our ancestors and is probably of considerable antiquity.

The earliest entry of it upon the Registers of the Stationers' Company is to William Griffith in 1564, but no such edition is known to bibliographers. It is possible, however, that Puttenham may have found the line quoted above—

" I hope I shall be hanged to-morrow "

in that edition.

It belongs to the large class of tales in which the sovereign is

---

* Nor in that of the *Barker* mentioned below.
[† Vol. iii. Book 2, No. 20.]

made to converse on terms of good fellowship with a humble subject.

The interesting ballad of *John the Reeve* referred to by Percy is printed for the first time in Hales and Furnivall's edition of the Folio Manuscript (vol. ii. p. 550.)

The Tanner of Tamworth is introduced into the first part of Heywood's *Edward IV*. The ballad *Under the greenwood tree*, among the Ashmole MSS. at Oxford, *Robin Hood and the Curtal Friar*, and *Robin Hood and the Monk*, all begin with the same words as this ballad—

"In summer time when leaves grow green."

The present version is an eclectic copy, polished and reversified by Percy.]

N summer time, when leaves grow greene,
    And blossoms bedecke the tree,
  King Edward wolde a hunting ryde,
    Some pastime for to see.

With hawke and hounde he made him bowne,[1] 5
  With horne, and eke with bowe;
To Drayton Basset he tooke his waye,
  With all his lordes a rowe.

And he had ridden ore dale and downe
  By eight of clocke in the day,   10
When he was ware of a bold tannèr,
  Come ryding along the waye.

A fayre russet coat the tanner had on
  Fast buttoned under his chin,
And under him a good cow-hide,   15
  And a mare of four shilling.*

---

* In the reign of Edward IV. Dame Cecill, lady of Torboke, in her will dated March 7, A.D. 1466; among many other bequests

[1 ready.]

Nowe stand you still, my good lordes all,
    Under the grene wood spraye;
And I will wend to yonder fellowe,
    To weet[1] what he will saye.   20

God speede, God speede thee, said our king,
    Thou art welcome, sir, sayd hee.
" The readyest waye to Drayton Basset
    I praye thee to shewe to mee."

" To Drayton Basset woldst thou goe,   25
    Fro the place where thou dost stand?
The next payre of gallowes thou comest unto,
    Turne in upon thy right hand."

That is an unreadye waye, sayd our king,
    Thou doest but jest I see :   30
Nowe shewe me out the nearest waye,
    And I pray thee wend with mee.

Awaye with a vengeance ! quoth the tanner :
    I hold thee out of thy witt :
All daye have I rydden on Brocke my mare,   35
    And I am fasting yett.

" Go with me downe to Drayton Basset,
    No daynties we will spare ;
All daye shalt thou eate and drinke of the best,
    And I will paye thy fare."   40

Gramercye[2] for nothing, the tanner replyde,
    Thou payest no fare of mine :
I trowe I've more nobles in my purse,
    Than thou hast pence in thine.

---

has this, " Also I will that my sonne Thomas of Torboke have
13*s*. 4*d*. to buy him an horse." Vid. Harleian Catalog. 2176. 27.—
Now if 13*s*. 4*d*. would purchase a steed fit for a person of quality,
a tanner's horse might reasonably be valued at four or five shillings.

    [1 know.   2 thank you.]

God give thee joy of them, sayd the king,   45
    And send them well to priefe.[1]
The tanner wolde faine have beene away,
    For he weende he had beene a thiefe.

What art thou, hee sayde, thou fine fellòwe,
    Of thee I am in great feare,   50
For the cloathes, thou wearest upon thy backe,
    Might beseeme a lord to weare.

I never stole them, quoth our king,
    I tell you, sir, by the roode.
" Then thou playest, as many an unthrift doth,   55
    And standest in midds of thy goode."*

What tydinges heare you, sayd the kynge,
    As you ryde farre and neare?
" I heare no tydinges, sir, by the masse,
    But that cowe-hides are deare."   60

" Cowe-hides ! cowe-hides ! what things are those?
    I marvell what they bee?"
What art thou a foole ? the tanner reply'd;
    I carry one under mee.

What craftsman art thou, said the king,   65
    I praye thee tell me trowe.
" I am a barker,† sir, by my trade ;
    Nowe tell me what art thou ? "

I am a poore courtier, sir, quoth he,
    That am forth of service worne ;   70
And faine I wolde thy prentise bee,
    Thy cunninge for to learne.

---

* *i.e.* hast no other wealth, but what thou carriest about thee.
† *i.e.* a dealer in bark.

[¹ prove.]

're heaven forfend,[1] the tanner replyde,
ιt thou my prentise were :
woldst spend more good than I shold winne 75
'ortye shilling a yere.

ιt one thinge wolde I, sayd our king,
  If thou wilt not seeme strange :
Thoughe my horse be better than thy mare,
  Yet with thee I faine wold change.   80

"Why if with me thou faine wilt change,
  As change full well maye wee,
By the faith of my bodye, thou proude fellòwe,
  I will have some boot[2] of thee."

That were against reason, sayd the king,   85
  I sweare, so mote I thee :[3]
My horse is better than thy mare,
  And that thou well mayst see.

"Yea, sir, but Brocke is gentle and mild,
  And softly she will fare :   90
Thy horse is unrulye and wild, I wiss ;
  Aye skipping here and theare."

What boote wilt thou have? our king reply'd ;
  Now tell me in this stound.[4]
"Noe pence, nor half pence, by my faye,   95
  But a noble in gold so round."

"Here's twentye groates of white moneyè,
  Sith thou will have it of mee."
I would have sworne now, quoth the tanner,
  Thou hadst not had one penniè.   100

[[1] avert it.   [2] profit.   [3] so may I thrive.
  [4] moment.]

But since we two have made a change,
  A change we must abide,
Although thou hast gotten Brocke my mare,
  Thou gettest not my cowe-hide.

I will not have it, sayd the kynge,   105
  I sweare, so mought I thee ;
Thy foule cowe-hide I wolde not beare,
  If thou woldst give it to mee.

The tanner hee tooke his good cowe-hide,
  That of the cow was hilt ;   110
And threwe it upon the king's sadèlle,
  That was soe fayrelye gilte.

" Now help me up, thou fine fellòwe,
  'Tis time that I were gone :
When I come home to Gyllian my wife,   115
  Sheel say I am a gentilmon."

The king he tooke him up by the legge ;
  The tanner a f ** lett fall.
Nowe marrye, good fellowe, sayd the kyng,
  Thy courtesye is but small.   120

When the tanner he was in the kinges sadèlle,
  And his foote in the stirrup was ;
He marvelled greatlye in his minde,
  Whether it were golde or brass.

But when his steede saw the cows taile wagge, 125
  And eke the blacke cowe-horne ;
He stamped, and stared, and awaye he ranne,
  As the devill had him borne.

The tanner he pulld, the tanner he sweat,
  And held by the pummil fast :   130
At length the tanner came tumbling downe ;
  His necke he had well-nye brast.[1]

[1 broken.]

Take thy horse again with a vengeance, he sayd,
   With mee he shall not byde.
" My horse wolde have borne thee well enoughe, 135
   But he knewe not of thy cowe-hide.

Yet if againe thou faine woldst change,
   As change full well may wee,
By the faith of my bodye, thou jolly tannèr,
   I will have some boote of thee."   140

What boote wilt thou have, the tanner replyd,
   Nowe tell me in this stounde ?
" Noe pence nor halfpence, sir, by my faye,
   But I will have twentye pound."

" Here's twentye groates out of my purse ;   145
   And twentye I have of thine :
And I have one more, which we will spend
   Together at the wine."

The king set a bugle horne to his mouthe,
   And blewe both loude and shrille :   150
And soone came lords, and soone came knights,
   Fast ryding over the hille.

Nowe, out alas ! the tanner he cryde,
   That ever I sawe this daye !
Thou art a strong thiefe, yon come thy fellowes 155
   Will beare my cowe-hide away.

They are no thieves, the king replyde,
   I sweare, soe mote I thee :
But they are the lords of the north countrèy,
   Here come to hunt with mee.   160

And soone before our king they came,
   And knelt downe on the grounde :
Then might the tanner have beene awaye,
   He had lever than twentye pounde.

A coller, a coller, here : sayd the king,   165
    A coller he loud gan crye ;
Then woulde he lever then twentye pound,
    He had not beene so nighe.

A coller, a coller, the tanner he sayd,
    I trowe it will breed sorrowe :   170
After a coller commeth a halter,
    I trow I shall be hang'd to-morrowe.

Be not afraid Tanner, said our king ;
    I tell thee, so mought I thee,
Lo here I make thee the best esquire   175
    That is in the North countrie.*

For Plumpton-parke I will give thee,
    With tenements faire beside :
'Tis worth three hundred markes by the yeare,
    To maintaine thy good cowe-hide.   180

Gramercye, my liege, the tanner replyde,
    For the favour thou hast me showne ;
If ever thou comest to merry Tamwòrth,
    Neates leather shall clout thy shoen.[1]   ***

---

* This stanza is restored from a quotation of this ballad in Selden's *Titles of Honour*, who produces it as a good authority to prove, that one mode of creating *Esquires* at that time, was by the imposition of a *Collar*. His words are, " Nor is that old pamphlet of the Tanner of Tamworth and King Edward the Fourth so contemptible, but that wee may thence note also an observable passage, wherein the use of making Esquires, by giving Collars, is expressed." (Sub Tit. Esquire ; & vide in Spelmanni Glossar. Armiger.)   This form of creating Esquires actually exists at this day among the Serjeants at Arms, who are invested with a Collar (which they wear on Collar Days) by the King himself.

This information I owe to Samuel Pegge, Esq. to whom the publick is indebted for that curious work the *Curialia*, 4to.

[1 cow hide shall mend thy shoes.]

XVI.

AS YE CAME FROM THE HOLY LAND.

DIALOGUE BETWEEN A PILGRIM AND TRAVELLER.

THE scene of this song is the same as in Num. XIV. The pilgrimage to Walsingham suggested the plan of many popular pieces. In the Pepys collection, vol. i. p. 226, is a kind of Interlude in the old ballad style, of which the first stanza alone is worth reprinting.

> "As I went to Walsingham,
>   To the shrine with speede,
> Met I with a jolly palmer
>   In a pilgrimes weede.
> Now God you save, you jolly palmer!
>   'Welcome, lady gay,
> Oft have I sued to thee for love.'
>   —Oft have I said you nay."

The pilgrimages undertaken on pretence of religion, were often productive of affairs of gallantry, and led the votaries to no other shrine than that of Venus.*

The following ballad was once very popular; it is quoted in Fletcher's *Knt. of the burning pestle*, act ii. sc. ult. and in another old play, called, *Hans Beer-pot, his invisible Comedy, &c.* 4to. 1618; act i.—The copy below was communicated to the Editor by the late Mr. Shenstone as corrected by him from an ancient copy, and supplied with a concluding stanza.

We have placed this, and *Gentle Herdsman*, &c. thus early in the volume, upon a presumption that they must have been written,

---

* Even in the time of Langland, pilgrimages to Walsingham were not unfavourable to the rites of Venus. Thus in his *Visions of Pierce Plowman*, fo. 1.

> " Hermets on a heape, with hoked staves,
>   Wenten to Walsingham, and her† wenches after."

† *i.e.* their.

if not before the dissolution of the monasteries, yet while the remembrance of them was fresh in the minds of the people.

[Although Percy does not mention his folio MS. this song is there,
and a copy from it is now printed at the end of Percy's version.
With the exception of the last three lines there are little but verbal
differences, but these are numerous.   The ending is strikingly inferior to that of the MS. and does very little credit to Shenstone's
poetical taste.   A copy of the song in the Bodleian library (MS.
Rawl. 85 fol. 124) is signed W. R., and Dr. Bliss in consequence
claimed it for Sir Walter Raleigh in his edition of Wood's *Athenæ.*
It is inserted in the Oxford edition of Raleigh's Works, vol. viii.
p. 733, with the title—*False Love and True Love.*   Dr. Hannah
also includes it in his edition of the *Courtly Poets,* but believes
it highly improbable that Raleigh wrote the song.

Mr. Chappell points out that the first line of the ballad quoted
above is introduced in Nashe's *Have with you to Saffron Walden,*
1596.   In *The Weakest goes to the Wall,* 1600, we read

" King Richard's gone to Walsingham, to the Holy Land."

The tune of *Walsingham* was highly popular, and numerous songs
have been set to it.]

S ye came from the holy land
  Of blessed Walsingham,
 O met you not with my true love
  As by the way ye came ?

" How should I know your true love,   5
  That have met many a one,
As I came from the holy land,
  That have both come and gone ? "

My love is neither white*, nor browne,
  But as the heavens faire ;   10
There is none hath her form divine,
  Either in earth, or ayre.

---

* sc. pale.

"Such an one did I meet, good sir,
  With an angelicke face;
Who like a nymphe, a queene appeard   15
  Both in her gait, her grace."

Yes: she hath cleane forsaken me,
  And left me all alone;
Who some time loved me as her life,
  And called me her owne.   20

"What is the cause she leaves thee thus,
  And a new way doth take,
That some times loved thee as her life,
  And thee her joy did make?"

I that loved her all my youth,   25
  Growe old now as you see;
Love liketh not the falling fruite,
  Nor yet the withered tree.

For love is like a carelesse childe,
  Forgetting promise past: 30
He is blind, or deaf, whenere he list;
  His faith is never fast.

His fond desire is fickle found,
  And yieldes a trustlesse joye;
Wonne with a world of toil and care,   35
  And lost ev'n with a toye.

Such is the love of womankinde,
  Or Loves faire name abusde,
Beneathe which many vaine desires,
  And follyes are excusde.   40

' But true love is a lasting fire,
  [Which viewless vestals * tend,
That burnes for ever in the soule,
  And knowes nor change, nor end.']   *⁎*

---

* sc. angels.

HE following version is reprinted from the **Folio MS.**
(ed. Hales and Furnivall, vol. iii. p. 471.)

" As : yee came ffrom the holy Land
    of Walsingham,
Mett you not with my true loue
    by the way as you came ? "   4
" how shold I know your true loue,
    that haue mett many a one
as I cam ffrom the holy Land,
    that haue come, that haue gone ? "   8

" Shee is neither white nor browne,
    but as the heauens ffaire ;
there is none hathe their fforme diuine
    on the earth or the ayre."   12
" such a one did I meete, good Sir,
    with an angellike fface,
who like a nimph, like a queene, did appeare
    in her gate, in her grace."   16

" Shee hath left me heere alone,
    all alone as vnknowne,
who sometime loued me as her liffe
    and called me her owne."   20
" What is the cause shee hath left thee alone,
    and a new way doth take,
that sometime did loue thee as her selfe,
    and her ioy did thee make ? "   24

" I haue loued her all my youth,
    but now am old, as you see.
loue liketh not the ffalling ffruite
    nor the whithered tree ;   28
for loue is like a carlesse child,
    and fforgetts promise past :
he is blind, he is deaffe when he list,
    and infaith neuer ffast ;   32

" his desire is ffickle, ffond,
    and a trustles ioye ;
he is won with a world of dispayre,
    and lost with a toye.   36

such is the [fate of all man] kind,
   or the word loue abused,
under which many childish desires
   and conceipts are excused."   40

" But loue is a durabler ffyer
   in the mind euer Burninge,
euer sicke, neuer dead, neuer cold,
   ffrom itt selfe neuer turninge."   ffinis.]   44

XVII.

HARDYKNUTE.

A Scottish Fragment.

AS this fine morsel of heroic poetry hath generally past for ancient, it is here thrown to the end of our earliest pieces; that such as doubt of its age, may the better compare it with other pieces of genuine antiquity. For after all, there is more than reason to suspect, that it owes most of its beauties (if not its whole existence) to the pen of a lady, within the present century. The following particulars may be depended on. Mrs. Wardlaw, whose maiden name was Halket (aunt to the late Sir Peter Halket, of Pitferran, in Scotland, who was killed in America, along with general Bradock, in 1755), pretended she had found this poem, written on shreds of paper, employed for what is called the bottoms of clues. A suspicion arose that it was her own composition. Some able judges asserted it to be modern. The lady did in a manner acknowledge it to be so. Being desired to shew an additional stanza, as a prooi of this, she produced the 2 last beginning with " *There's nae light,*" &c. which were not in the copy that was first printed. The late Lord President Forbes, and Sir Gilbert Elliot of Minto (late Lord Justice Clerk for Scotland) who had believed it ancient, contributed to the expence of publishing the first edition, in folio, 1719. —This account was transmitted from Scotland by Sir David Dalrymple, the late Lord Hailes, who yet was of opinion, that part ot the ballad may be ancient; but retouched and much enlarged by the lady abovementioned. Indeed he had been informed, that the late William Thomson, the Scottish musician, who published the *Orpheus Caledonius*, 1733, 2 vols. 8vo. declared he had heard fragments of it repeated in his infancy, before Mrs. Wardlaw's copy was heard of.

The poem is here printed from the original edition, as it was prepared for the press with the additional improvements.

In an elegant publication, intitled, *Scottish Tragic Ballads*, printed by and for J. Nichols, 1781, 8vo. may be seen a continuation of the Ballad of *Hardyknute*, by the addition of a *Second Part*, which hath since been acknowledged to be his own composition, by the ingenious Editor [John Pinkerton]—To whom the late Sir D. Dalrymple communicated (subsequent to the account drawn up above) extracts of a letter from Sir John Bruce, of Kinross, to Lord Binning, which plainly proves the pretended discoverer of the fragment of *Hardyknute* to have been Sir John Bruce himself. His words are, "To perform my promise, I send you a true copy of the Manuscript I found some weeks ago in a vault at Dumferline. It is written on vellum in a fair Gothic character, but so much defaced by time, as you'll find that the tenth part is not legible." He then gives the whole fragment as it was first published in 1719, save one or two stanzas, marking several passages as having perished by being illegible in the old MS. Hence it appears, that Sir John was the author of *Hardyknute*, but afterwards used Mrs. Wardlaw to be the midwife of his poetry, and suppressed the story of the vault; as is well observed by the Editor of the *Tragic Ballads*, and of Maitland's *Scot. Poets*, vol. i. p. cxxvii.

To this gentleman we are indebted for the use of the copy, whence the second edition was afterwards printed, as the same was prepared for the press by John Clerk, M.D. of Edinburgh, an intimate companion of Lord President Forbes.

The title of the first edition was, "*Hardyknute, a Fragment*. Edinburgh, printed for James Watson, &c. 1719," folio, 12 pages.

Stanzas not in the first edition are, Nos. 17, 18, 20, 21, 22, 23, 34, 35, 36, 37, 41, 42.

In the present impression the orthography of Dr. Clerk's copy has been preserved, and his readings carefully followed, except in a few instances, wherein the common edition appeared preferable: *viz.* He had in ver. 20. *but.*—v. 56. *of harm.*—v. 64. *every.*—v. 67. *lo down.*—v. 83. *That* omitted.—v. 89. *And* omitted.—v. 143. *With argument but vainly strave Lang.*—v. 148. *say'd.*—v. 155. *incampit on the plain.*—v. 156. *Norse squadrons.*—v. 158. *regand revers.*— v. 170. *his strides he bent.*—v. 171. *minstrals playand Pibrochs fine.* —v. 172. *stately went.*—v. 182. *mon.*—v. 196. *sharp and fatal.*— v. 219. *which.*—v. 241. *stood wyld.*—Stanza 39 preceded stanza 38.—v. 305. *There.*—v. 313. *blew westling.*—v. 336. had originally been, *He fear'd a' cou'd be fear'd.*

The Editor was also informed, on the authority of Dr. David Clerk, M.D. of Edinburgh (son of the aforesaid Dr. John Clerk), that between the present stanzas 36 and 37, the two following had been intended, but were on maturer consideration omitted, and do not now appear among the MS. additions:

> " Now darts flew wavering through slaw speed,
>   Scarce could they reach their aim;
> Or reach'd, scarce blood the round point drew,
>   'Twas all but shot in vain :
> Right strengthy arms forfeebled grew,
>   Sair wreck'd wi' that day's toils:
> E'en fierce-born minds now lang'd for peace,
>   And curs'd war's cruel broils.

> " Yet still wars horns sounded to charge,
>   Swords clash'd and harness rang;
> But saftly sae ilk blaster blew
>   The hills and dales fraemang.
> Nae echo heard in double dints,
>   Nor the lang-winding horn,
> Nae mair she blew out brade as she
>   Did eir that summers morn."

[Elizabeth Halket, second daughter of Sir Charles Halket of Pitfirrane, Fife, and wife of Sir Henry Wardlaw of Pitrivie, Fife and Balmulie near Dunfermline, who was born in the year 1677, married in 1696, and died in 1727, is now known to have been the authoress of *Hardyknute*, although it was many years before the question of the authorship was finally settled.

Mr. David Laing once possessed a copy of this ballad printed in a duodecimo of eight pages without date, which is supposed to be the original edition. Besides various differences, some important and others minute, it does not contain stanzas 27, 28 and 40, which are printed in the folio of 1719. It was reprinted several times before Percy included it in his book, and its antiquity does not seem to have been doubted, for the editor of the edition of 1740 speaks of it as a specimen of the true sublime, and believes that "it can only be the work of an author highly smitten with the fury of a poetical genius." Allan Ramsay's *Evergreen*, 1724, vol. ii. contains this ballad with the twelve additional stanzas noted above by Percy.

When Percy first printed the ballad suspicions of its authenticity had been expressed, which soon led to the discovery of the writer, but after having stated who was the real author, he threw doubts upon his statement on account of Pinkerton's truthless report. Pinkerton was never to be depended upon, and he had previously affirmed that the common people of Lanarkshire "repeat scraps of *both parts*," although the second was his own composition. Sir John Hope Bruce had nothing to do with the composition of the ballad, and it is even doubtful whether his supposed letter to Lord Binning ever had any existence. If it had, it was merely a mystification. On the second of December, 1785, Lord Hailes wrote to Pinkerton as follows, " You mistook if you suppose that I reckoned Sir John Bruce to be the author of *Hardyknute*. It is his sister-in-law, Lady Wardlaw, who is said to have been the author." Yet Pinkerton made Percy believe that Bruce was the author. Great difference of opinion has been expressed as to the merit of the ballad by various critics. Mathias was fascinated with it, and printed it privately with an encomiastic criticism. Scott wrote on the fly-leaf of his copy of Ramsay's *Evergreen*, " *Hardyknute* was the first poem I ever learnt—the last that I shall forget," and in his *Minstrelsy of the Border* he terms it " a most spirited and beautiful imitation of the ancient ballad." Thomas Warton was deceived by it, and describes it as genuine in the first edition of his *Observations on Spenser*. In the second edition he assigns the ballad to its true author, but adds, " I am apt to think that the first stanza is old and gave the hint for writing the rest." On the other side Dr. Johnson considered it to have " no great merit," and Aytoun esteemed it a very poor performance. It has not been popular with the ordinary devourers of ballads, and Mr. James Maidment never had the good luck to pick up a stall copy—he writes, " The flying stationers, the best judges of what suited their customers, not considering it an eligible republication." The ballad is supposed to refer to the battle of Largs, fought on the second of October, 1263, between the invading force led by Haco, King of Norway, and the Scottish army commanded in person by Alexander III., but it would, in fact, suit any conflict between Scots and Northmen. The effect of this battle was the loss to Scandinavia of the Hebrides and the Isle of Man, which dependencies were relinquished to Alexander III. by terms of a treaty concluded in 1266, with Magnus, the successor of Haco. The victory was largely due to the Lord High Steward of Scotland, who is supposed to be represented by Hardyknute. Mr. Gilfillan notes that " Fairly Castle, the residence of Hardyknute, stands three miles south of the battle field. It is a single square tower, by the side of a wild stream tumbling over a rock into a deep ravine."]

I.

STATELY stept he east the wa',[1]
　　And stately stept he west,
　　Full seventy years he now had seen,
　　Wi' scarce seven years of rest.
He liv'd when Britons breach of faith　　　　5
　　Wrought Scotland mickle wae :
And ay his sword tauld to their cost,
　　He was their deadlye fae.

II.

High on a hill his castle stood,
　　With ha's[2] and tow'rs a height,　　　　10
And goodly chambers fair to se,
　　Where he lodged mony a knight.
His dame sae peerless anes and fair,
　　For chast and beauty deem'd,
Nae marrow[3] had in all the land,　　　　15
　　Save Elenor* the queen.

III.

Full thirteen sons to him she bare,
　　All men of valour stout ;
In bloody fight with sword in hand
　　Nine lost their lives bot[4] doubt :　　　　20
Four yet remain, lang may they live
　　To stand by liege and land ;
High was their fame, high was their might,
　　And high was their command.

[* Margaret was the name of the queen of Alexander III. Her mother was Eleanor, Queen of England.
[1] wall or rampart of the castle.　　　　[2] halls.
[3] match or equal.　　　　[4] without.]

IV.

Great love they bare to Fairly fair,   25
   Their sister saft and dear,
Her girdle shaw'd her middle gimp,[1]
   And gowden glist[2] her hair.
What waefu' wae her beauty bred?
   Waefu' to young and auld,   30
Waefu' I trow to kyth and kin,
   As story ever tauld.

V.

The king of Norse in summer tyde,
   Puff'd up with pow'r and might,
Landed in fair Scotland the isle   35
   With mony a hardy knight.
The tydings to our good Scots king
   Came, as he sat at dine,
With noble chiefs in brave aray,
   Drinking the blood-red wine   40

VI.

" To horse, to horse, my royal liege,
   Your faes stand on the strand,
Full twenty thousand glittering spears
   The king of Norse commands."
Bring me my steed Mage dapple gray,   4
   Our good king rose and cry'd,
A trustier beast in a' the land
   A Scots king nevir try'd.

VII.

Go little page, tell Hardyknute,
   That lives on hill sae hie,
To draw his sword, the dread of faes,
   And haste and follow me.

[1 slender.   2 shone like gold.]

The little page flew swift as dart
    Flung by his master's arm,
" Come down, come down, lord Hardyknute, 55
    And rid your king frae harm."

VIII.

Then red red grew his dark-brown cheeks,
    Sae did his dark-brown brow ;
His looks grew keen, as they were wont
    In dangers great to do ;   60
He's ta'en a horn as green as grass,
    And gi'en five sounds sae shill,[1]
That trees in green wood shook thereat,
    Sae loud rang ilka hill.

IX.

His sons in manly sport and glee,   65
    Had past that summer's morn,
When low down in a grassy dale,
    They heard their father's horn.
That horn, quo' they, ne'er sounds in peace,
    We've other sport to bide.   70
And soon they hy'd them up the hill,
    And soon were at his side.

X.

" Late late the yestreen[2] I ween'd in peace
    To end my lengthened life,
My age might well excuse my arm   75
    Frae manly feats of strife ;
But now that Norse do's proudly boast
    Fair Scotland to inthrall,
It's ne'er be said of Hardyknute,
    He fear'd to fight or fall.   80

[1 so shrill.   2 yester even.]

XI.

" Robin of Rothsay, bend thy bow
  Thy arrows shoot sae leel,[1]
That mony a comely countenance
  They've turnd to deadly pale.
Brade[2] Thomas take you but your lance,   85
  You need nae weapons mair,
If you fight wi't as you did anes
  'Gainst Westmoreland's fierce heir.

XII.

" And Malcolm, light of foot as stag
  That runs in forest wild,   90
Get me my thousands three of men
  Well bred to sword and shield :
Bring me my horse and harnisine,[3]
  My blade of mettal clear.
If faes but ken'd the hand it bare,   95
  They soon had fled for fear.

XIII.

" Farewell my dame sae peerless good,
  (And took her by the hand),
Fairer to me in age you seem,
  Than maids for beauty fam'd.   100
My youngest son shall here remain
  To guard these stately towers,
And shut the silver bolt that keeps
  Sae fast your painted bowers."

XIV.

And first she wet her comely cheiks,   105
  And then her boddice green,
Her silken cords of twirtle twist,[4]
  Well plett with silver sheen ;

[[1] true.   [2] broad.   [3] armour.   [4] twirled twist.]

And apron set with mony a dice
   Of needle-wark sae rare, 110
Wove by nae hand, as ye may guess,
   Save that of Fairly fair.

xv.

And he has ridden o'er muir and moss,
   O'er hills and mony a glen,
When he came to a wounded knight 115
   Making a heavy mane ;
" Here maun I lye, here maun I dye,
   By treacherie's false guiles ;
Witless I was that e'er ga faith
   To wicked woman's smiles." 120

xvi.

" Sir knight, gin you were in my bower,
   To lean on silken seat,
My lady's kindly care you'd prove,
   Who ne'er knew deadly hate :
Herself wou'd watch you a' the day, 125
   Her maids a dead of night ;
And Fairly fair your heart wou'd chear,
   As she stands in your sight.

xvii.

" Arise young knight, and mount your stead,
   Full lowns the shynand day :[1] 130
Choose frae my menzie[2] whom ye please
   To lead you on the way."
With smileless look, and visage wan
   The wounded knight reply'd,
" Kind chieftain, your intent pursue, 13
   For here I maun abyde.

[[1] full calm the shining day becomes.   [2] retinue.]

XVIII.

To me nae after day nor night
    Can e're be sweet or fair,
But soon beneath some draping tree,
    Cauld death shall end my care."   140
With him nae pleading might prevail ;
    Brave Hardyknute to gain
With fairest words, and reason strong,
    Strave courteously in vain.

XIX.

Syne he has gane far hynd out o'er[1]   145
    Lord Chattan's land sae wide ;
That lord a worthy wight was ay,
    When faes his courage sey'd :[2]
Of Pictish race by mother's side,
    When Picts rul'd Caledon,   150
Lord Chattan claim'd the princely maid,
    When he sav'd Pictish crown.

XX.

Now with his fierce and stalwart train,
    He reach'd a rising hight,
Quhair braid encampit on the dale,   155
    Norss menzie[3] lay in sicht.
" Yonder my valiant sons and feirs[4]
    Our raging revers[5] wait
On the unconquert Scottish sward
    To try with us their fate.   160

XXI.

" Make orisons to him that sav'd
    Our sauls upon the rude ;[6]
Syne[7] bravely shaw your veins are fill'd
    With Caledonian blude."

[[1] gone far over the country. [2]   tried.   [3] the horse army.
[4] companions.   [5] spoilers or robbers.   [6] cross.   [7] then.]

Then furth he drew his trusty glave,[1] 165
 While thousands all around
Drawn frae their sheaths glanc'd in the sun ;
 And loud the bougles sound.

XXII.

To joyn his king adoun the hill
 In hast his merch he made, 170
While, playand pibrochs, minstralls meit[2]
 Afore him stately strade.
" Thrice welcome valiant stoup of weir,[3]
 Thy nations shield and pride ;
Thy king nae reason has to fear 175
 When thou art by his side."

XXIII.

When bows were bent and darts were thrawn ;
 For thrang scarce cou'd they flee ;
The darts clove arrows as they met,
 The arrows dart[4] the tree. 180
Lang did they rage and fight fu' fierce,
 With little skaith to mon,
But bloody bloody was the field,
 Ere that lang day was done.

XXIV.

The king of Scots, that sindle[5] brook'd 185
 The war that look'd like play,
Drew his braid sword, and brake his bow,
 Sin bows seem'd but delay.
Quoth noble Rothsay, " Mine I'll keep,
 I wat it's bled a score." 190
Haste up my merry men, cry'd the king,
 As he rode on before.

[[1] sword. [2] proper. [3] pillar of war. [4] hit [5] seldom.]

XXV.

The king of Norse he sought to find,
　With him to mense[1] the faught,
But on his forehead there did light　　　　195
　A sharp unsonsie[2] shaft ;
As he his hand put up to feel
　The wound, an arrow keen,
O waefu' chance ! there pinn'd his hand
　In midst between his een.　　　　　　　200

XXVI.

" Revenge, revenge, cry'd Rothsay's heir,
　Your mail-coat sha' na bide
The strength and sharpness of my dart:"
　Then sent it through his side.
Another arrow well he mark'd,　　　　　205
　It pierc'd his neck in twa,
His hands then quat[3] the silver reins,
　He low as earth did fa'.

XXVII.

" Sair bleids my liege, sair, sair he bleeds ! "
　Again wi' might he drew　　　　　　　210
And gesture dread his sturdy bow,
　Fast the braid arrow flew :
Wae to the knight he ettled at;[4]
　Lament now queen Elgreed ;
High dames too wail your darling's fall,　215
　His youth and comely meed.

XXVIII.

" Take aff, take aff his costly jupe[5]
　(Of gold well was it twin'd,
Knit like the fowler's net, through quhilk,
　His steelly harness shin'd)　　　　　　220

[¹ to measure or try the battle.　² unlucky.　³ quitted.
⁴ aimed at.　　　⁵ upper garment.]

Take, Norse, that gift frae me, and bid
　　Him venge the blood it bears;
Say, if he face my bended bow,
　　He sure nae weapon fears."

XXIX.

Proud Norse with giant body tall,　　　225
　　Braid shoulders and arms strong,
Cry'd, "Where is Hardyknute sae fam'd,
　　And fear'd at Britain's throne:
Tho' Britons tremble at his name,
　　I soon shall make him wail,　　　230
That e'er my sword was made sae sharp,
　　Sae saft his coat of mail."

XXX.

That brag his stout heart cou'd na bide,
　　It lent him youthfu' micht:
" I'm Hardyknute; this day, he cry'd,　　　235
　　To Scotland's king I heght[1]
To lay thee low, as horses hoof;
　　My word I mean to keep."
Syne with the first stroke e'er he strake,
　　He garr'd[2] his body bleed.　　　240

XXXI.

Norss' een like gray gosehawk's stair'd wyld,
　　He sigh'd wi' shame and spite;
" Disgrac'd is now my far-fam'd arm
　　That left thee power to strike:"
Then ga' his head a blow sae fell,　　　245
　　It made him doun to stoup,
As laigh as he to ladies us'd
　　In courtly guise to lout.[3]

[¹ promised.　　² made.　　³ bend low.]

XXXII.

Fu' soon he rais'd his bent body,
    His bow he marvell'd sair,   250
Sin blows till then on him but darr'd[1]
    As touch of Fairly fair :
Norse marvell'd too as sair as he
    To see his stately look ;
Sae soon as e'er he strake a fae,   255
    Sae soon his life he took.

XXXIII.

Where like a fire to heather set,
    Bauld Thomas did advance,
Ane sturdy fae with look enrag'd
    Up toward him did prance ;   260
He spurr'd his steid through thickest ranks
    The hardy youth to quell,
Wha stood unmov'd at his approach
    His fury to repell.

XXXIV.

" That short brown shaft sae meanly trimm'd, 265
    Looks like poor Scotlands gear,
But dreadfull seems the rusty point ! "
    And loud he leugh in jear.[2]
" Oft Britons b[l]ood has dimm'd its shine ;
    This point cut short their vaunt : "   270
Syne pierc'd the boasters bearded cheek ;
    Nae time he took to taunt.

XXXV.

Short while he in his saddle swang,
    His stirrup was nae stay,
Sae feeble hang his unbent knee   275
    Sure taiken he was fey :[3]

[[1] hit.   [2] in derision.   [3] sure token he was doomed to death.]

Swith[1] on the harden't clay he fell,
  Right far was heard the thud :
But Thomas look't nae as he lay
  All waltering in his blud :　　　　　280

XXXVI.

With careless gesture, mind unmov't,
  On rode he north the plain ;
His seem in throng of fiercest strife,
  When winner ay the same :
Not yet his heart dames dimplet cheek　285
  Could mease[2] soft love to bruik,
Till vengefu' Ann return'd his scorn,
  Then languid grew his luik.

XXXVII.

In thraws of death, with walowit[3] cheik
  All panting on the plain,　　　　　290
The fainting corps of warriours lay,
  Ne're to arise again ;
Ne're to return to native land,
  Nae mair with blithsome sounds
To boast the glories of the day,　　　295
  And shaw their shining wounds.

XXXVIII.

On Norways coast the widowit dame
  May wash the rocks with tears,
May lang luik ow'r the shipless seas
  Befor her mate appears.　　　　　300
Cease, Emma, cease to hope in vain ;
  Thy lord lyes in the clay ;
The valiant Scots nae revers thole[4]
  To carry life away.

[[1] at once.　　　[2] mollify.　　　[3] faded.　　　[4] suffer.

XXXIX.

Here on a lee, where stands a cross   305
    Set up for monument,
Thousands fu' fierce that summer's day
    Fill'd keen war's black intent.
Let Scots, while Scots, praise Hardyknute,
    Let Norse the name ay dread,   310
Ay how he faught, aft how he spar'd,
    Shall latest ages read.

XL.

Now loud and chill blew th' westlin wind,
    Sair beat the heavy shower,
Mirk¹ grew the night ere Hardyknute   315
    Wan² near his stately tower.
His tow'r that us'd wi' torches blaze
    To shine sae far at night,
Seem'd now as black as mourning weed,
    Nae marvel sair he sigh'd.   320

XLI.

" There's nae light in my lady's bower,
    There's nae light in my ha' ;
Nae blink shines round my Fairly fair,
    Nor ward³ stands on my wa'.
" What bodes it ? Robert, Thomas, say ;"— 325
    Nae answer fitts their dread.
" Stand back, my sons, I'le be your guide ;"
    But by they past with speed.

[¹ dark.   ² drew near.   ³ warden.]

XLII.

" As fast I've sped owre Scotlands faes,"—
  There ceas'd his brag of weir,   330
Sair sham'd to mind ought but his dame,
  And maiden Fairly fair.
Black fear he felt, but what to fear
  He wist nae yet; wi' dread
Sair shook his body, sair his limbs,   335
  And a' the warrior fled.

    *   *   *   *   *

THE END OF THE FIRST BOOK.

RELIQUES OF ANCIENT POETRY, ETC.

SERIES THE SECOND.

BOOK II.

I.

A BALLAD OF LUTHER, THE POPE, A CARDINAL, AND A HUSBANDMAN.

N the former Book we brought down this second Series of poems, as low as about the middle of the sixteenth century. We now find the Muses deeply engaged in religious controversy. The sudden revolution, wrought in the opinions of mankind by the Reformation, is one of the most striking events in the history of the human mind. It could not but engross the attention of every individual in that age, and therefore no other writings would have any chance to be read, but such as related to this grand topic. The alterations made in the established religion by Henry VIII., the sudden changes it underwent in the three succeeding reigns within so short a space as eleven or twelve years, and the violent struggles between expiring Popery, and growing Protestantism, could not but interest all mankind. Accordingly every pen was engaged in the dispute. The followers of the Old and New Profession (as they were called) had their respective Ballad-makers; and every day produced some popular sonnet for or against the Reformation. The following ballad, and that intitled *Little John Nobody*, may serve for specimens of the writings of each party. Both were written in the reign of Edward VI.; and are not the worst that were composed upon the occasion. Controversial divinity is no friend to poetic flights. Yet this ballad of *Luther and the Pope* is not altogether devoid of spirit; it is of the dramatic kind, and the characters are tolerably well sustained; especially that of Luther, which is made to speak in a manner not unbecoming the spirit and courage of that vigorous Reformer. It is printed from the original black-letter copy (in the Pepys collection, vol. i. folio,) to which is prefixed a large wooden cut, designed and executed by some eminent master.

We are not to wonder that the ballad-writers of that age should be inspired with the zeal of controversy, when the very stage teemed with polemic divinity.   I have now before me two very ancient quarto black-letter plays : the one published in the time of Henry VIII., intitled, *Every Man ;* the other called *Lusty Juventus,* printed in the reign of Edward VI.   In the former of these, occasion is taken to inculcate great reverence for old mother church and her superstitions :* in the other, the poet (one *R. Wever*) with great success attacks both.   So that the Stage in those days literally was, what wise men have always wished it, a supplement to the pulpit :—This was so much the case, that in the play of *Lusty Juventus,* chapter and verse are every where quoted as formally as in a sermon ; take an instance :

> " The Lord by his prophet Ezechiel sayeth in this wise playnlye,
> As in the xxxiij chapter it doth appere :
> Be converted, O ye children, &c."

From this play we learn that most of the young people were New Gospellers, or friends to the Reformation ; and that the old were tenacious of the doctrines imbibed in their youth : for thus the Devil is introduced lamenting the downfal of superstition :

---

* Take a specimen from his high encomiums on the priesthood.

> " There is no emperour, kyng, duke, ne baron
> That of God hath commissyon,
> As hath the leest preest in the world beynge.
>   *   *   *   *   *
> God hath to them more power gyven,
> Than to any aungell, that is in heven ;
> With v. words he may consecrate
> Goddes body in fleshe and blode to take,
> And handeleth his maker bytwene his handes.
> The preest byndeth and unbindeth all bandes,
> Bothe in erthe and in heven.—
> Thou ministers all the sacramentes seven.
> Though we kyst thy fete thou were worthy ;
> Thou art the surgyan that cureth synne dedly ;
> No remedy may we fynde under God,
> But alone on preesthode.
> —— God gave preest that dignitè,
> And letteth them in his stede amonge us be,
> Thus be they above aungels in degre."
>   See Hawkins's *Orig. of Eng. Drama,* vol. i. p. 61.

> " The olde people would believe stil in my lawes,
> But the yonger sort leade them a contrary way,
> They wyl not beleve, they playnly say,
> In olde traditions, and made by men, &c."

And in another place Hypocrisy urges,

> " The worlde was never meri
> Since chyldren were so boulde :
> Now every boy will be a teacher,
> The father a foole, the chyld a preacher."

Of the plays abovementioned, to the first is subjoined the following Printer's Colophon, ¶ Thus endeth this moral playe of Every Man, ¶ Imprynted at London in Powles chyrche yarde by me John Skot.   In Mr. Garrick's collection is an imperfect copy of the same play, printed by Richarde Pynson.

The other is intitled, *An enterlude called Lusty Juventus :* and is thus distinguished at the end : Finis. quod R. Wever. Imprinted at London in Paules churche yeard, by Abraham Vele at the signe of the Lambe.   Of this too Mr. Garrick has an imperfect copy of a different edition.

Of these two plays the reader may find some further particulars in the former volume, Appendix II., see *The Essay on the Origin of the English Stage;* and the curious reader will find the plays themselves printed at large in Hawkins's *Origin of the English Drama*, 3 vols. Oxford, 1773, 12mo.

THE HUSBANDMAN.

LET us lift up our hartes all,
  And prayse the lordes magnificence,
 Which hath given the wolues a fall,
  And is become our strong defence :
For they thorowe a false pretens
From Christes bloude dyd all us leade,*   5
 Gettynge from every man his pence,
As satisfactours for the deade.

---

* *i.e.* denied us the cup, see below, ver. 94.

For what we with our Flayles coulde get
   To kepe our house, and servauntes;   10
That did the Freers[1] from us fet,
   And with our soules played the merchauntes:
   And thus they with theyr false warrantes
Of our sweate have easelye lyved,
   That for fatnesse theyr belyes pantes,   15
So greatlye have they us deceaued.

They spared not the fatherlesse,
   The carefull, nor the pore wydowe ;
They wolde have somewhat more or lesse,
   If it above the ground did growe :   20
   But now we Husbandmen do knowe
Al their subteltye, and their false caste ;[2]
   For the lorde hath them overthrowe
With his swete word now at the laste.

Doctor Martin Luther.

Thou antichrist, with thy thre crownes,   25
   Hast usurped kynges powers,
As having power over realmes and townes,
   Whom thou oughtest to serve all houres:
   Thou thinkest by thy jugglyng colours
Thou maist lykewise Gods word oppresse;   30
   As do the deceatful foulers,
When they theyr nettes craftelye dresse.

Thou flatterest every prince, and lord,
   Thretening poore men with swearde and fyre;
All those, that do followe Gods worde,   35
   To make them cleve to thy desire,
   Theyr bokes thou burnest in flaming fire;
Cursing with boke, bell, and candell,
   Such as to reade them have desyre,
Or with them are wyllynge to meddell.   40

[1 friars.   2 stratagem.]

Thy false power wyl I bryng down,
  Thou shalt not raygne many a yere,
I shall dryve the from citye and towne,
  Even with this PEN that thou seyste here :
  Thou fyghtest with swerd, shylde, and speare,   45
But I wyll fyght with Gods worde ;
  Which is now so open and cleare,
That it shall brynge the under the borde.*

THE POPE.

Though I brought never so many to hel,
  And to utter dampnacion,   50
Throughe myne ensample, and consel,
  Or thorow any abhominacion,
  Yet doth our lawe excuse my fashion.
And thou, Luther, arte accursed ;
  For blamynge me, and my condicion,   55
The holy decres have the condempned.

Thou stryvest against my purgatory,
  Because thou findest it not in scripture ;
As though I by myne auctorite
  Myght not make one for myne honoure.   60
  Knowest thou not, that I have power
To make, and mar, in heaven and hell,
  In erth, and every creature ?
Whatsoever I do it must be well.

As for scripture, I am above it ;   65
  Am not I Gods hye vicare ?
Shulde I be bounde to folowe it,
  As the carpenter his ruler?†
  Nay, nay, hereticks ye are,
That will not obey my auctoritie.   70
  With this SWORDE I wyll declare,
That ye shal al accursed be.

---

* *i.e.* make thee knock under the table.   † *i.e.* his rule.

THE CARDINAL.

I am a Cardinall of Rome,
 Sent from Christes hye vicary,
To graunt pardon to more, and sume,   75
 That wil Luther resist strongly :
 He is a greate hereticke treuly,
And regardeth to much the scripture ;
 For he thinketh onely thereby
To subdue the popes high honoure.   80

Receive ye this PARDON devoutely,
 And loke that ye agaynst him fight ;
Plucke up youre herts, and be manlye,
 For the pope sayth ye do but ryght :
 And this be sure, that at one flyghte,   85
Allthough ye be overcome by chaunce,
 Ye shall to heaven go with greate myghte ;
God can make you no resistaunce.

But these heretikes for their medlynge
 Shall go down to hel every one ;   90
For they have not the popes blessynge,
 Nor regarde his holy pardòn :
 They thinke from all destruction
By Christes bloud to be saved,
 Fearynge not our excommunicacion,   95
Therefore shall they al be dampned.

II.

JOHN ANDERSON MY JO.

A Scottish Song.

WHILE in England verse was made the vehicle of controversy, and popery was attacked in it by logical argument, or stinging satire; we may be sure the zeal of the Scottish Reformers would not suffer their pens to be idle, but many a pasquil was discharged at the Romish priests, and their enormous encroachments on property. Of this kind perhaps is the following, (preserved in Maitland's MS. Collection of Scottish poems in the Pepysian library :)

> "Tak a Wobster, that is leill,
> And a Miller, that will not steill,
> With ane Priest, that is not gredy,
> And lay ane deid corpse thame by,
> And, throw virtue of thame three,
> That deid corpse sall qwyknit be."

Thus far all was fair : but the furious hatred of popery led them to employ their rhymes in a still more licentious manner. It is a received tradition in Scotland, that at the time of the Reformation, ridiculous and obscene songs were composed to be sung by the rabble to the tunes of the most favourite hymns in the Latin service. *Green sleeves and pudding pies* (designed to ridicule the popish clergy) is said to have been one of these metamorphosed hymns : *Maggy Lauder* was another : *John Anderson my jo* was a third. The original music of all these burlesque sonnets was very fine. To give a specimen of their manner, we have inserted one of the least offensive. The reader will pardon the meanness of the composition for the sake of the anecdote, which strongly marks the spirit of the times.

In the present Edition this song is much improved by some new readings communicated by a friend; who thinks by the "Seven Bairns," in st. 2d. are meant the Seven Sacraments; five of which were the spurious offspring of Mother Church: as the first stanza contains a satirical allusion to the luxury of the popish clergy.

The adaptation of solemn church music to these ludicrous pieces and the jumble of ideas thereby occasioned, will account for the following fact.—From the Records of the General Assembly in Scotland, called, *The Book of the Universal Kirk*, p. 90, 7th July, 1568, it appears, that Thomas Bassendyne printer in Edinburgh, printed "a psalme buik, in the end whereof was found printit ane baudy sang, called, *Welcome Fortunes.*" *

[In the first edition of the *Reliques* the number of the bairns is fixed at five instead of seven, and the rhyme to five is thrive instead of threven. The last line is

" For four of them were gotten, quhan Willie was awa."

The present copy has thus been altered to support the untenable position that the seven bairns were meant to represent the seven sacraments.

According to tradition John Anderson was formerly the town crier of Kelso, and the song is not of any great antiquity, for it is first found in the Skene MS., the date of which Dauney (*Ancient Scottish Melodies*, p. 219) fixes at the beginning of the seventeenth century, but which includes, according to Mr. Chappell, an English country dance that first appeared in 1698 (*Popular Music of the Olden Time*, vol. ii. p. 770).

Burns wrote his song—

" John Anderson my jo John
When we were first acquent,"

to the old tune, for Johnson's *Musical Museum*.]

WOMAN.

OHN Anderson my jo, cum in as ye gae bye,
And ye sall get a sheips heid weel baken in a pye;
Weel baken in a pye, and the haggis in a pat:
John Anderson my jo, cum in, and ye's get that.

* See also *Biograph. Britan.* 1st edit. vol. i. p. 177.

MAN.

And how doe ye, Cummer?[1] and how hae ye threven?
And how mony bairns hae ye? WOM. Cummer, I hae
    seven.
MAN. Are they to your awin gude man? WOM. Na,
    Cummer, na;
For five of tham were gotten, quhan he was awa.'

III.

LITTLE JOHN NOBODY.

WE have here a witty libel on the Reformation under
king Edward VI. written about the year 1550, and preserved in the Pepys collection, British Museum, and
Strype's *Mem. of Cranmer*. The author artfully declines
entering into the merits of the cause, and wholly reflects on the lives
and actions of many of the Reformed. It is so easy to find flaws and
imperfections in the conduct of men, even the best of them, and
still easier to make general exclamations about the profligacy of
the present times, that no great point is gained by arguments
of that sort, unless the author could have proved that the principles of the Reformed Religion had a natural tendency to produce a corruption of manners: whereas he indirectly owns,
that their *reverend father* [archbishop Cranmer] had used the
most proper means to stem the torrent, by giving the people
access to the Scriptures, by teaching them to pray with understanding, and by publishing homilies, and other religious tracts.
It must however be acknowledged, that our libeller had at that
time sufficient room for just satire. For under the banners of the
Reformed had enlisted themselves, many concealed papists, who
had private ends to gratify; many that were of no religion; many
greedy courtiers, who thirsted after the possessions of the church;
and many dissolute persons, who wanted to be exempt from all
ecclesiastical censures. And as these men were loudest of all
others in their cries for Reformation, so in effect, none obstructed
the regular progress of it so much, or by their vicious lives brought

[1 gossip.]

vexation and shame more on the truly venerable and pious Reformers.

The reader will remark the fondness of our satirist for alliteration: in this he was guilty of no affectation or singularity; his
versification is that of *Pierce Plowman's Visions*, in which a recurrence of similar letters is essential: to this he has only superadded
rhyme, which in his time began to be the general practice. See
an *Essay* on this very peculiar kind of metre, in the appendix to
this Volume.

N december, when the dayes draw to be
   short,
   After november, when the nights wax noy-
    some and long;
As I past by a place privily at a port,
I saw one sit by himself making a song:
His last* talk of trifles, who told with his tongue
That few were fast i'th' faith. I 'freyned'† that freake,[1]
Whether he wanted wit, or some had done him wrong.
He said, he was little John Nobody, that durst not
  speake.

John Nobody, quoth I, what news? thou soon note
  and tell
What maner men thou meane, thou are so mad.
He said, These gay gallants, that wil construe the
  gospel,
As Solomon the sage, with semblance full sad;
To discusse divinity they nought adread;
More meet it were for them to milk kye at a fleyke.[2]
Thou lyest, quoth I, thou losel,[3] like a leud lad.
He said, he was little John Nobody, that durst not
  speake.

---

  * Perhaps "he left talk."   † feyned, MSS. and *PC*.
[1] asked that man. [2] cows at a hurdle. [3] worthless fellow.]

Its meet for every man on this matter to talk,
And the glorious gospel ghostly to have in mind;
It is sothe said, that sect but much unseemly skalk,
As boyes babble in books, that in scripture are
    blind:
Yet to their fancy soon a cause will find;
As to live in lust, in lechery to leyke:[1]
Such caitives count to be come of Cains kind;
    But that I little John Nobody durst not speake.

For our reverend father hath set forth an order,
Our service to be said in our seignours tongue;
As Solomon the sage set forth the scripture;
Our suffrages, and services, with many a sweet song,
With homilies, and godly books us among,
That no stiff, stubborn stomacks we should freyke:[2]
But wretches nere worse to do poor men wrong;
    But that I little John Nobody dare not speake.

For bribery was never so great, since born was our
    Lord,
And whoredom was never les hated, sith Christ har-
    rowed[3] hel,
And poor men are so sore punished commonly through
    the world,
That it would grieve any one, that good is, to hear
    tel.
For al the homilies and good books, yet their hearts
    be so quel,[4]
That if a man do amisse, with mischiefe they wil him
    wreake;[5]

Ver. 3. *Cain's kind.*] So in *Pierce the Plowman's Creed*, the
proud friars are said to be

"Of Caymes kind."—*Vid.* Sig. C ii. *b*.

[[1] play.   [2] humour.   [3] harassed.   [4] cruel.
[5] pursue revengefully.]

The fashion of these new fellows it is so vile and fell:
But that I little John Nobody dare not speake.

Thus to live after their lust, that life would they have,
And in lechery to leyke al their long life ;
For al the preaching of Paul, yet many a proud knave
Wil move mischiefe in their mind both to maid and
    wife
To bring them in advoutry,[1] or else they wil strife,
And in brawling about baudery, Gods command-
    ments breake :
But of these frantic il fellowes, few of them do thrife ;
Though I little John Nobody dare not speake.

If thou company with them, they wil currishly carp,[2]
    and not care
According to their foolish fantacy ; but fast wil they
    naught :
Prayer with them is but prating ; therefore they it
    forbear :
Both almes deeds, and holiness, they hate it in their
    thought :
Therefore pray we to that prince, that with his bloud
    us bought,
That he wil mend that is amiss : for many a manful
    freyke[3]
Is sorry for these sects, though they say little or
    nought ;
And that I little John Nobody dare not once speake.

Thus in NO place, this NOBODY, in NO time I met,
Where NO man, ' ne'* NOUGHT was, nor NOTHING did
    appear;
Through the sound of a synagogue for sorrow I swett,
That ' Aeolus'† through the eccho did cause me to
    hear.

---

* then, MSS. and *PC.*   † Hercules, MSS. and *PC.*
[1 adultery.   2 censure.   3 strong man.]

Then I drew me down into a dale, whereas the dumb
    deer
Did shiver for a shower; but I shunted[1] from a freyke:
For I would no wight in this world wist who I were,
    But little John Nobody, that dare not once speake.

IV.

Q. ELIZABETH'S VERSES, WHILE PRISONER AT WOODSTOCK,

WRIT WITH CHARCOAL ON A SHUTTER,

RE preserved by Hentzner, in that part of his *Travels*
which has been reprinted in so elegant a manner at
Strawberry-hill. In Hentzner's book they were wretch-
edly corrupted, but are here given as amended by his
ingenious editor. The old orthography, and one or two ancient
readings of Hentzner's copy, are here restored.

H, Fortune! how thy restlesse wavering
    state
    Hath fraught with cares my troubled
    witt!
Witnes this present prisonn, whither fate
    Could beare me, and the joys I quit.

Ver. 4. "Could beare," is an ancient idiom, equivalent to "did
bear" or "hath borne." See below the *Beggar of Bednal Green*,
Book 2, No. x. v. 57. "Could say."

[¹ shunned.]

Thou causedest the guiltie to be losed 5
From bandes, wherein are innocents inclosed :
  Causing the guiltles to be straite reserved,
  And freeing those that death had well deserved.
But by her envie can be nothing wroughte,
So God send to my foes all they have thoughte. 10

A.D. MDLV.   ELIZABETHE, PRISONNER.

V.

THE HEIR OF LINNE.

THE original of this ballad is found in the Editor's folio MS., the breaches and defects in which rendered the insertion of supplemental stanzas necessary. These, it is hoped, the reader will pardon, as indeed the completion of the story was suggested by a modern ballad on a similar subject.

From the Scottish phrases here and there discernible in this poem, it should seem to have been originally composed beyond the Tweed.

The Heir of Linne appears not to have been a Lord of Parliament, but a Laird, whose title went along with his estate.

[In the folio MS. Percy wrote the following note : " This old copy (tho' a very indifferent fragment) I thought deserving ot some attention. I have therefore bestowed an entire revisal of the subject for my *Reliques*, &c." In this revisal, the Bishop swelled out the 125 lines of the original into the 216 of his own version. It has, therefore, been necessary to print a copy of the original at the end of the present ballad. The modern ballad referred to above is the *Drunkard's Legacy*, printed in J. H. Dixon's *Ballads of the Peasantry*, but it is only comparatively modern, as it dates back to a period long before Percy's time. The portion which Percy interpolated and took from this ballad, forms the end of the first part and beginning of the second part of the following version.

The incident by which the hidden treasure is discovered occurs in one of the stories of Cinthio's *Heccatomithi* (Dec. ix. Nov. 8), but the arguments of the two tales are in other respects different.

The Scotch claim this ballad as their own. Some suppose the hero to have been an Ayrshire laird, and others that he was from Galloway. Motherwell gives the following verses as the commencement of the traditionary version extant in Scotland:

> " The bonnie heir, the weel-faur'd heir,
>   And the weary heir o' Linne,
> Yonder he stands at his father's gate,
>   And naebody bids him come in,
> O see whare he gaup and see whare he stands,
>   The weary heir o' Linne,
> O see whare he stands on the cauld causey,
>   Some ane wuld ta'en him in.
> But if he had been his father's heir,
>   Or yet the heir o' Linne,
> He wadna stand on the cauld causey,
>   Some ane wuld ta'en him in."]

PART THE FIRST.

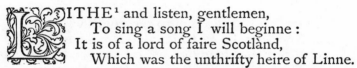

ITHE[1] and listen, gentlemen,
    To sing a song I will beginne :
It is of a lord of faire Scotland,
    Which was the unthrifty heire of Linne.

His father was a right good lord,   5
    His mother a lady of high degree ;
But they, alas! were dead, him froe,
    And he lov'd keeping companie.

To spend the daye with merry cheare,
    To drinke and revell every night,   10
To card and dice from eve to morne,
    It was, I ween, his hearts delighte

To ride, to runne, to rant, to roare,
    To alwaye spend and never spare,
I wott, an' it were the king himselfe,   15
    Of gold and fee he mote be bare.

[1 attend.]

Soe fares the unthrifty lord of Linne
 Till all his gold is gone and spent;
And he maun sell his landes so broad,
 His house, and landes, and all his rent. **20**

His father had a keen stewàrde,
 And John o' the Scales was called hee:
But John is become a gentel-man,
 And John has gott both gold and fee.[1]

Sayes, Welcome, welcome, lord of Linne, **25**
 Let nought disturb thy merry cheere;
Iff thou wilt sell thy landes soe broad,
 Good store of gold Ile give thee heere.

My gold is gone, my money is spent;
 My lande nowe take it unto the: **30**
Give me the golde, good John o' the Scales,
 And thine for aye my lande shall bee.

Then John he did him to record draw,
 And John he cast him a gods-pennie;*
But for every pounde that John agreed, **35**
 The lande, I wis, was well worth three.

He told him the gold upon the borde,
 He was right glad his land to winne:
The gold is thine, the land is mine,
 And now Ile be the lord of Linne. **40**

Thus he hath sold his land soe broad,
 Both hill and holt,[2] and moore and fenne,
All but a poore and lonesome lodge,
 That stood far off in a lonely glenne.

---

* *i.e.* earnest-money; from the French *Denier à Dieu.* At this
day, when application is made to the Dean and Chapter of Car-
lisle to accept an exchange of the tenant under one of their leases,
a piece of silver is presented by the new tenant, which is still
called a "Gods-penny."

   [1 property.   2 forest.]

For soe he to his father hight.   45
  My sonne, when I am gonne, sayd hee,
Then thou wilt spend thy lande so broad,
  And thou wilt spend thy gold so free :

But sweare me nowe upon the roode,
  That lonesome lodge thou'lt never spend ;   50
For when all the world doth frown on thee,
  Thou there shalt find a faithful friend.

The heire of Linne is full of golde :
  And come with me, my friends, sayd hee,
Let's drinke, and rant, and merry make,   55
  And he that spares, ne'er mote he thee.

They ranted, drank, and merry made,
  Till all his gold it waxed thinne ;
And then his friendes they slunk away ;
  They left the unthrifty heire of Linne.   60

He had never a penny left in his purse,
  Never a penny left but three,
And one was brass, another was lead,
  And another it was white monèy.

Nowe well-aday, sayd the heire of Linne,   65
  Nowe well-aday, and woe is mee,
For when I was the lord of Linne,
  I never wanted gold nor fee.

But many a trustye friend have I,
  And why shold I feel dole or care ?   70
Ile borrow of them all by turnes,
  Soe need I not be never bare.

But one, I wis, was not at home ;
  Another had payd his gold away ;
Another call'd him thriftless loone,   75
  And bade him sharpely wend his way.

Ver. 63, 4, 5, &c. *Sic* MS.

Now well-aday, sayd the heire of Linne,
  Now well-aday, and woe is me!
For when I had my landes so broad,
  On me they liv'd right merrilee.   80

To beg my bread from door to door
  I wis, it were a brenning shame:
To rob and steal it were a sinne:
  To worke my limbs I cannot frame.

Now Ile away to lonesome lodge,   85
  For there my father bade me wend;
When all the world should frown on mee,
  I there shold find a trusty friend.

Part the Second.

AWAY then hyed the heire of Linne
  O'er hill and holt,[1] and moor and fenne,
Untill he came to lonesome lodge,
  That stood so lowe in a lonely glenne.

He looked up, he looked downe,   5
  In hope some comfort for to winne:
But bare and lothly[2] were the walles.
  Here's sorry cheare, quo' the heire of Linne.

The little windowe dim and darke
  Was hung with ivy, brere, and yewe;   10
No shimmering sunn here ever shone;
  No halesome breeze here ever blew.

No chair, ne table he mote spye,
  No chearful hearth, ne welcome bed,
Nought save a rope with renning noose,   15
  That dangling hung up o'er his head.

[1 forest   2 loathsome.]

And over it in broad lettèrs,
  These words were written so plain to see :
"Ah! gracelesse wretch, hast spent thine all,
  And brought thyselfe to penurìe ?   20

"And this my boding mind misgave,
  I therefore left this trusty friend :
Let it now sheeld thy foule disgrace,
  And all thy shame and sorrows end."

Sorely shent[1] wi' this rebuke,   25
  Sorely shent was the heire of Linne ;
His heart, I wis, was near to brast
  With guilt and sorrowe, shame and sinne.

Never a word spake the heire of Linne,
  Never a word he spake but three :   30
"This is a trusty friend indeed,
  And is right welcome unto mee."

Then round his necke the corde he drewe,
  And sprang aloft with his bodìe :
When lo! the ceiling burst in twaine,   35
  And to the ground came tumbling hee.

Astonyed lay the heire of Linne,
  Ne knewe if he were live or dead :
At length he looked, and sawe a bille,[2]
  And in it a key of gold so redd.   40

He took the bill, and lookt it on,
  Strait good comfort found he there :
Itt told him of a hole in the wall,
  In which there stood three chests in-fere.*

---

* in-fere, *i.e.* together.

[1 abashed.   2 letter.]

Two were full of the beaten golde,   45
   The third was full of white monèy ;
And over them in broad lettèrs
   These words were written so plaine to see:

" Once more, my sonne, I sette thee clere ;
   Amend thy life and follies past ;   50
For but thou amend thee of thy life,
   That rope must be thy end at last."

And let it bee, sayd the heire of Linne ;
   And let it bee, but if I amend :*
For here I will make mine avow,   55
   This reade† shall guide me to the end.

Away then went with a merry cheare,
   Away then went the heire of Linne ;
I wis, he neither ceas'd ne blanne,[1]
   Till John o' the Scales house he did winne.   60

And when he came to John o' the Scales,
   Upp at the speere‡ then looked hee ;
There sate three lords upon a rowe,
   Were drinking of the wine so free.

And John himself sate at the bord-head,   65
   Because now lord of Linne was hee.
I pray thee, he said, good John o' the Scales,
   One forty pence for to lend mee.

Ver. 60. an old northern phrase.

   * *i.e.* unless I amend.   † *i.e.* advice, counsel.

   ‡ Perhaps the hole in the door or window, by which it was speered, *i.e.* sparred, fastened, or shut.   In Bale's second part of the *Acts of Eng. Votaries,* we have this phrase (f. 38), " The dore therof oft tymes opened and *speared* agayne."

        [1 lingered.]

Away, away, thou thriftless loone ;
   Away, away, this may not bee :   70
For Christs curse on my head, he sayd,
   If ever I trust thee one pennìe.

Then bespake the heire of Linne,
   To John o' the Scales wife then spake he :
Madame, some almes on me bestowe,   75
   I pray for sweet saint Charitìe.

Away, away, thou thriftless loone,
   I swear thou gettest no almes of mee ;
For if we shold hang any losel[1] heere,
   The first we wold begin with thee.   8ɔ

Then bespake a good fellòwe,
   Which sat at John o' the Scales his bord ;
Sayd, Turn againe, thou heire of Linne ;
   Some time thou wast a well good lord :

Some time a good fellow thou hast been,   85
   And sparedst not thy gold and fee ;
Therefore Ile lend thee forty pence,
   And other forty if need bee.

And ever, I pray thee, John o' the Scales,
   To let him sit in thy companie :   90
For well I wot thou hadst his land,
   And a good bargain it was to thee.

Up then spake him John o' the Scales,
   All wood[2] he answer'd him againe :
Now Christs curse on my head, he sayd,   95
   But I did lose by that bargàine.

[1 worthless fellow.   2 furious.]

And here I proffer thee, heire of Linne,
  Before these lords so faire and free,
Thou shalt have it backe again better cheape,
  By a hundred markes, than I had it of thee.   100

I drawe you to record, lords, he said.
  With that he cast him a gods pennie:
Now by my fay, sayd the heire of Linne,
  And here, good John, is thy monèy.

And he pull'd forth three bagges of gold,   105
  And layd them down upon the bord:
All woe begone was John o' the Scales,
  Soe shent he cold say never a word.

He told him forth the good red gold,
  He told it forth [with] mickle dinne.   110
The gold is thine, the land is mine,
  And now Ime againe the lord of Linne.

Sayes, Have thou here, thou good fellòwe,
  Forty pence thou didst lend mee:
Now I am againe the lord of Linne,   115
  And forty pounds I will give thee.

Ile make the keeper of my forrest,
  Both of the wild deere and the tame;
For but[1] I reward thy bounteous heart,
  I wis, good fellowe, I were to blame.   120

Now welladay! sayth Joan o' the Scales:
  Now welladay! and woe is my life!
Yesterday I was lady of Linne,
  Now Ime but John o' the Scales his wife.

Ver. 34, 102. cast, is the reading of the MS.

[1 unless.]

Now fare thee well, sayd the heire of Linne;　125
　Farewell now, John o' the Scales, said hee :
Christs curse light on me, if ever again
　I bring my lands in jeopardy.　　****

†‡† In the present edition of this ballad several ancient readings
are restored from the folio MS.

T HE following original version of the *Heir of Linne* is
reprinted from Hales and Furnivall's edition of the folio
MS. vol. i. p. 174 :

Off all the lords in faire Scottland
　a song I will begin :
amongst them all there dweld a Lord
　which was the vnthrifty Lord of linne.　　4

his father & mother were dead him froe,
　& soe was the head of all his kinne ;
he did neither cease nor bl[i]nne
　to the cards & dice that he did run,　　8

to drinke the wine that was soe cleere,
　with euery man he wold make merry.
and then bespake him John of the Scales,
　vnto the heire of Linne sayd hee,　　12

sayes, "how dost thou, Lord of Linne,
　doest either want gold or fee ?
wilt thou not sell thy lands soe brode
　to such a good fellow as me ?　　16

"ffor . . I . ." he said,
　"my land, take it vnto thee,
I draw you to record, my Lord[e]s all :"
　with that he cast him a good-se peny,　　20

he told him the gold vpon the bord,
　it wanted neuer a bare penny.
"that gold is thine, the land is mine,
　the heire of Linne I wilbee."　　24

"heeres gold inoughe," saithe the heire of Linne,
　"both for me & my company."
he drunke the wine that was soe cleere,
　& with euery man he made merry.　　28

with-in 3 quarters of a yeere
 his gold & fee it waxed thinne,
his merry men were from him gone,
 & left him himselfe all alone.   32

he had neuer a penny left in his pursse,
 neuer a penny but 3,
& one was brasse, & another was lead,
 & another was white mony.   36

" Now well-a day ! " said the heire of **Linne,**
 " now welladay, & woe is mee !
for when I was the lord of Linne,
 I neither wanted gold nor fee ;   40

" for I haue sold my lands soe broad,
 & haue not left me one penny !
I must goe now & take some read
 vnto Edenborrow, & begg my bread." 44

he had not beene in Edenborrow
 not 3 qwarters of a yeere,
but some did giue him & some said nay,
 & some bid " to the deele gang yee ! 48

" for if we shold hang any Land selfeer,
 the first we wold begin with thee."
" Now welladay ! " said the heire of Linne,
 no[w] welladay, & woe is mee !   52

" for now I have sold my lands soe broad,
 that mery man is irke with mee ;
but when that I was the Lord of Linne,
 then on my land I liued merrily ;   56

" & now I have sold my land soe broade
 that I haue not left me one pennye !
god be with my father ! " he said,
 " on his land he liued merrily."   60

Still in a study there as he stood,
 he vnbethought him of [a] bill
[he vnbethought him of a bill]
 which his father had left with him, 64

bade him he shold neuer on it looke
 till he was in extreame neede,
" & by my faith," said the heire of Linne,
 "then now I had neuer more neede." 68

he tooke the bill, & looked it on,
   good comfort that he found there ;
itt told him of a Castle wall
   where there stood 3 chests in feare: 72

2 were full of the beaten gold,
   the 3 was full of white mony.
he turned then downe his baggs of bread,
   & filled them full of gold soe red ;   76

then he did neuer cease nor blinne
   till John of the Scales house he did winne.
when that he came to John of the Scalels,
   vpp at the speere he looked then: 80
there sate 3 lords vpon a rowe,
   and John o the Scales sate at the bords head,
[and John o the Scales sate at the bords head]
   because he was the Lord of Linne.   84

and then bespake the heire of Linne,
   to John o the Scales wiffe thus sayd hee :
sayd, " Dame, wilt thou not trust me one shott
   that I may sitt downe in this company ? "   88

" now, christs curse on my head," shee said,
   if I do trust thee one pennye."
then bespake a good fellowe,
   which sate by John o the Scales his knee,   2

Said, " haue thou here, thou heire of linne,
   40 pence I will lend thee,—
some time a good fellow thou hast beene,—
   & other 40 if neede bee,"   96

thé druken wine that was soe cleere,
   & euery man thé made merry ;
& then bespake him John o the Scales,
   vnto the Lord of linne said hee :   10

said, " how doest thou, heire of Linne,
   since I did buy thy Lands of thee ?
I will sell it to thee 20^{li} better cheepe
   nor euer I did buy it of thee.   104

" I draw you to recorde, lord[e]s all;"
   with that he cast him gods penny ;
then he tooke to his baggs of bread,
   & they were full of the gold soe redd,   108

he told him the gold then over the borde;
    it wanted neuer a broad pennye:
"that gold is thine, the land is mine,
    & the heire of Linne againe I wilbee."   112

" Now welladay !" said John o the Scales wife,
    " welladay, & woe is me !
Yesterday I was the lady of Linne,
    & now I am but John o the Scales wiffe !"   116

saies, "haue thou heere, thou good fellow,
    40 pence thou did lend me,
[40 pence thou did lend me,]
    & 40^{s}. I will giue thee,   120
Ile make thee keeper of my forrest,
    both of the wild deere & the tame."

but then bespake the heire of Linne,
    these were the words, & thus said hee,   124
" Christs curse light vpon my crowne
    if ere my land stand in any Jeopardye !"

                               ffins]

VI.

GASCOIGNE'S PRAISE OF THE FAIR BRIDGES, AFTERWARDS LADY SANDES,

On Her having a Scar in Her Forehead.

GEORGE GASCOIGNE was a celebrated poet in the early part of Queen Elizabeth's reign, and appears to great advantage among the miscellaneous writers of that age. He was author of three or four plays, and of many smaller poems; one of the most remarkable of which is a satire in blank verse, called the *Steele-glass*, 1576, 4to.

Gascoigne was born in Essex, educated in both universities, whence he removed to Gray's-inn; but, disliking the study of the law, became first a dangler at court, and afterwards a soldier in the wars of the Low Countries. He had no great success in any of these pursuits, as appears from a poem of his, intitled "Gascoigne's Wodmanship, written to lord Gray of Wilton." Many of his epistles dedicatory are dated in 1575, 1576, from "his poore house in Walthamstoe:" where he died a middle-aged man in 1578, according to Anth. Wood: or rather in 1577, if he is the person meant in an old tract, intitled, "A remembrance of the well employed Life and godly End of Geo. Gascoigne, Esq.; who deceased at Stamford in Lincolnshire, Oct. 7, 1577, by Geo. Whetstone, Gent. an eye-witness of his godly and charitable end in this world," 4to. no date. [From a MS. of Oldys.]

Mr. Thomas Warton thinks "Gascoigne has much exceeded all the poets of his age, in smoothness and harmony of versification."* But the truth is, scarce any of the earlier poets of Q. Elizabeth's time are found deficient in harmony and smoothness, tho' those qualities appear so rare in the writings of their successors. In the *Paradise of Dainty Devises,*† (the *Dodsley's Miscellany* of those times) will hardly be found one rough, or inharmonious line:‡ whereas the numbers of Jonson, Donne, and most of their contemporaries, frequently offend the ear like the filing of a saw. Perhaps this is in some measure to be accounted for from the growing pedantry of that age, and from the writers affecting to run their lines into one another, after the manner of the Latin and Greek poets.

The following poem (which the elegant writer above quoted hath recommended to notice, as possessed of a delicacy rarely to be seen in that early state of our poetry) properly consists of Alexandrines of twelve and fourteen syllables, and is printed from two quarto black-letter collections of Gascoigne's pieces; the first intitled, "A hundreth sundrie flowres, bounde up in one small posie, &c. London, imprinted for Richarde Smith:" without date, but from a letter of H. W. (p. 202), compared with the printer's epist. to the reader, it appears to have been published in 1572, or 3. The other is intitled, "The Posies of George Gascoigne, Esq.; corrected, perfected, and augmented by the author; 1575.—Printed at Lond. for Richard Smith, &c." No year, but the epist. dedicat. is dated 1576.

In the title-page of this last (by way of printer's,§ or bookseller's device) is an ornamental wooden cut, tolerably well

---

* Observations on the *Faerie Queen*, vol. ii. p. 168.

† Printed in 1576, 1577, 1578, 1580, 1585, 1596, 1600, and perhaps oftener, in 4to. black-letter.

‡ The same is true of most of the poems in the *Mirrour of Magistrates*, 1563, 4to. and also of Surrey's Poems, 1557.

§ Henrie Binneman.

executed, wherein Time is represented drawing the figure of Truth out of a pit or cavern, with this legend, *Occulta veritas tempore patet* [R. S.] This is mentioned because it is not improbable but the accidental sight of this or some other title-page containing the same device, suggested to Rubens that well-known design of a similar kind, which he has introduced into the Luxemburg gallery,* and which has been so justly censured for the unnatural manner of its execution.

The lady here celebrated was Catharine, daughter of Edmond second Lord Chandos, wife of William Lord Sands. See Collins's *Peerage*, vol. ii. p. 133, ed. 1779.

[George Gascoigne, soldier and poet, had many enemies, and when objection was made to the Privy Council against his return as a burgess for Midhurst, they termed him " a common rymer, ruffian, atheist," &c. Mr. W. C. Hazlitt printed a complete collection of his poems in the Roxburghe Library, 2 vols. London, 1869-70.]

N court whoso demaundes
 What dame doth most excell ;
For my conceit I must needes say,
 Faire Bridges beares the bel.

Upon whose lively cheeke,   5
 To prove my judgment true,
The rose and lillie seeme to strive
 For equall change of hewe :

And therewithall so well
 Hir graces all agree ;   10
No frowning cheere dare once presume
 In hir sweet face to bee.

Although some lavishe lippes
 Which like some other best,
Will say, the blemishe on hir browe 15
 Disgraceth all the rest.

---

* Le Tems découvre la Vérité.

Thereto I thus replie ;
   God wotte, they little knowe
The hidden cause of that mishap,
   Nor how the harm did growe :   20

For when dame Nature first
   Had framde hir heavenly face,
And thoroughly bedecked it
   With goodly gleames of grace ;

It lyked hir so well :   25
   Lo here, quod she, a peece
For perfect shape, that passeth all
   Appelles' worke in Greece.

This bayt may chaunce to catche
   The greatest God of love,   30
Or mightie thundring Jove himself,
   That rules the roast above.

But out, alas ! those wordes
   Were vaunted all in vayne ;
And some unseen wer present there,   35
   Pore Bridges, to thy pain.

For Cupide, crafty boy,
   Close in a corner stoode,
Not blyndfold then, to gaze on hir :
   I gesse it did him good.   40

Yet when he felte the flame
   Gan kindle in his brest,
And herd dame Nature boast by hir
   To break him of his rest,

His hot newe-chosen love   45
   He chaunged into hate,
And sodeynly with mightie mace
   Gan rap hir on the pate.

It greeved Nature muche
  To see the cruell deede :   50
Mee seemes I see hir, how she wept
  To see hir dearling bleede.

Wel yet, quod she, this hurt
  Shal have some helpe I trowe :
And quick with skin she coverd it,   55
  That whiter is than snowe.

Wherwith Dan Cupide fled,
  For feare of further flame,
When angel-like he saw hir shine,
  Whome he had smit with shame.   60

Lo, thus was Bridges hurt
  In cradel of hir kind.
The coward Cupide brake hir browe
  To wreke his wounded mynd.

The skar still there remains ;   65
  No force, there let it bee :
There is no cloude that can eclipse
  So bright a sunne, as she.

VII.

FAIR ROSAMOND.

OST of the circumstances in this popular story of king
Henry II. and the beautiful Rosamond have been
taken for fact by our English historians ; who, unable to
account for the unnatural conduct of queen Eleanor in
stimulating her sons to rebellion, have attributed it to jealousy,

---

Ver. 62. In cradel of hir kind : *i.e.* in the cradle of her family.
See Warton's *Observations*, vol. ii. p. 137.

and supposed that Henry's amour with Rosamond was the object of that passion.

Our old English annalists seem, most of them, to have followed Higden the monk of Chester, whose account, with some enlargements, is thus given by Stow:—" Rosamond the fayre daughter of Walter lord Clifford, concubine to Henry II. (poisoned by queen Elianor, as some thought) dyed at Woodstocke [A.D. 1177] where king Henry had made for her a house of wonderfull working; so that no man or woman might come to her, but he that was instructed by the king, or such as were right secret with him touching the matter. This house after some was named Labyrinthus, or Dedalus worke, which was wrought like unto a knot in a garden, called a maze;* but it was commonly said, that lastly the queene came to her by a clue of thridde, or silke, and so dealt with her, that she lived not long after: but when she was dead, she was buried at Godstow in an house of nunnes, beside Oxford, with these verses upon her tombe:—

' Hic jacet in tumba, Rosa mundi, non Rosa munda :
   Non redolet, sed olet, quæ redolere solet.'

" In English thus :—

' The rose of the world, but not the cleane flowre,
   Is now here graven; to whom beauty was lent:
In this grave full darke nowe is her bowre,
   That by her life was sweete and redolent:
But now that she is from this life blent,
   Though she were sweete, now foully doth she stinke.
A mirrour good for all men, that on her thinke.'"
                            STOWE's *Annals*, ed. 1631, p. 154.

How the queen gained admittance into Rosamond's bower is differently related. Hollinshed speaks of it, as "the common report of the people, that the queene . . . founde hir out by a silken thread, which the king had drawne after him out of hir chamber with his foot, and dealt with hir in such sharpe and cruell wise, that she lived not long after." Vol. iii. p. 115. On the other hand, in Speede's *Hist.* we are told that the jealous queen found her out " by a clew of silke, fallen from Rosamund's lappe, as shee sate to take ayre, and suddenly fleeing from the sight of the searcher, the end of her silke fastened to her foot, and

---

* Consisting of vaults under ground, arched and walled with brick and stone, according to Drayton. See note on his Epistle of Rosamond.

the clew still unwinding, remained behinde: which the queene followed, till she had found what she sought, and upon Rosamund so vented her spleene, as the lady lived not long after." 3rd edit. p. 509. Our ballad-maker with more ingenuity, and probably as much truth, tells us the clue was gained by surprise, from the knight who was left to guard her bower.

It is observable, that none of the old writers attribute Rosamond's death to poison (Stow, above, mentions it merely as a slight conjecture); they only give us to understand, that the queen treated her harshly; with furious menaces, we may suppose, and sharp expostulations, which had such effect on her spirits, that she did not long survive it. Indeed on her tomb-stone, as we learn from a person of credit,* among other fine sculptures, was engraven the figure of a cup. This, which perhaps at first was an accidental ornament (perhaps only the chalice) might in after times suggest the notion that she was poisoned; at least this construction was put upon it, when the stone came to be demolished after the nunnery was dissolved. The account is, that " the tomb-stone of Rosamund Clifford was taken up at Godstow, and broken in pieces, and that upon it were interchangeable weavings drawn out and decked with roses red and green, and the picture of the *cup*, out of which she drank the poison given her by the queen, carved in stone."

Rosamond's father having been a great benefactor to the nunnery of Godstow, where she had also resided herself in the innocent part of her life, her body was conveyed there, and buried in the middle of the choir; in which place it remained till the year 1191, when Hugh bishop of Lincoln caused it to be removed. The fact is recorded by Hoveden, a contemporary writer, whose words are thus translated by Stow: " Hugh bishop of Lincolne came to the abbey of nunnes, called Godstow, ... and when he had entred the church to pray, he saw a tombe in the middle of the quire, covered with a pall of silke, and set about with lights of waxe : and demanding whose tomb it was, he was answered, that it was the tombe of Rosamond, that was some time lemman to Henry II. . . . . who for the love of her had done much good to that church. Then quoth the bishop, take out of this place the harlot, and bury her without the church, lest christian religion should grow in contempt, and to the end that, through example of her, other women being made afraid may beware, and keepe themselves from unlawfull and advouterous company with men."— *Annals*, p. 159.

---

* Tho. Allen of Gloc. Hall, Oxon. who died in 1632, aged 90. See Hearne's rambling discourse concerning Rosamond, at the end of *Gul. Neubrig. Hist.* vol. iii. p. 739.

History further informs us, that king John repaired Godstow nunnery, and endowed it with yearly revenues, "that these holy virgins might releeve with their prayers, the soules of his father king Henrie, and of lady Rosamund there interred."* . . . . In what situation her remains were found at the dissolution of the nunnery, we learn from Leland : "Rosamundes tumbe at Godstowe nunnery was taken up [of] late; it is a stone with this inscription, TUMBA ROSAMUNDÆ. Her bones were closid in lede, and withyn that bones were closyd yn lether. When it was opened a very swete smell came owt of it."† See Hearne's discourse above quoted, written in 1718; at which time he tells us, were still seen by the pool at Woodstock the foundations of a very large building, which were believed to be the remains of Rosamond's labyrinth.

To conclude this (perhaps too prolix) account, Henry had two sons by Rosamond, from a computation of whose age, a modern historian has endeavoured to invalidate the received story. These were William Longue-espé (or Long-sword), earl of Salisbury, and Geoffrey, bishop of Lincolne.‡ Geoffrey was the younger of Rosamond's sons, and yet is said to have been twenty years old at the time of his election to that see in 1173. Hence this writer concludes, that king Henry fell in love with Rosamond in 1149, when in king Stephen's reign he came over to be knighted by the king of Scots; he also thinks it probable that Henry's commerce with this lady "broke off upon his marriage with Eleanor (in 1152) and that the young lady, by a natural effect of grief and resentment at the defection of her lover, entered on that occasion into the nunnery of Godstowe, where she died probably before the rebellion of Henry's sons in 1173." (Carte's *Hist.* vol. i. p. 652.) But let it be observed, that Henry was but sixteen years old when he came over to be knighted; that he staid but eight months in this island, and was almost all the time with the king of Scots; that he did not return back to England till 1153, the year after his marriage with Eleanor; and that no writer drops the least hint of Rosamond's having ever been abroad with her lover, nor indeed is it probable that a boy of sixteen should venture to carry over a mistress to his mother's court. If all these circumstances are considered, Mr. Carte's account will be found more incoherent

---

* Vid. reign of Henry II. in Speed's *Hist.* writ by Dr. Barcham, Dean of Bocking.

† This would have passed for miraculous, if it had happened in the tomb of any clerical person, and a proof of his being a saint.

‡ Afterwards Archbishop of York, temp. Rich. I.

and improbable than that of the old ballad; which is also countenanced by most of our old historians.

Indeed the true date of Geoffrey's birth, and consequently of Henry's commerce with Rosamond, seems to be best ascertained from an ancient manuscript in the Cotton library: wherein it is thus registered of Geoffrey Plantagenet: "Natus est 5° Hen. II. [1159.]　Factus est miles 25° Hen. II. [1179.]　Elect. in Episcop. Lincoln. 28° Hen. II. [1182]." Vid. *Chron. de Kirkstall* (Domitian XII.)　Drake's *Hist. of York*, p. 422.

The ballad of *Fair Rosamond* appears to have been first published in "Strange Histories, or Songs and Sonnets, of Kinges, Princes, Dukes, Lords, Ladyes, Knights, and Gentlemen, &c. By Thomas Delone. Lond. 1607." 12mo.

It is here printed (with conjectural emendations), from four ancient copies in black-letter; two of them in the Pepys library.

[It is also printed in the *Crown Garland of Golden Roses, and Garland of Goodwill.*　Reprinted by the Percy Society.

In the *Collection of Old Ballads*, 1723, vol. i. p. 1, is another ballad on the same subject, with the title, *The Unfortunate Concubine, or Rosamond's Overthrow.*

The story is also treated in Warner's *Albion's England* (ch. 41).]

HEN as king Henry rulde this land,
　　The second of that name,
　Besides the queene, he dearly lovde
　　A faire and comely dame.

Most peerlesse was her beautye founde,　　　5
　　Her favour, and her face;
A sweeter creature in this worlde
　　Could never prince embrace.

Her crisped lockes like threads of golde
　　Appeard to each mans sight;　　　10
Her sparkling eyes, like Orient pearles,
　　Did cast a heavenlye light.

The blood within her crystal cheekes
  Did such a colour drive,
As though the lillye and the rose   15
  For mastership did strive.

Yea Rosamonde, fair Rosamonde,
  Her name was called so,
To whom our queene, dame Ellinor,
  Was known a deadlye foe.   20

The king therefore, for her defence,
  Against the furious queene,
At Woodstocke builded such a bower,
  The like was never seene.

Most curiously that bower was built   25
  Of stone and timber strong,
An hundered and fifty doors
  Did to this bower belong:

And they so cunninglye contriv'd
  With turnings round about,   30
That none but with a clue of thread,
  Could enter in or out.

And for his love and ladyes sake,
  That was so faire and brighte,
The keeping of this bower he gave   35
  Unto a valiant knighte.

But fortune, that doth often frowne
  Where she before did smile,
The kinges delighte and ladyes joy
  Full soon shee did beguile: 4

For why, the kinges ungracious sonne,
  Whom he did high advance,
Against his father raised warres
  Within the realme of France.

But yet before our comelye king   45
   The English land forsooke,
Of Rosamond, his lady faire,
   His farewelle thus he tooke :

" My Rosamonde, my only Rose,
   That pleasest best mine eye :   50
The fairest flower in all the worlde
   To feed my fantasye :

The flower of mine affected heart,
   Whose sweetness doth excelle :
My royal Rose, a thousand times   55
   I bid thee nowe farwelle !

For I must leave my fairest flower,
   My sweetest Rose, a space,
And cross the seas to famous France,
   Proud rebelles to abase.   60

But yet, my Rose, be sure thou shalt
   My coming shortlye see,
And in my heart, when hence I am,
   Ile beare my Rose with mee."

When Rosamond, that ladye brighte,   65
   Did heare the king saye soe,
The sorrowe of her grieved heart
   Her outward lookes did showe ;

And from her cleare and crystall eyes
   The teares gusht out apace,   70
Which like the silver-pearled dewe
   Ranne downe her comely face.

Her lippes, erst like the corall redde,
   Did waxe both wan and pale,
And for the sorrow she conceivde   75
   Her vitall spirits faile ;

And falling down all in a swoone
   Before king Henryes face,
Full oft he in his princelye armes
   Her bodye did embrace :   80

And twentye times, with watery eyes,
   He kist her tender cheeke,
Untill he had revivde againe
   Her senses milde and meeke.

Why grieves my Rose, my sweetest Rose ?   85
   The king did often say.
Because, quoth shee, to bloodye warres
   My lord must part awaye.

But since your grace on forrayne coastes
   Amonge your foes unkinde   90
Must goe to hazard life and limbe,
   Why should I staye behinde ?

Nay rather, let me, like a page,
   Your sworde and target beare ;
That on my breast the blowes may lighte,   95
   Which would offend you there.

Or lett mee, in your royal tent,
   Prepare your bed at nighte,
And with sweete baths refresh your grace,
   At your returne from fighte.   100

So I your presence may enjoye
   No toil I will refuse ;
But wanting you, my life is death ;
   Nay, death Ild rather chuse!

" Content thy self, my dearest love ;   105
   Thy rest at home shall bee
In Englandes sweet and pleasant isle ;
   For travell fits not thee.

Faire ladies brooke not bloodye warres ;
　　Soft peace their sexe delightes ;　　　110
' Not rugged campes, but courtlye bowers ;
　　Gay feastes, not cruell fightes.'

My Rose shall safely here abide,
　　With musicke passe the daye ;
Whilst I, amonge the piercing pikes,　　115
　　My foes seeke far awaye.

My Rose shall shine in pearle, and golde,
　　Whilst Ime in armour dighte ;
Gay galliards here my love shall dance,
　　Whilst I my foes goe fighte.　　　120

And you, sir Thomas, whom I truste
　　To bee my loves defence ;
Be carefull of my gallant Rose
　　When I am parted hence."

And therewithall he fetcht a sigh,　　125
　　As though his heart would breake :
And Rosamonde, for very griefe,
　　Not one plaine word could speake.

And at their parting well they mighte
　　In heart be grieved sore :　　　130
After that daye faire Rosamonde
　　The king did see no more.

For when his grace had past the seas,
　　And into France was gone ;
With envious heart, queene Ellinor,　　135
　　To Woodstocke came anone.

And forth she calles this trustye knighte,
　　In an unhappy houre ;
Who with his clue of twined thread,
　　Came from this famous bower.　　　140

And when that they had wounded him,
  The queene this thread did gette,
And went where ladye Rosamonde
  Was like an angell sette.

But when the queene with stedfast eye   145
  Beheld her beauteous face,
She was amazed in her minde
  At her exceeding grace.

Cast off from thee those robes, she said,
  That riche and costlye bee ;   150
And drinke thou up this deadlye draught,
  Which I have brought to thee.

Then presentlye upon her knees
  Sweet Rosamonde did falle ;
And pardon of the queene she crav'd   155
  For her offences all.

" Take pitty on my youthfull yeares,
  Faire Rosamonde did crye ;
And lett mee not with poison stronge
  Enforced bee to dye.   160

I will renounce my sinfull life,
  And in some cloyster bide ;
Or else be banisht, if you please,
  To range the world soe wide.

And for the fault which I have done,   165
  Though I was forc'd theretoe,
Preserve my life, and punish mee
  As you thinke meet to doe."

And with these words, her lillie handes
  She wrunge full often there ;   170
And downe along her lovely face
  Did trickle many a teare.

But nothing could this furious queene
   Therewith appeased bee;
The cup of deadlye poyson stronge,   175
   As she knelt on her knee,

Shee gave this comelye dame to drinke;
   Who tooke it in her hand,
And from her bended knee arose,
   And on her feet did stand: 180

And casting up her eyes to heaven,
   Shee did for mercye calle;
And drinking up the poyson stronge,
   Her life she lost withalle.

And when that death through everye limbe   185
   Had showde its greatest spite,
Her chiefest foes did plaine confesse
   Shee was a glorious wighte.

Her body then they did entomb,
   When life was fled away,   190
At Godstowe, neare to Oxford towne,
   As may be seene this day.

*

VIII.

QUEEN ELEANOR'S CONFESSION.

"ELEANOR, the daughter and heiress of William duke of Guienne, and count of Poictou, had been married sixteen years to Louis VII. king of France, and had attended him in a croisade, which that monarch commanded against the infidels; but having lost the affections of her husband, and even fallen under some suspicions of gallantry with a handsome Saracen, Louis, more delicate than politic, procured a divorce from her, and restored her those rich provinces, which by her marriage she had annexed to the crown of France. The young count of Anjou, afterwards Henry II. king of England, tho' at that time but in his nineteenth year, neither discouraged by the disparity of age, nor by the reports of Eleanor's gallantry, made such successful courtship to that princess, that he married her six weeks after her divorce, and got possession of all her dominions as a dowery. A marriage thus founded upon interest was not likely to be very happy: it happened accordingly, Eleanor, who had disgusted her first husband by her gallantries, was no less offensive to her second by her jealousy : thus carrying to extremity, in the different parts of her life, every circumstance of female weakness. She had several sons by Henry, whom she spirited up to rebel against him ; and endeavouring to escape to them disguised in man's apparel in 1173, she was discovered and thrown into a confinement, which seems to have continued till the death of her husband in 1189. She however survived him many years: dying in 1204, in the sixth year of the reign of her youngest son, John." See Hume's *Hist.* 4to. vol. i. pp. 260, 307. Speed, Stow, &c.

It is needless to observe, that the following ballad (given, with some corrections, from an old printed copy) is altogether fabulous ; whatever gallantries Eleanor encouraged in the time of her first husband, none are imputed to her in that of her second.

[The idea of the unlucky shrift exhibited in the following ballad is taken from some old story-teller. It occurs among the tales of Boccaccio, Bandello, Barbazan, La Fontaine, and several other writers.

A copy of this ballad, differing very considerably from the present version, is to be found in Kinloch's *Ancient Scottish Ballads.* The first stanza is as follows :—

> "The queen fell sick, and very, very sick
> She was sick and like to dee
> And she sent for a frier oure frae France
> Her confessour to be."

The last stanza but four reads :—

> " And do you see yon pretty little girl
> That's a beclad in green ?
> She's a friar's daughter oure in France
> And I hoped to see her a queen."

And the end as follows :—

" The king look'd over his left shoulder,
   An angry man was he :—
An it werna for the oath I sware
   Earl Marshall, thou shouldst dee."

Another version, recovered from recitation, and more like
Percy's than Kinloch's, is printed by Motherwell in his *Minstrelsy*,
under the title of " Earl Marshall."]

UEENE Elianor was a sicke womàn.
   And afraid that she should dye :
Then she sent for two fryars of France
   To speke with her speedilye.

The king calld downe his nobles all,   5
   By one, by two, by three ;
" Earl marshall, Ile goe shrive the queene,
   And thou shalt wend with mee."

A boone, a boone ; quoth earl marshàll,
   And fell on his bended knee ;   10
That whatsoever queene Elianor saye,
   No harme therof may bee.

Ile pawne my landes, the king then cryd,
   My sceptre, crowne, and all,
That whatsoere queen Elianor sayes   15
   No harme thereof shall fall.

Do thou put on a fryars coat,
   And Ile put on another ;
And we will to queen Elianor goe
   Like fryar and his brother.   20

Thus both attired then they goe :
   When they came to Whitehall,
The bells did ring, and the quiristers sing,
   And the torches did lighte them all.

When that they came before the queene   25
  They fell on their bended knee ;
A boone, a boone, our gracious queene,
  That you sent so hastilee.

Are you two fryars of France, she sayd,
  As I suppose you bee,   30
But if you are two Englishe fryars,
  You shall hang on the gallowes tree.

We are two fryars of France, they sayd,
  As you suppose we bee,
We have not been at any masse   35
  Sith we came from the sea.

The first vile thing that ever I did
  I will to you unfolde ;
Earl marshall had my maidenhed,
  Beneath this cloth of golde.   40

Thats a vile sinne, then sayd the king ;
  May God forgive it thee !
Amen, amen, quoth earl marshall ;
  With a heavye heart spake hee.

The next vile thing that ever I did,   45
  To you Ile not denye,
I made a boxe of poyson strong,
  To poison king Henrye.

Thats a vile sinne, then sayd the king,
  May God forgive it thee !   50
Amen, amen, quoth earl marshall ;
  And I wish it so may bee.

The next vile thing that ever I did,
  To you I will discover ;
I poysoned fair Rosamonde,   55
  All in fair Woodstocke bower.

Thats a vile sinne, then sayd the king;
　　May God forgive it thee!
Amen, amen, quoth earl marshall;
　　And I wish it so may bee.　　　　　　　60

Do you see yonders little boye,
　　A tossing of the balle?
That is earl marshalls eldest sonne,
　　And I love him the best of all.

Do you see yonders little boye,　　　　65
　　A catching of the balle?
That is king Henryes youngest sonne,
　　And I love him the worst of all.

His head is fashyon'd like a bull;　　　70
　　His nose is like a boare.
No matter for that, king Henrye cryd,
　　I love him the better therfore.

The king pulled off his fryars coate,
　　And appeared all in redde:　　　　　75
She shrieked, and cryd, and wrung her hands,
　　And sayd she was betrayde.

The king lookt over his left shoulder,
　　And a grimme look looked hee,
Earl marshall, he sayd, but for my oathe,　　80
　　Or hanged thou shouldst bee.

Ver. 63, 67. She means that the eldest of these two was by the
earl marshall, the youngest by the king.

IX.

THE STURDY ROCK.

HIS poem, subscribed M. T. (perhaps invertedly for T. Marshall*) is preserved in *The Paradise of Daintie Devises.* The two first stanzas may be found accompanied with musical notes in "An howres recreation in musicke, &c. by Richard Alison, Lond. 1606, 4to." usually bound up with three or four sets of "Madrigals set to music by Tho. Weelkes, Lond. 1597, 1600, 1608, 4to." One of these madrigals is so compleat an example of the bathos, that I cannot forbear presenting it to the reader :—

"Thule, the period of cosmographie,
  Doth vaunt of Hecla, whose sulphureous fire
Doth melt the frozen clime, and thaw the skie,
  Trinacrian Ætna's flames ascend not hier :
These things seeme wondrous, yet more wondrous I,
Whose heart with feare doth freeze, with love doth fry.

"The Andelusian merchant, that returnes
  Laden with cutchinele and china dishes,
Reports in Spaine, how strangely Fogo burnes
  Amidst an ocean full of flying fishes :
These things seeme wondrous, yet more wondrous I,
Whose heart with feare doth freeze, with love doth fry."

Mr. Weelkes seems to have been of opinion, with many of his brethren of later times, that nonsense was best adapted to display the powers of musical composure.

[Percy's conjecture that the author is Marshall is not a happy one. Sir Egerton Brydges, in his edition of the *Paradise,* 1810 (*British Bibliographer,* vol. iii.), attributes it to M. Thorn, whose name is signed to another poem, numbered 52 :—

  "Now mortall man beholde and see,
  This worlde is but a vanitie,"

written in much the same spirit. The heading to the *Sturdy Rock* is :—

  "Man's flitting life fyndes surest stay,
  Where sacred vertue beareth sway."]

---

* Vid. *Athen. Oxon.* pp. 152, 316.

HE sturdy rock for all his strength
　　By raging seas is rent in twaine :
The marble stone is pearst at length,
　　With little drops of drizling rain :
The oxe doth yeeld unto the yoke,　　　　　5
The steele obeyeth the hammer stroke.

The stately stagge, that seemes so stout,
　　By yalping hounds at bay is set :
The swiftest bird, that flies about,
　　Is caught at length in fowlers net :　　　10
The greatest fish, in deepest brooke,
Is soon deceived by subtill hooke.

Yea man himselfe, unto whose will
　　All things are bounden to obey,
For all his wit and worthie skill,　　　　　15
　　Doth fade at length, and fall away.
There is nothing but time doeth waste ;
The heavens, the earth consume at last.

But vertue sits triumphing still
　　Upon the throne of glorious fame :　　　20
Though spiteful death mans body kill,
　　Yet hurts he not his vertuous name :
By life or death what so betides,
The state of vertue never slides.

X.

THE BEGGAR'S DAUGHTER OF
BEDNALL-GREEN.

THIS popular old ballad was written in the reign of Elizabeth, as appears not only from ver. 23, where the arms of England are called the "Queenes armes;" but from its tune's being quoted in other old pieces, written in her time. See the ballad on *Mary Ambree* in this volume. The late Mr. Guthrie assured the editor that he had formerly seen another old song on the same subject, composed in a different measure from this; which was truly beautiful, if we may judge from the only stanza he remembered. In this it was said of the old beggar, that "down his neck

> " —— his reverend lockes
> In comelye curles did wave;
> And on his aged temples grewe
> The blossomes of the grave."

The following ballad is chiefly given from the Editor's folio MS. compared with two ancient printed copies: the concluding stanzas, which contain the old beggar's discovery of himself, are not however given from any of these, being very different from those of the vulgar ballad. Nor yet does the Editor offer them as genuine, but as a modern attempt to remove the absurdities and inconsistencies, which so remarkably prevailed in this part of the song, as it stood before: whereas by the alteration of a few lines, the story is rendered much more affecting, and is reconciled to probability and true history. For this informs us, that at the decisive battle of Evesham (fought Aug. 4, 1265), when Simon de Montfort, the great Earl of Leicester, was slain at the head of the barons, his eldest son Henry fell by his side, and in consequence of that defeat, his whole family sunk for ever, the king bestowing their great honours and possessions on his second son, Edmund earl of Lancaster.

[This charming old ballad has enjoyed a long life of popularity, and according to Mr. Chappell it is still kept in print in Seven Dials, and sung about the country. As it is to be found in most collections, it has not been thought necessary to take note of the various trifling alterations which Percy made, but the six stanzas which he ejected in favour of the eight between brackets are printed at the end. A few of the alterations are improvements, but most of them are the reverse; thus, in place of the received reading of verse 28,

> " Was straightway in love with pretty Bessee,"

Percy prints

> " Was straightway enamourd of pretty Bessee."

Mr. John Pickford (*Notes and Queries*, 4th Series, vol. ix. p. 64) once possessed an old mezzotint engraving of the Blind Beggar of a large folio size, on the margin of which were inscribed the lines referred to above. In Robert Greene's *Pandosto* (1588), from which Shakspere drew the plot of his *Winter's Tale*, there is the same simile as is used in these verses. Egistus says:—"Thou seest my white hayres are blossomes for the grave."

Pepys in his Diary (25th June, 1663), speaks of going to dinner with Sir William and Lady Batten and Sir J. Minnes to Sir William Ryder's at Bethnall Green, and adds : "This very house was built by the blind beggar of Bednall Green, so much talked of and sang in ballads, but they say it was only some outhouse of it." The mansion was built by John Kirby, a citizen of London, in the reign of Queen Elizabeth, and afterwards became the residence ot Sir Hugh Platt, author of *The Jewell House of Art and Nature*, 1594; *The Garden of Eden*, &c. Ryder died there in 1669.]

PART THE FIRST.

ITT was a blind beggar, had long lost his sight,
　　　He had a faire daughter of bewty most bright ;
And many a gallant brave suiter had shee,
For none was soe comelye as pretty Bessee.

And though shee was of favor most faire,　　　　5
Yett seeing shee was but a poor beggars heyre,
Of ancyent housekeepers despised was shee,
Whose sonnes came as suitors to prettye Bessee.

Wherefore in great sorrow faire Bessy did say,
Good father, and mother, let me goe away   10
To seeke out my fortune, whatever itt bee.
This suite then they granted to prettye Bessee.

Then Bessy, that was of bewtye soe bright,
All cladd in gray russett, and late in the night
From father and mother alone parted shee;   15
Who sighed and sobbed for prettye Bessee.

Shee went till shee came to Stratford-le-Bow;
Then knew shee not whither, nor which way to goe:
With teares shee lamented her hard destinìe,
So sadd and soe heavy was pretty Bessee.   20

Shee kept on her journey untill it was day,
And went unto Rumford along the hye way;
Where at the Queenes armes entertained was shee:
Soe faire and wel favoured was pretty Bessee.

Shee had not beene there a month to an end,   25
But master and mistres and all was her friend:
And every brave gallant, that once did her see,
Was straight-way enamourd of pretty Bessee.

Great gifts they did send her of silver and gold,
And in their songs daylye her love was extold;   30
Her beawtye was blazed in every degree;
Soe faire and soe comelye was pretty Bessee.

The young men of Rumford in her had their joy;
Shee shewed herself curteous, and modestlye coye;
And at her commandment still wold they bee;   35
Soe fayre and soe comlye was pretty Bessee.

Foure suitors att once unto her did goe;
They craved her favor, but still she sayd noe;
I wold not wish gentles to marry with mee.
Yett ever they honored prettye Bessee.   40

The first of them was a gallant young knight,
And he came unto her disguisde in the night :
The second a gentleman of good degree,
Who wooed and sued for prettye Bessee.

A merchant of London, whose wealth was not small, 45
He was the third suiter, and proper withall :
Her masters own sonne the fourth man must bee,
Who swore he would dye for pretty Bessee.

And, if thou wilt marry with mee, quoth the knight,
Ile make thee a ladye with joy and delight ;   50
My hart's so inthralled by thy bewtìe,
That soone I shall dye for prettye Bessee.

The gentleman sayd, Come, marry with mee,
As fine as a ladye my Bessy shal bee :
My life is distressed : O heare me, quoth hee ;   55
And grant me thy love, my prettye Bessee.

Let me bee thy husband, the merchant cold say,
Thou shalt live in London both gallant and gay ;
My shippes shall bring home rych jewells for thee,
And I will for ever love pretty Bessee.   60

Then Bessy shee sighed, and thus shee did say,
My father and mother I meane to obey ;
First gett their good will, and be faithfull to mee,
And you shall enjoye your prettye Bessee.

To every one this answer shee made,   65
Wherfore unto her they joyfullye sayd,
This thing to fulfill wee all doe agree;
But where dwells thy father, my prettye Bessee ?

My father, shee said, is soone to be seene:
The seely blind beggar of Bednall-greene,   70
That daylye sits begging for charitìe,
He is the good father of pretty Bessee.

His markes and his tokens are knowen very well;
He alwayes is led with a dogg and a bell:
A seely olde man, God knoweth, is hee,   75
Yett hee is the father of pretty Bessee.

Nay then, quoth the merchant, thou art not for mee:
Nor, quoth the innholder, my wiffe thou shalt bee:
I lothe, sayd the gentle, a beggars degree,
And therefore, adewe, my pretty Bessee!   80

Why then, quoth the knight, hap better or worse,
I waighe not true love by the waight of the pursse,
And bewtye is bewtye in every degree;
Then welcome unto me, my pretty Bessee.

With thee to thy father forthwith I will goe.   85
Nay soft, quoth his kinsmen, it must not be soe;
A poor beggars daughter noe ladye shal bee,
Then take thy adew of pretty Bessee.

But soone after this, by breake of the day
The knight had from Rumford stole Bessy away.   90
The younge men of Rumford, as thicke [as] might bee,
Rode after to feitch againe pretty Bessee.

As swifte as the winde to ryde they were seene,
Untill they came neare unto Bednall-greene;
And as the knight lighted most courteouslìe,   95
They all fought against him for pretty Bessee.

But rescew came speedilye over the plaine,
Or else the young knight for his love had been slaine.
This fray being ended, then straitway he see
His kinsmen come rayling at pretty Bessee.   100

Then spake the blind beggar, Although I bee poore,
Yett rayle not against my child at my own doore:
Though shee be not decked in velvett and pearle,
Yett will I dropp angells with you for my girle.

And then, if my gold may better her birthe,   105
And equall the gold that you lay on the earth,
Then neyther rayle nor grudge you to see
The blind beggars daughter a lady to bee.

But first you shall promise, and have itt well knowne,
The gold that you drop shall all be your owne.   110
With that they replyed, Contented bee wee.
Then here's, quoth the beggar, for pretty Bessee.

With that an angell he cast on the ground,
And dropped in angels full three thousand* pound;
And oftentimes itt was proved most plaine,   115
For the gentlemens one the beggar dropt twayne:

Soe that the place, wherin they did sitt,
With gold it was covered every whitt.
The gentlemen then having dropt all their store,
Sayd, Now, beggar, hold, for wee have noe more.   120

Thou hast fulfilled thy promise arright.
Then marry, quoth he, my girle to this knight;
And heere, added hee, I will now throwe you downe
A hundred pounds more to buy her a gowne.

The gentlemen all, that this treasure had seene,   125
Admired the beggar of Bednall-greene:
And all those, that were her suitors before,
Their fleshe for very anger they tore.

Thus was faire Besse matched to the knight,
And then made a ladye in others despite: 130
A fairer ladye there never was seene,
Than the blind beggars daughter of Bednall-greene.

---

* In the Editor's folio MS. it is £500.

But of their sumptuous marriage and feast,
What brave lords and knights thither were prest,
The second fitt * shall set forth to your sight   135
With marveilous pleasure, and wished delight.

Part the Second.

FF a blind beggars daughter most bright,
That late was betrothed unto a younge
knight ;
All the discourse therof you did see ;
But now comes the wedding of pretty Bessee.

Within a gorgeous palace most brave,   5
Adorned with all the cost they cold have,
This wedding was kept most sumptuouslìe,
And all for the creditt of pretty Bessee.

All kind of dainties, and delicates sweete
Were bought for the banquet, as it was most meete ; 10
Partridge, and plover, and venison most free,
Against the brave wedding of pretty Bessee.

This marriage through England was spread by report,
Soe that a great number therto did resort
Of nobles and gentles in every degree ;   15
And all for the fame of prettye Bessee.

To church then went this gallant younge knight ;
His bride followed after, an angell most bright,
With troopes of ladyes, the like nere was seene
As went with sweete Bessy of Bednall-greene.   20

This marryage being solempnized then,
With musicke performed by the skilfullest men,
The nobles and gentles sate downe at that tyde,
Each one admiring the beautifull bryde.

---

* See an essay on the word *fit* at the end of the second part.

Now, after the sumptuous dinner was done,   25
To talke, and to reason a number begunn :
They talkt of the blind beggars daughter most bright,
And what with his daughter he gave to the knight.

Then spake the nobles, " Much marveil have wee,
This jolly blind beggar wee cannot here see."   30
My lords, quoth the bride, my father's so base,
He is loth with his presence these states to disgrace.

" The prayse of a woman in questyon to bringe
Before her own face, were a flattering thinge ;
But wee thinke thy father's baseness," quoth they, 35
" Might by thy bewtye be cleane put awaye."

They had noe sooner these pleasant words spoke,
But in comes the beggar cladd in a silke cloke ;
A faire velvet capp, and a fether had hee,
And now a musicyan forsooth he wold bee.   40

He had a daintye lute under his arme,
He touched the strings, which made such a charme,
Saies, Please you to heare any musicke of mee,
Ile sing you a song of pretty Bessee.

With that his lute he twanged straightway,   45
And thereon begann most sweetlye to play ;
And after that lessons were playd two or three,
He strayn'd out this song most delicatelie.

" A poore beggars daughter did dwell on a greene,
Who for her fairenesse might well be a queene :   50
A blithe bonny lasse, and a daintye was shee,
And many one called her pretty Bessee.

" Her father hee had noe goods, nor noe land,
But beggd for a penny all day with his hand ;
And yett to her marriage hee gave thousands three,* 55
And still he hath somewhat for pretty Bessee.

---

* So the folio MS.

"And if any one here her birth doe disdaine,
Her father is ready, with might and with maine,
To proove shee is come of noble degree :
Therfore never flout att prettye Bessee." 60

With that the lords and the companye round
With harty laughter were readye to swound ;
Att last said the lords, Full well wee may see,
The bride and the beggar's behoulden to thee.

On this the bride all blushing did rise, 65
The pearlie dropps standing within her faire eyes,
O pardon my father, grave nobles, quoth shee,
That throughe blind affection thus doteth on mee.

If this be thy father, the nobles did say,
Well may he be proud of this happy day ; 70
Yett by his countenance well may wee see,
His birth and his fortune did never agree :

And therfore, blind man, we pray thee bewray,
(And looke that the truth thou to us doe say)
Thy birth and thy parentage, what itt may bee ; 75
For the love that thou bearest to pretty Bessee."

" Then give me leave, nobles and gentles, each one,
One song more to sing, and then I have done ;
And if that itt may not winn good report,
Then doe not give me a *groat* for my sport. 80

" [Sir Simon de Montfort my subject shal bee ;
Once chiefe of all the great barons was hee,
Yet fortune so cruelle this lorde did abase,
Now loste and forgotten are hee and his race.

" When the barons in armes did king Henrye oppose,
Sir Simon de Montfort their leader they chose ; 86
A leader of courage undaunted was hee,
And oft-times he made their enemyes flee.

" At length in the battle on Eveshame plaine*
The barons were routed, and Montfort was slaine ;   90
Moste fatall that battel did prove unto thee,
Thoughe thou wast not borne then, my prettye Bessee !

" Along with the nobles, that fell at that tyde,
His eldest son Henrye, who fought by his side,
Was fellde by a blowe, he receivde in the fight !   95
A blowe that deprivde him for ever of sight.

" Among the dead bodyes all lifelesse he laye,
Till evening drewe on of the following daye,
When by a yong ladye discoverd was hee ;
And this was thy mother, my prettye Bessee !   100

" A baron's faire daughter stept forth in the nighte
To search for her father, who fell in the fight,
And seeing yong Montfort, where gasping he laye,
Was moved with pitye, and brought him awaye.

" In secrette she nurst him, and swaged his paine,   105
While he throughe the realme was beleevd to be
         slaine :
At lengthe his faire bride she consented to bee,
And made him glad father of prettye Bessee.

" And nowe lest oure foes our lives sholde betraye,
We clothed ourselves in beggars arraye ;   110
Her jewelles shee solde, and hither came wee :
All our comfort and care was our prettye Bessee.]

" And here have wee lived in fortunes despite,
Thoughe poore, yet contented with humble delighte :
Full forty winters thus have I beene   115
A silly blind beggar of Bednall-greene.

* The battle of Evesham was fought on August 4, 1265.

" And here, noble lordes, is ended the song
Of one, that once to your own ranke did belong :
And thus have you learned a secrette from mee,
That ne'er had beene knowne, but for prettye
     Bessee."

120

Now when the faire companye everye one,
Had heard the strange tale in the song he had showne,
They all were amazed, as well they might bee,
Both at the blinde beggar, and pretty Bessee.

With that the faire bride they all did embrace,   125
Saying, Sure thou art come of an honourable race,
Thy father likewise is of noble degree,
And thou art well worthy a lady to bee.

Thus was the feast ended with joye and delighte,
A bridegroome most happy then was the young
    knighte,
In joy and felicitie long lived hee,   130
All with his faire ladye, the pretty Bessee.

*_**

[THE following stanzas (ll. 217-240 of the whole ballad),
were rejected by Percy in favour of the verses above
which are between brackets, and were written by
Robert Dodsley, the bookseller and author :—

" When ffirst our king his ffame did Advance,
& fought for his title in delicate ffrance,
in many a place many perills past hee :
then was not borne my pretty Bessye.

" And then in those warres went over to fight
many a braue duke, a *Lord*, & a *Knigh*t,
& with them younge Mountford, his courage most free :
but then was not borne my pretty Bessye.

" Att Bloyes there chanced a terrible day,
where many braue ffrenchmen vpon the ground Lay ;

amonge them Lay Mountford for companye:
but then was not borne my pretty Bessye.*

" But there did younge Mountford, by blow on the face,
loose both his eyes in a very short space ;
& alsoe his liffe had beene gone w*i*th his sight,
had not a younge woman come forth in the night

" Amongst the slaine men, as fancy did moue,
to search & to seeke for her owne true loue ;
& seeing young Mountford there gasping to bee,
shee saued his liffe through charitye.

" And then all our vittalls, in Beggar attire
att hands of good people wee then did require.
att last into England, as now it is seene,
wee came, & remained att Bednall greene."†]

†‡† The word *fit*, for *part*, often occurs in our ancient ballads
and metrical romances : which being divided into several parts for
the convenience of singing them at public entertainments, were in
the intervals of the feast sung by fits, or intermissions.   So Puttenham in his *Art of English Poesie*, 1589, says : " the Epithalamie
was divided by breaches into three partes to serve for three several
fits, or times to be sung." P. 41.

From the same writer we learn some curious particulars relative
to the state of ballad-singing in that age, that will throw light on
the present subject : speaking of the quick returns of one manner
of tune in the short measures used by common rhymers ; these, he
says, " glut the eare, unless it be in small and popular musickes,
sung by these Cantabanqui, upon benches and barrels heads,
where they have none other audience then boys or countrey
fellowes, that passe by them in the streete ; or else by *blind
harpers*, or such like taverne minstrels, that give a *fit* of mirth for
a *groat*, . . their matter being for the most part stories of old
time, as the tale of *Sir Topas*, the reportes of *Bevis of Southampton, Guy of Warwicke, Adam Bell and Clymme of the Clough*, and
such other old romances or historical rimes, made purposely for
recreation of the common people at Christmasse dinners and
brideales, and in tavernes and alehouses, and such other places of
base resorte." P. 69.

This species of entertainment, which seems to have been
handed down from the ancient bards, was in the time of Putten-

---

[* This stanza is not in the ordinary versions.
† Bessie of Bednall, Percy folio MS., ed. Hales and Furnivall,
vol. ii. p. 279.]

ham falling into neglect; but that it was not, even then, wholly excluded from more genteel assemblies, he gives us room to infer from another passage : " We ourselves," says this courtly* writer, " have written for pleasure a little brief romance, or historical ditty in the English tong of the *Isle of Great Britaine* in short and long meetres, and by breaches or divisions (*i. e.* fits), to be more commodiously sung to the harpe in places of assembly, where the company shal be desirous to heare of old adventures, and valiaunces of noble knights in times past, as are those of *King Arthur and his Knights of the Round Table, Sir Bevys of Southampton, Guy of Warwicke,* and others like." P. 33.

In more ancient times no grand scene of festivity was compleat without one of these reciters to entertain the company with feats of arms, and tales of knighthood, or, as one of these old minstrels says, in the beginning of an ancient romance on *Guy and Colbronde,* in the Editor's folio MS. p. 349 [ed. Hales and Furnivall, vol. ii., p. 527]:

> " When meate and drinke is great plentyè,
> And lords and ladyes still wil bee,
>   And sitt and solace lythe ;†
> Then itt is time for mee to speake
> Of keene knightes, and kempès great,
>   Such carping for to kythe."

If we consider that a *groat* in the age of Elizabeth was more than equivalent to a shilling now, we shall find that the old harpers were even then, when their art was on the decline, upon a far more reputable footing than the ballad-singers of our time. The reciting of one such ballad as this of the *Beggar of Bednal Green,* in two parts, was rewarded with half-a-crown of our money. And that they made a very respectable appearance, we may learn from the dress of the old beggar, in the preceding ballad, p. 178, where he comes into company in the habit and character of one of these minstrels, being not known to be the bride's father till after her speech, ver. 63. The exordium of his song, and his claiming a groat for his reward, v. 76, are peculiarly characteristic of that profession. Most of the old ballads begin in a pompous manner, in order to captivate the attention of the audience, and induce them to purchase a recital of the song : and they seldom conclude the first part without large promises of still

---

* He was one of Q. Elizabeth's gent. pensioners, at a time when the whole band consisted of men of distinguished birth and fortune. Vid. *Ath. Ox.*

† Perhaps " blythe."

greater entertainment in the second. This was a necessary piece of art to incline the hearers to be at the expense of a second groat's-worth. Many of the old romances extend to eight or nine fits, which would afford a considerable profit to the reciter.

To return to the word *fit;* it seems at one time to have peculiarly signified the pause, or breathing-time, between the several parts (answering to Passus in the *Visions of Pierce Plowman*): thus in the ancient ballad of *Chevy-Chase* (vol. i. p. 27), the first part ends with this line :

> " The first *fit* here I fynde : "

i. e. here I come to the first pause or intermission. (See also vol. i. p. 44.) By degrees it came to signify the whole part or division preceding the pause. (See vol. i. pp. 162, 169.) This sense it had obtained so early as the time of Chaucer ; who thus concludes the first part of his rhyme of *Sir Thopas* (writ in ridicule of the old ballad romances) :—

> " Lo ! lordis mine, here is a *fitt;*
> If ye woll any more of it,
> To tell it woll I fonde."

The word *fit* indeed appears originally to have signified a poetic strain, verse, or poem ; for in these senses it is used by the Anglo-Saxon writers. Thus K. Ælfred in his *Boethius*, having given a version of lib. 3, metr. 5, adds, Ða ɼe piɼꝺom þa þaɼ ꝼɪττe aɼunȝen hæꝼꝺe, p. 65, *i. e.* " When wisdom had sung these (Fitts) verses." And in the proem to the same book, Fon on ꝼɪττe, " Put into (fitt) verse." So in Cedmon, p. 45. Feonꝺ on ꝼɪττe, seems to mean " composed a song," or " poem." The reader will trace this old Saxon phrase, in the application of the word *fond*, in the foregoing passage of Chaucer.

Spencer has used the word fit to denote " a strain of music ; " see his poem, intitled, *Collin Clout's come home again*, where he says :—

> " The Shepherd of the ocean [Sir Walt. Raleigh]
> Provoked me to play some pleasant *fit.*
> And when he heard the music which I made
> He found himself full greatlye pleas'd at it," &c.

It is also used in the old ballad of *K. Estmere*, vol. i. book 1, No. 6, v. 243.

From being applied to music, this word was easily transferred to dancing ; thus in the old play of *Lusty Juventus* (described in preiminary note to book 2, No. 1 in this volume), Juventus says :

> " By the masse I would fayne go daunce a *fitte*."

And from being used as a part or division in a ballad, poem, &c.
it is applied by Bale to a section or chapter in a book (though I
believe in a sense of ridicule or sarcasm), for thus he intitles two
chapters of his *English Votaryes*, part 2nd, viz. fol. 49, " The fyrst
fytt of Anselme with Kynge Wyllyam Rufus ;" fol. 50, " An other
Fytt of Anselme with kynge Wyllyam Rufus."

XI.

FANCY AND DESIRE.

By the Earl of Oxford.

DWARD Vere, Earl of Oxford, was in high fame for
his poetical talents in the reign of Elizabeth ; perhaps
it is no injury to his reputation that few of his compositions are preserved for the inspection of impartial
posterity. To gratify curiosity, we have inserted a sonnet of his,
which is quoted with great encomiums for its "excellencie and
wit," in Puttenham's *Arte of Eng. Poesie,** and found intire in the
Garland of Good-will. A few more of his sonnets (distinguished
by the initial letters E. O.), may be seen in the *Paradise of Daintie
Devises*. One of these is intitled *The Complaint of a Lover,
wearing blacke and tawnie*. The only lines in it worth notice are
these :—

> " A crowne of baies shall that man ' beare'
>   Who triumphs over me ;
> For black and tawnie will I weare,
>   Which mourning colours be."

We find in Hall's *Chronicle*, that when Q. Catharine of Arragon
dyed, Jan. 8, 1536, " Queen Anne (Bullen) ware *yellowe* for the
mourning." And when this unfortunate princess lost her head,
May 19, the same year, " on the ascencion day following, the kyng
for mourning ware *whyte*." Fol. 227, 228.

Edward, who was the seventeenth earl of Oxford, of the family

---

* Lond. 1589, p. 172.

of Vere, succeeded his father in his title and honours in 1563, and
died an aged man in 1604.   See Mr. Walpole's *Noble Authors*.
Athen. Oxon, &c.

[Walpole was in error when he stated that Lord Oxford died an
aged man, for that nobleman was only about sixty at the time of
his death.   Sir Egerton Brydges points out in his edition of the
Paradise of Dainty Devices (*British Bibliographer*, vol. iii.), that
the earl could not have been born earlier than 1540 or 1541,
because his elder half-sister Katherine, widow of Edward, Lord
Windsor, died in January, 1599, aged 60.   The chief events of his
life are these.   In 1585 he was the chief of those who embarked
with the Earl of Leicester for the relief of the states of Holland
and Zealand.   In 1586 he sat as Lord Great Chamberlain of England on the trial of Mary, Queen of Scots.   In 1588 he hired and
fitted out ships at his own charge against the Spanish Armada.   In
1589 he sat on the trial of Philip Howard, Earl of Arundel, and
in 1601 on the trials of the Earls of Essex and Southampton.
His private character was far from good, and his honour was tar-
nished by his dispute with Sir Philip Sidney.   He used his first
wife (a daughter of the great Burleigh) cruelly, in revenge for the
statesman's treatment of his great friend, Thomas, Duke of Norfolk.   In his early youth he travelled in Italy, and returned from
that country a finished coxcomb, bringing home with him Italian
dresses, perfumes, and embroidered gloves.   He presented a pair
of the latter to Queen Elizabeth, who was so pleased with them
that she was drawn with them on her hands.   The earl was buried
at Hackney, on the 6th of July, 1604.

Percy might have spared rather more praise for this pretty little
poem.]

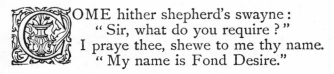

OME hither shepherd's swayne :
  " Sir, what do you require ? "
I praye thee, shewe to me thy name.
  " My name is Fond Desire."

When wert thou borne, Desire?   5
  " In pompe and pryme of may."
By whom, sweet boy, wert thou begot?
  " By fond Conceit men say."

Tell me, who was thy nurse?
  " Fresh Youth in sugred joy."   10
What was thy meate and dayly foode?
  " Sad sighes with great annoy."

What hadst thou then to drinke?
  " Unsavoury lovers teares."
What cradle wert thou rocked in?   15
  " In hope devoyde of feares."

What lulld thee then asleepe?
  " Sweete speech, which likes me best."
Tell me, where is thy dwelling place?
  " In gentle hartes I rest."   20

What thing doth please thee most?
  " To gaze on beautye stille."
Whom dost thou thinke to be thy foe?
  " Disdayn of my good wille."

Doth companye displease?   25
  " Yes, surelye, many one."
Where doth Desire delighte to live?
  " He loves to live alone."

Doth either tyme or age
  Bringe him unto decaye?   30
" No, no, Desire both lives and dyes
  Ten thousand times a daye."

Then, fond Desire, farewelle,
  Thou art no mate for mee;
I sholde be lothe, methinkes, to dwelle   35
  With such a one as thee.

XII.

SIR ANDREW BARTON.

 CANNOT give a better relation of the fact which is the subject of the following ballad, than in an extract from the late Mr. Guthrie's *Peerage*,* which was begun upon a very elegant plan, but never finished. Vol. i. 4to. p. 22.

"The transaction which did the greatest honour to the earl of Surrey† and his family at this time (A.D. 1511), was their behaviour in the case of Barton, a Scotch sea-officer. This gentleman's father having suffered by sea from the Portuguese, he had obtained letters of marque for his two sons to make reprisals upon the subjects of Portugal. It is extremely probable, that the court of Scotland granted these letters with no very honest intention. The council board of England, at which the earl of Surrey held the chief place, was daily pestered with complaints from the sailors and merchants, that Barton, who was called Sir Andrew Barton, under pretence of searching for Portuguese goods, interrupted the English navigation. Henry's situation at that time rendered him backward from breaking with Scotland, so that their complaints were but coldly received. The earl of Surrey, however, could not smother his indignation, but gallantly declared at the council board, that while he had an estate that could furnish out a ship, or a son that was capable of commanding one, the narrow seas should not be infested.

"Sir Andrew Barton, who commanded the two Scotch ships, had the reputation of being one of the ablest sea officers of his time. By his depredations, he had amassed great wealth, and his ships were very richly laden. Henry, notwithstanding his situation, could not refuse the generous offer made by the earl of Surrey. Two ships were immediately fitted out, and put to sea with letters of marque, under his two sons, Sir Thomas‡ and Sir Edward Howard. After encountering a great deal of foul weather,

---

[* Copied literally from Lord Herbert's (of Cherbury) *History of Henry VIII.*, p. 116.]

† Thomas Howard, afterwards created Duke of Norfolk.

‡ Called by old historians lord Howard, afterwards created earl of Surrey in his father's life-time. He was father of the poetical earl of Surrey.

Sir Thomas came up with the ' Lion,' which was commanded by
Sir Andrew Barton in person; and Sir Edward came up with the
' Union,' Barton's other ship (called by Hall, the ' Bark of Scotland.') The engagement which ensued was extremely obstinate
on both sides; but at last the fortune of the Howards prevailed.
Sir Andrew was killed fighting bravely, and encouraging his men
with his whistle, to hold out to the last; and the two Scotch ships
with their crews, were carried into the river Thames. (Aug. 2,
1511.)

"This exploit had the more merit, as the two English commanders were in a manner volunteers in the service, by their
father's order. But it seems to have laid the foundation of Sir
Edward's fortune; for, on the 7th of April, 1512, the king con-
stituted him (according to Dugdale) admiral of England,
Wales, &c

"King James 'insisted' upon satisfaction for the death of
Barton, and capture of his ship: tho' Henry had generously dis-
missed the crews, and even agreed that the parties accused might
appear in his courts of admiralty by their attornies, to vindicate
themselves." This affair was in a great measure the cause of the
battle of Flodden, in which James IV. lost his life.

In the following ballad will be found perhaps some few devia-
tions from the truth of history; to atone for which it has probably
recorded many lesser facts, which history hath not condescended
to relate. I take many of the little circumstances of the story to
be real, because I find one of the most unlikely to be not very
remote from the truth. In pt. 2, v. 156, it is said, that England
had before "but two ships of war." Now the "Great Harry" had
been built only seven years before, viz. in 1504: which "was
properly speaking the first ship in the English navy. Before this
period, when the prince wanted a fleet, he had no other expedient
but hiring ships from the merchants."—Hume.

This ballad, which appears to have been written in the reign of
Elizabeth, has received great improvements from the Editor's folio
MS. wherein was an ancient copy, which, though very incorrect,
seemed in many respects superior to the common ballad; the
latter being evidently modernized and abridged from it. The
following text is, however, in some places amended and improved
by the latter (chiefly from a black-letter copy in the Pepys collection), as also by conjecture.

[There is little to be added to the above preface, but those who
wish to read the Scottish version will find John Lesley's (Bishop
of Ross) account of the affair (*Historie of Scotland*, 1436-1561),
quoted in Mr. Furnivall's full preface to the ballad in the folio MS.
(vol. iii. p. 399). Percy fully explains how he made up his copy.

There is, in fact, hardly a line that has not been altered, and the notes at the foot of the page give the reader no idea of the changes that have been made.   To have noted all the differences would have loaded the page unnecessarily, and therefore in consideration of the interest of the ballad, a reprint of the folio copy has been added, although there are several printed copies.   It is difficult to understand what could have induced Percy to reject the pretty lines :

> " As itt beffell in Midsummer time
> When burds singe sweetlye on every tree,"

for the incongruous opening of Flora with her flowers, and Neptune with his showers.   The greatest alterations are in vv. 33-40, 129-136 ; part 2, vv. 1-8, 17-64, 89-94, 113-120, 145-176.]

The First Part.

WHEN Flora with her fragrant flowers
    ' Bedeckt the earth so trim and gaye,
    ' And Neptune with his daintye showers
       ' Came to present the monthe of Maye ;'*
King Henrye rode to take the ayre,   5
    Over the river of Thames past hee ;
When eighty merchants of London came,
    And downe they knelt upon their knee.

" O yee are welcome, rich merchànts ;
    Good saylors, welcome unto mee."   10
They swore by the rood, they were saylors good,
    But rich merchànts they cold not bee :
" To France nor Flanders dare we pass :
    Nor Bourdeaux voyage dare we fare ;
And all for a rover that lyes on the seas,   15
    Who robbs us of our merchant ware."

Ver. 15, 83. robber, MS.
* From the pr. copy.

King Henrye frownd, and turned him rounde,
  And swore by the Lord, that was mickle of might,
" I thought he had not beene in the world,
  Durst have wrought England such unright."   20
The merchants sighed, and said, alas !
  And thus they did their answer frame,
He is a proud Scott, that robbs on the seas,
  And Sir Andrewe Barton is his name.

The king lookt over his left shouldèr,   25
  And an angrye look then looked hee :
" Have I never a lorde in all my realme,
  Will feitch yond traytor unto mee ? "
Yea, that dare I ; lord Howard sayes ;
  Yea, that dare I with heart and hand ;   30
If it please your grace to give me leave,
  Myselfe wil be the only man.

Thou art but yong ; the kyng replyed :
  Yond Scott hath numbred manye a yeare.
" Trust me, my liege, Ile make him quail,   35
  Or before my prince I will never appeare."
Then bowemen and gunners thou shalt have,
  And chuse them over my realme so free ;
Besides good mariners, and shipp-boyes,
  To guide the great shipp on the sea.   40

The first man, that lord Howard chose,
  Was the ablest gunner in all the realm,
Thoughe he was threescore yeeres and ten :
  Good Peter Simon was his name.
Peter, sais hee, I must to the sea,   45
  To bring home a traytor live or dead :
Before all others I have chosen thee ;
  Of a hundred gunners to be the head.

Ver. 29. lord Charles Howard, MS.

If you, my lord, have chosen mee
    Of a hundred gunners to be the head,   **50**
Then hang me up on your maine-mast tree,
    If I misse my marke one shilling bread.✱
My lord then chose a boweman rare,
    Whose active hands had gained fame.†
In Yorkshire was this gentleman borne,   **55**
    And William Horseley was his name.‡

Horseley, sayd he, I must with speede
    Go seeke a traytor on the sea,
And now of a hundred bowemen brave
    To be the head I have chosen thee.   **60**
If you, quoth hee, have chosen mee
    Of a hundred bowemen to be the head ;
On your maine-màst Ile hanged bee,
    If I miss twelvescore one penny bread.✱

With pikes and gunnes, and bowemen bold,   **65**
    This noble Howard is gone to the sea ;
With a valyant heart and a pleasant cheare,
    Out at Thames mouth sayled he.
And days he scant had sayled three,
    Upon the ' voyage ' he tooke in hand,   **70**
But there he mett with a noble shipp,
    And stoutely made itt stay and stand.

Thou must tell me, lord Howard said,
    Now who thou art, and what's thy name ;
And shewe me where thy dwelling is :   **75**
    And whither bound, and whence thou came.

Ver. 70. Journey, MS.
  ✱ An old Eng. word for breadth.   † Pr. copy.
  ‡ Mr. Lambe, in his notes to the poem on the *Battle of Flodden Field*, contends that this expert bowman's name was not Horseley, but Hustler, of a family long seated near Stockton, in Cleveland, Yorkshire. Vid. p. 5.

My name is Henry Hunt, quoth hee
   With a heavye heart, and a carefull mind;
I and my shipp doe both belong
   To the Newcastle, that stands upon Tyne.   80

Hast thou not heard, nowe, Henrye Hunt,
   As thou hast sayled by daye and by night,
Of a Scottish rover on the seas;
   Men call him sir Andrew Barton, knight?
Then ever he sighed, and sayd alas!   85
   With a grieved mind, and well away!
But over-well I knowe that wight,
   I was his prisoner yesterday.

As I was sayling uppon the sea,
   A Burdeaux voyage for to fare;   90
To his hach-borde he clasped me,
   And robd me of all my merchant ware:
And mickle debts, Got wot, I owe,
   And every man will have his owne;
And I am nowe to London bounde,   95
   Of our gracious king to beg a boone.

That shall not need, lord Howard sais;
   Lett me but once that robber see,
For every penny tane thee froe
   It shall be doubled shillings three.   100
Nowe God forefend, the merchant said,
   That you shold seek soe far amisse!
God keepe you out of that traitors hands!
   Full litle ye wott what a man hee is.

Hee is brasse within, and steele without,   105
   With beames on his topcastle stronge;
And eighteen pieces of ordinance
   He carries on each side along:

Ver. 91. The MS. has here Archborde, but in pt. ii. ver. 5
Hachebord: [= ship or side of the ship.]

And he hath a pinnace deerlye dight,[1]
  St. Andrewes crosse that is his guide ;   110
His pinnace beareth ninescore men,
  And fifteen canons on each side.

Were ye twentye shippes, and he but one ;
  I sweare by kirke, and bower, and hall ;
He wold overcome them everye one,   115
  If once his beames they doe downe fall.*
This is cold comfort, sais my lord,
  To wellcome a stranger thus to the sea :
Yet Ile bring him and his shipp to shore,
  Or to Scottland hee shall carrye mee.   120

Then a noble gunner you must have,
  And he must aim well with his ee,
And sinke his pinnace into the sea,
  Or else hee never orecome will bee :
And if you chance his shipp to borde,   125
  This counsel I must give withall,
Let no man to his topcastle goe
  To strive to let his beams downe fall.

And seven pieces of ordinance,
  I pray your honour lend to mee,   130
On each side of my shipp along,
  And I will lead you on the sea.

---

* It should seem from hence, that before our marine artillery was brought to its present perfection, some naval commanders had recourse to instruments or machines, similar in use, though perhaps unlike in construction, to the heavy dolphins made of lead or iron used by the ancient Greeks ; which they suspended from beams or yards fastened to the masts, and which they precipitately let fall on the enemies ships, in order to sink them, by beating holes through the bottoms of their undecked triremes, or otherwise damaging them. These are mentioned by Thucydides, lib. vii. p. 256, ed. 1564, folio, and are more fully explained in *Schefferi de Militiâ Navali,* lib. ii. cap. v. p. 136, ed. 1653, 4to.
  N.B. It everywhere in the MS. seems to be written "beanes."

[1 richly fitted out.]

A glasse Ile sett, that may be seene,
  Whether you sayle by day or night,
And to-morrowe, I sweare, by nine of the clocke 135
  You shall meet with Sir Andrewe Barton knight.

THE SECOND PART.

THE merchant sett my lorde a glasse
  Soe well apparent in his sight,
And on the morrowe, by nine of the clocke,
  He shewed him Sir Andrewe Barton knight.
His hachebord it was 'gilt' with gold,   5
  Soe deerlye dight it dazzled the ee :
Nowe by my faith, lord Howarde sais,
  This is a gallant sight to see.

Take in your ancyents,[1] standards eke,
  So close that no man may them see ;   10
And put me forth a white willowe wand,
  As merchants use to sayle the sea.
But they stirred neither top, nor mast ;*
  Stoutly they past Sir Andrew by.
What English churles are yonder, he sayd,   15
  That can soe litle curtesye?

Now by the roode, three yeares and more
  I have beene admirall over the sea ;
And never an English nor Portingall
  Without my leave can passe this way.   20
Then called he forth his stout pinnàce ;
  "Fetch backe yond pedlars nowe to mee :
I sweare by the masse, yon English churles
  Shall all hang att my maine-mast tree."

Ver. 5. "hached with gold," MS.   * *i.e.* did not salute.

[¹ flags.]

With that the pinnace itt shott off,   25
   Full well lord Howard might it ken ;
For itt stroke down my lord's fore mast,
   And killed fourteen of his men.
Come hither, Simon, sayes my lord,
   Looke that thy word be true, thou said ;   30
For at my maine-mast thou shalt hang,
   If thou misse thy marke one shilling bread.

Simon was old, but his heart itt was bold.
   His ordinance he laid right lowe ;
He put in chaine full nine yardes long,   35
   With other great shott lesse, and moe ;
And he lette goe his great gunnes shott ;
   Soe well he settled itt with his ee,
The first sight that Sir Andrew sawe,
   He see his pinnace sunke in the sea.   40

And when he saw his pinnace sunke,
   Lord, how his heart with rage did swell !
" Nowe cutt my ropes, itt is time to be gon ;
   Ile fetch yond pedlars backe mysell."
When my Lord sawe Sir Andrewe loose,   45
   Within his heart hee was full faine :
" Nowe spread your ancyents, strike up drummes,
   Sound all your trumpetts out amaine."

Fight on, my men, Sir Andrewe sais,
   Weale howsoever this geere will sway ;   50
Itt is my lord admirall of Englànd,
   Is come to seeke mee on the sea.
Simon had a sonne, who shott right well,
   That did Sir Andrewe mickle scare ;
In att his decke he gave a shott,   55
   Killed threescore of his men of warre.

Ver. 35. *i. e.* discharged chain-shot.

Then Henrye Hunt with rigour hott
   Came bravely on the other side,
Soone he drove downe his fore-mast tree,
   And killed fourscore men beside.   60
Nowe, out alas! Sir Andrewe cryed,
   What may a man now thinke, or say?
Yonder merchant theefe, that pierceth mee,
   He was my prisoner yesterday.

Come hither to me, thou Gordon good,   65
   That aye wast readye att my call;
I will give thee three hundred markes,
   If thou wilt let my beames downe fall.
Lord Howard hee then calld in haste,
   " Horseley see thou be true in stead;   70
For thou shalt at the maine-mast hang,
   If thou misse twelvescore one penny bread."

Then Gordon swarved[1] the maine-mast tree,
   He swarved it with might and maine;
But Horseley with a bearing arrowe,   75
   Stroke the Gordon through the braine;
And he fell unto the haches again,
   And sore his deadlye wounde did bleed:
Then word went through Sir Andrews men,
   How that the Gordon hee was dead.   80

Come hither to mee, James Hambilton,
   Thou art my only sisters sonne,
If thou wilt let my beames downe fall,
   Six hundred nobles thou hast wonne.
With that he swarved the maine-mast tree,   85
   He swarved it with nimble art;
But Horseley with a broad arrowe
   Pierced the Hambilton through the heart:

Ver. 67. 84 pounds, MS.   V. 75. bearinge, sc. that carries well,
&c.

[1 climbed.]

And downe he fell upon the deck,
　　That with his blood did streame amaine :　　90
Then every Scott cryed, Well-away !
　　Alas a comelye youth is slaine !
All woe begone was Sir Andrew then,
　　With griefe and rage his heart did swell :
" Go fetch me forth my armour of proofe,　　95
　　For I will to the topcastle mysell.

" Goe fetch me forth my armour of proofe ;
　　That gilded is with gold soe cleare :
God be with my brother John of Barton !
　　Against the Portingalls hee it ware ;　　100
And when he had on this armour of proofe,
　　He was a gallant sight to see :
Ah ! nere didst thou meet with living wight,
　　My deere brothèr, could cope with thee."

Come hither Horseley, sayes my lord,　　105
　　And looke your shaft that itt goe right,
Shoot a good shoote in time of need,
　　And for it thou shalt be made a knight.
Ile shoot my best, quoth Horseley then,
　　Your honour shall see, with might and maine ; 110
But if I were hanged at your maine-mast,
　　I have now left but arrowes twaine.

Sir Andrew he did swarve the tree,
　　With right good will he swarved then :
Upon his breast did Horseley hitt,　　115
　　But the arrow bounded back agen.
Then Horseley spyed a privye place
　　With a perfect eye in a secrette part ;
Under the spole[1] of his right arme
　　He smote Sir Andrew to the heart.　　120

[1 shoulder.]

"Fight on, my men, Sir Andrew sayes,
　A little Ime hurt, but yett not slaine;
Ile but lye downe and bleede a while,
　And then Ile rise and fight againe.
Fight on, my men, Sir Andrew sayes,　　　　125
　And never flinche before the foe;
And stand fast by St. Andrewes crosse
　Untill you heare my whistle blowe." *

They never heard his whistle blow,——
　Which made their hearts waxe sore adread:　130
Then Horseley sayd, Aboard, my lord,
　For well I wott Sir Andrew's dead.
They boarded then his noble shipp,
　They boarded it with might and maine;
Eighteen score Scots alive they found,　　　135
　The rest were either maimed or slaine.

Lord Howard tooke a sword in hand,
　And off he smote Sir Andrewes head;
"I must have left England many a daye,
　If thou wert alive as thou art dead."　　　140
He caused his body to be cast
　Over the hatchbord into the sea,
And about his middle three hundred crownes:
　"Wherever thou land this will bury thee."

Thus from the warres lord Howard came,　　　145
　And backe he sayled ore the maine,
With mickle joy and triumphìng
　Into Thames mouth he came againe.
Lord Howard then a letter wrote,
　And sealed it with seale and ring;　　　150
"Such a noble prize have I brought to your grace,
　As never did subject to a king.

[* For a reference to whistles used by naval commanders, see
Statute of apparel, 24 Hen. VIII. c. 13 (Anstis's *Order of the
Garter*, vol. ii. p. 121.)]

" Sir Andrewes shipp I bring with mee ;
   A braver shipp was never none :
Nowe hath your grace two shipps of warr,   *155*
   Before in England was but one."
King Henryes grace with royall cheere
   Welcomed the noble Howard home,
And where, said he, is this rover stout,
   That I myselfe may give the doome ?   *160*

" The rover, he is safe, my leige,
   Full many a fadom in the sea ;
If he were alive as he is dead,
   I must have left England many a day :
And your grace may thank four men i' the ship   *165*
   For the victory wee have wonne,
These are William Horseley, Henry Hunt,
   And Peter Simon, and his sonne."

To Henry Hunt, the king then sayd,
   In lieu of what was from thee tane,   *170*
A noble a day now thou shalt have,
   Sir Andrewes jewels and his chayne.
And Horseley thou shalt be a knight,
   And lands and livings shalt have store ;
Howard shall be erle Surrye hight,   *175*
   As Howards erst have beene before.

Nowe, Peter Simon, thou art old,
   I will maintaine thee and thy sonne :
And the men shall have five hundred markes
   For the good service they have done.   *180*
Then in came the queene with ladyes fair
   To see Sir Andrewe Barton knight :
They weend that hee were brought on shore,
   And thought to have seen a gallant sight.

Ver. 175, 6. . . . Erle of Nottingham, And soe was **never**,
&c., MS.

But when they see his deadlye face,   185
   And eyes soe hollow in his head,
I wold give, quoth the king, a thousand markes,
   This man were alive as hee is dead :
Yett for the manfull part hee playd,
   Which fought soe well with heart and hand,   190
His men shall have twelvepence a day,
   Till they come to my brother kings high land.

❧

*_**

THE following version is reprinted from Hales and Furnivall's edition of the folio MS., vol. iii. p. 403 :—

As : itt beffell in M[i]dsumer time
   when burds singe sweetlye on euery tree,
our noble King, King Henery the 8th,
   ouer the riuer of Thames past hee.   4
hee was no sooner ouer the riuer,
   downe in a fforrest to take the ayre,
but 80 merchants of London cittye
   came kneeling before King Henery there :   8

"O yee are welcome, rich merchants,
   [Good saylors, welcome unto me !"]
they swore by the rood thé were saylers good,
   but rich merchants they cold not bee ;   12
"to ffrance nor fflanders dare we nott passe,
   nor Burdeaux voyage wee dare not ffare,
& all ffor a ffalse robber that lyes on the seas,
   & robb vs of our merchants ware."   16

King Henery was stout, & he turned him about,
   & swore by the Lord that was mickle of might,
"I thought he had not beene in the world throughout,
   that durst haue wrought England such vnright."   20
but euer they sighed, and said—alas !—
   vnto King Harry this answere againe
"he is a proud Scott that will robb vs all
   if wee were 20 shipps and hee but one."   24

The King looket ouer his left shoulder,
   amongst his Lords & Barrons soe ffree :
"haue I neuer Lord in all my realme
   will ffeitch yond traitor vnto mee?"   28

"yes, that dare I !" sayes my Lord Chareles Howard,
  neere to the King wheras hee did stand;
" If that your grace will giue me leaue,
  my selfe wilbe the only man."   32

"thou shalt haue 600 men," saith our King,
  " & chuse them out of my realme soe ffree ;
besids Marriners and boyes,
  to guide the great shipp on the sea."   36
"Ile goe speake with Sir Andrew," sais Charles, my Lord Haward;
  " vpon the sea, if hee be there,
I will bring him & his shipp to shore,
  or before my prince I will neuer come neere."   40

the ffirst of all my Lord did call,
  a noble gunner hee was one ;
this man was 60 yeeres and ten,
  & Peeter Simon was his name.   44
" Peeter," sais hee, " I must sayle to the sea
  to seeke out an enemye ; god be my speed !
before all others I haue chosen thee ;
  of a 100^d. guners thoust be my head."   48

" my Lord," sais hee, " if you haue chosen mee
  of a 100^d. gunners to be the head,
hange me att your maine-mast tree
  if I misse my marke past 3 pence bread."   52
The next of all my Lord he did call,
  a noble bowman hee was one ;
In yorekeshire was this gentleman borne,
  & william Horsley was his name.   56

" Horsley," sayes hee, " I must sayle to the sea
  to seeke out an enemye ; god be my speede !
before all others I haue chosen thee ;
  of a 100 bowemen thoust be my head."   60
" My Lord," sais hee, " if you haue chosen mee
  of a 100^d. bowemen to be they head,
hang me att your mainemast tree
  if I misse my marke past 12^d. bread."   64

with pikes, and gunnes, & bowemen bold,
  this Noble Howard is gone to the sea
on the day before Midsummer euen,
  & out att Thames mouth sayled they.   68
They had not sayled dayes 3
  vpon their Iourney they tooke in hand,
but there they mett with a Noble shipp,
  & stoutely made itt both stay & stand.   72

" thou must tell me thy name," sais Charles, my Lord Haward,
  " or who thou art, or ffrom whence thou came,
yea, & where thy dwelling is,
  to whom & where thy shipp does belong."   76
" My name," sayes hee, " is Henery Hunt,
  with a pure hart & a penitent mind ;
I and my shipp they doe belong
  vnto the New castle that stands vpon tine."   80

" Now thou must tell me, Harry Hunt,
  as thou hast sayled by day & by night,
hast thou not heard of a stout robber ?
  men calls him Sir Andrew Bartton, Knight."   84
but euer he sighed, & sayd, " alas !
  ffull well, my Lord, I know that wight !
he robd me of my merchants ware,
  & I was his prisoner but yesternight.   88

" as I was sayling vppon the sea,
  & Burdeaux voyage as I did ffare,
he Clasped me to his Archborde
  & robd me of all my merchants ware ;   92
& I am a man both poore & bare,
  & euery man will haue his owne of me,
& I am bound towards London to ffare,
  to complaine to my Prince Henerye."   96

" that shall not need," sais my Lord Haward ;
  " if thou canst lett me this robber see,
ffor euery peny he hath taken thee ffroe,
  thou shalt be rewarded a shilling," quoth hee.   100
" Now god ffore-fend," saies Henery Hunt,
  " my Lord, you shold worke soe ffarr amisse !
god keepe you out of that Traitors hands !
  for you wott ffull litle what a man hee is.   104

" hee is brasse within, & steele without,
  & beanes hee beares in his Topcastle stronge ;
his shipp hath ordinance cleane round about ;
  besids, my Lord, hee is verry well mand ;   108
he hath a pinnace is deerlye dight,
  Saint Andrews crosse, that is his guide ;
his pinnace beares 9 score men & more,
  besids 15 cannons on euery side.   112

" if you were 20 shippes, & he but one,
  either in charke-bord or in hall,
he wold ouercome you euerye one,
  & if his beanes they doe downe ffall."   116

" this is cold comfort," sais my Lord Haward,
  " to wellcome a stranger thus to the sea ;
Ile bring him & his shipp to shore,
  or else into Scottland hee shall carrye mee."   120

" then you must gett a noble gunner, my Lord,
  that can sett well with his eye
& sinke his pinnace into the sea,
  & soone then ouercome will hee bee   124
& when that you haue done this,
  if you chance Sir Andrew for to bord,
lett no man to his Topcastle goe ;
  & I will giue you a glasse, my Lord,   128

" & then you need to fferae no Scott,
  whether you sayle by day or by night;
& to-morrow by 7 of the clocke,
  you shall meete with Sir Andrew Bartton, Knight.   132
I was his prisoner but yester night,
  & he hath taken mee sworne ;" quoth hee,
" I trust my L[ord] god will me fforgiue
  & if that oath then broken bee.   136

" you must lend me six peeces, my Lord," quoth hee,
  "into my shipp to sayle the sea,
& to-morrow by 9 of the clocke
  your honour againe then will I see."   140
And the hache-bord where Sir Andrew Lay,
  is hached with gold deerlye dight :
" now by my ffaith," sais Charles, my Lord Haward,
  " then yonder Scott is a worthye wight ! "   144

2^d. parte
  { Take in your ancyents & your standards,
    yea that no man shall them see,
  & put me fforth a white willow wand,
    as Merchants vse to sayle the sea.   148
But they stirred neither top nor mast,
  but Sir Andrew they passed by.
" whatt English are yonder," said Sir Andrew,
  " that can so litle curtesye ?   152

" I haue beene Admirall ouer the sea
  more then these yeeres three ;
there is neuer an English dog, nor Portingall,
  can passe this way without leaue of mee.   156
But now yonder pedlers, they are past,
  which is no litle greffe to me :
ffeich them backe," sayes Sir Andrew Bartton,
  " they shall all hang att my maine-mast tree."   60

with that they pinnace itt shott of,
   that my Lord Haward might itt well ken,
itt strokes downe my Lords fforemast,
   & killed 14 of my Lord his men.   164
" come hither, Simon !" sayes my Lord Haward,
   "looke that thy words be true thou sayd ;
Ile hang thee att my maine-mast tree
   if thou misse thy marke past 12ᵈ. bread."   168

Simon was old, but his hart itt was bold,
   hee tooke downe a peece, & layd itt ffull lowe ;
he put in chaine yeards 9,
   besids other great shott lesse and more.   172
with that hee lett his gun shott goe ;
   soe well hee settled itt with his eye,
the ffirst sight that Sir Andrew sawe,
   hee see his pinnace sunke in the sea.   176

when hee saw his pinace sunke,
   Lord ! in his hart hee was not well :
" cutt my ropes ! itt is time to be gon !
   Ile goe ffeitch yond pedlers backe my selfe !"   180
when my Lord Haward saw Sir Andrew loose,
   lord ! in his hart that hee was ffaine :
" strike on your drummes, spread out your ancyents !
   sound out your trumpetts ! sound out amaine !"   184

"ffight on, my men !" sais Sir Andrew Bartton ;
   "weate, howsoeuer this geere will sway,
itt is my Lord Adm[i]rall of England
   is come to seeke mee on the sea."   188
Simon had a sonne, with shott of a gunn,—
   well Sir Andrew might itt Ken,—
he shott itt in att a priuye place,
   & killed 60 more of Sir Andrews men.   192

Harry Hunt came in att the other syde,
   & att Sir Andrew hee shott then,
he droue downe his fformost tree,
   & killed 80 more of Sir Andirwes men.   196
" I haue done a good turne," sayes Harry Hunt,
   "Sir Andrew is not our Kings ffreind ;
he hoped to haue vndone me yesternight,
   but I hope I haue quitt him well in the end."   200

" Euer alas !" sayd Sir Andrew Barton,
   " what shold a man either thinke or say ?
yonder ffalse theeffe is my strongest Enemye,
   who was my prisoner but yesterday.   204

come hither to me, thou Gourden good,
   & be thou readye att my call,
& I will giue thee 300ʰ.
   if thou wilt lett my beanes downe ffall."   208

with that hee swarned the maine-mast tree,
   soe did he itt with might and maine :
Horseley with a bearing arrow
   stroke the Gourden through the braine,   212
And he ffell into the haches againe,
   & sore of this wound that he did bleed.
then word went throug Sir Andrews men,
   that they Gourden hee was dead.   216

" come hither to me, Iames Hambliton,—
   thou art my sisters sonne, I haue no more,—
I will giue [thee] 600ʰ.
   If thou will lett my beanes downe ffall."   220
with that hee swarned the maine-mast tree,
   soe did hee itt with might and maine :
Horseley with an-other broad Arrow
   strake the yeaman through the braine,   224

that hee ffell downe to the haches againe :
   sore of his wound that hee did bleed.
itt is verry true, as the welchman sayd,
   couetousness getts no gaine.   228
but when hee saw his sisters sonne slaine,
   Lord ! in his heart hee was not well.
" goe ffeitch me downe my armour of proue,
   ffor I will to the topcastle my-selfe.   232

goe ffeitch me downe my armour of prooffe,
   for itt is guilded with gold soe cleere.
god be with my brother, Iohn of Bartton !
   amongst the Portingalls hee did itt weare."   236
but when hee had his armour of prooffe,
   & on his body hee had itt on,
euery man that looked att him
   sayd, " gunn nor arrow hee neede feare none !"   240

" come hither, Horsley !" sayes my Lord Haward,
   " & looke your shaft that itt goe right ;
shoot a good shoote in the time of need,
   & ffor thy shooting thoust be made a Knight."   244
" Ile doe my best," sayes Horslay then,
   " your honor shall see beffore I goe ;
if I shold be hanged att your mainemast,
   I haue in my shipp but arrowes tow."   248

but att Sir Andrew hee shott then ;
   hee made sure to hitt his marke ;
vnder the spole of his right arme
   hee smote Sir Andrew quite throw the hart.   252
yett ffrom the tree hee wold not start,
   but hee clinged to itt with might & maine.
vnder the coller then of his Iacke,
   he stroke Sir Andrew thorrow the braine.   256

" ffight on my men," sayes Sir Andrew Bartton,
   " I am hurt, but I am not slaine ;
Ile lay mee downe & bleed a-while,
   & then Ile rise & ffight againe.   260
ffight on my men," sayes Sir Andrew Bartton,
   " these English doggs they bite soe lowe ;
ffight on ffor Scottland & Saint Andrew
   till you heare my whistle blowe !"   264

but when thé cold not heare his whistle blow,
   sayes Harry Hunt, " Ile lay my head
you may bord yonder noble shipp, my Lord,
   for I know Sir Andrew hee is dead."   268
with that they borded this noble shipp,
   soe did they itt with might & maine ;
thé ffound 18 score Scotts aliue,
   besids the rest were maimed & slaine.   272

My Lord Haward tooke a sword in his hand,
   & smote of Sir Andrews head.
the Scotts stood by, did weepe & mourne,
   but neuer a word durst speake or say.   276
he caused his body to be taken downe,
   & ouer the hatch-bord cast into the sea,
& about his middle 300 crownes :
   " wheresoeuer thou lands, itt will bury thee."   280

with his head they sayled into England againe
   with right good will & fforce & meanye,
& the day beffore New yeeres euen
   & into Thames mouth againe they came.   284
My Lord Haward wrote to King Heneryes grace,
   with all the newes hee cold him bring :
" such a new yeeres gifft I haue brought to your gr[ace],
   As neuer did subiect to any King.   288

" ffor Merchandyes and Manhood,
   the like is nott to be ffound ;
the sight of these wold doe you good,
   ffor you haue not the Like in your English ground."   292

but when hee heard tell that they were come,
  full royally hee welcomed them home :
Sir Andrews shipp was the Kings New yeeres guifft ;
  A brauer shipp you neuer saw none.   296

Now hath our King Sir Andrews shipp
  besett with pearles and precyous stones ;
Now hath England 2 shipps of warr,
  2 shipps of warr, before but one.   300
"who holpe to this ?" sayes King Henerye,
  "that I may reward him ffor his paine,"
" Harry Hunt and Peeter Simon,
  William Horseleay, & I the same."   304

" Harry Hunt shall haue his whistle & chaine,
  & all his Iewells, whatsoeuer they bee,
& other rich giffts that I will not name,
  for his good service he hath done mee.   308
Horslay, right thoust be a Knight ;
  Lands and liuings thou shalt haue store.
Howard shalbe Erle of Nottingham,
  & soe was neuer Haward before.   312

" Now Peeter Simon, thou art old,
  I will maintaine thee & thy sonne,
thou shalt haue 500^li. all in gold
  ffor the good service that thou hast done."   316
then King Henerye shiffted his roome ;
  in came the Queene & ladyes bright ;
other arrands they had none
  but to see Sir Andrew Bartton, Knight.   320

but when they see his deadly fface,
  his eyes were hollow in his head,
" I wold giue a 100^li." sais King Henerye,
  " the man were aliue as hee is dead !   324
yett ffor the manfull part that hee hath playd
  both heere & beyond the sea
his men shall haue halfe a crowne a day
  to bring them to my brother King Iamye."   328
                              ffinis.]

XIII.

LADY ANNE BOTHWELL'S LAMENT.

A Scottish Song.

THE subject of this pathetic ballad the Editor once thought might possibly relate to the Earl of Bothwell, and his desertion of his wife Lady Jean Gordon, to make room for his marriage with the Queen of Scots. But this opinion he now believes to be groundless; indeed Earl Bothwell's age, who was upwards of 60 at the time of that marriage, renders it unlikely that he should be the object of so warm a passion as this elegy supposes. He has been since informed, that it entirely refers to a private story: A young lady of the name of *Bothwell*, or rather *Boswell*, having been, together with her child, deserted by her husband or lover, composed these affecting lines herself; which here are given from a copy in the Editor's folio MS. corrected by another in Allan Ramsay's *Miscellany*.

[The young lady alluded to above has since been set aside for the Hon. Anne Bothwell, daughter of Adam Bothwell, Bishop of Orkney. Mr. James Maidment, in his elegant edition of *Scottish Ballads and Songs* (vol. ii. 1868), writes: "The late Charles Kirkpatrick Sharpe, Esquire, whose knowledge of antiquated scandal was extraordinary, found in a MS. history of the family of Bothwell by Father Hay, that Adam Bothwell, Bishop of Orkney, had a daughter named 'Anne, who fell with child to a son of the Earl of Marre.'" Anne was the sister of the first Lord Holyroodhouse (created in 1607), and her seducer was Alexander, third son of John, seventh Earl of Mar, a cousin of her own, considered one of the handsomest men of his day. This is all very well for conjecture, but it is nothing more. The ballad does not appear to have been associated with a Bothwell, or in fact with any named person, until more than a century after it was written. In the Folio MS. it is simply called *Balowe*, and Percy therefore might well have hesitated before he gave it the heading he has, and before he Scotticised all the English words. The four earliest versions are in the following books: 1. Richard Brome's Comedy of the *Northern Lass, or the Nest of Fools*, printed in 1632, but acted somewhat earlier; 2. Percy Folio; 3. Pinkerton's MS. (1625-49), in the possession of David Laing; 4. John Gamble's MS., 1649;

5. Elizabeth Rogers' MS., 1658. Mr. Chappell drew up the following very valuable note for the edition of the Percy Folio (vol. iii. p. 518), which puts the matter very clearly:—

" Baloo is a sixteenth-century ballad, not a seventeenth. It is alluded to by several of our early dramatists, and the tune is to be found in an early Elizabethan MS. known as William Ballet's Lute Book, as well as in Morley's *Consort Lessons*, printed in 1599. The words and tune are together in John Gamble's Music Book, a MS. in the possession of Dr. Rimbault, (date 1649,) and in Elizabeth Rogers's Virginal Book, in the library of the British Museum (Addit. MS. 10,337). The last is dated 1658, but the copy may have been taken some few years after. Baloo was so popular a subject that it was printed as a street ballad, with additional stanzas, just as ' My lodging it is on the cold ground' and other popular songs were lengthened for the same purpose. It has been reprinted in that form by Evans, in his *Old Ballads, Historical and Narrative*, edit. 1810, vol. i. p. 259. The title is ' The New Balow ; or A Wenches Lamentation for the loss of her Sweetheart : he having left her a babe to play with, being the fruits of her folly.' The particular honour of having been the ' wench' in question was first claimed for ' Lady Anne Bothwell' in Part iii. of *Comic and Serious Scots Poems*, published by Watson in Edinburgh in 1711. Since that date Scotch antiquaries have been very busy in searching into the scandalous history of the Bothwell family, to find out which of the Lady Annes might have been halla-balooing.

" May we not release the whole race from this imputation ? The sole authority for the charge is Watson's *Collection !* the same book that ascribes to the unfortunate Montrose the song of ' My dear and only love, take heed,' and tacks it as a second part to his ' My dear and only love, I pray.' Shade of Montrose ! how must you be ashamed of your over-zealous advocate ! Let us examine whether the spirit of ' Lady Anne Bothwel' has more reason to be grateful. Among the stanzas ascribed to her by Watson are the two following, which are not to be found in any English copy :—

> ' I take my fate from best to worse
> That I must needs now be a nurse,
> And lull my young son in my lap.
> From me, sweet orphan, take the pap :
> Balow, my boy, thy mother mild
> Shall sing, as from all bliss exil'd.'

" In the second we find the inducement supposed to have been offered by Lady Anne's lover :

' I was too credulous at the first
To grant thee that a maiden durst,
And in thy bravery thou didst vaunt
That I no maintenance should want: (!)
Thou swear thou lov'd, thy mind is moved,
Which since no otherwise has proved.'

" Comment is unnecessary. Can any one believe that such
lines were written by or for any lady of rank? Yet they were
copied as Lady Anne's by Allan Ramsay, and polished in his
usual style. They have been polished and repolished by subsequent editors, but to little avail, for they remain great blots upon
a good English ballad. There is not a Scotch word, nor even one
peculiar to the North of England, in the whole of Watson's ver
sion."

This attempt to dispute the Scottish origin of the ballad is
strongly resented by the editor of the *Ballad Minstrelsy of Scotland*, Glasgow, 1871. At all events the fact remains that the title
" Lady Anne Bothwell's Balow" cannot be traced farther back
than Watson's *Collection*, published in 1711.]

BALOW,[1] my babe, lye still and sleipe !
It grieves me sair to see thee weipe :
If thoust be silent, Ise be glad,
Thy maining[2] maks my heart ful sad.
Balow, my boy, thy mothers joy,   5
Thy father breides me great annoy.
Balow, my babe, ly stil and sleipe,
It grieves me sair to see thee weepe.

Whan he began to court my luve,
And with his sugred wordes* to muve,   10

---

* When *sugar* was first imported into Europe, it was a very great
dainty ; and therefore the epithet *sugred* is used by all our old
writers metaphorically to express extreme and delicate sweetness.
(See above, No. XI. v. 10.) *Sugar* at present is cheap and common ; and therefore suggests now a coarse and vulgar idea.

[[1] hush.   [2] moaning.]

His faynings fals, and flattering cheire
To me that time did not appeire:
But now I see, most cruell hee
Cares neither for my babe nor mee.
                    Balow, &c.   15

Lye still, my darling, sleipe a while,
And when thou wakest, sweitly smile:
But smile not, as thy father did,
To cozen maids : nay God forbid!
Bot yett I feire, thou wilt gae neire   20
Thy fatheris hart, and face to beire.
                    Balow, &c.

I cannae chuse, but ever will
Be luving to thy father still :
Whair-eir he gae, whair-eir he ryde,   25
My luve with him doth still abyde :
In weil or wae, whair-eir he gae,
Mine hart can neire depart him frae.
                    Balow, &c.

Bot doe not, doe not, prettie mine,   30
To faynings fals thine hart incline:
Be loyal to thy luver trew,
And nevir change hir for a new :
If gude or faire, of hir have care,
For womens banning's[1] wonderous sair.   35
                    Balow, &c.

Bairne, sin thy cruel father is gane,
Thy winsome smiles maun eise my paine ;
My babe and I'll together live,
He'll comfort me when cares doe grieve :   40
My babe and I right saft will ly,
And quite forgeit man's cruelty.
                    Balow, &c

[1 cursing.]

Fareweil, fareweil, thou falsest youth,
That evir kist a womans mouth!   45
I wish all maides be warnd by mee
Nevir to trust mans curtesy;
For if we doe bot chance to bow,
They'le use us then they care not how.
   Balow, my babe, ly stil, and sleipe,   50
   It grives me sair to see thee weipe.

XIV.

THE MURDER OF THE KING OF SCOTS.

THE catastrophe of Henry Stewart, lord Darnley, the unfortunate husband of Mary Q. of Scots, is the subject
of this ballad. It is here related in that partial, imperfect manner in which such an event would naturally
strike the subjects of another kingdom, of which he was a native.
Henry appears to have been a vain, capricious, worthless young
man, of weak understanding, and dissolute morals. But the beauty
of his person, and the inexperience of his youth, would dispose
mankind to treat him with an indulgence, which the cruelty of his
murder would afterwards convert into the most tender pity and
regret: and then imagination would not fail to adorn his memory
with all those virtues he ought to have possessed. This will
account for the extravagant elogium bestowed upon him in the
first stanza, &c.

Henry lord Darnley was eldest son of the earl of Lennox, by
the lady Margaret Douglas, niece of Henry VIII. and daughter
of Margaret queen of Scotland by the earl of Angus, whom that
princess married after the death of James IV.—Darnley, who had
been born and educated in England, was but in his 21st year, when
he was murdered, Feb. 9, 1567-8. This crime was perpetrated by
the E. of Bothwell, not out of respect to the memory of Riccio,
but in order to pave the way for his own marriage with the queen

This ballad (printed, with a few corrections, from the Editor's
folio MS.) seems to have been written soon after Mary's escape
into England in 1568, see v. 65.—It will be remembered at v. 5,
that this princess was Q. dowager of France, having been first
married to Francis II. who died Dec. 4, 1560.

[In the above note Percy takes the ordinary unfavourable view of Darnley's character, which is not entirely borne out by contemporary evidence. Darnley was unfortunate both in having all Mary's friends as his enemies and in having no supporters among her opponents because he was a Roman Catholic. It is not fair to dispose of such a ballad as the present with the inference that the writer could know nothing of Darnley's character. It does not stand alone, and it appears from the broadsides that circulated through the country after his murder that the people had a real liking for him although he had been amongst them only a couple of years. Robert Lekprevik, the most celebrated Edinburgh printer of his time, printed in 1567, *The Testament and Tragedie of umquhile King Henrie Stewart of gude memorie,* a powerful poem, which discovers clearly the popular feeling against Mary. Mr. Froude also found one of these ballads among the Scottish State Papers, in which curses are heaped upon Mary, who is called Dalila, Clytemnestra and Semiramis for her murder of " ane bonny boy." One of the verses is as follows :—

> " At ten houris on Sunday late at een,
> When Dalila and Bothwell bade good night,
> Off her finger false she threw ane ring,
> And said, My Lord ane token you I plight."

If the circumstances of the English ballad are related in a partial and imperfect manner, what shall we say of the much more severe tone of those written in Scotland. Mr. Maidment[1] has gathered together a few facts that show how much may be said in favour of the unfortunate prince. It appears from Colville's *Historie and Life of King James the sext,* that Secretary Maitland inflamed Darnley's mind with the insinuation that Rizzio was too intimate with the queen. The criminal familiarity of her majesty with Rizzio appears to have been generally suspected, so that Darnley's conduct was that of a jealous husband who was fascinated with his wife. Colville gives the following portrait of him :—" He was a cumlie Prince, of a fayre and large stature of bodie, pleasant in countenance and affable to all men and devote, weill excercesit in martiall pastymis uponn horsback as ony prince of that age, bot was sa facile as he could concele no secreit although it myght tend to his awin weill."[2]

He was certainly accomplished and had been carefully educated.

---

[1] James Maidment's *Scottish Ballads and Songs,* 1868, vol. ii. p. 12.

[2] Quoted in Maidment's *Ballads,* 1868, vol. ii. p. 8.

He wrote a little tale called *Utopia Nova* when he was between eight and nine years of age, which he presented to his cousin, Mary Tudor. The queen in return presented him with a gold chain, which he acknowledged in a letter remarkable for the extreme beauty of its caligraphy. He also completed a translation into English of Valerius Maximus. Mr. Froude severely condemns the character of Darnley in the following terms: " He was at once meddlesome and incapable, weak and cowardly, yet insolent and unmanageable," and adds that Randolph described him as "a conceited, arrogant, intolerant fool." Nevertheless "the death of the husband of the Queen of Scots belongs to that rare class of incidents which, like the murder of Cæsar, have touched the interests of the entire educated world. Perhaps there is no single recorded act, arising merely out of private or personal passions, of which the public consequences have been so considerable."[1]

Darnley was the second son of the Earl and Countess of Lennox, and not, as stated above, by Percy, the eldest. Their first-born died on the 28th of November, 1545, nine months after his birth.

The following ballad is entitled *Earle Bodwell* in the Folio MS. (ed. Hales and Furnivall, vol. ii. p. 260). In the first three editions of the *Reliques* there were more alterations from the MS. than in the fourth, for in the latter Percy restored several of the old readings. The retained alterations are judicious, and no more than the Editor might well feel himself justified in making.]

OE worth, woe worth thee, false Scotlànde !
　　For thou hast ever wrought by sleight;
　The worthyest prince that ever was borne,
　　You hanged under a cloud by night.

The queene of France a letter wrote,　　　　5
　And sealed itt with harte and ringe ;
And bade him come Scotland within,
　And shee wold marry and crowne him kinge.

[Ver. 1. woe worth thee, woe worth thee, MS. V. 2. by a sleight. V. 3. for the worthyest. V. 8. wold marry him.
[1] Froude's *History of England* (Elizabeth), vol. iii. pp. 1-2.]

To be a king is a pleasant thing,
    To bee a prince unto a peere :   10
But you have heard, and soe have I too,
    A man may well buy gold too deare.

There was an Italyan in that place,
    Was as well beloved as ever was hee,
Lord David was his name,   15
    Chamberlaine to the queene was hee.

If the king had risen forth of his place,
    He wold have sate him downe in the cheare,
And tho itt beseemed him not so well,
    Altho the kinge had beene present there.   20

Some lords in Scotlande waxed wroth,
    And quarrelled with him for the nonce;
I shall you tell how it befell,
    Twelve daggers were in him att once.

When the queene saw her chamberlaine was slaine, 25
    For him her faire cheeks shee did weete,
And made a vowe for a yeare and a day
    The king and shee wold not come in one sheete.

Then some of the lords they waxed wrothe,
    And made their vow all vehementlye ;   30
For the death of the queenes chamberlaine,
    The king himselfe, how he shall dye.

With gun-powder they strewed his roome,
    And layd greene rushes in his way ;
For the traitors thought that very night   35
    This worthye king for to betray.

[Ver. 9. it is a pleasant.] V. 15. *sic* MS.   [V. 16. chamberlaine
unto. V. 17. ffor if the king. V. 18. have sitt him. V. 21. wonderous wroth. V. 24. all att once. V. 25. when this queene see
the chamberlaine. V. 26. her cheeks. V. 27. vow for a 12 month.
V. 29. Lords of Scottland waxed. V. 32. the king himselfe he shall
dye. V. 33. they strowed his chamber over with gunpowder.
V. 35. that night. V. 36. the worthye.]

To bedd the king he made him bowne;[1]
  To take his rest was his desire;
He was noe sooner cast on sleepe,
  But his chamber was on a blasing fire.   40

Up he lope,[2] and the window brake,
  And hee had thirtye foote to fall;
Lord Bodwell kept a privy watch,
  Underneath his castle wall.

Who have wee here? lord Bodwell sayd: 45
  Now answer me, that I may know.
" King Henry the eighth my uncle was;
  For his sweete sake some pitty show."

Who have we here? lord Bodwell sayd,
  Now answer me when I doe speake.   50
" Ah, lord Bodwell, I know thee well;
  Some pitty on me I pray thee take."

Ile pitty thee as much, he sayd,
  And as much favor show to thee,
As thou didst to the queenes chamberlaine,   55
  That day thou deemedst[3] him to die.*

Through halls and towers the king they ledd,
  Through towers and castles that were nye,
Through an arbor into an orchàrd,
  There on a peare-tree hanged him hye.   60

---

* Pronounced after the northern manner *dee.*

[Ver. 37. the worthy king made. V. 38. that was his desire.
V. 41. and a glasse window broke. V. 42. he had 30 foote for
to ffall. V. 45. sayd Lord Bodwell. V. 46. answer me, now I
doe call. V. 48. some pitty show for his sweet sake. V. 49, 50.
these two lines are not in the MS., but are here introduced to
equalize the stanzas. V. 54. Ile show to thee. V. 55. As thou
had on the. V. 57. this king. V. 58. through castles and towers
that were hye. V. 60. and there hanged him in a peare tree.
     [1] ready.   [2] leapt.   [3] doomedst.]

When the governor of Scotland heard
　How that the worthye king was slaine ;
He persued the queen so bitterlye,
　That in Scotland shee dare not remaine.

But she is fledd into merry England,　　　　65
　And here her residence hath taine ;
And through the queene of Englands grace,
　In England now shee doth remaine.

XV.

A SONNET BY Q. ELIZABETH.

HE following lines, if they display no rich vein of poetry, are yet so strongly characteristic of their great and spirited authoress, that the insertion of them will be pardoned. They are preserved in Puttenham's *Arte of English Poesie;* a book in which are many sly addresses to the queen's foible of shining as a poetess. The extraordinary manner in which these verses are introduced shews what kind of homage was exacted from the courtly writers of that age, viz.

"I find," says this antiquated critic, "none example in English metre, so well maintaining this figure [*Exargasia*, or the Gorgeous, Lat. *Expolitio*] as that dittie of her majesties owne making, passing sweete and harmonicall; which figure beyng as his very originall name purporteth the most bewtifull and gorgious of all others, it asketh in reason to be reserved for a last complement, and de-sciphred by a ladies penne herselfe beyng the most bewtifull, or rather bewtie of queenes.*   And this was the occasion: our sove-raigne lady perceiving how the Scottish queenes residence within this realme at so great libertie and ease (as were skarce meete for so great and dangerous a prysoner) bred secret factions among her people, and made many of the nobilitie incline to favour her partie: some of them desirous of innovation in the state: others aspiring

---

*   She was at this time near three-score.

[Ver. 61. Scotland he heard tell.   V. 62. that the worthye king he was slaine.   V. 64. he hath banished the queene.   V. 66. and Scottland to aside hath laine.   V. 67. good grace.   V. 68. now in England, MS.]

to greater fortunes by her libertie and life.   The queene our sove-
raigne ladie to declare that she was nothing ignorant of those secret
practizes, though she had long with great wisdome and pacience
dissembled it, writeth this dittie most sweete and sententious, not
hiding from all such aspiring minds the daunger of their ambition
and disloyaltie: which afterward fell out most truly by th' exem-
plary chastisement of sundry persons, who in fauour of the said Sc.
Q. declining from her Maiestie, sought to interrupt the quiet of the
Realme by many euill and vndutiful practizes." (p. 207.)

This sonnet was probably written in 1584, not long before Hen.
Percy 8th E. of Northumberland was imprisoned on suspicion of
plotting with F. Throckmorton, Tho. Lord Paget, and the Guises,
for invading England, and liberating the Q. of Scots, &c. (See
Collins's *Peerage*, 1779, ii. 405.)   The original is written in long
lines or alexandrines, each of which is here, on account of the
narrowness of the page, subdivided into two : but her majesty's
orthography, or at least that of her copyist, is exactly followed.

In the first edition of Harrington's *Nugæ Antiquæ*, 1st vol. 1769,
12mo. p. 58, is a copy of this poem, with great variations, the best
of which are noted below.   It is there accompanied with a very
curious letter, in which this sonnet is said to be " of her Highness
own enditing . . . My Lady Willoughby did covertly get it on her
Majesties tablet, and had much hazard in so doing ; for the Queen
did find out the thief, and chid for spreading evil bruit of her
writing such toyes, when other matters did so occupy her employ-
ment at this time ; and was fearful of being thought too lightly of
for so doing." * * *

HE doubt of future foes,
　　Exiles my present ioy,
And wit me warnes to shun such snares
　　As threaten mine annoy.

For falshood now doth flow,   5
　　And subiect faith doth ebbe,
Which would not be, if reason rul'd
　　Or wisdome weu'd the webbe.

But clowdes of iois vntried,
　　Do cloake aspiring mindes,   10

Ver. 1. dread, Harrington's ed.   V. 6. subjects, Har.   V. 7.
should, Har.   V. 8. wove, Har.

Which turne to raine of late repent,
  By course of changed windes.

The toppe of hope supposed,
  The roote of ruthe wil be,
And frutelesse all their graffed guiles,   1
  As shortly ye shall see.

Then dazeld eyes with pride,
  Which great ambition blinds,
Shalbe vnseeld by worthy wights,
  Whose foresight falshood finds.   20

The daughter of debate,*
  That eke discord doth sowe,
Shal reap no gaine where former rule
  Hath taught stil peace to growe.

No forreine bannisht wight   25
  Shall ancre in this port,
Our realme it brookes no strangers force,
  Let them elsewhere resort.

Our rusty sworde with rest,
  Shall first his edge employ,   30
To polle their toppes, that seeke such change,
  And gape for 'such like' ioy.

†‡† I cannot help subjoining to the above sonnet another distich of Elizabeth's preserved by Puttenham (p. 197) "which (says he) our soveraigne lady wrote in defiance of fortune."

  " Never thinke you, Fortune can beare the sway,
  Where Vertue's force can cause her to obay."

The slightest effusion of such a mind deserves attention.

---

* *Scil.* the Queen of Scots.
  Ver. 9. joys, Har.   V. 11. raigne, Puttenham.   V. 22. That discorde aye, Har.   V. 23. formor, Put.   V. 27. realme brookes no seditious Sects, Har.   V. 32. "such like" is supplied from Harrington's ed., in which are other variations, that seem meer mistakes of the transcriber or printer.

XVI.

KING OF SCOTS AND ANDREW BROWNE.

HIS ballad is a proof of the little intercourse that subsisted between the Scots and English, before the accession of James I. to the crown of England. The tale which is here so circumstantially related does not appear to have had the least foundation in history, but was probably built upon some confused hearsay report of the tumults in Scotland during the minority of that prince, and of the conspiracies formed by different factions to get possession of his person. It should seem from ver. 97 to have been written during the regency, or at least before the death, of the earl of Morton, who was condemned and executed June 2, 1581; when James was in his 15th year.

The original copy (preserved in the archives of the Antiquarian Society, London) is intitled, *A new Ballad, declaring the great treason conspired against the young king of Scots, and how one Andrew Browne an English-man, which was the king's chamberlaine, prevented the same. To the tune of Milfield, or els to Green-sleeves.* At the end is subjoined the name of the author " W. Elderton. Imprinted at London for Yarathe James, dwelling in Newgate Market, over against Ch. Church," in black-letter, folio.

This *Elderton,* who had been originally an attorney in the sheriffs' courts of London, and afterwards (if we may believe Oldys) a comedian, was a facetious fuddling companion, whose tippling and rhymes rendered him famous among his contemporaries. He was author of many popular songs and ballads: and probably other pieces in these volumes, besides the following, are of his composing. He is believed to have fallen a victim to his bottle before the year 1592. His epitaph has been recorded by Camden, and translated by Oldys:—

> " Hic situs est sitiens, atque ebrius Eldertonus,
> Quid dico hic situs est? hic potius sitis est."

> " Dead drunk here Elderton doth lie;
> Dead as he is, he still is dry:
> So of him it may well be said,
> Here he, but not his thirst, is laid."

See Stow's *Lond.* [*Guild Hall*].—*Biog. Brit.* [*Drayton,* by Oldys

Note B.] Ath. Ox.—Camden's *Remains.—The Exale-tation of Ale,* among Beaumont's *Poems,* 8vo. 1653.

[This ballad was licensed to Y. James on the 30th of May, 1581. Percy does not mention in the above note the fact that the ballad is included in the Folio MS., where it is entitled *Bishoppe and Browne* (ed. Hales and Furnivall, vol. ii. p. 265). It only consists of ten stanzas in place of fifteen, and two of them are incomplete. There is a sort of second part, probably also by Elderton, called *King James and Brown,* in the MS. (vol. i. p. 135), the villain of which is the same Douglas who is warned in the 98th verse of the present ballad to "take heede you do not offend the king."]

UT alas!' what a griefe is this
  That princes subjects cannot be true,
But still the devill hath some of his,
  Will play their parts whatsoever ensue;
Forgetting what a grievous thing   5
It is to offend the anointed king?
  Alas for woe, why should it be so,
  This makes a sorrowful heigh ho.

In Scotland is a bonnie kinge,
  As proper a youth as neede to be,   10
Well given to every happy thing,
  That can be in a kinge to see :
Yet that unluckie country still,
Hath people given to craftie will.
  Alas for woe, &c.   15

On Whitsun eve it so befell,
  A posset was made to give the king,
Whereof his ladie nurse hard tell,
  And that it was a poysoned thing :
She cryed, and called piteouslie ;   20
Now help, or els the king shall die!
  Alas for woe, &c.

One Browne, that was an English man,
  And hard the ladies piteous crye,
Out with his sword, and bestir'd him than,   25
  Out of the doores in haste to flie;
But all the doores were made so fast,
Out of a window he got at last.
    Alas for woe, &c.

He met the bishop coming fast,   30
  Having the posset in his hande:
The sight of Browne made him aghast,
  Who bad him stoutly staie and stand.
With him were two that ranne awa,
For feare that Browne would make a fray.   35
    Alas for woe, &c.

Bishop, quoth Browne, what hast thou there?
  Nothing at all, my friend, sayde he;
But a posset to make the king good cheere.
  Is it so? sayd Browne, that will I see,   40
First I will have thyself begin,
Before thou go any further in;
    Be it weale or woe, it shall be so,
    This makes a sorrowful heigh ho.

The bishop sayde, Browne I doo know,   45
  Thou art a young man poore and bare;
Livings on thee I will bestowe:
  Let me go on, take thou no care.
No, no, quoth Browne, I will not be
A traitour for all Christiantie: 50
    Happe well or woe, it shall be so,
    Drink now with a sorrowfull, &c.

The bishop dranke, and by and by
  His belly burst and he fell downe:
A just rewarde for his traitery.   55
    This was a posset indeed, quoth Brown!

He serched the bishop, and found the keyes,
To come to the kinge when he did please.
    Alas for woe, &c.

As soon as the king got word of this,   60
    He humbly fell uppon his knee,
And praysed God that he did misse
    To tast of that extremity:
For that he did perceive and know,
His clergie would betray him so: 65
    Alas for woe, &c.

Alas, he said, unhappie realme,
    My father, and grandfather slaine:
My mother banished, O extreame!
    Unhappy fate, and bitter bayne!   70
And now like treason wrought for me,
What more unhappie realme can be!
    Alas for woe, &c.

The king did call his nurse to his grace,
    And gave her twenty poundes a yeere;   75
And trustie Browne too in like case,
    He knighted him with gallant geere;
And gave him 'lands and' livings great,
For dooing such a manly feat,
    As he did showe, to the bishop's woe,   80
    Which made, &c.

When all this treason done and past,
    Tooke not effect of traytery;
Another treason at the last,
    They sought against his majestie: 85

Ver. 67. His father was Henry Lord Darnley. His grandfather
the old Earl of Lenox, regent of Scotland, and father of Lord
Darnley, was murdered at Stirling, Sept. 5, 1571.

How they might make their kinge away,
By a privie banket[1] on a daye.
    Alas for woe, &c.

'Another time' to sell the king
  Beyonde the seas they had decreede :   90
Three noble Earles heard of this thing,
  And did prevent the same with speede.
For a letter came, with such a charme,
That they should doo their king no harme :
    For further woe, if they did soe,   95
    Would make a sorrowful heigh hoe.

The Earle Mourton told the Douglas then,
  Take heede you do not offend the king ;
But shew yourselves like honest men
  Obediently in every thing :   100
For his godmother* will not see
Her noble childe misus'd to be
    With any woe; for if it be so,
    She will make, &c.

God graunt all subjects may be true,   105
  In England, Scotland, every where :
That no such daunger may ensue,
  To put the prince or state in feare :
That God the highest king may see
Obedience as it ought to be,   110
    In wealth or woe, God graunt it be so
    To avoide the sorrowful heigh ho.

---

* Q. Elizabeth.

[1 banquet.]

XVII.

THE BONNY EARL OF MURRAY

A Scottish Song.

IN December, 1591, Francis Stewart, Earl of Bothwell, had made an attempt to seize on the person of his sovereign James VI., but being disappointed, had retired towards the north. The king unadvisedly gave a commission to George Gordon Earl of Huntley, to pursue Bothwell and his followers with fire and sword. Huntley, under cover of executing that commission, took occasion to revenge a private quarrel he had against James Stewart Earl of Murray, a relation of Bothwell's. In the night of Feb. 7, 1592, he beset Murray's house, burnt it to the ground, and slew Murray himself; a young nobleman of the most promising virtues, and the very darling of the people. See Robertson's *Hist.*

The present Lord Murray hath now in his possession a picture of his ancestor naked and covered with wounds, which had been carried about, according to the custom of that age, in order to inflame the populace to revenge his death. If this picture did not flatter, he well deserved the name of the *bonny Earl*, for he is there represented as a tall and comely personage. It is a tradition in the family, that Gordon of Bucky gave him a wound in the face: Murray half expiring, said, "You hae spilt a better face than your awin." Upon this, Bucky pointing his dagger at Huntley's breast, swore, "You shall be as deep as I;" and forced him to pierce the poor defenceless body.

K. James, who took no care to punish the murtherers, is said by some to have privately countenanced and abetted them, being stimulated by jealousy for some indiscreet praises which his Queen had too lavishly bestowed on this unfortunate youth. See the preface to the next ballad. See also Mr. Walpole's *Catalogue of Royal Auth.* vol. i. p. 42.

[James Stewart, son of Sir James Stewart of Doune, acquired the earldom of Murray by his marriage with Elizabeth, eldest daughter and heiress of the Regent Murray. The earl was only twenty-one years of age at the time of his murder, which was perpetrated at Dinnibrissel, the seat of his mother, where he was on a visit. Doune Castle in Menteith is now in ruins, but it is

still the property of the family, and gives the title of Viscount to
the eldest son of the Earl of Murray. The Earl of Huntley,
instead of being punished for his crime, was created a marquis,
and King James made the young earl of Murray marry the eldest
daughter of his father's murderer.

There is another version of this ballad given in Finlay's *Scottish
Ballads* (ii. 21), which commences—

> " Open the gates
> And let him come in ;
> He is my brother Huntly,
> He'll do me nae harm."

The author of this seems to have supposed that Murray married a
sister of Huntley.]

E highlands, and ye lawlands,
    Oh ! quhair hae ye been ?
    They hae slaine the Earl of Murray,
      And hae laid him on the green.

Now wae be to thee, Huntley !   5
    And quhairfore did you sae !
I bade you bring him wi' you,
    But forbade you him to slay.

He was a braw gallant,
    And he rid at the ring ;   10
And the bonny Earl of Murray,
    Oh ! he might hae been a king.

He was a braw gallant,
    And he playd at the ba' ;
And the bonny Earl of Murray   15
    Was the flower among them a'.

He was a braw gallant,
    And he playd at the gluve ;
And the bonny Earl of Murray,
    Oh ! he was the Queenes luve.   20

Oh ! lang will his lady
Luke owre the castle downe,*
Ere she see the Earl of Murray
Cum sounding throw the towne.

XVIII.

YOUNG WATERS.

A SCOTTISH BALLAD.

T has been suggested to the Editor, that this ballad covertly alludes to the indiscreet partiality, which Q. Anne of Denmark is said to have shewn for the *bonny Earl of Murray;* and which is supposed to have influenced the fate of that unhappy nobleman. Let the reader judge for himself.

The following account of the murder is given by a contemporary writer, and a person of credit, Sir James Balfour, knight, Lyon King of Arms, whose MS. of the Annals of Scotland is in the Advocates library at Edinburgh.

" The seventh of Febry, this yeire, 1592, the Earle of Murray was cruelly murthered by the Earle of Huntley at his house in Dunibrissel in Fyffe-shyre, and with him Dumbar, shriffe of Murray.   It [was] given out and publickly talked, that the Earle of Huntley was only the instrument of perpetrating this facte, to satisfie the King's jealousie of Murray, quhum the Queine more rashely than wyslie, some few dayes before had commendit in the King's heiringe, with too many epithets of a proper and gallant man.   The reasons of these surmises proceidit from pro-clamatione of the Kings, the 18 of Marche following ; inhibiting the younge Earle of Murray to persue the Earle of Huntley, for his father's slaughter, in respect he being wardit [imprisoned] in the castell of Blacknesse for the same murther, was willing to abide his tryall, averring that he had done nothing bot by the King's

---

* *Castle downe* here has been thought to mean the *Castle of Downe,* a seat belonging to the family of Murray.

majesties commissione; and was neither airt nor part of the murther."*

The following ballad is here given from a copy printed not long since at Glasgow, in one sheet 8vo. The world was indebted for its publication to the lady Jean Hume, sister to the Earl of Hume, who died at Gibraltar [in 1761].

[Buchan, who printed a longer version of this ballad in thirty-nine stanzas, believed young Waters to have been David Graham of Fintray, who was found guilty of being concerned in a Popish plot, and beheaded on the 16th of February, 1592. Chambers supposed that the fate of some one of the Scottish nobles executed by James I. after his return from captivity in England is alluded to. The various conflicting conjectures are none of them very probable, and there is nothing in the ballad that would conclusively connect it with authentic Scottish history. Percy's suggestion is peculiarly unfortunate, as young Waters was publicly executed at Stirling. Mr. Maidment points out (*Scottish Ballads and Songs*, vol. i. p. 62) that the first edition appeared under the following title, *Young Waters, an Ancient Scotish Poem, never before printed. Glasgow : printed and sold by Robert and Andrew Foulis, MDCCLV.* sm. 4to. pp. 8 ; and he suggests that Lord Hailes was the editor of it.]

BOUT Yule, quhen the wind blew cule,
    And the round tables began,
    A' ! there is cum to our kings court
    Mony a well-favourd man.

The queen luikt owre the castle wa,   5
    Beheld baith dale and down,
And then she saw young Waters
    Cum riding to the town.

His footmen they did rin before,
    His horsemen rade behind,   10
Ane mantel of the burning gowd
    Did keip him frae the wind.

Gowden graith'd[1] his horse before
 And siller shod behind,
The horse yong Waters rade upon **15**
 Was fleeter than the wind.

But then spake a wylie lord,
 Unto the queen said he,
O tell me quha's the fairest face
 Rides in the company. **20**

I've sene lord, and I've sene laird,
 And knights of high degree;
Bot a fairer face than young Watèrs
 Mine eyne did never see.

Out then spack the jealous king, **25**
 (And an angry man was he)
O, if he had been twice as fair,
 You micht have excepted me.

You're neither laird nor lord, she says,
 Bot the king that wears the crown; **30**
Ther is not a knight in fair Scotland
 Bot to thee maun bow down.

For a' that she could do or say,
 Appeasd he wad nae bee;
Bot for the words which she had said **35**
 Young Waters he maun dee.

They hae taen young Waters, and
 Put fetters to his feet;
They hae taen young Waters, and
 Thrown him in dungeon deep. **40**

[1 caparisoned with golden accoutrements.]

Aft I have ridden thro' Stirling town
　In the wind both and the weit ;
Bot I neir rade thro' Stirling town
　Wi fetters at my feet.

Aft have I ridden thro' Stirling town　　45
　In the wind both and the rain ;
Bot I neir rade thro' Stirling town
　Neir to return again.

They hae taen to the heiding-hill*
　His young son in his craddle,　　50
And they hae taen to the heiding-hill,
　His horse both and his saddle.

They hae taen to the heiding-hill
　His lady fair to see.
And for the words the Queen had spoke,　　55
　Young Waters he did dee.

XIX.

MARY AMBREE.

N the year 1584, the Spaniards, under the command of
Alexander Farnese, prince of Parma, began to gain
great advantages in Flanders and Brabant, by re-
covering many strong holds and cities from the Hol-
landers, as Ghent, (called then by the English *Gaunt,*) Antwerp,
Mechlin, &c. See Stow's *Annals*, p. 711. Some attempt made
with the assistance of English volunteers to retrieve the former of
those places probably gave occasion to this ballad. I can find no
mention of our heroine in history, but the following rhymes rendered her famous among our poets. Ben Jonson often mentions her,

---

* *Heiding-hill; i.e.* heading [beheading] hill. The place of execution was anciently an artificial hillock.

and calls any remarkable virago by her name. See his *Epicœne*, first acted in 1609, act iv. sc. 2. His *Tale of a Tub*, act i. sc. 2. And his masque intitled the *Fortunate Isles*, 1626, where he quotes the very words of the ballad,

> —— " *Mary Ambree*,
> (Who marched so free
> To the siege of Gaunt,
> And death could not daunt,
> As the ballad doth vaunt)
> Were a braver wight, &c."

She is also mentioned in Fletcher's *Scornful Lady*, act v. *sub finem*.

—— "My large gentlewoman, my *Mary Ambree*, had I but seen into you, you should have had another bed-fellow."——

It is likewise evident, that she is the virago intended by Butler in *Hudibras* (p. i. c. iii. v. 365), by her being coupled with *Joan a'Arc*, the celebrated *Pucelle d'Orleans*.

> " A bold virago stout and tall
> As *Joan* of France, or English *Mall*."

This ballad is printed from a black letter copy in the Pepys Collection, improved from the Editor's folio MS. and by conjecture. The full title is, *The valorous acts performed at Gaunt by the brave bonnie lass Mary Ambree, who in revenge of her lovers death did play her part most gallantly*. The tune is, *The blind beggar, &c.*"

[The copy from the MS., which is printed at the end, will be found to differ considerably from the following version.]

WHEN captain's couragious, whom death cold
      not daunte,
   Did march to the siege of the citty of Gaunt,
   They mustred their souldiers by two and
      by three,
And the formost in battle was Mary Ambree.

When brave Sir John Major* was slaine in her sight, 5
Who was her true lover, her joy, and delight,

---

* So MS. *Serjeant Major* in *PC*.

Because he was slaine most treacherouslie,
Then vowd to revenge him Mary Ambree.

She clothed herselfe from the top to the toe
In buffe of the bravest, most seemelye to showe; 10
A faire shirt of male* then slipped on shee ;
Was not this a brave bonny lass, Mary Ambree ?

A helmett of proofe shee strait did provide,
A strong arminge sword shee girt by her side,
On her hand a goodly faire gauntlett put shee ; 15
Was not this a brave bonny lass, Mary Ambree ?

Then tooke shee her sworde and her targett in hand,
Bidding all such, as wold, bee of her band ;
To wayte on her person came thousand and three :
Was not this a brave bonny lass, Mary Ambree ? 20

My soldiers, she saith, soe valiant and bold,
Nowe followe your captaine, whom you doe beholde ;
Still foremost in battel myselfe will I bee :
Was not this a brave bonny lasse, Mary Ambree ?

Then cryed out her souldiers, and loude they did say, 25
Soe well thou becomest this gallant array,
Thy harte and thy weapons soe well do agree,
There was none ever like Mary Ambree.

Shee cheared her souldiers, that foughten for life,
With ancyent and standard, with drum and with fyfe, 30
With brave clanging trumpetts, that sounded so free ;
Was not this a brave bonny lasse, Mary Ambree ?

Before I will see the worst of you all
To come into danger of death, or of thrall,
This hand and this life I will venture so free : 35
Was not this a brave bonny lasse, Mary Ambree ?

---

* A peculiar kind of armour, composed of small rings of iron,
and worn under the cloaths. It is mentioned by Spencer, who
speaks of the Irish Gallowglass or Foot-soldier as " armed in a
long Shirt of Mayl." (*View of the State of Ireland.*)

Shee led upp her souldiers in battaile array,
Gainst three times theyr number by breake of the daye;
Seven howers in skirmish continued shee :
Was not this a brave bonny lasse, Mary Ambree ? 40

She filled the skyes with the smoke of her shott,
And her enemyes bodyes with bullets soe hott;
For one of her owne men a score killed shee :
Was not this a brave bonny lasse, Mary Ambree ?

And when her false gunner, to spoyle her intent, 45
Away all her pellets and powder had sent,
Straight with her keen weapon shee slasht him in three :
Was not this a brave bonny lasse, Mary Ambree ?

Being falselye betrayed for lucre of hyre,
At length she was forced to make a retyre ; 50
Then her souldiers into a strong castle drew shee :
Was not this a brave bonny lasse, Mary Ambree ?

Her foes they besett her on everye side,
As thinking close siege shee cold never abide ;
To beate down the walles they all did decree : 55
But stoutlye deffyd them brave Mary Ambree.

Then tooke shee her sword and her targett in hand,
And mounting the walls all undaunted did stand,
There daring their captaines to match any three :
O what a brave captaine was Mary Ambree ! 60

Now saye, English captaine, what woldest thou give
To ransome thy selfe, which else must not live ?
Come yield thy selfe quicklye, or slaine thou must bee.
Then smiled sweetlye brave Mary Ambree.

Ye captaines couragious, of valour so bold, 65
Whom thinke you before you now you doe behold ?
A knight, sir, of England, and captaine soe free,
Who shortelye with us a prisoner must bee.

No captaine of England; behold in your sight
Two brests in my bosome, and therfore no knight: 70
Noe knight, sirs, of England, nor captaine you see,
But a poor simple lass, called Mary Ambree.

But art thou a woman, as thou dost declare,
Whose valor hath provd so undaunted in warre?
If England doth yield such brave lasses as thee,   75
Full well may they conquer, faire Mary Ambree.

The prince of Great Parma heard of her renowne,
Who long had advanced for Englands faire crowne;
Hee wooed her and sued her his mistress to bee,
And offerd rich presents to Mary Ambree.   80

But this virtuous mayden despised them all,
Ile nere sell my honour for purple nor pall:
A mayden of England, sir, never will bee
The whore of a monarcke, quoth Mary Ambree.

Then to her owne country shee backe did returne, 85
Still holding the foes of faire England in scorne:
Therfore English captaines of every degree
Sing forth the brave valours of Mary Ambree.

[THE following version is reprinted from Hales and Furnivall's edition of the folio MS. vol. i. p. 516.

> Captaine couragious, whome death cold daunte,
> beseeged the Citye brauelye, the citty of Gaunt!
> they mustered their soliders by 2 & by 3:
> & the fformost in Battele was Mary Aumbree!   4
>
> When braue Sir Iohn Maior was slaine in that fight,
> that was her true louer, her Ioy & delight,
> shee swore his death vnreuenged shold not bee;
> was not this a braue, bonye lasse, Mary Aumbree?   8

The death of her trueloue shee meant to requite
with fire & ffamine [&] sword shining bright,
which lately was slaine most villanouslye;
was not this a braue, bonnye Lasse, Mary Aumbree?   12

Shee cladd her selfe from the top to the toe
in buffe of the brauest most seemlye to show,
& a faire shirt of Male slipped on shee;
was not this a braue, bonye lasse, Mary Aumbree?   16

A helmett of proofe shee tooke on her head,
& a strong arminge sword shee wore by her side;
a goodly fayre gauntlett on her hand put shee;
was not this a braue, bonye lasse, Mary Aumbree?   20

Shee tooke her sword & her targett in hand,
bidding all such as wold, wayte on her band.
to waite on her person there came 1000^{ds} 3:
was not this a braue, bonye lasse, Mary Aumbree?   24

" My soldiers," shee saith, " soe valiant and bold,
now ffollow your Captain which you doe beholde;
in the fight formost my selfe will I bee !"
was not this a brave, bonye lasse, Mary Aumbree?   28

Then cryed out her souldiers, & loude thé did say,
" soe well thou becomes this gallant array,
thy hands & thy weapons doe well soe agree,
there was neuer none like to Mary Aumbree !"   32

Shee cheared her good souldiers that foughten for life,
with the cominge of Ancyents, with drum & with fife,
that braue sonding trumpetts with ingines soe free,
att last thé made mention of Mary Aumbree.   36

" Before that I doe see the worst of you all
come in the danger of your enemyes thrall,
this hand & this sword shall first sett him free;"
was not this a braue bonye lasse, Mary Aumbree?   40

Shee forward went on in Battaile array,
& straight shee did make her foes flye away;
7 houres in sckirmish continued shee;
was not this a braue bonye lasse, Mary Aumbree?   44

The skyes shee did fill with the smoke of her shott,
in her enemies bodyes with bulletts soe hott;
for one of her owne men, a sckore killed shee;
was not this a braue bonye lasse, Mary Aumbree?   48

Then did her gunner spoyle her intent,
pelletts & powder away had he sent:
then with her sword shee cutt him in 3,
was not this a braue bonye lasse, Mary Aumbree?   52

Then was shee caused to make a retyre,
being falsely betrayd, as itt doth appeare;
then to saue her selfe into a castle went shee;
was not this a braue bonye lasse, Mary Aumbree?   56

Her foes thé besett her on euerye side,
thinking in that castle shee wold not abyde;
to beate downe those walls they all did agree;
was not that a braue bonye lasse, Mary Aumbree?   60

She tooke her sword & her targett in hand,
shee came to the walls, and vpon them did stand,
their daring their Captaine to match any 3,
was not that a braue bonye lasse, Mary Aumbree?   64

" Thou English Captain, what woldest thou giue
to ransome thy liffe which else must not liue?
come downe quickly, & yeeld thee to mee!"
then smiled sweetlye Mary Aumbree;   68

" Good gentle Captain, what thinke you by mee,
or whom in my likenesse you take mee to bee?"
" a knight, sir, of England, & Captain soe free,
that I meane to take away prisoner with me."   72

" Good gentle Captain, behold in your sight
2 brests in my bosome, & therfore no knight;
noe knight, Sir, of England, nor Captain soe free,
but eue[n]e a pore bony Lasse, Mary Aumbree."   76

" If thou beest a woman as thou dost declare,
that hast mangled our soliders, & made them soe bare;
the like in my liffe I neuer did see;
therfore Ile honor thee, Mary Aumbree."   80

" Giue I be a woman, as well thou doest see,
Captain, thou gettst noe redemption of mee
without thou wilt fight with blowes 2 or 3."
was not this a braue bonye lasse, Mary Aumbree?   84

God send in warrs, such euent I abide,
god send such a solider to stand by my side!
then safely preserued my person wilbe;
there was neuer none like to Mary Aumbree!]   88

XX.

BRAVE LORD WILLOUGHBEY.

PEREGRINE BERTIE, lord Willoughby of Eresby, had, in the year 1586, distinguished himself at the siege of Zutphen, in the Low Countries. He was the year after made general of the English forces in the United Provinces, in room of the earl of Leicester, who was recalled. This gave him an opportunity of signalizing his courage and military skill in several actions against the Spaniards. One of these, greatly exaggerated by popular report, is probably the subject of this old ballad, which, on account of its flattering encomiums on English valour, hath always been a favourite with the people.

" My lord Willoughbie (says a contemporary writer) was one of the queenes best swordsmen : . . . he was a great master of the art military . . . I have heard it spoken, that had he not slighted the court, but applied himself to the queene, he might have enjoyed a plentifull portion of her grace; and it was his saying, and it did him no good, that he was none of the *Reptilia;* intimating, that he could not creepe on the ground, and that the court was not his element; for indeed, as he was a great souldier, so he was of suitable magnanimitie, and could not brooke the obsequiousnesse and assiduitie of the courte." (*Naunton.*)

Lord Willoughbie died in 1601.—Both Norris and Turner were famous among the military men of that age.

The subject of this ballad (which is printed from an old black-letter copy, with some conjectural emendations,) may possibly receive illustration from what *Chapman* says in the Dedicat. to his version of Homer's *Frogs and Mice*, concerning the brave and memorable Retreat of Sir John Norris, with only 1000 men, thro' the whole Spanish army, under the duke of Parma, for three miles together.

[Lord Willoughby was the son of Katherine, daughter of Lord Willoughby of Eresby and widow of Charles Brandon, Duke of Suffolk, and of her second husband, Richard Bertie. They were protestants and were forced to fly from persecution in 1553, taking refuge first in the Low Countries and afterwards in Poland. They called their son in consequence Peregrine, a name that has ever since remained in the family. Mr. Hales has drawn my attention to the fact that Spenser, when in Ireland, named one of his sons Peregrine for a similar reason. A ballad was written entitled *The Duchess of Suffolk's Calamity*, which contains these lines :

" A sonne she had in Germanie,
  Peregrine Bartue cald by name,
Surnamde The Good Lord Willobie,
  Of courage great and worthie fame."

Mr. Chappell informs us that the tune of the following ballad
occurs in Lady Neville's Virginal Book (MS. 1591), and in Robin-
son's *School of Music* (1603), where it is called " Lord Willobie's
Welcome Home."]

THE fifteenth day of July,
  With glistering spear and shield,
A famous fight in Flanders
  Was foughten in the field :
The most couragious officers   5
  Were English captains three ;
But the bravest man in battel
  Was brave lord Willoughbèy.

The next was captain Norris,
  A valiant man was hee :   10
The other captain Turner,
  From field would never flee.
With fifteen hundred fighting men,
  Alas ! there were no more,
They fought with fourteen thousand then, 15
  Upon the bloody shore.

Stand to it noble pikemen,
  And look you round about :
And shoot you right you bow-men,
  And we will keep them out :   20
You musquet and calliver¹ men,
  Do you prove true to me,
I'le be the formost man in fight,
  Says brave lord Willoughbèy.

[¹ a large pistol or blunderbuss.]

And then the bloody enemy 25
   They fiercely did assail,
And fought it out most furiously,
   Not doubting to prevail ;
The wounded men on both sides fell
   Most pitious for to see, 30
Yet nothing could the courage quell
   Of brave lord Willoughbèy.

For seven hours to all mens view
   This fight endured sore,
Until our men so feeble grew 35
   That they could fight no more ;
And then upon dead horses
   Full savourly they eat,
And drank the puddle water,
   They could no better get. 40

When they had fed so freely,
   They kneeled on the ground,
And praised God devoutly
   For the favour they had found ;
And beating up their colours, 45
   The fight they did renew,
And turning tow'rds the Spaniard,
   A thousand more they slew.

The sharp steel-pointed arrows,
   And bullets thick did fly ; 50
Then did our valiant soldiers
   Charge on most furiously ;
Which made the Spaniards waver,
   They thought it best to flee,
They fear'd the stout behaviour 55
   Of brave lord Willoughbèy.

Then quoth the Spanish general,
   Come let us march away,
I fear we shall be spoiled all
   If here we longer stay ; 60

For yonder comes lord Willoughbey
  With courage fierce and fell,
He will not give one inch of way
  For all the devils in hell.

And then the fearful enemy   65
  Was quickly put to flight,
Our men persued couragiously,
  And caught their forces quite;
But at last they gave a shout,
  Which ecchoed through the sky,   70
God, and St. George for England!
  The conquerers did cry.

This news was brought to England
  With all the speed might be,
And soon our gracious queen was told 75
  Of this same victory.
O this is brave lord Willoughbey,
  My love that ever won,
Of all the lords of honour
  'Tis he great deeds hath done.   80

To the souldiers that were maimed,
  And wounded in the fray,
The queen allowed a pension
  Of fifteen pence a day;
And from all costs and charges   85
  She quit and set them free:
And this she did all for the sake
  Of brave lord Willoughbèy.

Then courage, noble Englishmen,
  And never be dismaid;   90
If that we be but one to ten,
  We will not be afraid
To fight with foraign enemies,
  And set our nation free.
And thus I end the bloody bout   95
  Of brave lord Willoughbèy.

XXI.

VICTORIOUS MEN OF EARTH.

THIS little moral sonnet hath such a pointed application to the heroes of the foregoing and following ballads, that I cannot help placing it here, tho' the date of its composition is of a much later period. It is extracted from *Cupid and Death, a masque by J. S. (James Shirley) presented Mar. 26, 1653. London printed 1653, 4to.*

[Dr. Rimbault informs us that this masque was represented at the Military Ground in Leicester Fields, with music by Matthew Locke and Dr. Christopher Gibbons. (*Musical Illustrations*, p. 22.)]

VICTORIOUS men of earth, no more
    Proclaim how wide your empires are ;
    Though you binde in every shore,
    And your triumphs reach as far
        As night or day ;   5
Yet you proud monarchs must obey,
And mingle with forgotten ashes, when
Death calls yee to the croud of common men.

Devouring famine, plague, and war,
    Each able to undo mankind,   10
Death's servile emissaries are :
    Nor to these alone confin'd,
        He hath at will
    More quaint and subtle wayes to kill ;
A smile or kiss, as he will use the art,   15
Shall have the cunning skill to break a heart.

XXII.

THE WINNING OF CALES.

HE subject of this ballad is the taking of the city of *Cadiz*, (called by our sailors corruptly *Cales*) on June 21, 1596, in a descent made on the coast of Spain, under the command of the Lord Howard admiral, and the earl of Essex general.

The valour of Essex was not more distinguished on this occasion than his generosity: the town was carried sword in hand, but he stopt the slaughter as soon as possible, and treated his prisoners with the greatest humanity, and even affability and kindness. The English made a rich plunder in the city, but missed of a much richer, by the resolution which the Duke of Medina, the Spanish admiral, took, of setting fire to the ships, in order to prevent their falling into the hands of the enemy [see v. 27]. It was computed, that the loss which the Spaniards sustained from this enterprize, amounted to twenty millions of ducats. See Hume's *Hist.*

The Earl of Essex knighted on this occasion not fewer than sixty persons, which gave rise to the following sarcasm:

> " A gentleman of Wales, a knight of Cales,
>   And a laird of the North country;
> But a yeoman of Kent with his yearly rent
>   Will buy them out all three."

The ballad is printed, with some corrections, from the Editor's folio MS. and seems to have been composed by some person, who was concerned in the expedition. Most of the circumstances related in it will be found supported by history.

[Philip II. was meditating the dispatch of a second armada, but before he could set his schemes in motion his strongest fortress was razed to the ground. Macaulay calls this " the most brilliant military exploit that was achieved on the continent by English arms during the long interval which elapsed between the battle of Agincourt and that of Blenheim." No wonder then that the English sang with enthusiasm of the glories of their success. Raleigh and Sir Francis Vere were among the leaders under Essex.

It will be seen by the foot notes that Percy follows his MS. original pretty faithfully. Child prints a version from Deloney's *Garland of Goodwill* as reprinted by the Percy Society (vol. xxx. p. 113). The earliest notice of the tune (the new Tantara) to which this ballad was to be sung is in the year 1590.]

ONG the proud Spaniards had vaunted to
    conquer us,
      Threatning our country with fyer and
      sword ;
Often preparing their navy most sumptuous
  With as great plenty as Spain could afford.
    Dub a dub, dub a dub, thus strike their drums ;
    Tantara, tantara, the Englishman comes.   6

To the seas presentlye went our lord admiral,
  With knights couragious and captains full good ;
The brave Earl of Essex, a prosperous general,
  With him prepared to pass the salt flood.   10
    Dub a dub, &c.

At Plymouth speedilye, took they ship valiantlye,
  Braver ships never were seen under sayle,
With their fair colours spread, and streamers ore their
    head,
  Now bragging Spaniards, take heed of your tayle.
    Dub a dub, &c.   16

Unto Cales cunninglye, came we most speedilye,
  Where the kinges navy securelye did ryde ;
Being upon their backs, piercing their butts of sacks,
  Ere any Spaniards our coming descryde.   20
    Dub a dub, &c.

Great was the crying, the running and ryding,
  Which at that season was made in that place ;
The beacons were fyred, as need then required ;
  To hyde their great treasure they had little space.
    Dub a dub, &c.   26

[Ver. 6. tantara, ra-ra, MS. V. 22. *the* before *running* not
in MS.]

There you might see their ships, how they were fyred
    fast,
  And how their men drowned themselves in the sea;
There might you hear them cry, wayle and weep
    piteously,
  When they saw no shift to scape thence away.   30
  Dub a dub, &c.

The great St. Phillip, the pryde of the Spaniards,
  Was burnt to the bottom, and sunk in the sea;
But the St. Andrew, and eke the St. Matthew,
  Wee took in fight manfullye and brought away. 35
  Dub a dub, &c.

The Earl of Essex most valiant and hardye,
  With horsemen and footmen march'd up to the
    town;
The Spanyards, which saw them, were greatly
    alarmed,
  Did fly for their savegard, and durst not come down.
  Dub a dub, &c.
                         41

Now, quoth the noble Earl, courage my soldiers all,
  Fight and be valiant, the spoil you shall have;
And bè well rewarded all from the great to the small;
  But looke that the women and children you save.
  Dub a dub, &c.
                         46

The Spaniards at that sight, thinking it vain to fight,
  Hung upp flags of truce and yielded the towne;
Wee marched in presentlye, decking the walls on hye,
  With English colours which purchas'd renowne. 50
  Dub a dub, &c.

[Ver. 35. brought *them* away, MS.   V. 38. marched toward the
town.   V. 44. *all* not in MS.   V. 45. no *the* in MS.   V. 47.
thought in vaine twas to fight.   V. 48. *and* not in MS.   V. 50. with
our English.]

Entering the houses then, of the most richest men,
 For gold and treasure we searched eche day ;
In sòme places wè did find, pyes baking left behind,
 Meate at fire rosting, and folkes run away. 55
  Dub a dub, &c.

Full of rich merchandize, every shop catch'd our eyes,
 Damasks and sattens and velvets full fayre :
Which soldiers mèasur'd out by the length of their
  swords ;
 Of all commodities eche had a share. 60
  Dub a dub, &c.

Thus Cales was taken, and our brave general
 March'd to the market-place, where he did stand :
There many prisoners fell to our several shares,
 Many crav'd mercye, and mercye they fannd. 65
  Dub a dub, &c.

When our brave general saw they delayed all,
 And would not ransome their towne as they said,
With their fair wanscots, their presses and bedsteds,
 Their joint-stools and tables a fire we made ; 70
 And when the town burned all in a flame,
 With tara, tantara, away wee all came.

[Ver. 54. baking in the oven. V. 55. meate att the fire rosting
& ffolkes ffled away. V. 57. shop wee did see. V. 60. each one.
V. 64. prisoners of good account were tooke. V. 65. they found.
V. 67. delayed time. V. 70. a ffire were made. V. 72. away wee
came.]

XXIII.

THE SPANISH LADY'S LOVE.

HIS beautiful old ballad most probably took its rise from one of these descents made on the Spanish coasts in the time of queen Elizabeth; and in all likelihood from that which is celebrated in the foregoing ballad.

It was a tradition in the West of England, that the person admired by the Spanish lady was a gentleman of the Popham family [Sir John Popham], and that her picture, with the pearl necklace mentioned in the ballad, was not many years ago preserved at Littlecot, near Hungerford, Wilts, the seat of that respectable family.

Another tradition hath pointed out Sir Richard Levison, of Trentham, in Staffordshire, as the subject of this ballad; who married Margaret daughter of Charles Earl of Nottingham; and was eminently distinguished as a naval officer and commander in all the expeditions against the Spaniards in the latter end of Q. Elizabeth's reign, particularly in that to Cadiz in 1596, when he was aged 27. He died in 1605, and has a monument, with his effigy in brass, in Wolverhampton church.

It is printed from an ancient black-letter copy, corrected in part by the Editor's folio MS.

[Sir John Popham and Sir Richard Levison are not the only candidates for the honour of being associated with the Spanish Lady, for strong claims have also been brought forward in favour of Sir Urias Legh of Adlington, Cheshire, and of Sir John Bolle of Thorpe Hall, Lincolnshire. A descendant of the latter worthy wrote a letter in his favour, which appeared in the *Times* of May 1, 1846, and from which the following particulars are extracted:—
" In Illingworth's *Topographical Account of Scampton, with Anecdotes of the family of Bolles*, it is stated, 'the portrait of Sir John, drawn in 1596, at the age of thirty-six years, having on him the gold chain given him by the Spanish Lady, &c., is still in the possession of Captain Birch.' That portrait is now in the possession of Captain Birch's successor, Thomas Bosvile Bosvile, Esq., of Ravensfield Park, Yorkshire." The writer of the letter signs himself Charles Lee, and dates from Coldrey, Hants. He adds another extract from Illingworth's *Scampton*, which is as follows: " On Sir John Bolle's departure from Cadiz, the Spanish Lady sent as presents to his wife, a profusion of jewels, and other

valuables, amongst which was her portrait, drawn in green, plate, money, and other treasure. Some articles are still in the possession of the family, though her picture was unfortunately and by accident, disposed of about half a century since. This portrait being drawn in green, gave occasion to her being called in the neighbourhood of Thorpe Hall, the Green Lady, where to this day there is a traditionary superstition among the vulgar that Thorpe Hall was haunted by the Green Lady, who used nightly to take her seat in a particular tree near the mansion."

Mr. Chappell points out that this ballad is quoted in *Cupid's Whirligig*, 1616, and parodied in Rowley's *A Match at Midnight*, 1633. It is also quoted in Mrs. Behn's Comedy, *The Rovers, or the banished Cavaliers*, and in Richard Brome's *Northern Lasse.*

Shenstone was not satisfied with the beautiful simplicity of this charming ballad, and attempted in his *Moral Tale of Love and Honour* to place it before his readers " in less grovelling accents than the simple guise of ancient record." The mode he adopted was to spin it out by the frequent introduction of *Ah me* and *'tis true*, and addresses to the "generous maid," Elvira, Iberia, &c. Wordsworth acted far differently, when he founded his exquisite *Armenian Lady's Love* upon this ballad :

> " You have heard of a Spanish Lady,
> How she wooed an English man ;
> Hear now of a fair Armenian,
> Daughter of the proud Soldàn."

The copy in the folio MS. (ed. Hales and Furnivall, vol. iii. p. 393) begins with verse 33, the early part having been torn out.]

ILL you hear a Spanish lady,
How she wooed an English man ?
Garments gay as rich as may be
Decked with jewels she had on.
Of a comely countenance and grace was she,   5
And by birth and parentage of high degree.

As his prisoner there he kept her,
In his hands her life did lye ;
Cupid's bands did tye them faster
By the liking of an eye.   10

In his courteous company was all her joy,
To favour him in any thing she was not coy.

But at last there came commandment
   For to set the ladies free,
With their jewels still adorned,   15
   None to do them injury.
Then said this lady mild, Full woe is me;
O let me still sustain this kind captivity!

Gallant captain, shew some pity
   To a ladye in distresse;   20
Leave me not within this city,
   For to dye in heavinesse:
Thou hast set this present day my body free,
But my heart in prison still remains with thee.

" How should'st thou, fair lady, love me,   25
   Whom thou knowst thy country's foe?
Thy fair wordes make me suspect thee:
   Serpents lie where flowers grow."
All the harm I wishe to thee, most courteous knight,
God grant the same upon my head may fully light. 30

Blessed be the time and season,
   That you came on Spanish ground;
If our foes you may be termed,
   Gentle foes we have you found:
With our city, you have won our hearts eche one, 35
Then to your country bear away, that is your owne.

" Rest you still, most gallant lady;
   Rest you still, and weep no more;
Of fair lovers there is plenty,
   Spain doth yield a wonderous store."   40
Spaniards fraught with jealousy we often find,
But Englishmen through all the world are counted
    kind.

Leave me not unto a Spaniard,
  You alone enjoy my heart;
I am lovely, young, and tender,   45
  Love is likewise my desert :
Still to serve thee day and night my mind is prest ;
The wife of every Englishman is counted blest.

" It wold be a shame, fair lady,
  For to bear a woman hence;   50
English soldiers never carry
  Any such without offence."
I'll quickly change myself, if it be so,
And like a page Ile follow thee, where'er thou go.

" I have neither gold nor silver   55
  To maintain thee in this case,
And to travel is great charges,
  As you know in every place."
My chains and jewels every one shal be thy own,
And eke five hundred* pounds in gold that lies un-
      known.   60

" On the seas are many dangers,
  Many storms do there arise,
Which wil be to ladies dreadful,
  And force tears from watery eyes."
Well in troth I shall endure extremity,   65
For I could find in heart to lose my life for thee.

" Courteous ladye, leave this fancy,
  Here comes all that breeds the strife;
I in England have already
  A sweet woman to my wife :   70
I will not falsify my vow for gold nor gain,
Nor yet for all the fairest dames that live in Spain."

---

* So the MS., 10,000*l.* *PC.*

[Ver. 54. whersoere thou go.] V. 65. Well in worth [I will],
MS. [V. 66. find my heart.   V. 68. that breakes.]

O how happy is that woman
    That enjoys so true a friend!
Many happy days God send her;   75
    Of my suit I make an end:
On my knees I pardon crave for my offence,
Which did from love and true affection first commence.

Commend me to thy lovely lady,
    Bear to her this chain of gold;   80
And these bracelets for a token;
    Grieving that I was so bold:
All my jewels in like sort take thou with thee,
For they are fitting for thy wife, but not for me.

I will spend my days in prayer,   85
    Love and all her laws* defye;
In a nunnery will I shroud mee
    Far from any companye:
But ere my prayers have an end, be sure of this,
To pray for thee and for thy love I will not miss. 90

Thus farewell, most gallant captain!
    Farewell too my heart's content!
Count not Spanish ladies wanton,
    Though to thee my love was bent:
Joy and true prosperity goe still with thee!   95
" The like fall ever to thy share, most fair ladìe."

---

* So the folio MS.   Other editions read *his laws*.

[Ver. 75. many dayes of joy god send you.   V. 76. Ile make.
V. 77. upon my knees I pardon crave for this offence.   V. 78.
which love and true affectyon did ffirst commence.   V. 80. a
chaine.   V. 83. take with thee.   V. 84. these are . . . and not for
me.   V. 88. from other.   V. 92. and ffarwell my.   V. 95. be still.]

XXIV.

ARGENTILE AND CURAN,

S extracted from an ancient historical poem in XIII. Books, intitled, *Albion's England*, by *William Warner:* "An author (says a former editor,) only unhappy in the choice of his subject, and measure of his verse. His poem is an epitome of the British history, and written with great learning, sense, and spirit. In some places fine to an extraordinary degree, as I think will eminently appear in the ensuing episode (of Argentile and Curan). A tale full of beautiful incidents in the romantic taste, extremely affecting, rich in ornament, wonderfully various in style; and in short, one of the most beautiful pastorals I ever met with." (*Muses Library*, 1738, 8vo.) To his merit nothing can be objected unless perhaps an affected quaintness in some of his expressions, and an indelicacy in some of his pastoral images.

Warner is said, by A. Wood,[*] to have been a Warwickshire man, and to have been educated in Oxford, at Magdalene-hall: as also in the latter part of his life to have been retained in the service of Henry Cary Lord Hunsdon, to whom he dedicates his poem. However that may have been, new light is thrown upon his history, and the time and manner of his death are now ascertained, by the following extract from the parish register book of Amwell, in Hertfordshire; which was obligingly communicated to the Editor by Mr. *Hoole*, the very ingenious translator of Tasso, &c.

(1608—1609.) "Master William Warner, a man of good yeares and of honest reputation; by his profession an Atturnye of the Common Pleas; author of *Albions England*, diynge suddenly in the night in his bedde, without any former complaynt or sicknesse, on thursday night beeinge the 9th daye of March; was buried the saturday following, and lyeth in the church at the corner under the stone of Walter Ffader." Signed *Tho. Hassall Vicarius.*

Though now Warner is so seldom mentioned, his contemporaries ranked him on a level with Spenser, and called them the Homer and Virgil of their age.[†] But Warner rather resembled *Ovid*, whose *Metamorphoses* he seems to have taken for his model, having deduced a perpetual poem from the deluge down to the æra of

---

[*] Athen. Oxon.　　　　　　　　[†] *Ibid.*

Elizabeth, full of lively digressions and entertaining episodes. And though he is sometimes harsh, affected, and obscure, he often displays a most charming and pathetic simplicity : as where he describes Eleanor's harsh treatment of Rosamond :

> " With that she dasht her on the lippes
> So dyed double red :
> Hard was the heart that gave the blow,
> Soft were those lippes that bled."

The edition of *Albion's England* here followed was printed in 4to. 1602; said in the title-page to have been "first penned and published by William Warner, and now revised and newly enlarged by the same author." The story of *Argentile and Curan* is I believe the poet's own invention; it is not mentioned in any of our chronicles. It was however so much admired, that not many years after he published it, came out a larger poem on the same subject in stanzas of six lines, intitled, *The most pleasant and delightful historie of Curan a prince of Danske, and the fayre princesse Argentile, daughter and heyre to Adelbright, sometime king of Northumberland, &c. by* William Webster, *London,* 1617, in 8 sheets 4to. An indifferent paraphrase of the following poem.—This episode of Warner's has also been altered into the common ballad, *of the two young Princes on Salisbury Plain,* which is chiefly composed of Warner's lines, with a few contractions and interpolations, but all greatly for the worse. See the collection of *Hist. Ballads,* 1727, 3 vols. 12mo.

[Percy had already in the first volume quoted from Warner's poem the story of the *Patient Countess.*]

HE Bruton's 'being' departed hence seaven
   kingdoms here begonne,
  Where diversly in divers broyles the
   Saxons lost and wonne.
King Edel and king Adelbright in Diria jointly raigne;
In loyal concorde during life these kingly friends
  remaine.
When Adelbright should leave his life, to Edel thus
  he sayes ;   5
By those same bondes of happie love, that held us
  friends alwaies ;

By our by-parted crowne, of which the moyetie is
    mine ;
By God, to whom my soule must passe, and so in time
    may thine ;
I pray thee, nay I cònjure thee, to nourish, as thine
    owne,
Thy niece, my daughter Argentile, till she to age be
    growne ;   10
And then, as thou receivest it, resigne to her my
    throne.
A promise had for his bequest, the testatòr he dies ;
But all that Edel undertooke, he afterwards denies.
Yet well he ' fosters for ' a time the damsell that was
    growne
The fairest lady under heaven ; whose beautie being
    knowne,   15
A many princes seeke her love ; but none might her
    obtaine ;
For grippell[1] Edel to himselfe her kingdome sought
    to gaine ;
And for that cause from sight of such he did his ward
    restraine.
By chance one Curan, sonne unto a prince in Danske,[2]
    did see
The maid, with whom he fell in love, as much as man
    might bee.   20
Unhappie youth, what should he doe ? his saint was
    kept in mewe ;[3]
Nor he, nor any noble-man admitted to her vewe.
One while in melancholy fits he pines himselfe awaye ;
Anon he thought by force of arms to win her if he
    maye :
And still against the kings restraint did secretly
    invay.   25

[[1] griping or miserly.   [2] Denmark.   [3] in confinement.]

At length the high controller Love, whom none may
 disobay,
Imbased him from lordlines into a kitchen drudge,
That so at least of life or death she might become
 his judge.
Accesse so had to see and speake, he did his love
 bewray,
And tells his birth : her answer was, she husbandles
 would stay.   30
Meane while the king did beate his braines, his booty
 to atchieve,
Nor caring what became of her, so he by her might
 thrive ;
At last his resolution was some pessant should her
 wive.
And (which was working to his wish) he did observe
 with joye
How Curan, whom he thought a drudge, scapt many
 an amorous toye.*   35
The king, perceiving such his veine, promotes his
 vassal still,
Lest that the basenesse of the man should lett,[1] per-
 haps, his will.
Assured therefore of his love, but not suspecting who
The lover was, the king himselfe in his behalf did
 woe.
The lady resolute from love, unkindly takes that he 40
Should barre the noble, and unto so base a match
 agree :
And therefore shifting out of doores, departed thence
 by stealth ;
Preferring povertie before a dangerous life in wealth.

---

 * The construction is, " How that many an amorous toy, or
foolery of love, 'scaped Curan ;" *i.e.* escaped from him, being off
his guard.

     [1 hinder.]

When Curan heard of her escape, the anguish in his
    hart
Was more than much, and after her from court he
    did depart ;   45
Forgetfull of himselfe, his birth, his country, friends,
    and all,
And only minding (whom he mist) the foundresse of
    his thrall.
Nor meanes he after to frequent or court, or stately
    townes,
But solitarily to live amongst the country grownes.[1]
A brace of years he lived thus, well pleased so to
    live,   50
And shepherd-like to feed a flocke himselfe did wholly
    give.
So wasting, love, by worke, and want, grew almost to
    the waine :
But then began a second love, the worser of the twaine.
A country wench, a neatherds maid, where Curan kept
    his sheepe,
Did feed her drove : and now on her was all the
    shepherds keepe.   55
He borrowed on the working daies his holy russets oft,
And of the bacon's fat, to make his startops[2] blacke
    and soft.
And least his tarbox[3] should offend, he left it at the
    folde :
Sweete growte,[4] or whig,[5] his bottle had, as much as
    it might holde.
A sheeve[6] of bread as browne as nut, and cheese as
    white as snow,   60

Ver. 56. *i.e.* holy-day russets [or best clothes.]

[1 grounds.   2 buskins or half boots.
3 used for anointing sores in sheep, &c.   4 small beer.
5 whey or buttermilk.   6 slice.]

And wildings,[1] or the seasons fruit he did in scrip
    bestow,
And whilst his py-bald curre did sleepe, and sheep-
    hooke lay him by,
On hollow quilles of oten straw he piped melody
But when he spyed her his saint, he wip'd his greasie
    shooes,
And clear'd the drivell from his beard, and thus the
    shepheard wooes.   65
" I have, sweet wench, a peece of cheese, as good as
    tooth may chawe,
And bread and wildings souling[2] well, (and there-
    withall did drawe
His lardrie) and in ' yeaning' see yon crumpling[3] ewe,
    quoth he,
Did twinne this fall, and twin shouldst thou, if I might
    tup[4] with thee.
Thou art too elvish, faith thou art, too elvish and too
    coy :   70
Am I, I pray thee, beggarly, that such a flock enjoye ?
I wis I am not : yet that thou doest hold me in dis-
    daine
Is brimme[5] abroad, and made a gybe to all that keepe
    this plaine.
There be as quaint[6] (at least that thinke themselves
    as quaint) that crave
The match, that thou, I wot not why, maist, but mis-
    lik'st to have.   75
How wouldst thou match ? (for well I wot, thou art a
    female) I,
Her know not here that willingly with maiden-head
    would die.

Ver. 68. Eating. *PCC.* V. 77. Her know I not her that.
1602.

[1 crab apples.   2 victualling.   3 crooked horned.
4 ram.   5 public.   6 nice or prudent.]

The plowmans labour hath no end, and he a churle
    will prove :
The craftsman hath more worke in hand then fitteth
    unto love :
The merchant, traffiquing abroad, suspects his wife at
    home :   80
A youth will play the wanton ; and an old man prove
    a mome.[1]
Then chuse a shepheard : with the sun he doth his
    flocke unfold,
And all the day on hill or plaine he merrie chat can
    hold ;
And with the sun doth folde againe ; then jogging
    home betime,
He turnes a crab, or turnes a round, or sings some
    merry ryme.   85
Nor lacks he gleeful tales, whilst round the nut-brown
    bowl doth trot ;
And sitteth singing care away, till he to bed be got :
Theare sleepes he soundly all the night, forgetting
    morrow-cares :
Nor feares he blasting of his corne, nor uttering of
    his wares ;
Or storms by seas, or stirres on land, or cracke of
    credit lost ;   90
Not spending franklier than his flocke, shall still de-
    fray the cost.
Well wot I, sooth they say, that say more quiet
    nights and daies
The shepheard sleeps and wakes, than he whose
    cattel he doth graize.
Beleeve me, lasse, a king is but a man, and so am I :

Ver. 85. *i.e.* roasts a crab, or apple.   V. 86. to tell, whilst
round the bole doth trot.   Ed. 1597.

[1 blockhead.]

Content is worth a monarchie, and mischiefs hit the
    hie;   95
As late it did a king and his not dwelling far from
    hence,
Who left a daughter, save thyselfe, for fair a match-
    less wench."—
Here did he pause, as if his tongue had done his
    heart offence.
The neatresse,[1] longing for the rest, did egge him on
    to tell
How faire she was, and who she was. "She bore,
    quoth he, the bell   100
For beautie: though I clownish am, I know what
    beautie is;
Or did I not, at seeing thee, I senceles were to mis.
      *   *   *   *
Her stature comely, tall; her gate well graced; and
    her wit
To marvell at, not meddle with, as matchless I omit.
A globe-like head, a gold-like haire, a forehead
    smooth, and hie,   105
An even nose; on either side did shine a grayish eie:
Two rosie cheeks, round ruddy lips, white just-set
    teeth within;
A mouth in meane;[2] and underneathe a round and
    dimpled chin.
Her snowie necke, with blewish veines, stood bolt
    upright upon
Her portly shoulders: beating balles her veined
    breasts, anon   110
Adde more to beautie. Wand-like was her middle
    falling still,
And rising whereas women rise: * * * — imagine
    nothing ill.

[1 female keeper of herds.   2 middle sized.]

And more, her long, and limber armes had white and
    azure wrists;
And slender fingers aunswere to her smooth and lillie
    fists.
A legge in print, a pretie foot; conjecture of the rest:
For amorous eies, observing forme, think parts ob-
    scured best. 116
With these, O raretie! with these her tong of speech
    was spare;
But speaking, Venus seem'd to speake, the balle from
    Ide to bear.
With Phœbe, Juno, and with both herselfe contends
    in face;
Wheare equall mixture did not want of milde and
    stately grace. 120
Her smiles were sober, and her lookes were chearefull
    unto all:
Even such as neither wanton seeme, nor waiward;
    mell,[1] nor gall.
A quiet minde, a patient moode, and not disdaining
    any;
Not gybing, gadding, gawdy: and sweete faculties
    had many.
A nimph, no tong, no heart, no eie, might praise,
    might wish, might see; 125
For life, for love, for forme; more good, more worth,
    more faire than shee.
Yea such an one, as such was none, save only she was
    such:
Of Argentile to say the most, were to be silent much."
I knew the lady very well, but worthles of such
    praise,
The neatresse said: and muse I do, a shepheard thus
    should blaze 130

[1 honey.]

The 'coate' of beautie*. Credit me, thy latter speech
    bewraies
Thy clownish shape a coined shew. But wherefore
    dost thou weepe ?
The shepheard wept, and she was woe, and both
    doe silence keepe.
" In troth, quoth he, I am not such, as seeming I
    professe :
But then for her, and now for thee, I from myselfe
    digresse.   135
Her loved I (wretch that I am a recreant to be)
I loved her, that hated love, but now I die for thee.
At Kirkland is my fathers court, and Curan is my
    name,
In Edels court sometimes in pompe, till love coun-
    trould the same :
But now—what now ?—deare heart, how now ?
    what ailest thou to weepe ? "   140
The damsell wept, and he was woe, and both did
    silence keepe.
I graunt, quoth she, it was too much that you did love
    so much :
But whom your former could not move, your second
    love doth touch.
Thy twice-beloved argentile submitteth her to thee,
And for thy double love presents herself a single fee,
In passion not in person chang'd, and I, my lord, am
    she.   146
They sweetly surfeiting in joy, and silent for a space,
When as the extasie had end, did tenderly imbrace ;
And for their wedding, and their wish got fitting time
    and place.
Not England (for of Hengist then was named so this
    land)   150

---

   * *i.e.* emblazon beauty's coat. Ed. 1597, 1602, 1612, read
Coote.

Then Curan had an hardier knight; his force could
    none withstand :
Whose sheep-hooke laid apart, he then had higher
    things in hand.
First, making knowne his lawfull claime in Argentile
    her right,
He warr'd in Diria*, and he wonne Bernicia* too in
    fight :
And so from trecherous Edel tooke at once his life
    and crowne,   155
And of Northumberland was king, long raigning in
    renowne.†

* * During the Saxon heptarchy, the kingdom of Northumberland (consisting of 6 northern counties, besides part of Scotland)
was for a long time divided into two lesser sovereignties, viz. Deira
(called here Diria) which contained the southern parts, and Bernicia, comprehending those which lay north.

XXV.

CORIN'S FATE.

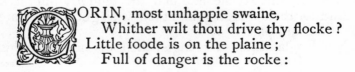 NLY the three first stanzas of this song are ancient;
these are extracted from a small quarto MS. in the
Editor's possession, written in the time of Q. Elizabeth.
As they seemed to want application, this has been attempted by a modern hand.

ORIN, most unhappie swaine,
    Whither wilt thou drive thy flocke ?
Little foode is on the plaine ;
    Full of danger is the rocke :

[† This poem was subdivided into stanzas by Percy, and is so
printed in previous editions of the *Reliques*.]

Wolfes and beares doe kepe the woodes ;   5
  Forests tangled are with brakes :
Meadowes subject are to floodes ;
  Moores are full of miry lakes.

Yet to shun all plaine, and hill,
  Forest, moore, and meadow-ground,   10
Hunger will as surely kill :
  How may then reliefe be found ?

[Such is hapless Corins fate :
  Since my waywarde love begunne,
Equall doubts begett debate   15
  What to seeke, and what to shunne.

Spare to speke, and spare to speed ;
  Yet to speke will move disdaine :
If I see her not I bleed,
  Yet her sight augments my paine.   20

What may then poor Corin doe ?
  Tell me, shepherdes, quicklye tell ;
For to linger thus in woe
  Is the lover's sharpest hell.]

⁎

XXVI.

JANE SHORE.

THOUGH so many vulgar errors have prevailed concerning this celebrated courtezan, no character in history has been more perfectly handed down to us. We have her portrait drawn by two masterly pens ; the one has delineated the features of her person, the other those of her character and story. Sir Thomas More drew from the life, and Drayton has copied an original picture of her. The reader will pardon the length of the quotations, as they serve to correct many popular mistakes relating to her catastrophe. The first is from Sir Thomas More's *History of Richard III.* written in 1513, about thirty years after the death of Edw. IV.

"Now then by and by, as it wer for anger, not for covetise, the protector sent into the house of Shores wife (for her husband dwelled not with her) and spoiled her of al that ever she had, (above the value of 2 or 3 thousand marks) and sent her body to prison. And when he had a while laide unto her, for the maner sake, that she went about to bewitch him, and that she was of counsel with the lord chamberlein to destroy him: in conclusion when that no colour could fasten upon these matters, then he layd heinously to her charge the thing that herselfe could not deny, that al the world wist was true, and that natheles every man laughed at to here it then so sodainly so highly taken,—that she was naught of her body. And for thys cause (as a goodly continent prince, clene and fautless of himself, sent oute of heaven into this vicious world for the amendment of mens maners) he caused the bishop of London to put her to open pennance, going before the crosse in procession upon a sonday with a taper in her hand. In which she went in countenance and pace demure so womanly; and albeit she was out of al array save her kyrtle only, yet went she so fair and lovely, namelye, while the wondering of the people caste a comly rud in her chekes (of which she before had most misse) that her great shame wan her much praise among those that were more amorous of her body, then curious of her soule. And many good folke also, that hated her living, and glad wer to se sin corrected, yet pittied thei more her penance then rejoiced therin, when thei considred that the protector procured it more of a corrupt intent, then any virtuous affeccion.

"This woman was born in London, worshipfully frended, honestly brought up, and very wel maryed, saving somewhat too soone; her husbande an honest citizen, yonge, and goodly, and of good substance. But forasmuche as they were coupled ere she wer wel ripe, she not very fervently loved, for whom she never longed. Which was happely the thinge, that the more easily made her encline unto the king's appetite, when he required her. Howbeit the respect of his royaltie, the hope of gay apparel, ease, plesure, and other wanton welth, was able soone to perse a soft tender hearte. But when the king had abused her, anon her husband (as he was an honest man, and one that could his good, not presuming to touch a kinges concubine) left her up to him al together. When the king died, the lord chamberlen [Hastings] toke her:* which

---

* After the death of Hastings, she was kept by the marquis of Dorset, son to Edward IV.'s queen. In Rymer's *Fœdera* is a pro-

in the kinges daies, albeit he was sore enamoured upon her, yet he forbare her, either for reverence, or for a certain friendly faithfulness.

"Proper she was, and faire : nothing in her body that you wold have changed, but if you would have wished her somewhat higher. Thus say thei that knew her in her youthe. Albeit some that *now see her* (*for yet she liveth*) deme her never to have bene wel visaged. Whose jugement seemeth me somewhat like, as though men should gesse the bewty of one longe before departed, by her scalpe taken out of the charnel-house; for now is she old, lene, withered, and dried up, nothing left but ryvilde skin, and hard bone. And yet being even such, whoso wel advise her visage, might gesse and devise which partes how filled, wold make it a fair face.

"Yet delited not men so much in her bewty, as in her pleasant behaviour. For a proper wit had she, and could both rede wel and write; mery in company, redy and quick of aunswer, neither mute nor ful of bable; sometime taunting without displeasure, and not without disport. The king would say, That he had three concubines, which in three divers properties diversly excelled. One the meriest, another the wiliest, the thirde the holiest harlot in his realme, as one whom no man could get out of the church lightly to any place, but it were to his bed. The other two wer somwhat greater personages, and natheles of their humilite content to be nameles, and to forbere the praise of those properties; but the meriest was the Shoris wife, in whom the king therfore toke

---

clamation of Richard's, dated at Leicester, Oct. 23, 1483, wherein a reward of 1000 marks in money, or 100 a year in land is offered for taking " Thomas late marquis of Dorset," who, " not having the fear of God, nor the salvation of his own soul, before his eyes, has damnably debauched and defiled many maids, widows, and wives, and *lived in actual adultery with the wife of Shore.*" Buckingham was at that time in rebellion, but as Dorset was not with him, Richard could not accuse him of treason, and therefore made a handle of these pretended debaucheries to get him apprehended. Vide *Rym. Fœd.* tom. xij. pag. 204.

[The Rev. Mark Noble writes as follows of the charge made by Richard of Dorset's living in adultery with Jane Shore.—" It could not be before she was taken by Edward; it could not be during that king's life; it could not be afterwards, by Richard's own account, for by his proclamation she then was the mistress of Hastings to the night preceding his being put to death. It could not be after that catastrophe, for ever after then Richard kept her either in the Tower or in Ludgate a close prisoner."—*Brayley's Graphic and Historical Illustrator,* 1834, p. 55.]

special pleasure. For many he had, but her he loved, whose favour, to sai the trouth (for sinne it wer to belie the devil) she never abused to any mans hurt, but to many a mans comfort and relief. Where the king toke displeasure, she would mitigate and appease his mind : where men were out of favour, she wold bring them in his grace : for many, that had highly offended, shee obtained pardon : of great forfeitures she gate men remission : and finally in many weighty sutes she stode many men in gret stede, either for none or very smal rewardes, and those rather gay than rich : either for that she was content with the dede selfe well done, or for that she delited to be sued unto, and to show what she was able to do wyth the king, or for that wanton women and welthy be not alway covetous.

"I doubt not some shal think this woman too sleight a thing to be written of, and set amonge the remembraunces of great matters : which thei shal specially think, that happely shal esteme her only by that thei *now see her*. But me semeth the chaunce so much the more worthy to be remembred, in how much she is *now* in the more beggerly condicion, unfrended and worne out of acquaintance, after good substance, after as grete favour with the prince, after as grete sute and seeking to with al those, that in those days had busynes to spede, as many other men were in their times, which be now famouse only by the infamy of their il dedes. Her doinges were not much lesse, albeit thei be muche lesse remembred because thei were not so evil. For men use, if they have an evil turne, to write it in marble ; and whoso doth us a good tourne, we write it in duste.* Which is not worst proved by her ; for *at this daye* shee beggeth of many at this daye living, that at this day had begged, if shee had not bene." See More's *workes*, folio, bl. let. 1557, pp. 56, 57.

Drayton has written a poetical epistle from this lady to her royal lover, and in his notes thereto he thus draws her portrait : " Her stature was meane, her haire of a dark yellow, her face round and full, her eye gray, delicate harmony being betwixt each part's proportion, and each proportion's colour, her body fat, white and smooth, her countenance cheerfull and like to her condition. The picture which I have seen of hers was such as she rose out of her bed in the

---

* These words of Sir Thomas More probably suggested to Shakespeare that proverbial reflection in *Hen. VIII.* act iv. sc. 2.

" Men's evill manners live in brass : their virtues
We write in water."

Shakesp. in his play of *Rich. III.* follows More's *Hist.* of that reign, and therefore could not but see this passage.

morning, having nothing on but a rich mantle cast under one arme over her shoulder, and sitting on a chaire, on which her naked arm did lie. What her father's name was, or where she was borne, is not certainly knowne: but Shore, a young man of right goodly person, wealth and behaviour, abandoned her bed after the king had made her his concubine. Richard III. causing her to do open penance in Paul's church-yard, *commanded that no man should relieve her*, which the tyrant did, not so much for his hatred to sinne, but that by making his brother's life odious. he might cover his horrible treasons the more cunningly." See *England's Heroical Epistles*, by Mich. Drayton, Esq; Lond. 1637, 12mo.

An original picture of *Jane Shore* almost naked is preserved in the Provost's Lodgings at Eton; and another picture of her is in the Provost's Lodge at King's College, Cambridge: to both which foundations she is supposed to have done friendly offices with *Edward IV.* A small quarto Mezzotinto print was taken from the former of these by *J. Faber.*

The history of *Jane Shore* receives new illustration from the following letter of *K. Richard III.* which is preserved in the *Harl. MSS.* Num. 433, Art. 2378, but of which the copy transmitted to the Editor has been reduced to modern orthography, &c. It is said to have been addressed to *Russel* bp. of Lincoln, lord chancellor, Anno 1484.

By the *King.*

" Right Reverend Father in God, &c. signifying unto you, that it is shewed unto us, that our Servant and Solicitor Thomas Lynom, marvellously blinded and abused with the late Wife of William Shore, now living in Ludgate by our commandment, hath made Contract of Matrimony with her, as it is said, and intendeth, to our full great marvel, to effect the same. WE, for many causes, would be sorry that he should be so disposed; pray you therefore to send for him, and in that ye goodly may, exhort, and stir him to the contrary: And if ye find him utterly set for to marry her, and none otherwise would be advertized, then, if it may stand with the laws of the church, we be content the time of marriage be deferred to our coming next to London; that upon sufficient Surety found of her good abearing, ye do so send for her Keeper, and discharge him of our said commandment, by Warrant of these, committing her to the rule, and guiding of her Father, or any other, by your direction, in the mean season. Given, &c.

" *RIC.* Rex."

It appears from two articles in the same MS. that K. Richard had granted to the said *Thomas Linom* the office of King's Solicitor (Art. 134.), and also the Manor of Colmeworth, com. Bedf. to him and his Heirs Male (Art. 596.)

The following ballad is printed (with some corrections) from an old black-letter copy in the Pepys collection.　Its full title is, *The woefull lamentation of Jane Shore, a goldsmith's wife in London, sometime king Edward IV. his concubine.* To the tune of *Live with me, &c.* (See the first volume.)　To every stanza is annexed the following burthen :

> " Then maids and wives in time amend,
> For love and beauty will have end."

[The tale of Jane Shore's sufferings has found frequent narrators. The first known ballad upon her story was written by Thomas Churchyard (who died in 1604) and is included in the *Mirror for Magistrates.* The ballad here printed is attributed to Thomas Deloney, and was entered on the books of the Stationers' Company to William White, printer, on the 11th of June, 1603, but no copy of this edition is known to exist.　Mr. Chappell remarks that no copy in any of the collections can be dated " earlier than Charles the Second's time, or at most than the Protectorate" (*Roxburghe Ballads*, vol. i. p. 479).　It is printed in the *Collection of Old Ballads*, 1723 (vol. i. p. 145), and in the same collection is a burlesque song called *King Edward and Jane Shore* (vol. i. p. 153).　The Roxburghe copy has a second part which Mr. Chappell says is " probably by another hand and of later date."　Deloney has paid very little attention to facts, and many of his statements are groundless, for instance no one was hanged for succouring Jane (vv. 105-112), and instead of dying of hunger in a ditch (vv. 125-132), she survived her penance nearly fifty years. (She died in the 18th year of Henry VIII.'s reign.)　Her husband is named Matthew Shore in verse 13, but we have the best authority for affirming that his true name was William. Richard III. followed Jane Shore with unrelenting hate, and not content with making her do penance, clapping her in prison and depriving her of all her property, which amounted to the value of 3000 marks, equal to about £20,000 of our present money, he prevented her from marrying a respectable man.

There is no date to the paper printed above, but as John Russell, D.D., Bishop of Lincoln, was Richard's Chancellor only from Nov. 1484 to July 1485, we can fix it pretty closely.

According to Mr. Nugent Bell, in his *Huntingdon Peerage*, the name of the father of Jane Shore was Thomas Wainstead.　Granger says that the Duchess of Montagu had a lock of her hair which looked as if it had been powdered with gold dust.　For further information, see *Some Particulars of the Life of Jane Shore*, by the Rev. Mark Noble, in Brayley's *Graphic Illustrator*, pp. 49-64.]

F Rosamonde that was so faire,
Had cause her sorrowes to declare,
Then let Jane Shore with sorrowe sing,
That was beloved of a king.

In maiden yeares my beautye bright 5
Was loved dear of lord and knight;
But yet the love that they requir'd,
It was not as my friends desir'd.

My parents they, for thirst of gaine,
A husband for me did obtaine; 10
And I, their pleasure to fulfille,
Was forc'd to wedd against my wille.

To Matthew Shore I was a wife,
Till lust brought ruine to my life;
And then my life I lewdlye spent, 15
Which makes my soul for to lament.

In Lombard-street I once did dwelle,
As London yet can witness welle;
Where many gallants did beholde
My beautye in a shop of golde. 20

I spred my plumes, as wantons doe,
Some sweet and secret friende to wooe,
Because chast love I did not finde
Agreeing to my wanton minde.

At last my name in court did ring 25
Into the eares of Englandes king,
Who came and lik'd, and love requir'd,
But I made coye what he desir'd:

Yet Mistress Blague, a neighbour neare,
Whose friendship I esteemed deare, 30
Did saye, It was a gallant thing
To be beloved of a king.

By her persuasions I was led,
For to defile my marriage-bed,
And wronge my wedded husband Shore,   35
Whom I had married yeares before.

In heart and mind I did rejoyce,
That I had made so sweet a choice;
And therefore did my state resigne.
To be king Edward's concubine.   40

From city then to court I went,
To reape the pleasures of content;
There had the joyes that love could bring,
And knew the secrets of a king.

When I was thus advanc'd on highe   45
Commanding Edward with mine eye,
For Mrs. Blague I in short space
Obtainde a livinge from his grace.

No friende I had but in short time
I made unto a promotion climbe;   50
But yet for all this costlye pride,
My husbande could not mee abide.

His bed, though wronged by a king,
His heart with deadlye griefe did sting;
From England then he goes away   55
To end his life beyond the sea.

He could not live to see his name
Impaired by my wanton shame;
Although a prince of peerlesse might
Did reape the pleasure of his right.   60

Long time I lived in the courte,
With lords and ladies of great sorte;
And when I smil'd all men were glad,
But when I frown'd my prince grewe sad.

But yet a gentle minde I bore 65
To helplesse people, that were poore;
I still redrest the orphans crye,
And sav'd their lives condemnd to dye.

I still had ruth on widowes tears,
I succour'd babes of tender yeares; 70
And never look'd for other gaine
But love and thankes for all my paine.

At last my royall king did dye,
And then my dayes of woe grew nighe;
When crook-back Richard got the crowne, 75
King Edwards friends were soon put downe.

I then was punisht for my sin,
That I so long had lived in;
Yea, every one that was his friend,
This tyrant brought to shamefull end. 80

Then for my lewd and wanton life,
That made a strumpet of a wife,
I penance did in Lombard-street,
In shamefull manner in a sheet.

Where many thousands did me viewe, 85
Who late in court my credit knewe;
Which made the teares run down my face,
To thinke upon my foul disgrace.

Not thus content, they took from mee
My goodes, my livings, and my fee, 90
And charg'd that none should me relieve,
Nor any succour to me give.

Then unto Mrs. Blague I went,
To whom my jewels I had sent,
In hope therebye to ease my want, 95
When riches fail'd, and love grew scant:

But she denyed to me the same
When in my need for them I came;
To recompence my former love,
Out of her doores shee did me shove.   100

So love did vanish with my state,
Which now my soul repents too late;
Therefore example take by mee,
For friendship parts in povertie.

But yet one friend among the rest,   105
Whom I before had seen distrest,
And sav'd his life, condemn'd to die,
Did give me food to succour me :

For which, by lawe, it was decreed
That he was hanged for that deed;   110
His death did grieve me so much more,
Than had I dyed myself therefore.

Then those to whom I had done good,
Durst not afford me any food;
Whereby I begged all the day,   115
And still in streets by night I lay.

My gowns beset with pearl and gold,
Were turn'd to simple garments old;
My chains and gems and golden rings,
To filthy rags and loathsome things.   120

Thus was I scorn'd of maid and wife,
For leading such a wicked life;
Both sucking babes and children small,
Did make their pastime at my fall.

I could not get one bit of bread,   125
Whereby my hunger might be fed :
Nor drink, but such as channels yield,
Or stinking ditches in the field.

Thus, weary of my life, at lengthe
I yielded up my vital strength 130
Within a ditch of loathsome scent,
Where carrion dogs did much frequent:

The which now since my dying daye,
Is Shoreditch call'd, as writers saye*;
Which is a witness of my sinne, 135
For being concubine to a king.

You wanton wives, that fall to lust,
Be you assur'd that God is just;
Whoredome shall not escape his hand,
Nor pride unpunish'd in this land. 140

If God to me such shame did bring,
That yielded only to a king,
How shall they scape that daily run
To practise sin with every one?

You husbands, match not but for love, 145
Lest some disliking after prove;
Women, be warn'd when you are wives,
What plagues are due to sinful lives:
 Then, maids and wives, in time amend,
 For love and beauty will have end. 150

---

* But it had this name long before; being so called from its
being a common Sewer (vulgarly Shore) or drain. See Stow.
[Weever states that it was named from the Lord of the Manor.
Sir John de Sordig was Ambassador from Edward III. to the Pope,
to remonstrate with his Holiness on his claim to present foreigners
to English livings.]

XXVII.

CORYDON'S DOLEFUL KNELL.

HIS little simple elegy is given, with some corrections, from two copies, one of which is in *The golden garland of princely delights.*

The burthen of the song, *Ding Dong*, &c. is at present appropriated to burlesque subjects, and therefore may excite only ludicrous ideas in a modern reader; but in the time of our poet it usually accompanied the most solemn and mournful strains. Of this kind is that fine aërial Dirge in Shakespear's *Tempest:*

" Full fadom five thy father lies,
    Of his bones are corrall made;
Those are pearles that were his eyes;
    Nothing of him, that doth fade,
But doth suffer a sea-change
    Into something rich and strange:
Sea-nymphs hourly ring his knell,
    Harke now I heare them, Ding dong bell.
            " Burthen, Ding Dong."

I make no doubt but the poet intended to conclude the above air in a manner the most solemn and expressive of melancholy.

Y Phillida, adieu love!
    For evermore farewel!
Ay me! I've lost my true love,
    And thus I ring her knell,
Ding dong, ding dong, ding dong,   5
    My Phillida is dead!
I'll stick a branch of willow
    At my fair Phillis' head.

For my fair Phillida
    Our bridal bed was made: 10
But 'stead of silkes so gay,
    She in her shroud is laid.
            Ding, &c.

Her corpse shall be attended
By maides in fair array,
Till the obsequies are ended,
And she is wrapt in clay.
Ding, &c.

15

Her herse it shall be carried
By youths, that do excell;
And when that she is buried,
I thus will ring her knell,
Ding, &c.

20

A garland shall be framed
By art and natures skill,
Of sundry-colour'd flowers,
In token of good-will*:
Ding, &c.

And sundry-colour'd ribbands
On it I will bestow;
But chiefly black and yellowe†:
With her to grave shall go.
Ding, &c.

25

I'll decke her tomb with flowers,
The rarest ever seen,
And with my tears, as showers,
I'll keepe them fresh and green.
Ding, &c.

30

Instead of fairest colours,
Set forth with curious art‡,

---

* It is a custom in many parts of England, to carry a flowery garland before the corpse of a woman who dies unmarried. [For further note on this custom, see *The Bride's Burial*, vol iii. Book II. No. 13.]

† See above, preface to No. XI. Book II.

‡ This alludes to the painted effigies of alabaster, anciently erected upon tombs and monuments.

Ding, &c.
Her image shall be painted 35
On my distressed heart.

And thereon shall be graven
Her epitaph so faire,
" Here lies the loveliest maiden,
That e'er gave shepheard care." 40
Ding, &c.

In sable will I mourne;
Blacke shall be all my weede;
Ay me ! I am forlorne,
Now Phillida is dead!
Ding dong, ding dong, ding dong,
My Phillida is dead! 46
I'll stick a branch of willow
At my fair Phillis' head

THE END OF THE SECOND BOOK.

RELIQUES OF ANCIENT POETRY, ETC

SERIES THE SECOND.

BOOK III.

I.

THE COMPLAINT OF CONSCIENCE.

I SHALL begin this third book with an old allegoric Satire; a manner of moralizing, which, if it was not first introduced by the author of *Pierce Plowman's Visions*,* was at least chiefly brought into repute by that ancient Satirist. It is not so generally known that the kind of verse used in this ballad hath any affinity with the peculiar metre of that writer, for which reason I shall throw together some cursory remarks on that very singular species of versification, the nature of which has been so little understood.†

The following Song, intitled, *The Complaint of Conscience*, is printed from the Editor's folio Manuscript: Some corruptions in the old copy are here corrected; but with notice to the Reader, wherever it was judged necessary, by inclosing the corrections between inverted 'commas.'

[This poem entitled *Conscience* is printed in Hales and Furnivall's edition of the Percy folio MS. (vol. ii. p. 174), with a long preface by Mr. Furnivall, on the earnest side of Early English literature.

It will be seen from the foot-notes that Percy left many of his corrections unnoticed.]

---

* [The correct title is *William's Vision of Piers Plowman*. It is William (the author) who has the vision of Piers Plowman.

† This essay is printed as an Appendix.]

S I walked of late by ' an ' wood side,
 To God for to meditate was my entent;
 Where under a hawthorne I suddenlye
  spyed
A silly poore creature ragged and rent,
With bloody teares his face was besprent,   5
 His fleshe and his color consumed away,
 And his garments they were all mire, mucke, and
  clay.

This made me muse, and much ' to ' desire
To know what kind of man hee shold bee;
I stept to him straight, and did him require 10
His name and his secretts to shew unto mee.
His head he cast up, and wooful was hee,
 My name, quoth he, is the cause of my care,
 And makes me scorned, and left here so bare.

Then straightway he turn'd him, and pray'd ' me ' sit
 downe,   15
And I will, saithe he, declare my whole greefe ;
My name is called CONSCIENCE :—wheratt he did
 frowne,
He pined to repeate it, and grinded his teethe,
' Thoughe now, silly wretche, I'm denyed all releef,'
 ' Yet ' while I was young, and tender of yeeres, 20
 I was entertained with kinges, and with peeres.

Ver. 1. one, MS. [V. 3. espyed, MS. Between vv. 5, 6 the
MS. has this line, "with turning and winding his bodye was toste."
After v. 7, the MS. has the following lines :—

 " good lord ! of my liffe deprive me, I pray
  for I silly wretch am ashamed of my name !
 my name," quoth hee, " is the cause of my care,
  and I cursse my godfathers that gave me the same ! "

Percy omits three of these, and transfers the third line to v. 13.]
V. 15. him, MS. V. 19. not in MS. [V. 20. *for* in place of *yet*, MS.]

There was none in the court that lived in such fame,
For with the kings councell ' I ' sate in commission ;
Dukes, earles, and barrons esteem'd of my name ;
And how that I liv'd there needs no repetition : 25
I was ever holden in honest condition,
 For howsoever the lawes went in Westminster-hall,
 When sentence was given, for me they wold call.

No incomes at all the landlords wold take,
But one pore peny, that was their fine ; 30
And that they acknowledged to be for my sake.
The poore wold doe nothing without councell mine :
I ruled the world with the right line :
 For nothing was passed betweene foe and friend,
 But Conscience was called to bee at ' the ' end. 35

Noe bargaines, nor merchandize merchants wold make
But I was called a wittenesse therto :
No use for noe money, nor forfett wold take,
But I wold controule them, if that they did soe :
' And ' that makes me live now in great woe, 40
 For then came in Pride, Sathan's disciple,
 That is now entertained with all kind of people.

He brought with him three, whose names ' thus they
        call '
That is Covetousnes, Lecherye, Usury, beside :
They never prevail'd, till they had wrought my
    downefall ; 45
Soe Pride was entertained, but Conscience decried,
And ' now ever since ' abroad have I tryed
 To have had entertainment with some one or other ;
 But I am rejected, and scorned of my brother.

[Ver. 22. in all the court.] V. 23. he sate, MS. [V. 34. that
was passed.] V. 35. an end, MS. [V. 36. Noe merchandize nor
bargaines the merchants wold make. V. 42. now is.] V. 43. they
be these, MS. V. 46. was deride, MS. [V. 47. Yet still abroad
have I tried.]

Then went I to the Court the gallants to winn,   50
But the porter kept me out of the gate :
To Bartlemew Spittle[1] to pray for my sinne,
They bade me goe packe, it was fitt for my state ;
Goe, goe, threed-bare Conscience, and seeke thee a
    mate.
    Good Lord, long preserve my king, prince, and
      queene,   55
    With whom evermore I esteemed have been.

Then went I to London, where once I did ' dwell ' :
But they bade away with me, when they knew my
    name ;
For he will undoe us to bye and to sell !   59
They bade me goe packe me, and hye me for shame ;
They lought[2] at my raggs, and there had good game;
    This is old threed-bare Conscience, that dwelt
      with saint Peter :
    But they wold not admitt me to be a chimney-
      sweeper.

Not one wold receive me, the Lord ' he ' doth know;
I having but one poor pennye in my purse,   65
On an awle and some patches I did it bestow ;
' For ' I thought better cobble shooes than doe worse.
Straight then all the coblers began for to curse,
    And by statute wold prove me a rogue, and forlorne,
    And whipp me out of towne to ' seeke ' where I
      was borne.   70

    [Ver. 51. gates. V. 52. sinnes.] V. 53. packe me, MS. [V. 56.
have esteemed.] V. 57. wonne, MS. [V. 64. the Lord God doth.
V. 66. of an. V. 67. I thought better to cobble shoes than to doe
worse. V. 68. all they cobblers. V. 69. and by statute thé wold
prove me I was a rouge and forlorne. V. 70. And they whipt me
out of towne to see where I was borne.]

    [[1] St. Bartholomew's Hospital.   [2] laughed.]

Then did I remember, and call to my minde,
The Court of Conscience where once I did sit:
Not doubting but there I some favor shold find,
For my name and the place agreed soe fit;
But there of my purpose I fayled a whit,   75
  For 'thoughe' the judge us'd my name in everye
    'commission,'
  The lawyers with their quillets[1] wold get 'my'
    dismission.

Then Westminster-hall was noe place for me ;
Good lord ! how the Lawyers began to assemble,
And fearfull they were, lest there I shold bee !   80
The silly poore clarkes began for to tremble ;
I showed them my cause, and did not dissemble ;
  Soe they gave me some money my charges to beare,
  But swore me on a booke I must never come there.

Next the Merchants said, Counterfeite, get thee
    away,   85
Dost thou remember how wee thee found ?
We banisht thee the country beyond the salt sea,
And sett thee on shore in the New-found land ;
And there thou and wee most friendly shook hand,
  And we were right glad when thou didst refuse us ;
  For when we wold reape profitt here thou woldst
    accuse us.   91

Then had I noe way, but for to goe on
To Gentlemens houses of an ancyent name ;
Declaring my greeffes, and there I made moane,
'Telling' how their forefathers held me in fame :   95

[Ver. 72. they Court.   V. 73. some favor I.   V. 76. did use my
name in everye condicion.   V. 77. for lawyers get a.   V. 79. good
god.   V. 83. soe then they.   V. 85. then the merchants.   V. 89.
hands.   V. 90. verry glad . . . did . . .   V. 91. wold.   V. 92.
goe an.   V. 95. and how . . . had held, MS.]

[[1] quibbles.]

And at letting their farmes 'how always I came'.
  They sayd, Fye upon thee! we may thee curse :
  'Theire' leases continue, and we fare the worse.

And then I was forced a begging to goe
To husbandmens houses, who greeved right sore, 100
And sware that their landlords had plagued them so
That they were not able to keepe open doore,
Nor nothing had left to give to the poore :
  Therefore to this wood I doe me repayre,
  Where hepps and hawes, that is my best fare. 105

Yet within this same desert some comfort I have
Of Mercy, of Pittye, and of Almes-deeds ;
Who have vowed to company me to my grave.
Wee are 'all' put to silence, and live upon weeds,
'And hence such cold house-keeping proceeds' : 110
  Our banishment is its utter decay,
  The which the riche glutton will answer one day.

Why then, I said to him, me-thinks it were best
To goe to the Clergie ; for dailye they preach
Eche man to love you above all the rest ;   115
Of Mercye, and Pittie, and Almes-'deeds', they teach.
O, said he, noe matter of a pin what they preach,
  For their wives and their children soe hange them
    upon,
  That whosoever gives almes they will* give none.

---

* We ought in justice and truth to read ' *can*.'

[Ver. 96. and in letting of their ffarmes I always used the same.
V. 98. they have leases.   V. 101. who sware . . . so sore.   V. 103.
thé had.   V. 104. doe repayre.]   V. 109. ill, MS.   V. 110. not in
MS.   [V. 111. their utter.   V. 115. of pittie and of almes they doe
teach.   V. 117. doe preach.   V. 118. hangs.]   V. 119. almes-
deeds, MS.

Then laid he him down, and turned him away,   120
'And' prayd me to goe, and leave him to rest.
I told him, I haplie might yet see the day
For him and his fellowes to live with the best.
First, said he, banish Pride, then all England were
 blest ;
 For then those wold love us, that now sell their
  land,   125
 And then good 'house-keeping wold revive' out
  of hand.

II.

PLAIN TRUTH AND BLIND IGNORANCE.

HIS excellent old ballad is preserved in the little ancient miscellany, intitled, *The Garland of Goodwill.—Ignorance* is here made to speak in the broad Somersetshire dialect. The scene we may suppose to be Glastonbury Abbey.

TRUTH.

OD speed you, ancient father,
 And give you a good daye ;
What is the cause, I praye you
 So sadly here you staye ?
And that you keep such gazing   5
 On this decayed place,
The which, for superstition,
 Good princes down did raze ?

[Ver. 122. I might happen to see. V. 123. to have him. V. 124. you must banish pride and then. V. 125. and then . . . sells their lands.] V. 126. houses every where wold be kept, MS.

IGNORANCE.

Chill[1] tell thee, by my vazen*,
  That zometimes che[2] have knowne   10
A vair and goodly abbey
  Stand here of bricke and stone;
And many a holy vrier,[3]
  As ich[4] may say to thee,
Within these goodly cloysters
  Che did full often zee.   15

TRUTH.

Then I must tell thee, father,
  In truthe and veritiè,
A sorte of greater hypocrites
  Thou couldst not likely see;   20
Deceiving of the simple
  With false and feigned lies:
But such an order truly
  Christ never did devise.

IGNORANCE.

Ah! ah! che zmell thee now, man;   25
  Che know well what thou art;
A vellow of mean learning,
  Thee was not worth a vart:
Vor when we had the old lawe,
  A merry world was then;   30
And every thing was plenty
  Among all zorts of men.

---

* *i. e.* faithen: as in the Midland counties they say housen, closen, for houses, closes. *A.*

[[1] I will.   [2] I.   [3] friar.   [4] I.]

Truth.

Thou givest me an answer,
  As did the Jewes sometimes
Unto the prophet Jeremye,   35
  When he accus'd their crimes;
'Twas merry, sayd the people,
  And joyfull in our rea'me,
When we did offer spice-cakes
  Unto the queen of heav'n.   40

Ignorance.

Chill tell thee what, good vellowe,
  Before the vriers went hence,
A bushell of the best wheate
  Was zold vor vourteen pence;
And vorty egges a penny,   45
  That were both good and newe;
And this che zay my zelf have zeene,
  And yet ich am no Jewe.

Truth.

Within the sacred bible
  We find it written plain,   50
The latter days should troublesome
  And dangerous be, certaine;
That we should be self-lovers,
  And charity wax colde;
Then 'tis not true religion   55
  That makes thee grief to holde.

Ignorance.

Chill tell thee my opinion plaine,
  And choul'd[1] that well ye knewe,
Ich care not for the bible booke;
  Tis too big to be true.

[1 I would.]

Our blessed ladyes psalter
  Zhall for my money goe;
Zuch pretty prayers, as there bee*,
  The bible cannot zhowe.

TRUTH.

Nowe hast thou spoken trulye,   65
  For in that book indeede
No mention of our lady,
  Or Romish saint we read:
For by the blessed Spirit
  That book indited was,   70
And not by simple persons,
  As was the foolish masse.

IGNORANCE.

Cham[1] zure they were not voolishe
  That made the masse, che trowe;
Why, man, 'tis all in Latine,   75
  And vools no Latine knowe.
Were not our fathers wise men,
  And they did like it well;
Who very much rejoyced
  To heare the zacring bell?[2]   80

TRUTH.

But many kinges and prophets,
  As I may say to thee,
Have wisht the light that you have,
  And could it never see:
For what art thou the better   85
  A Latin song to heare,
And understandest nothing,
  That they sing in the quiere?

---

* Probably alluding to the illuminated Psalters, Missals, &c.

[[1] I am.   [2] the sacring bell was rung to give notice of the elevation of the host.]

IGNORANCE.

O hold thy peace, che pray thee,
   The noise was passing trim   90
To heare the vriers zinging,
   As we did enter in ;
And then to zee the rood-loft
   Zo bravely zet with zaints ;—
But now to zee them wandring   95
   My heart with zorrow vaints.

TRUTH.

The Lord did give commandment,
   No image thou shouldst make,
Nor that unto idolatry
   You should your self betake :   100
The golden calf of Israel
   Moses did therefore spoile ;
And Baal's priests and temple
   Were brought to utter foile.

IGNORANCE.

But our lady of Walsinghame   105
   Was a pure and holy zaint,
And many men in pilgrimage
   Did shew to her complaint.
Yea with zweet Thomas Becket,
   And many other moe :   110
The holy maid of Kent* likewise
   Did many wonders zhowe.

TRUTH.

Such saints are well agreeing
   To your profession sure ;
And to the men that made them   115
   So precious and so pure ;

---

* By name Eliz. Barton, executed Apr. 21, 1534. Stow, p. 570.

The one for being a traytoure,
  Met an untimely death ;
The other eke for treason
  Did end her hateful breath.   120

IGNORANCE.

Yea, yea, it is no matter,
  Dispraise them how you wille :
But zure they did much goodnesse ;
  Would they were with us stille !
We had our holy water,   125
  And holy bread likewise,
And many holy reliques
  We zaw before our eyes.

TRUTH.

And all this while they fed you
  With vain and empty showe,   130
Which never Christ commanded,
  As learned doctors knowe :
Search then the holy scriptures,
  And thou shalt plainly see
That headlong to damnation   135
  They alway trained thee.

IGNORANCE.

If it be true, good vellowe,
  As thou dost zay to mee,
Unto my heavenly fader
  Alone then will I flee :   140
Believing in the Gospel,
  And passion of his zon,
And with the zubtil papistes
  Ich have for ever done.

III.

THE WANDERING JEW.

THE story of the Wandering Jew is of considerable antiquity: it had obtained full credit in this part of the world before the year 1228, as we learn from Mat. Paris. For in that year, it seems, there came an Armenian archbishop into England, to visit the shrines and reliques preserved in our churches; who, being entertained at the monastery of St. Albans, was asked several questions relating to his country, &c. Among the rest a monk, who sat near him, inquired, "if he had ever seen or heard of the famous person named Joseph, that was so much talked of; who was present at our Lord's crucifixion and conversed with him, and who was still alive in confirmation of the Christian faith." The archbishop answered, That the fact was true. And afterwards one of his train, who was well known to a servant of the abbot's, interpreting his master's words, told them in French, "That his lord knew the person they spoke of very well: that he had dined at his table but a little while before he left the East: that he had been Pontius Pilate's porter, by name Cartaphilus; who, when they were dragging Jesus out of the door of the Judgment-hall, struck him with his fist on the back, saying, 'Go faster, Jesus, go faster: why dost thou linger?' Upon which Jesus looked at him with a frown and said, 'I indeed am going, but thou shalt tarry till I come.' Soon after he was converted, and baptized by the name of Joseph. He lives for ever, but at the end of every hundred years falls into an incurable illness, and at length into a fit or ecstacy, out of which when he recovers, he returns to the same state of youth he was in when Jesus suffered, being then about thirty years of age. He remembers all the circumstances of the death and resurrection of Christ, the saints that arose with him, the composing of the apostles' creed, their preaching, and dispersion; and is himself a very grave and holy person." This is the substance of Matthew Paris's account, who was himself a monk of St. Albans, and was living at the time when this Armenian archbishop made the above relation.

Since his time several impostors have appeared at intervals under the name and character of the *Wandering Jew;* whose several histories may be seen in Calmet's *Dictionary of the Bible.* See also the *Turkish Spy,* vol. ii. book 3, let. 1. The story that is copied in the following ballad is of one, who appeared at Hamburgh in 1547, and pretended he had been a Jewish shoemaker at the time of Christ's crucifixion.—The ballad however seems to be of later date. It is preserved in black-letter in the Pepys collection.

[This wondrous myth has found its way into many literatures, and numerous theories have been brought forward to account for its universality; but the only foundation for it appears to be in Christ's words—"tarry till I come." Mons. Paul Lacroix, however, suggests that it took its rise in a grand and beautiful allegory in which the Hebrew race were personified under the figure of the Everlasting Wanderer. Professor Child makes the following pertinent remark in his *English and Scottish Ballads* (vol. viii. p. 78). "It will be noticed that in the second form of the legend, the punishment of perpetual existence, which gives rise to the old names, *Judæus non mortalis, Ewiger Jude*, is aggravated by a condemnation to incessant change of place, which is indicated by a corresponding name, *Wandering Jew, Juif Errant*, &c."

In the Middle Ages it was supposed by some that Cain was the Wandering Jew, but the Mahometan belief was fixed upon Samiri, who, during the absence of Moses, enticed the people to worship the golden calf. In G. Weil's *The Bible, the Koran, and the Talmud*, 1846 (p. 127), we read, "Moses then summoned Samiri, and would have put him to death instantly, but Allah directed that he should be sent into banishment. Ever since that time he roams like a wild beast throughout the world; everyone shuns him and purifies the ground on which his feet have stood; and he himself, whenever he approaches men, exclaims, 'Touch me not.'" (Quoted in Buckle's *Common Place Book. Works*, vol. ii. p. 502, 1872.)

The legend has been localized in various parts of the world and connected with other myths. According to Mr. Baring Gould, a similar curse to that under which the Wandering Jew is living is supposed to have been inflicted upon the gipsies, on account of their refusal to shelter the Virgin and Child in the flight into Egypt.

The last recorded appearance of the Wandering Jew was at Brussels in April, 1774, and the wanderer's name was Isaac Laquedem. The name of the Hamburgh impostor, mentioned above by Percy, was Ahasuerus.]

WHEN as in faire Jerusalem
　　Our Saviour Christ did live,
And for the sins of all the worlde
　　His own deare life did give;
The wicked Jewes with scoffes and scornes　5
　　Did dailye him molest,
That never till he left his life,
　　Our Saviour could not rest.

When they had crown'd his head with thornes,
　　And scourg'd him to disgrace,　　　10
In scornfull sort they led him forthe
　　Unto his dying place;
Where thousand thousands in the streete
　　Beheld him passe along,
Yet not one gentle heart was there,　　15
　　That pityed this his wrong.

Both old and young reviled him,
　　As in the streete he wente,
And nought he found but churlish tauntes,
　　By every ones consente:　　　20
His owne deare crosse he bore himselfe,
　　A burthen far too great,
Which made him in the street to fainte,
　　With blood and water sweat.

Being weary thus, he sought for rest,　　25
　　To ease his burthened soule,
Upon a stone; the which a wretch
　　Did churlishly controule;
And sayd, Awaye, thou king of Jewes,
　　Thou shalt not rest thee here;　　30
Pass on; thy execution place
　　Thou seest nowe draweth neare.

And thereupon he thrust him thence;
   At which our Saviour sayd,
I sure will rest, but thou shalt walke,   35
   And have no journey stayed.
With that this cursed shoemaker,
   For offering Christ this wrong,
Left wife and children, house and all,
   And went from thence along.   40

Where after he had seene the bloude
   Of Jesus Christ thus shed,
And to the crosse his bodye nail'd,
   Awaye with speed he fled
Without returning backe againe   45
   Unto his dwelling place,
And wandred up and downe the worlde,
   A runnagate most base.

No resting could he finde at all,
   No ease, nor hearts content;   50
No house, nor home, nor biding place :
   But wandring forth he went
From towne to towne in foreigne landes,
   With grieved conscience still,
Repenting for the heinous guilt   55
   Of his fore-passed ill.

Thus after some fewe ages past
   In wandring up and downe ;
He much again desired to see
   Jerusalems renowne,   60
But finding it all quite destroyd,
   He wandred thence with woe,
Our Saviours wordes, which he had spoke,
   To verifie and showe.

" I'll rest, sayd hee, but thou shalt walke,"   65
   So doth this wandring Jew

From place to place, but cannot rest
    For seeing countries newe ;
Declaring still the power of him,
    Whereas he comes or goes,   70
And of all things done in the east,
    Since Christ his death, he showes.

The world he hath still compast round
    And seene those nations strange,
That hearing of the name of Christ,   75
    Their idol gods doe change :
To whom he hath told wondrous thinges
    Of time forepast, and gone,
And to the princes of the worlde
    Declares his cause of moane :   80

Desiring still to be dissolv'd,
    And yeild his mortal breath ;
But, if the Lord hath thus decreed,
    He shall not yet see death.
For neither lookes he old nor young,   85
    But as he did those times,
When Christ did suffer on the crosse
    For mortall sinners crimes.

He hath past through many a foreigne place,
    Arabia, Egypt, Africa,   90
Grecia, Syria, and great Thrace,
    And throughout all Hungaria.
Where Paul and Peter preached Christ,
    Those blest apostles deare ;
There he hath told our Saviours wordes,   95
    In countries far, and neare.

And lately in Bohemia,
    With many a German towne ;
And now in Flanders, as tis thought,
    He wandreth up and downe :   100

Where learned men with him conferre
   Of those his lingering dayes,
And wonder much to heare him tell
   His journeyes, and his wayes.

If people give this Jew an almes,   105
   The most that he will take
Is not above a groat a time :
   Which he, for Jesus' sake,
Will kindlye give unto the poore,
   And thereof make no spare,   110
Affirming still that Jesus Christ
   Of him hath dailye care.

He ne'er was seene to laugh nor smile,
   But weepe and make great moane ;
Lamenting still his miseries,   115
   And dayes forepast and gone :
If he heare any one blaspheme,
   Or take God's name in vaine,
He telles them that they crucifie
   Their Saviour Christe againe.   120

If you had seene his death, saith he,
   As these mine eyes have done,
Ten thousand thousand times would yee
   His torments think upon :
And suffer for his sake all paine   125
   Of torments, and all woes.
These are his wordes and eke his life
   Whereas he comes or goes.

IV.

THE LYE,

BY SIR WALTER RALEIGH,

S found in a very scarce miscellany intitled "*Davison's Poems, or a poeticall Rapsodie divided into sixe books* . . . The 4th impression newly corrected and augmented, and put into a forme more pleasing to the reader. Lond. 1621, 12mo." This poem is reported to have been written by its celebrated author the night before his execution, Oct. 29, 1618. But this must be a mistake, for there were at least two editions of Davison's poems before that time, one in 1608,* the other in 1611.† So that unless this poem was an after-insertion in the 4th edit. it must have been written long before the death of Sir Walter: perhaps it was composed soon after his condemnation in 1603. See Oldys's *Life of Sir W. Raleigh*, p. 173, fol.

[Hallam asserted that this favourite poem had been ascribed to Raleigh without evidence and without probability. Ritson affirmed that F. Davison was the author, and Ellis supported the claims of Joshua Sylvester, but Dr. Hannah has proved conclusively that it was really written by Raleigh. It was certainly composed before 1608, and probably about the period of its author's marriage and his consequent imprisonment in the Tower. Dr. Hannah has brought together a large amount of illustrative evidence in his interesting edition of the *Courtly Poets* (1872), and he shows that the answerers of the poem attributed it to Raleigh. One of the answers commences as follows—

" Go, echo of the mind, a careless truth protest ;
Make answer that rude Rawly no stomach can digest."

He also draws attention to a transcript of the poem among the Chetham MSS., made not long after Raleigh's death, and signed " Wa. Raleigh."

In that remarkable book, *Sylvester's Remains*, printed at the end of the translation of Du Bartas, 1641, *The Soules Errand* is inserted with some poor additional verses.]

---

* *Catalog. of T. Rawlinson*, 1727.
† *Cat. of Sion coll. library.* This is either lost or mislaid.

GOE, soule, the bodies guest,
Upon a thankelesse arrant;
Feare not to touche the best,
The truth shall be thy warrant:
Goe, since I needs must dye,   5
And give the world the lye.

Goe tell the court, it glowes
And shines like rotten wood;
Goe tell the church it showes
What's good, and doth no good: 10
If church and court reply,
Then give them both the lye.

Tell potentates they live
Acting by others actions;
Not lov'd unlesse they give,   15
Not strong but by their factions;
If potentates reply,
Give potentates the lye.

Tell men of high condition,
That rule affairs of state,   20
Their purpose is ambition,
Their practise onely hate;
And if they once reply,
Then give them all the lye.

Tell them that brave it most,   25
They beg for more by spending,
Who in their greatest cost
Seek nothing but commending;
And if they make reply,
Spare not to give the lye.   30

Tell zeale, it lacks devotion;
    Tell love it is but lust;
Tell time, it is but motion;
    Tell flesh, it is but dust;
        And wish them not reply,   35
        For thou must give the lye.

Tell age, it daily wasteth;
    Tell honour, how it alters;
Tell beauty, how she blasteth;
    Tell favour, how she falters;   40
        And as they shall reply,
        Give each of them the lye.

Tell wit, how much it wrangles
    In tickle points of nicenesse;
Tell wisedome, she entangles   45
    Herselfe in over-wisenesse;
        And if they do reply,
        Straight give them both the lye.

Tell physicke of her boldnesse;
    Tell skill, it is pretension;   50
Tell charity of coldness;
    Tell law, it is contention;
        And as they yield reply,
        So give them still the lye.

Tell fortune of her blindnesse;   55
    Tell nature of decay;
Tell friendship of unkindnesse;
    Tell justice of delay:
        And if they dare reply,
        Then give them all the lye.   60

Tell arts, they have no soundnesse,
    But vary by esteeming;

Tell schooles, they want profoundnesse,
  And stand too much on seeming :
    If arts and schooles reply,   65
    Give arts and schooles the lye.

Tell faith, it's fled the citie ;
  Tell how the countrey erreth ;
Tell, manhood shakes off pitie ;
  Tell, vertue least preferreth :   70
    And, if they doe reply,
    Spare not to give the lye.

So, when thou hast, as I
  Commanded thee, done blabbing,
Although to give the lye   75
  Deserves no less than stabbing,
    Yet stab at thee who will,
    No stab the soule can kill.

V.

VERSES BY KING JAMES I.

N the first edition of this book were inserted, by way of specimen of his majesty's poetic talents, some Punning Verses made on the disputations at Sterling : but it having been suggested to the Editor, that the king only gave the quibbling commendations in prose, and that some obsequious court-rhymer put them into metre ;* it was thought proper to exchange them for two *Sonnets* of K. James's own composition. James was a great versifier, and therefore out of the multitude of his poems we have here selected two, which (to shew our impartiality) are written in his best and his worst manner. The first would not dishonour any writer of that time ; the second is a most complete example of the Bathos.

---

* See a folio intitled *The Muses welcome to King James.*

[James I. commenced the practice of poetry at an early age, and his first book was printed at Edinburgh by T. Vautroullier, in 1584, under the title of *The Essays of a Prentise in the divine art of Poesie.* The king's next poetical venture was entitled, *His Majesty's Poeticall Exercises at Vacant Houres.* Printed at Edinburgh, by Robert Waldegrave, printer to the King's Majesty in 1591.]

A Sonnet addressed by King James to his son Prince Henry.

From K. James's works in folio : Where is also printed another called *his Majesty's* own *Sonnet ;* it would perhaps be too cruel to infer from thence that this was *not* his Majesty's *own* Sonnet.

GOD gives not kings the stile of Gods in vaine,
⠀⠀For on his throne his scepter do they
⠀⠀⠀⠀swey :
⠀⠀And as their subjects ought them to obey,
So kings should feare and serve their God againe.

If then ye would enjoy a happie reigne,
⠀⠀Observe the statutes of our heavenly king ;
⠀⠀And from his law make all your laws to spring ;
Since his lieutenant here ye should remaine.

Rewarde the just, be stedfast, true and plaine ;
⠀⠀Represse the proud, maintayning aye the right ;
⠀⠀Walke always so, as ever in HIS sight,
Who guardes the godly, plaguing the prophane.
⠀⠀And so ye shall in princely vertues shine,
⠀⠀Resembling right your mightie king divine.

A Sonnet occasioned by the bad Weather which hindred the Sports at New-market in January 1616.

This is printed from Drummond of Hawthornden's works, folio: where also may be seen some verses of Lord Stirling's upon this Sonnet, which concludes with the finest Anticlimax I remember to have seen.

HOW cruelly these catives do conspire?
    What loathsome love breeds such a bale-
      ful band
    Betwixt the cankred king of Creta land,*
That melancholy old and angry sire,

And him, who wont to quench debate and ire   5
    Among the Romans, when his ports were clos'd?†
But now his double face is still dispos'd,
With Saturn's help, to freeze us at the fire.

The earth ore-covered with a sheet of snow,
Refuses food to fowl, to bird, and beast: 10
    The chilling cold lets every thing to grow,
And surfeits cattle with a starving feast.
    Curs'd be that love and mought‡ continue short,
    Which kills all creatures, and doth spoil our sport.

---

* Saturn.   † Janus.   ‡ *i.e.* may it.

VI.

K. JOHN AND THE ABBOT OF CANTERBURY.

HE common popular ballad of *King John and the Abbot* seems to have been abridged and modernized about the time of James I. from one much older, intitled, *King John and the Bishop of Canterbury.* The Editor's folio MS. contains a copy of this last, but in too corrupt a state to be reprinted; it however afforded many lines worth reviving, which will be found inserted in the ensuing stanzas.

The archness of the following questions and answers hath been much admired by our old ballad-makers; for besides the two copies above mentioned, there is extant another ballad on the same subject (but of no great antiquity or merit), intitled, *King Olfrey and the Abbot.** Lastly, about the time of the civil wars, when the cry ran against the Bishops, some Puritan worked up the same story into a very doleful ditty, to a solemn tune, concerning *King Henry and a Bishop*, with this stinging moral:

> "Unlearned men hard matters out can find,
> When learned bishops princes eyes do blind."

[All the copies of this ballad are of late date, but Mr. Chappell says that the story upon which it is founded can be traced back to the fifteenth century, and Dr. Rimbault so traces it to the *Adventures of Howleglas*, printed in the Lower Saxon dialect in 1483. Wynkyn de Worde printed in 1511 a collection of riddles translated from the French, with the title *Demaundes Joyous*, which are like those propounded by King John to the Abbot. Prof. Child points out that by this link the ballad is connected with a tolerably large literature of wit combats of the middle ages. (See *English and Scottish Ballads*, vol. viii. p. 3.)

Copies of the puritan ballad referred to above are in the Pepys, Douce, and Roxburghe collections. It commences as follows—

---

* See the collection of *Hist. Ballads*, 3 vols. 1727. Mr. Wise supposes *Olfrey* to be a corruption of *Alfred*, in his pamphlet concerning the *White Horse* in Berkshire, p. 15.

" In Popish times, when bishops proud
  In England did bear sway,
Their lordships did like princes live,
  And kept all at obey."

The ballad entitled *King John and Bishoppe*, in the folio MS. to which Percy refers, is printed at the end of the following ballad.]

*The following is chiefly printed from an ancient black-letter copy, to
  " The tune of Derry down."*

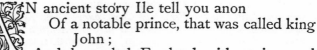N ancient story Ile tell you anon
        Of a notable prince, that was called king
          John ;
       And he ruled England with maine and
          with might,
For he did great wrong, and maintein'd little right.

And Ile tell you a story, a story so merrye,   5
Concerning the Abbot of Canterbùrye ;
How for his house-keeping, and high renowne,
They rode poste for him to fair London towne.

An hundred men, the king did heare say,
The abbot kept in his house every day ;   10
And fifty golde chaynes, without any doubt,
In velvet coates waited the abbot about.

How now, father abbot, I heare it of thee,
Thou keepest a farre better house than mee,
And for thy house-keeping and high renowne,   15
I feare thou work'st treason against my crown.

My liege, quo' the abbot, I would it were knowne,
I never spend nothing, but what is my owne ;
And I trust, your grace will doe me no deere,[1]
For spending of my owne true-gotten geere.   20

[1 harm.]

Yes, yes, father abbot, thy fault it is highe,
And now for the same thou needest must dye;
For except thou canst answer me questions three,
Thy head shall be smitten from thy bodie.

And first, quo' the king, when I'm in this stead,   25
With my crowne of golde so faire on my head,
Among all my liege-men so noble of birthe,
Thou must tell me to one penny what I am worthe.

Secondlye, tell me, without any doubt,
How soone I may ride the whole worlde about.   30
And at the third question thou must not shrink,
But tell me here truly what I do think.

O, these are hard questions for my shallow witt,
Nor I cannot answer your grace as yet:
But if you will give me but three weekes space,   35
Ile do my endeavour to answer your grace.

Now three weeks space to thee will I give,
And that is the longest time thou hast to live;
For if thou dost not answer my questions three,
Thy lands and thy livings are forfeit to mee.   40

Away rode the abbot all sad at that word,
And he rode to Cambridge, and Oxenford;
But never a doctor there was so wise,
That could with his learning an answer devise.

Then home rode the abbot of comfort so cold,   45
And he mett his shepheard a going to fold:
How now, my lord abbot, you are welcome home;
What newes do you bring us from good king John?

" Sad newes, sad newes, shepheard, I must give;
That I have but three days more to live: 50
For if I do not answer him questions three,
My head will be smitten from my bodie.

The first is to tell him there in that stead,
With his crowne of golde so fair on his head,
Among all his liege men so noble of birth,   55
To within one penny of what he is worth.

The seconde, to tell him, without any doubt,
How soone he may ride this whole world about:
And at the third question I must not shrinke,
But tell him there truly what he does thinke."   60

Now cheare up, sire abbot, did you never hear yet,
That a fool he may learn a wise man witt?
Lend me horse, and serving men, and your apparel,
And I'll ride to London to answere your quarrel.

Nay frowne not, if it hath bin told unto mee,   65
I am like your lordship, as ever may bee:
And if you will but lend me your gowne,
There is none shall knowe us at fair London towne.

"Now horses, and serving-men thou shalt have,
With sumptuous array most gallant and brave;   70
With crozier, and miter, and rochet, and cope,
Fit to appeare 'fore our fader the pope."

Now welcome, sire abbot, the king he did say,
Tis well thou'rt come back to keepe thy day;
For and if thou canst answer my questions three,   75
Thy life and thy living both saved shall bee.

And first, when thou seest me here in this stead,
With my crown of golde so fair on my head,
Among all my liege-men so noble of birthe,
Tell me to one penny what I am worth.   80

" For thirty pence our Saviour was sold
Amonge the false Jewes, as I have bin told;
And twenty nine is the worth of thee,
For I thinke, thou art one penny worser than hee."

The king he laughed, and swore by St. Bittel*,   85
I did not think I had been worth so littel!
—Now secondly tell me, without any doubt,
How soone I may ride this whole world about.

" You must rise with the sun, and ride with the same,
Until the next morning he riseth againe ;   90
And then your grace need not make any doubt,
But in twenty-four hours you'll ride it about."

The king he laughed, and swore by St. Jone,
I did not think, it could be gone so soone!
—Now from the third question thou must not shrinke,
But tell me here truly what I do thinke.   96

" Yea, that shall I do, and make your grace merry :
You thinke I'm the abbot of Canterbùry ;
But I'm his poor shepheard, as plain you may see,
That am come to beg pardon for him and for mee."

The king he laughed, and swore by the masse,   101
Ile make thee lord abbot this day in his place!
" Now naye, my liege, be not in such speede,
For alacke I can neither write, ne reade."

Four nobles a weeke, then I will give thee,   105
For this merry jest thou hast showne unto mee ;
And tell the old abbot when thou comest home,
Thou hast brought him a pardon from good king John.

*_**

---

* Meaning probably St. Botolph.

HE following version is reprinted from Hales and Furnivall's edition of the Percy Folio, vol. i. p. 508.

Off an ancient story Ile tell you anon,
of a notable prince that was called King Iohn,
in England was borne, with maine and with might
hee did much wrong, and mainteined litle right.   4

this noble prince was vexed in veretye,
for he was angry with the bishopp of canterbury
ffor his house-keeping and his good cheere,
the rode post for him, as you shall heare;   8

they rode post for him very hastilye;
the King sayd the bishopp kept a better house then hee;
a 100 men euen, as I say,
the Bishopp kept in his house euerye day,   12

and 50 gold chaines without any doubt,
in veluett coates waited the Bishopp about.
the Bishopp, he came to the court anon
before his prince that was called King Iohn.   1

as soone as the Bishopp the King did see,
" O," quoth the King, "Bishopp, thou art welcome to mee!
there is noe man soe welcome to towne
as thou that workes treason against my crowne."   20

" My leege," quoth the Bishopp, "I wold it were knowne;
I spend, your grace, nothing but that thats my owne;
I trust your grace will doe me noe deare
for spending my owne trew gotten geere."   24

" Yes," quoth the King, " Bishopp, thou must needs dye:
eccept thou can answere mee questions 3,
thy head shalbe smitten quite from thy bodye,
and all thy liuing remayne vnto mee.   28

" first," quoth the King, " tell me in this steade,
with this crowne of gold heere vpon my head,
amongst my Nobilitye with Ioy and much Mirth,
lett me know within one pennye what I am worth: 32

Secondlye, tell me without any dowbt
how soone I may goe the whole world about:

and thirdly, tell mee or euer I stinte,
what is the thing, Bishopp, that I doe thinke.   36
20 dayes pardon thoust haue trulye,
and come againe and answere mee."

the Bishopp bade the King 'god night' att a word.
he rode betwixt Cambridge and Oxenford,   40
but neuer a Doctor there was soe wise
cold shew him these questions or enterprise;

wherewith the Bishopp was nothing gladd,
but in his hart was heauy and sadd,   44
and hyed him home to a house in the countrye
To ease some part of his Melanchollye.

his halfe brother dwelt there, was feirce & fell,
noe better but a shepard to the Bishoppe him-sell;   48
the shepard came to the Bishopp anon,
saying, "my Lord, you are welcome home!

what ayles you," quoth the shepard, "that you are soe sadd,
and had wonte to haue beene soe merry & gladd?"   52
"Nothing," quoth the Bishopp, "I ayle att this time,
will not thee availe to know, Brother mine."

"Brother," quoth the Shepeard, "you haue heard itt,
that a ffoole may teach a wisemane witt;   56
say me therfore what-soeuer you will,
and if I doe you noe good, Ile doe you noe ill."

Quoth the Bishop: "I have beene att thy court anon,
before my prince is called King Iohn,   60
and there he hath charged mee
against his crowne with traitorye;

if I cannot answer his misterye,
3 questions hee hath propounded to mee,   64
he will haue my Land soe faire and free,
and alsoe the head from my bodye.

the first question was, 'to tell him in that stead
with the crowne of gold vpon his head,   68
amongst his nobilitye with Ioy & much mirth,
to lett him know within one penye what hee is worth;'

and secondlye 'to tell him with-out any doubt
how soone he may goe the whole world about;'   72
and thirdlye, 'to tell him, or ere I stint,
what is the thing that he does thinke.'"

"Brother," quoth the shepard, "you are a man of Learninge;
what neede you stand in doubt of soe small a thinge?   76
lend me," quoth the shepard, " your ministers apparrell,
Ile ryde to the court and answere your quarrell;

lend me your serving men, say me not nay;
with all your best horsses that ryd on the way,   80
Ile to the court, this matter to stay;
Ile speake with King Iohn & heare what heele say."

the Bishopp with speed prepared then
to sett forth the shepard with horsse and man;   84
the shepard was liuely with-out any doubt;
I wott a royall companye came to the court.

the shepard hee came to the court anon
before (his) prince that was called King Iohn.   88
as soone as the king the shepard did see,
"O," quoth the king, " Bishopp, thou art welcome to me!"

the shepard was soe like the Bishopp his brother,
the King cold not know the one from the other.   92
Quoth the King, "Bishopp, thou art welcome to me
if thou can answer me my questions 3!"

said the shepeard, " if it please your grace,
show mee what the first quest[i]on was."   96
"first" quoth the king, "tell mee in this stead
with the crowne of gold vpon my head,

amongst my nobilitye with Ioy and much mirth,
within one pennye what I am worth."   100
Quoth the shepard, " to make your grace noe offence,
I thinke you are worth 29 pence;

for our Lord Iesus, that bought vs all,
for 30 pence was sold into thrall   104
amongst the cursed Iewes, as I to you doe showe;
but I know christ was one penye better then you."

then the King laught, and swore by St Andrew
he was not thought to bee of such a small value.   108
' Secondlye, tell mee with-out any doubt
how soone I may goe the world round about,"

saies the shepard, " it is noe time with your grace to scorne;
but rise betime with the sun in the morne,   112
and follow his course till his vprising,
and then you may know with-out any Leasing—

and this your grace shall proue the same—
you are come to the same place from whence you came;   116
24 houres, with-out any doubt,
your grace may the world goe round about;

the world round about, euen as I doe say,
if with the sun you can goe the next way."   120
" and thirdlye tell me or euer I stint,
what is the thing, Bishoppe, that I doe thinke."

" that shall I doe," quoth the shepeard, " for veretye
you thinke I am the Bishopp of Canterburye,"   124
" why? art not thou? the truth tell to me;
for I doe thinke soe," quoth the king, " by St. Marye."

" not soe," quoth the shepeard ; " the truth shalbe knowne,
I am his poore shepeard ; my brother is att home."   128
" why," quoth the King, " if itt soe bee,
Ile make thee Bishopp here to mee."

" Noe Sir " quoth the shepard, " I pray you be still,
for Ile not bee Bishop but against my will;   132
for I am not fitt for any such deede,
for I can neither write nor reede."

" why then," quoth the king, " Ile giue thee cleere
a patten of 300 pound a yeere ;   136
that I will giue thee franke and free ;
take thee that, shepard, for coming to me :

free pardon Ile giue," the kings grace said,
" to saue the Bishopp, his land and his head ;   140
with him nor thee Ile be nothing wrath ;
here is the pardon for him and thee both."

then the shepard he had noe more to say,
but tooke the pardon and rode his way.   144
when he came to the Bishopps place,
the Bishopp asket anon how all things was :

" Brother," quoth the Shepard, " I haue well sped,
for I haue saued both your Land & your head ;   148
the King with you is nothing wrath,
for heere is the pardon for you and mee both."

then the Bishopes hart was of a merry cheere,
" brother, thy paines Ile quitt them cleare,   152
for I will giue thee a patent to thee & to thine
of 50 li. a yeere land good and fine."

" I will to thee noe longer croche nor creepe,
nor Ile serue thee noe more to keepe thy sheepe."   56
whereeuer wist you shepard before,
that had in his head witt such store

to pleasure a Bishopp in such a like case,
to answer 3 questions to the Kings grace?   60
whereeuer wist you shepard gett cleare
350 ⁰ pound a yeere?

I neuer hard of his fellow before,
nor I neuer shall. now I need to say noe more: 64
I neuer knew shepeard that gott such a liuinge
But David the shepeard that was a King.

                                        ffins.]

VII.

YOU MEANER BEAUTIES.

HIS little Sonnet was written by Sir *Henry Wotton,*
Knight, on that amiable Princess, Elizabeth daughter
of James I. and wife of the Elector Palatine, who
was chosen King of Bohemia, Sept. 5, 1619.   The
consequences of this fatal election are well known : Sir Henry
Wotton, who in that and the following year was employed in
several embassies in Germany on behalf of this unfortunate lady,
seems to have had an uncommon attachment to her merit and
fortunes, for he gave away a jewel worth a thousand pounds, that
was presented to him by the Emperor, " because it came from an
enemy to his royal mistress the Queen of Bohemia."   See *Biog.
Britan.*
    This song is printed from the *Reliquiæ Wottonianæ,* 1651, with
some corrections from an old MS. copy.

[This elegant little poem in praise of the Queen of Bohemia
(who was called by those who knew her and were won by her
sweetness, spirit, wit, and unselfishness—the Queen of Hearts) has
been very frequently reprinted.   The unfortunate princess was
also named the *Snow Queen* and her husband the *Winter King,*
in allusion to the fact that their reign at Prague only lasted one
winter.   The poem first appeared, according to Dr. Rimbault, in
" The Sixt Set of Bookes, wherein are Anthemes for Versus and

Chorus of 5 and 6 Parts; apt for Violls and Voyces: newly composed by Michaell Est, Bachelor of Musicke, and Master of the
Choristers of the Cathedrall Church in Litchfield," London, 1624,
4to. It is printed in *Wit's Recreations,* 1640, and *Wit's Inter-
preter,* 1671, and in "Songs and Fancies to severall Musicall parts,
both apt for Voices and Viols," Aberdeen, 1682. Alterations
were made in the various copies, and in the latter book a wretched
second part, quite out of harmony with the original, was added.
It has found its way, with some variations, among Montrose's poems
(see Napier's *Life of Montrose,* 1856, *Appendix,* p. xl.), and Robert
Chambers (ignorant of the Englishman Sir Henry Wotton's claim
to the authorship) actually printed it in his *Scottish Songs* (vol. ii.
p. 631) as if "written by Darnley in praise of the beauty of Queen
Mary before their marriage."

Percy, while copying from the *Reliquiæ Wottonianæ,* 1651,
transposed stanzas 2 and 3. In Abp. Sancroft's MS. (Tanner, 465,
fol. 43) the following verses occur as stanzas 4 and 6 of the whole
poem :—

> " You rubies, that do gems adorn,
>   And sapphires with your azure hue
> Like to the skies, or blushing morn,
>   How pale's your brightness in our view
>   When diamonds are mixed with you.

> " The rose, the violet, all the spring
>   Unto her breath, for sweetness run;
> The diamond's dark'ned in the ring
>   If she appear, the moon's undone,
>   As in the presence of the Sun."]

OU meaner beauties of the night,
   That poorly satisfie our eies
More by your number, than your light ;
   You common people of the skies,
   What are you when the Moon shall rise ?   5

Ye violets that first appeare,
   By your pure purple mantles known
Like the proud virgins of the yeare,
   As if the Spring were all your own ;
   What are you when the Rose is blown?   10

Ye curious chaunters of the wood,
   That warble forth dame Nature's layes,
Thinking your passions understood
   By your weak accents : what's your praise,
   When Philomell her voyce shall raise ?   15

So when my mistris shal be seene
   In sweetnesse of her looks and minde ;
By virtue first, then choyce a queen ;
   Tell me, if she was not design'd
   Th' eclipse and glory of her kind ?   20

VIII.

THE OLD AND YOUNG COURTIER.

THIS excellent old song, the subject of which is a comparison between the manners of the old gentry, as still subsisting in the times of Elizabeth, and the modern refinements affected by their sons in the reigns of her successors, is given, with corrections, from an ancient black-letter copy in the Pepys collection, compared with another printed among some miscellaneous " poems and songs" in a book intitled, *Le Prince d'amour*, or *The Prince of Love*, 1660, 8vo.

[This was one of the most popular of old songs, and Dr. King in his Preface to the *Art of Cookery* places it by the side of *Chevy Chase* as one of the ballads to be hung up over the carved mantel-piece in the homes of old British hospitality. It is to be found in broadside in nearly all the collections, and appears to have been printed for the first time in the reign of James I. by T. Symcocke. Pepys notices it in his *Diary* under the date 16th June, 1668— " Come to Newbery, and there dined—and musick : a song of the old Courtier of Queen Elizabeth's, and how he was changed upon the coming in of the King, did please me mightily, and I did cause W. Hewer to write it out."

The song was parodied and altered into many forms. About the middle of the last century it was revived and sung by Mr. Vernon in Shadwell's comedy, *The Squire of Alsatia*, with a new burden, "moderation and alteration," and finally it has been again revived in the present century, with still greater alterations, under the title of *The Old English Gentleman*.

Mr. Chappell has the following note on the object of the song :— "Southey remarks very justly on the complaints of the decay of hospitality, that ' while rents were received in kind they must have been chiefly consumed in kind ; at least there could be no accumulation of disposable wealth.' He supposes this mode of payment to have fallen generally into disuse during the reign of James I. Without doubt, many of the poor would feel the change." *Popular Music of the Olden Time*, vol. ii. p. 778.]

N old song made by an aged old pate,
  Of an old worshipful gentleman, who had
   a greate estate,
  That kept a brave old house at a bountiful
   rate,
And an old porter to relieve the poor at his gate ;
  Like an old courtier of the queen's,
  And the queen's old courtier.

With an old lady, whose anger one word asswages ;
They every quarter paid their old servants their wages,
And never knew what belong'd to coachmen, foot-
  men, nor pages,
But kept twenty old fellows with blue coats and
  badges ;
  Like an old courtier, &c.

With an old study fill'd full of learned old books,
With an old reverend chaplain, you might know him
  by his looks.
With an old buttery hatch worn quite off the hooks,
And an old kitchen, that maintain'd half a dozen old
  cooks :
  Like an old courtier, &c.

With an old hall, hung about with pikes, guns, and
    bows,
With old swords, and bucklers, that had borne many
    shrewde blows,
And an old frize coat, to cover his worship's trunk
    hose,
And a cup of old sherry, to comfort his copper nose ;
        Like an old courtier, &c.

With a good old fashion, when Christmasse was come,
To call in all his old neighbours with bagpipe and
    drum,
With good chear enough to furnish every old room,
And old liquor able to make a cat speak, and man
    dumb,
        Like an old courtier, &c.

With an old falconer, huntsman, and a kennel of
    hounds,
That never hawked, nor hunted, but in his own
    grounds,
Who, like a wise man, kept himself within his own
    bounds,
And when he dyed gave every child a thousand good
    pounds ;
        Like an old courtier, &c.

But to his eldest son his house and land he assign'd,
Charging him in his will to keep the old bountifull
    mind,
To be good to his old tenants, and to his neighbours
    be kind :
But in the ensuing ditty you shall hear how he was
    inclin'd ;
        Like a young courtier of the king's,
        And the king's young courtier.

Like a flourishing young gallant, newly come to his
    land,
Who keeps a brace of painted madams at his com-
    mand,
And takes up a thousand pound upon his father's land,
And gets drunk in a tavern, till he can neither go nor
    stand;
        Like a young courtier, &c.

With a new-fangled lady, that is dainty, nice, and spare,
Who never knew what belong'd to good house-keep-
    ing, or care,
Who buyes gaudy-color'd fans to play with wanton air,
And seven or eight different dressings of other
    womens hair;
        Like a young courtier, &c.

With a new-fashion'd hall, built where the old one
    stood,
Hung round with new pictures, that do the poor no
    good,
With a fine marble chimney, wherein burns neither
    coal nor wood,
And a new smooth shovelboard, whereon no victuals
    ne'er stood;
        Like a young courtier, &c.

With a new study, stuft full of pamphlets, and plays,
And a new chaplain, that swears faster than he prays,
With a new buttery hatch, that opens once in four or
    five days,
And a new French cook, to devise fine kickshaws,
    and toys;
        Like a young courtier, &c.

With a new fashion, when Christmas is drawing on,
On a new journey to London straight we all must
    begone,

And leave none to keep house, but our new porter
John,
Who relieves the poor with a thump on the back with
a stone ;
    Like a young courtier, &c.

With a new gentleman-usher, whose carriage is compleat,
With a new coachman, footmen, and pages to carry
up the meat,
With a waiting-gentlewoman, whose dressing is very
neat,
Who when her lady has din'd, lets the servants not
eat ;
    Like a young courtier, &c.

With new titles of honour bought with his father's
old gold,
For which sundry of his ancestors old manors are
sold ;
And this is the course most of our new gallants hold,
Which makes that good house-keeping is now grown
so cold,
    Among the young courtiers of the king,
    Or the king's young courtiers.

                                          ⁎

IX.

SIR JOHN SUCKLING'S CAMPAIGNE.

WHEN the Scottish covenanters rose up in arms, and
advanced to the English borders in 1639, many of
the courtiers complimented the king by raising forces
at their own expence.   Among these none were more
distinguished than the gallant Sir John Suckling, who raised a
troop of horse, so richly accoutred, that it cost him £12,000.
The like expensive equipment of other parts of the army, made

the king remark, that "the Scots would fight stoutly, if it were but for the Englishmen's fine cloaths." (Lloyd's *Memoirs*.) When they came to action, the rugged Scots proved more than a match for the fine shewy English: many of whom behaved remarkably ill, and among the rest this splendid troop of Sir John Suckling's.

This humorous pasquil has been generally supposed to have been written by Sir John, as a banter upon himself. Some of his contemporaries however attributed it to Sir John Mennis, a wit of those times, among whose poems it is printed in a small poetical miscellany, intitled, *Musarum deliciæ: or the Muses recreation, containing several pieces of poetique wit*, 2d edition.—By Sir J. M. (*Sir John Mennis*) and Ja. S. (*James Smith*.) Lond. 1656, 12mo.— (See Wood's *Athenæ*. ii. 397, 418.) In that copy is subjoined an additional stanza, which probably was written by this Sir John Mennis, viz.:—

> " But now there is peace, he's return'd to increase
>   His money, which lately he spent-a,
> But his lost honour must lye still in the dust ;
>   At Barwick away it went-a."

[This song is a parody of the famous old song, *John Dory*, commencing:—
> " As it fell on a holiday
>   And upon a holytide-a
> John Dory bought him an ambling nag
>   To Paris for to ride-a."

Suckling's satirical powers made him peculiarly odious to the Parliamentarians, as they were turned against them, and consequently Mennis's lampoon was a great favourite with the Roundheads. In *Le Prince d'Amour*, 1660, there is a song *Upon Sir John Suckling's* 100 *Horse*, and the following are two of the seven stanzas of which it consists:—

> " I tell thee, Jack, thou gav'st the king
> So rare a present, that nothing
>   Could welcomer have been ;
> A hundred horse! beshrew my heart,
> It was a brave heroic part,
>   The like will scarce be seen.

> " For ev'ry horse shall have on's back
> A man as valiant as Sir Jack,
>   Although not half so witty :
> Yet I did hear the other day
> Two tailors made seven run away
>   Good faith, the more's the pity."

The uniform adopted by Suckling for his troop consisted of a white doublet, and scarlet coat and breeches, with a scarlet feather in the bonnet. The men were vigorous, well mounted and armed, and these famous 100 horsemen were considered to be the finest sight in his majesty's army. Mr. W. C. Hazlitt points out that the earliest news of them appears to be in a letter of Jan. 29, 1638-9, from the Earl of Northumberland to Lord Conway, in which the writer speaks of Suckling having then engaged himself to raise the troop "within these three days." (*Calendar of State Papers (Domestic,*) 1638-9, p. 378.) The army was badly commanded, and no greater disgrace attached to Suckling's troop than to the rest.]

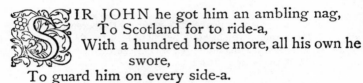IR JOHN he got him an ambling nag,
    To Scotland for to ride-a,
    With a hundred horse more, all his own he
        swore,
  To guard him on every side-a.

No Errant-knight ever went to fight   5
  With halfe so gay a bravada,
Had you seen but his look, you'ld have sworn on a
    book,
  Hee'ld have conquer'd a whole armada.

The ladies ran all to the windows to see
  So gallant and warlike a sight-a,   10
And as he pass'd by, they said with a sigh,
  Sir John, why will you go fight-a?

But he, like a cruel knight, spurr'd on;
  His heart would not relent-a,
For, till he came there, what had he to fear?   15
  Or why should he repent-a?

The king (God bless him!) had singular hopes
  Of him and all his troop-a:
The borderers they, as they met him on the way,
  For joy did hollow, and whoop-a.   20

None lik'd him so well, as his own colonell,
Who took him for John de Wert-a;
But when there were shows of gunning and blows,
My gallant was nothing so pert-a.

For when the Scots army came within sight, 25
And all prepared to fight-a,
He ran to his tent, they ask'd what he meant,
He swore he must needs goe sh*te-a.

The colonell sent for him back agen,
To quarter him in the van-a, 30
But Sir John did swear, he would not come there,
To be kill'd the very first man-a.

To cure his fear, he was sent to the reare,
Some ten miles back, and more-a;
Where Sir John did play at trip and away, 35
And ne'er saw the enemy more-a.

X.

TO ALTHEA FROM PRISON.

HIS excellent sonnet, which possessed a high degree of fame among the old Cavaliers, was written by Colone, Richard Lovelace during his confinement in the gate, house, Westminster : to which he was committed by the House of Commons, in April 1642, for presenting a petition from the county of Kent, requesting them to restore the king to his rights, and to settle the government. See Wood's *Athenæ*, vol. ii. p. 228, and Lysons' *Environs of London*, vol. i. p. 109 ; where may be seen at large the affecting story of this elegant writer, who after

---

Ver. 22. *John de Wert* was a German general of great reputation, and the terror of the French in the reign of Louis XIII. Hence his name became proverbial in France, where he was called *De Vert*. See Bayle's *Dict*.

having been distinguished for every gallant and polite accomplishment, the pattern of his own sex, and the darling of the ladies, died in the lowest wretchedness, obscurity, and want, in 1658.

This song is printed from a scarce volume of his poems intitled, *Lucasta*, 1649, 12mo. collated with a copy in the Editor's folio MS.

[As Percy mentions, the folio MS. collations have been added from it (ed. Hales and Furnivall, vol. ii. p. 17), but it will at once be seen that they are of little value. The music to this most exquisite of prison songs was composed by the celebrated Dr. John Wilson, and first printed (according to Dr. Rimbault) in his *Cheerful Ayres or Ballads set for three Voices*, Oxford, 1660.

Lucasta (= Lux casta, Lucy Sacheverell), misled by a report that Lovelace had died of his wounds received at Dunkirk while commanding a regiment of his own forming in the service of the French king, married another lover.

Although doubtless Lovelace died in great trouble, we may hope that Wood's account of his extreme poverty is exaggerated, for his daughter and sole heir married the son of Lord Chief Justice Coke, and brought to her husband the estates of her father at Kingsdown in Kent.]

HEN love with unconfined wings
    Hovers within my gates,
  And my divine Althea brings
    To whisper at my grates ;
When I lye tangled in her haire,   5
  And fetter'd with her eye,
The birds that wanton in the aire,
  Know no such libertye.

When flowing cups run swiftly round
  With no allaying Thames,   10
Our carelesse heads with roses crown'd,
  Our hearts with loyal flames ;

[Ver. 8, 16, 24. enjoyes such lybertye, MS.] V. 10. with woe-allaying theames, MS. Thames is here used for water in general.

When thirsty griefe in wine we steepe,
  When healths and draughts goe free,
Fishes, that tipple in the deepe,   15
  Know no such libertìe.

When, linnet-like, confined I
  With shriller note shall sing
The mercye, sweetness, majestye,
  And glories of my king;   20
When I shall voyce aloud how good
  He is, how great should be,
Th' enlarged windes, that curle the flood,
  Know no such libertìe.

Stone walls doe not a prison make,   25
  Nor iron barres a cage,
Mindes, innocent, and quiet, take
  That for an hermitage:
If I have freedom in my love,
  And in my soule am free,   30
Angels alone, that soare above,
  Enjoy such libertìe.

XI.

THE DOWNFALL OF CHARING-CROSS.

HARING-CROSS, as it stood before the civil wars, was one of those beautiful Gothic obelisks erected to conjugal affection by Edward I., who built such a one wherever the herse of his beloved Eleanor rested in its way from Lincolnshire to Westminster. But neither its ornamental situation, the beauty of its structure, nor the noble design

[Ver. 13. thirsty soules, MS. V. 14. when cupps and bowles goe free. V. 19. the mercy, goodnesse, maiestye. V. 20. glory. V. 23. curles the floods. V. 27. the spotlesse soule and inocent. V. 28. Calls this an. V. 31. sores. V. 32. enjoyes. The second and third stanzas are transposed in the MS.]

of its erection (which did honour to humanity), could preserve it from the merciless zeal of the times: For, in 1647, it was demolished by order of the House of Commons, as popish and superstitious.   This occasioned the following not unhumorous sarcasm, which has been often printed among the popular sonnets of those times.

The plot referred to in ver. 17, was that entered into by Mr. Waller the poet, and others, with a view to reduce the city and tower to the service of the king ; for which two of them, Nath. Tomkins and Rich. Chaloner, suffered death July 5, 1643.   Vid. *Ath. Ox.* ii. 24.

Whitlocke says, " May 3, 1643, Cheapside cross and other crosses were voted down," &c.—But this Vote was not put in execution with regard to *Charing Cross* till four years after, as appears from Lilly's *Observations on the Life, &c. of K. Charles,* viz. " Charing-Cross, we know, was pulled down, 1647, in June, July, and August.   Part of the Stones were converted to pave before Whitehall.   I have seen Knife-hafts made of some of the stones, which, being well-polished, looked like marble." Ed. 1715, p. 18, 12mo.

[In Laud's *Diary* it is written, " 1643 Maii 2 Tuesday The cross in Cheapside taken down."]

See an Account of the pulling down Cheapside Cross, in the Supplement to *Gent. Mag.* 1764.

[Charing Cross was the largest and most beautiful of the series of Eleanor crosses, and the architects employed in the construction of it were paid £450.   The work was formerly attributed to Cavalini, but that artist was not born until the year 1279, and was therefore about eleven years old when the Queen died.   Since the publication of the very interesting rolls of payments made by the executors of Queen Eleanor (*Manners and Household Expenses of England in the 13th and 15th centuries.* Roxburghe Club, 1841), it has been known that Charing Cross was commenced by Richard de Crundale and completed, after his death, by Roger de Crundale.

The site of the old cross was made use of as a place of execution, and several of the regicides were put to death there.

The Cheapside cross, which was taken down in 1643, was the third which occupied the site, and it had only been erected in 1600. The original cross was found to be in a bad condition in 1441, and a new one was therefore commenced, which was not finished until 1486.   This was replaced in 1600 by the third cross.

Dr. Rimbault informs us that this ballad is printed with the music for three voices by " Mr. F. Farmeloe " in " The Second Book of the *Pleasant Musical Companion*," 1687.]

NDONE, undone the lawyers are,
 They wander about the towne,
 Nor can find the way to Westminster,
  Now Charing-cross is downe :
At the end of the Strand, they make a stand,   5
 Swearing they are at a loss,
And chaffing say, that's not the way,
 They must go by Charing-cross.

The parliament to vote it down
 Conceived it very fitting,   10
For fear it should fall, and kill them all,
 In the house, as they were sitting.
They were told god-wot, it had a plot,
 Which made them so hard-hearted,
To give command, it should not stand,   15
 But be taken down and carted.

Men talk of plots, this might have been worse
 For any thing I know,
Than that Tomkins, and Chaloner,
 Were hang'd for long agoe.   20
Our parliament did that prevent,
 And wisely them defended,
For plots they will discover still,
 Before they were intended.

But neither man, woman, nor child,   25
 Will say, I'm confident,
They ever heard it speak one word
 Against the parliament.
An informer swore, it letters bore,
 Or else it had been freed ;   30
I'll take, in troth, my Bible oath,
 It could neither write, nor read.

The committee said, that verily
    To popery it was bent;
For ought I know, it might be so,   35
    For to church it never went.
What with excise, and such device,
    The kingdom doth begin
To think you'll leave them ne'er a cross,
    Without doors nor within.   40

Methinks the common-council shou'd
    Of it have taken pity,
'Cause, good old cross, it always stood
    So firmly to the city.
Since crosses you so much disdain,   45
    Faith, if I were as you,
For fear the king should rule again,
    I'd pull down Tiburn too.

XII.

LOYALTY CONFINED.

HIS excellent old song is preserved in David Lloyd's *Memoires of those that suffered in the cause of Charles I.* Lond. 1668, fol. p. 96. He speaks of it as the composition of a worthy personage, who suffered deeply in those times, and was still living with no other reward than the conscience of having suffered. The author's name he has not mentioned, but, if tradition may be credited, this song was written by Sir *Roger L'Estrange.*—Some mistakes in Lloyd's copy are corrected by two others, one in MS. the other in the *Westminster Drollery, or a choice Collection of Songs and Poems,* 1671, 12mo.

[The ascription of this song to L'Estrange is improbable, and we must therefore seek elsewhere for an author.]

EAT on, proud billows; Boreas blow;
    Swell, curled waves, high as Jove's
       roof;
    Your incivility doth show,
  That innocence is tempest proof;
Though surly Nereus frown, my thoughts are calm; 5
Then strike, Affliction, for thy wounds are balm.

  That which the world miscalls a jail,
    A private closet is to me:
  Whilst a good conscience is my bail,
    And innocence my liberty: 10
Locks, bars, and solitude, together met,
Make me no prisoner, but an anchoret.

  I, whilst I wisht to be retir'd,
    Into this private room was turn'd;
  As if their wisdoms had conspir'd   15
    The salamander should be burn'd;
Or like those sophists, that would drown a fish,
I am constrain'd to suffer what I wish.

  The cynick loves his poverty;
    The pelican her wilderness;   20
  And 'tis the Indian's pride to be
    Naked on frozen Caucasus:
Contentment cannot smart, Stoicks we see
Make torments easie to their apathy.

  These manacles upon my arm   25
    I, as my mistress' favours, wear;
  And for to keep my ancles warm,
    I have some iron shackles there:
These walls are but my garrison; this cell,
Which men call jail, doth prove my citadel.   30

I'm in the cabinet lockt up,
   Like some high-prized margarite,[1]
Or, like the great mogul or pope,
   Am cloyster'd up from publick sight :
Retiredness is a piece of majesty,   35
And thus, proud sultan, I'm as great as thee.

Here sin for want of food must starve,
   Where tempting objects are not seen ;
And these strong walls do only serve
   To keep vice out, and keep me in :   40
Malice of late's grown charitable sure,
I'm not committed, but am kept secure.

So he that struck at Jason's life,*
   Thinking t' have made his purpose sure,
By a malicious friendly knife   45
   Did only wound him to a cure :
Malice, I see, wants wit ; for what is meant
Mischief, oft-times proves favour by th' event.

When once my prince affliction hath,
   Prosperity doth treason seem ;   50
And to make smooth so rough a path,
   I can learn patience from him :
Now not to suffer shews no loyal heart,
When kings want ease subjects must bear a part.

What though I cannot see my king   55
   Neither in person or in coin ;
Yet contemplation is a thing
   That renders what I have not, mine ;
My king from me what adamant can part,
Whom I do wear engraven on my heart ?   60

---

* See this remarkable story in *Cicero de Nat. Deorum*, lib. 3,
c. 28. *Cic. de Offic.* lib. 1, c. 30 ; see also *Val. Max.* 1, 8.

[1 pearl.]

Have you not seen the nightingale,
  A prisoner like, coopt in a cage,
How doth she chaunt her wonted tale
  In that her narrow hermitage ?
Even then her charming melody doth prove,   65
That all her bars are trees, her cage a grove.

I am that bird, whom they combine
  Thus to deprive of liberty ;
But though they do my corps confine,
  Yet maugre hate, my soul is free :   70
And though immur'd, yet can I chirp, and sing
Disgrace to rebels, glory to my king.

My soul is free, as ambient air,
  Although my baser part's immew'd,
Whilst loyal thoughts do still repair   75
  T' accompany my solitude :
Although rebellion do my body binde,
My king alone can captivate my minde.

XIII.

VERSES BY K. CHARLES I.

"THIS prince, like his father, did not confine himself to prose: Bishop Burnet has given us a pathetic elegy, said to be written by Charles in Carisbrook castle (in 1648). The poetry is most uncouth and unharmonious, but there are strong thoughts in it, some good sense, and a strain of majestic piety." Mr. Walpole's *Royal and Noble Authors*, vol. i.

It is in his *Memoirs of the Duke of Hamilton*, p. 379, that Burnet hath preserved this elegy, which he tells us he had from a gentleman, who waited on the king at the time when it was written, and copied it out from the original. It is there intitled, *Majesty in Misery: or An Imploration to the King of Kings.*

Hume hath remarked of these stanzas, " that the truth of the sentiment, rather than the elegance of the expression, renders them very pathetic." See his *Hist.* 1763, 4to. vol. v. pp. 437, 442, which is no bad comment upon them.—These are almost the only verses known of Charles's composition. Indeed a little Poem *On a quiet Conscience*, printed in the *Poetical Calendar*, 1763, vol. viii. is attributed to *K. Charles I.;* being reprinted from a thin 8vo. published by Nahum Tate, called *Miscellanea Sacra, or Poems on Divine and Moral Subjects.*

GREAT monarch of the world, from whose
   power springs
  The potency and power of kings,
  Record the royal woe my suffering sings ;

And teach my tongue, that ever did confine
Its faculties in truth's seraphick line,   5
To track the treasons of thy foes and mine.

Nature and law, by thy divine decree,
(The only root of righteous royaltie)
With this dim diadem invested me :

With it, the sacred scepter, purple robe,   10
The holy unction, and the royal globe :
Yet am I levell'd with the life of Job.

The fiercest furies, that do daily tread
Upon my grief, my grey discrowned head,
Are those that owe my bounty for their bread. 15

They raise a war, and christen it THE CAUSE,
While sacrilegious hands have best applause,
Plunder and murder are the kingdom's laws ;

Tyranny bears the title of taxation,
Revenge and robbery are reformation,   20
Oppression gains the name of sequestration.

My loyal subjects, who in this bad season
Attend me (by the law of God and reason),
They dare impeach, and punish for high treason.

Next at the clergy do their furies frown,   25
Pious episcopacy must go down,
They will destroy the crosier and the crown.

Churchmen are chain'd, and schismaticks are freed,
Mechanicks preach, and holy fathers bleed,
The crown is crucified with the creed.   30

The church of England doth all factions foster,
The pulpit is usurpt by each impostor,
Extempore excludes the *Paternoster*.

The Presbyter, and Independent seed
Springs with broad blades.   To make religion bleed
Herod and Pontius Pilate are agreed.   36

The corner stone's misplac'd by every pavier:
With such a bloody method and behaviour
Their ancestors did crucifie our Saviour.

My royal consort, from whose fruitful womb   40
So many princes legally have come,
Is forc'd in pilgrimage to seek a tomb.

Great Britain's heir is forced into France,
Whilst on his father's head his foes advance:
Poor child! he weeps out his inheritance.   45

With my own power my majesty they wound,
In the king's name the king himself's uncrown'd:
So doth the dust destroy the diamond.

With propositions daily they enchant
My people's ears, such as do reason daunt,   50
And the Almighty will not let me grant.

They promise to erect my royal stem,
To make me great, t' advance my diadem,
If I will first fall down, and worship them!

But for refusal they devour my thrones,　　　　55
Distress my children, and destroy my bones ;
I fear they'll force me to make bread of stones.

My life they prize at such a slender rate,
That in my absence they draw bills of hate,
To prove the king a traytor to the state.　　　　60

Felons obtain more privilege than I,
They are allow'd to answer ere they die ;
'Tis death for me to ask the reason, why.

But, sacred Saviour, with thy words I woo
Thee to forgive, and not be bitter to　　　　65
Such, as thou know'st do not know what they do.

For since they from their lord are so disjointed,
As to contemn those edicts he appointed,
How can they prize the power of his anointed ?

Augment my patience, nullifie my hate,　　　　70
Preserve my issue, and inspire my mate,
Yet, though we perish, BLESS THIS CHURCH and STATE.

XIV.

THE SALE OF REBELLIOUS
HOUSHOLD-STUFF.

THIS sarcastic exultation of triumphant loyalty, is printed
from an old black-letter copy in the Pepys collection,
corrected by two others, one of which is preserved in
A choice collection of 120 *loyal songs, &c.* 1684, 12mo.—
To the tune of *Old Simon the king.*

[This triumph over the downfall of the Rump Parliament is one
of the best of the numerous songs that were set to the favourite
tune of *Old Simon the King,* the full burden of which is—

" Says old Sir Symon the King,
Says old Sir Symon the King,
With his threadbare clothes
And his malmsey nose
Sing hey ding, ding a ding, ding."]

REBELLION hath broken up house,
    And hath left me old lumber to sell;
Come hither, and take your choice,
    I'll promise to use you well:
Will you buy the old speaker's chair?   5
    Which was warm and easie to sit in,
And oft hath been clean'd I declare,
    When as it was fouler than fitting.
        Says old Simon the king, &c.

Will you buy any bacon-flitches,   10
    The fattest, that ever were spent?
They're the sides of the old committees,
    Fed up in the long parliament.
Here's a pair of bellows, and tongs,
    And for a small matter I'll sell ye 'um;   15
They are made of the presbyters lungs,
    To blow up the coals of rebellion.
        Says old Simon, &c.

I had thought to have given them once
    To some black-smith for his forge;   20
But now I have considered on't,
    They are consecrate to the church:
So I'll give them unto some quire,
    They will make the big organs roar,
And the little pipes to squeeke higher,   25
    Than ever they could before.
        Says old Simon, &c.

Here's a couple of stools for sale,
　　One's square, and t'other is round;
Betwixt them both the tail　　　　　　　　30
　　Of the RUMP fell down to the ground.
Will you buy the states council-table,
　　Which was made of the good wain Scot?
The frame was a tottering Babel
　　To uphold the Independent plot,　　　35
　　　　Says old Simon, &c.

Here's the beesom of Reformation,
　　Which should have made clean the floor,
But it swept the wealth out of the nation,
　　And left us dirt good store.　　　　　40
Will you buy the states spinning-wheel,
　　Which spun for the ropers trade?
But better it had stood still,
　　For now it has spun a fair thread.
　　　　Says old Simon, &c.　　　　　45

Here's a glyster-pipe well try'd,
　　Which was made of a butcher's stump,*
And has been safely apply'd,
　　To cure the colds of the rump.
Here's a lump of Pilgrims-Salve,　　　　50
　　Which once was a justice of peace,
Who Noll and the Devil did serve;
　　But now it is come to this.
　　　　Says old Simon, &c.

Here's a roll of the states tobacco,　　　55
　　If any good fellow will take it;
No Virginia had e'er such a smack-o,
　　And I'll tell you how they did make it:

---

* Alluding probably to Major-General Harrison a butcher's son, who assisted Cromwell in turning out the long parliament, April 20, 1653.

'Tis th' Engagement, and Covenant cookt
 Up with the Abjuration oath ;   60
And many of them, that have took't,
 Complain it was foul in the mouth.
  Says old Simon, &c.

Yet the ashes may happily serve
 To cure the scab of the nation,   65
Whene'er 't has an itch to swerve
 To Rebellion by innovation.
A Lanthorn here is to be bought,
 The like was scarce ever gotten,
For many plots it has found out   70
 Before they ever were thought on.
  Says old Simon, &c.

Will you buy the RUMP's great saddle,
 With which it jocky'd the nation ?
And here is the bitt, and the bridle,   75
 And curb of Dissimulation :
And here's the trunk-hose of the RUMP,
 And their fair dissembling cloak,
And a Presbyterian jump,
 With an Independent smock.   80
  Says old Simon, &c.

Will you buy a Conscience oft turn'd,
 Which serv'd the high-court of justice,
And stretch'd until England it mourn'd :
 But Hell will buy that if the worst is.   85
Here's Joan Cromwell's kitching-stuff tub,
 Wherein is the fat of the Rumpers,
With which old Noll's horns she did rub,
 When he was got drunk with false bumpers.
  Says old Simon, &c.   90

Ver. 86. This was a cant name given to Cromwell's wife by the
Royalists, though her name was Elizabeth. She was taxed with

Here's the purse of the public faith ;
Here's the model of the Sequestration,
When the old wives upon their good troth,
Lent thimbles to ruine the nation.
Here's Dick Cromwell's Protectorship, 95
 And here are Lambert's commissions,
And here is Hugh Peters his scrip
 Cramm'd with the tumultuous Petitions.
  Says old Simon, &c.

And here are old Noll's brewing vessels, 100
 And here are his dray, and his slings ;
Here are Hewson's awl, and his bristles ;
 With diverse other odd things :
And what is the price doth belong
 To all these matters before ye ? 105
I'll sell them all for an old song,
 And so I do end my story.
  Says old Simon, &c.

XV.

THE BAFFLED KNIGHT, OR LADY'S
POLICY.

IVEN (with some corrections) from a MS. copy, and
collated with two printed ones in Roman character in
the Pepys collection.

[There are several versions of this story, but the earliest known
to Mr. Chappell is the one printed by Ritson in his *Ancient Songs*
(vol. ii. ed. 1829, p. 54), beginning—

---

exchanging the kitchen-stuff for the candles used in the Protector's
houshold, &c. See *Gent. Mag.* for March, 1788, p. 242.
 Ver. 94. See Grey's *Hudibras*, pt. i. cant. 2, ver. 570, &c.
V. 100, 102. Cromwell had in his younger years followed the
brewing trade at Huntingdon. Col. Hewson is said to have been
originally a cobler.

          " Yonder comes a courteous knight,"

with the burden, *Then she sang Downe a downe, hey downe derry.*
It is from *Deuteromelia, or the second part of Musicks melodie or
melodious Musicke, London,* 1609. Others are in *Pills to purge
Melancholy* (iii. 1707, or v. 1719), and in *A Complete Collection
of old and new English and Scotch Songs,* 8vo., 1735. The copy in
the Roxburghe collection is entitled *The Politick Maid,* beginning
" There was a knight was wine dronke." Ritson says, " Bp. Percy
found the subject worthy of his best improvements."]

HERE was a knight was drunk with wine,
     A riding along the way, sir ;
   And there he met with a lady fine,
     Among the cocks of hay, sir.

Shall you and I, O lady faire,   5
   Among the grass lye down-a :
And I will have a special care
   Of rumpling of your gowne-a.

Upon the grass there is a dewe,
   Will spoil my damask gowne, sir :   10
My gowne, and kirtle they are newe,
   And cost me many a crowne, sir.

I have a cloak of scarlet red,
   Upon the ground I'll throwe it ;
Then, lady faire, come lay thy head ;   15
   We'll play, and none shall knowe it.

O yonder stands my steed so free
   Among the cocks of hay, sir ;
And if the pinner[1] should chance to see,
   He'll take my steed away, sir.   20

Upon my finger I have a ring,
   Is made of finest gold-a ;
And, lady, it thy steed shall bring
   Out of the pinner's fold-a.

[1 pinder or impounder of cattle.]

O go with me to my father's hall;   25
　Fair chambers there are three, sir :
And you shall have the best of all,
　And I'll your chamberlaine bee, sir.

He mounted himself on his steed so tall,
　And her on her dapple gray, sir :   30
And there they rode to her father's hall,
　Fast pricking along the way, sir.

To her father's hall they arrived strait ;
　'Twas moated round about-a ;
She slipped herself within the gate,   35
　And lockt the knight without-a.

Here is a silver penny to spend,
　And take it for your pain, sir ;
And two of my father's men I'll send
　To wait on you back again, sir.   40

He from his scabbard drew his brand,
　And wiped it upon his sleeve-a :
And cursed, he said, be every man,
　That will a maid believe-a !

She drew a bodkin from her haire,   45
　And whip'd it upon her gown-a ;
And curs'd be every maiden faire,
　That will with men lye down-a !

A herb there is, that lowly grows,
　And some do call it rue, sir :   50
The smallest dunghill cock that crows,
　Would make a capon of you, sir.

A flower there is, that shineth bright,
　Some call it mary gold-a :
He that wold not when he might,   55
　He shall not when he wold-a.

The knight was riding another day,
  With cloak and hat and feather:
He met again with that lady gay,
  Who was angling in the river.   60

Now, lady faire, I've met with you,
  You shall no more escape me;
Remember, how not long agoe
  You falsely did intrap me.

The lady blushed scarlet red,   65
  And trembled at the stranger:
How shall I guard my maidenhead
  From this approaching danger?

He from his saddle down did light,
  In all his riche attyer;   70
And cryed, As I am a noble knight,
  I do thy charms admyer.

He took the lady by the hand,
  Who seemingly consented;
And would no more disputing stand: 75
  She had a plot invented.

Looke yonder, good sir knight, I pray,
  Methinks I now discover
A riding upon his dapple gray,
  My former constant lover.   80

On tip-toe peering stood the knight,
  Fast by the rivers brink-a;
The lady pusht with all her might:
  Sir knight, now swim or sink-a.

O'er head and ears he plunged in,   85
  The bottom faire he sounded;
Then rising up, he cried amain,
  Help, helpe, or else I'm drownded!

Now, fare-you-well, sir knight, adieu!
   You see what comes of fooling :   90
That is the fittest place for you ;
   Your courage wanted cooling.

Ere many days, in her fathers park,
   Just at the close of eve-a,
Again she met with her angry sparke ;   95
   Which made this lady grieve-a.

False lady, here thou'rt in my powre,
   And no one now can hear thee :
And thou shalt sorely rue the hour,
   That e'er thou dar'dst to jeer me.   100

I pray, sir knight, be not so warm
   With a young silly maid-a :
I vow and swear I thought no harm,
   'Twas a gentle jest I playd-a.

A gentle jest, in soothe ! he cry'd,   105
   To tumble me in and leave me :
What if I had in the river dy'd ?——
   That fetch will not deceive me.

Once more I'll pardon thee this day,
   Tho' injur'd out of measure ;   110
But then prepare without delay
   To yield thee to my pleasure.

Well then, if I must grant your suit,
   Yet think of your boots and spurs, sir ·
Let me pull off both spur and boot,   115
   Or else you cannot stir, sir.

He set him down upon the grass,
   And begg'd her kind assistance :
Now, smiling thought this lovely lass,
   I'll make you keep your distance.   120

Then pulling off his boots half-way;
  Sir knight, now I'm your betters:
You shall not make of me your prey;
  Sit there like a knave in fetters.

The knight when she had served soe,   125
  He fretted, fum'd, and grumbled:
For he could neither stand nor goe,
  But like a cripple tumbled.

Farewell, sir knight, the clock strikes ten,
  Yet do not move nor stir, sir: 130
I'll send you my father's serving men,
  To pull off your boots and spurs, sir.

This merry jest you must excuse,
  You are but a stingless nettle:
You'd never have stood for boots or shoes,   135
  Had you been a man of mettle.

All night in grievous rage he lay,
  Rolling upon the plain-a;
Next morning a shepherd past that way,
  Who set him right again-a.   140

Then mounting upon his steed so tall,
  By hill and dale he swore-a:
I'll ride at once to her father's hall;
  She shall escape no more-a.

I'll take her father by the beard,   145
  I'll challenge all her kindred;
Each dastard soul shall stand affeard;
  My wrath shall no more be hindred.

He rode unto her father's house,
  Which every side was moated: 150
The lady heard his furious vows,
  And all his vengeance noted.

Thought shee, sir knight, to quench your rage,
   Once more I will endeavour :
This water shall your fury 'swage,   155
   Or else it shall burn for ever.

Then faining penitence and feare,
   She did invite a parley :
Sir knight, if you'll forgive me heare,
   Henceforth I'll love you dearly.   160

My father he is now from home,
   And I am all alone, sir :
Therefore a-cross the water come ;
   And I am all your own, sir.

False maid, thou canst no more deceive ;   165
   I scorn the treacherous bait-a :
If thou would'st have me thee believe,
   Now open me the gate-a.

The bridge is drawn, the gate is barr'd,
   My father he has the keys, sir.   170
But I have for my love prepar'd
   A shorter way and easier.

Over the moate I've laid a plank
   Full seventeen feet in measure :
Then step a-cross to the other bank,   175
   And there we'll take our pleasure.

These words she had no sooner spoke,
   But strait he came tripping over :
The plank was saw'd, it snapping broke ;
   And sous'd the unhappy lover.   180

⁎

XVI.

WHY SO PALE?

FROM Sir John Suckling's *Poems*. This sprightly knight was born in 1613, and cut off by a fever about the 29th year of his age. See above, Song IX. of this Book.

[This celebrated song occurs in the tragedy of *Aglaura*, where it is sung by Orsames, a young lord, who says—"It is a little foolish counsel I gave a friend of mine four or five years ago when he was falling into a consumption."

Dr. Rimbault (*Musical Illustrations*, p. 29) writes, "The original air is here given from a MS. volume of old songs with the music, *temp.* Charles II. in the collection of the Editor. It was originally in the Library at Staunton Harold, Leicestershire, the seat of Earl Ferrers. This beautiful lyric was sung by Mrs. Cross in the *Mock Astrologer*, to an air composed by Lewis Ramondon. It was afterwards reset by Dr. Arne."

The date of the poet's birth given above is incorrect. Suckling was baptized on the tenth of February, 1608-9, and his mother died in 1613. Reduced in fortune and an alien, he died of poison bought by him of an apothecary at Paris. The date of his death is not known, but it probably took place in 1641, and he certainly was dead before the year 1642 had ended.]

WHY so pale and wan, fond lover?
    Prethee, why so pale?
Will, when looking well can't move her,
    Looking ill prevail?
    Prethee, why so pale?   5

Why so dull and mute, young sinner?
    Prethee why so mute?
Will, when speaking well can't win her,
    Saying nothing doe't?
    Prethee why so mute?   10

Quit, quit for shame ; this will not move,
  This cannot take her ;
If of herself she will not love,
  Nothing can make her.
The devil take her !   15

XVII.

OLD TOM OF BEDLAM.

MAD SONG THE FIRST.

T is worth attention, that the English have more songs
and ballads on the subject of madness, than any of
their neighbours. Whether there be any truth in the
insinuation, that we are more liable to this calamity
than other nations, or that our native gloominess hath peculiarly
recommended subjects of this cast to our writers ; we certainly do
not find the same in the printed collections of French, Italian
Songs, &c.

Out of a much larger quantity, we have selected half a dozen
mad songs for these volumes. The three first are originals in
their respective kinds ; the merit of the three last is chiefly that
of imitation. They were written at considerable intervals of time ;
but we have here grouped them together, that the reader may the
better examine their comparative merits. He may consider them
as so many trials of skill in a very peculiar subject, as the contest
of so many rivals to shoot in the bow of Ulysses. The two first
were probably written about the beginning of the last century ; the
third about the middle of it ; the fourth and sixth towards the
end ; and the fifth within this present century.

This is given from the Editor's folio MS. compared with two
or three old printed copies.—With regard to the author of this old
rhapsody, in Walton's *Compleat Angler*, cap. 3, is a song in praise
of angling, which the author says was made at his request " by
Mr. *William Basse,* one that has made the choice songs of the
Hunter in his career, and of *Tom of Bedlam,* and many others
of note," p. 84. See Sir *John Hawkins's* curious Edition, 8vo. of
that excellent old book.

[The madness here referred to was sometimes real, but more

often shammed. These "mad rascals" were so numerous a class
that they obtained the distinctive names of Bedlam beggars, and
Abraham men. Dekker describes their tricks in his *Bellman of
London*, 1616, where he says, " he calls himself by the name of
Poor Tom, and coming near any body, cries out, ' Poor Tom is a
cold ;' " the very expression used by Edgar when he appears in
the disguise of a madman (*King Lear*). Mr. Chappell observes
that there is great uncertainty as to the authorship, for there are so
many Tom of Bedlam songs that it is impossible to determine from
the passage in the *Complete Angler* to which of them Walton refers.
It is also doubtful to whom we are indebted for the tune. Mr.
Chappell thinks that probably it was by Henry Lawes's master, John
Cooper, called Cuperario after his visit to Italy. It has been
attributed, without authority, to Henry Purcell and Henry Lawes.]

ORTH from my sad and darksome cell,
Or from the deepe abysse of hell,
Mad Tom is come into the world againe
To see if he can cure his distempered braine.

Feares and cares oppresse my soule ;   5
Harke, howe the angrye Fureys houle !
Pluto laughes, and Proserpine is gladd
To see poore naked Tom of Bedlam madd.

Through the world I wander night and day
    To seeke my straggling senses,   10
In an angrye moode I mett old Time,
    With his pentarchye of tenses :[1]

When me he spyed,
Away he hyed,
For time will stay for no man :   15

[Ver. 2. *or* not in MS. V. 4. can ease. V. 5. ffeare & dispayre
pursue. V. 7. *and* not in MS. V. 9. through woods. V. 11. I
found out time. V. 13. he spyes. V. 14. he fflyes. V. 15. *for*
not in MS.]

[[1] five tenses.]

In vaine with cryes
I rent the skyes,
For pity is not common.

Cold and comfortless I lye:
Helpe, oh helpe! or else I dye!   20
Harke! I heare Apollo's teame,
The carman 'gins to whistle;
Chast Diana bends her bowe,
The boare begins to bristle.

Come, Vulcan, with tools and with tackles,   25
To knocke off my troublesome shackles;
Bid Charles make ready his waine
To fetch me my senses againe.

Last night I heard the dog-star bark;
Mars met Venus in the darke;   30
Limping Vulcan het[1] an iron barr,
And furiouslye made at the god of war:

Mars with his weapon laid about,
But Vulcan's temples had the gout,
For his broad horns did so hang in his light, 35
He could not see to aim his blowes aright:

Mercurye the nimble post of heaven,
Stood still to see the quarrell;
Gorrel-bellyed[2] Bacchus, gyant-like,
Bestryd a strong-beere barrell.   40

To mee he dranke,
I did him thanke,
But I could get no cyder;

[Ver. 17. hee rends.   V. 18. *for* not in MS.   V. 26. and knocke.
V. 28. my five sences.   V. 31. heates.   V. 32. runs att.   V. 33.
weapons.   V. 35. hang soe.   V. 36. that hee cold not see to aime
arright.   V. 38. stayd to see.]

[1 heated.   2 very fat bellied.]

He dranke whole butts
Till he burst his gutts,
But mine were ne'er the wyder.   45

Poore naked Tom is very drye:
A little drinke for charitye!

Harke, I hear Acteon's horne!
The huntsmen whoop and hallowe: 50
Ringwood, Royster, Bowman, Jowler,
All the chase do followe.

The man in the moone drinkes clarret,
Eates powder'd beef, turnip, and carret,
But a cup of old Malaga sack   55
Will fire the bushe at his backe.

XVIII.

THE DISTRACTED PURITAN,

MAD SONG THE SECOND,

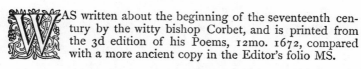AS written about the beginning of the seventeenth century by the witty bishop Corbet, and is printed from the 3d edition of his Poems, 12mo. 1672, compared with a more ancient copy in the Editor's folio MS.

[This song was printed in *Le Prince d'Amour*, 1660, with three other songs entitled *Tom of Bedlam*. It was also printed in the *Rump Songs*, 1662, but not in the edition of 1660.

The copy in the folio MS. (ed. Hales and Furnivall, vol. iii. p. 269) has several alterations. Stanza 5 was taken by Percy from the MS., where it occurs as stanza 8.

Richard Corbet, successively Bishop of Oxford and Norwich, was born at Ewell in Surrey in 1582. He died in 1635. He was a humorous man, and many pleasant stories are told of him, but Aubrey describes his appearance as "grave and venerable."]

A M I mad, O noble Festus,
    When zeal and godly knowledge
        Have put me in hope
        To deal with the pope,
As well as the best in the college?   5
        Boldly I preach, hate a cross, hate a surplice,
            Mitres, copes, and rochets;
        Come hear me pray nine times a day,
            And fill your heads with crochets.

In the house of pure Emanuel*   10
I had my education,
    Where my friends surmise
    I dazel'd my eyes
With the sight of revelation.
        Boldly I preach, &c.

They bound me like a bedlam,   15
They lash'd my four poor quarters;
    Whilst this I endure,
    Faith makes me sure
To be one of Foxes martyrs.
        Boldly I preach, &c.

These injuries I suffer   20
Through antichrist's perswasion:

---

* Emanuel college, Cambridge, was originally a seminary of
Puritans.

[Fuller has left us the following anecdote of Sir Walter Mildmay,
the founder of Emanuel, in his *History of the University of Cambridge.*
" Coming to court after he had founded his college, the queen told
him, 'Sir Walter, I hear you have erected a Puritan foundation.'
'No madam,' saith he, 'far be it from me to countenance anything contrary to your established laws; but I have set an acorn,
which, when it becomes an oak, God alone knows what will be the
fruit thereof.' "]

Take off this chain,
Neither Rome nor Spain
Can resist my strong invasion.
    Boldly I preach, &c.

Of the beast's ten horns (God bless us !)   25
I have knock'd off three already;
    If they let me alone
    I'll leave him none :
But they say I am too heady.
    Boldly I preach, &c.

When I sack'd the seven-hill'd city,   30
I met the great red dragon ;
    I kept him aloof
    With the armour of proof,
Though here I have never a rag on.
    Boldly I preach, &c.

With a fiery sword and target,   35
There fought I with this monster :
    But the sons of pride
    My zeal deride,
And all my deeds misconster.
    Boldly I preach, &c.

I un-hors'd the Whore of Babel,   40
With the lance of Inspiration ;
    I made her slink,
    And spill the drink
In her cup of abomination.
    Boldly I preach, &c.

I have seen two in a vision   45
With a flying-book* between them.

---

* Alluding to some visionary exposition of Zech. ch. v. ver. 1 ;
or, if the date of this song would permit, one might suppose it
aimed at one *Coppe*, a strange enthusiast, whose life may be seen

I have been in despair
Five times in a year,
And been cur'd by reading Greenham.*
   Boldly I preach, &c.

I observ'd in Perkin's tables†   50
The black line of damnation;
   Those crooked veins
   So stuck in my brains,
That I fear'd my reprobation.
   Boldly I preach, &c.

In the holy tongue of Canaan   55
I plac'd my chiefest pleasure:
   Till I prick'd my foot
   With an Hebrew root,
That I bled beyond all measure.
   Boldly I preach, &c.

---

in Wood's *Athen.* vol. ii. p. 501.   He was author of a book, intitled, *The Fiery Flying Roll:* and afterwards published a Re-
cantation, part of whose title is, *The Fiery Flying Roll's Wings
clipt,* &c.

   * See Greenham's *Works,* fol. 1605, particularly the tract intitled, *A sweet Comfort for an afflicted Conscience.*

   [Richard Greenham was born *circa* 1531 and died in 1591. He
was a singularly ardent preacher, and Brook, in his *Lives of the
Puritans,* says, that "in addition to his public ministerial labours
he had a remarkable talent for comforting afflicted consciences."
His *Works* were first collected in 1599.]

   † See Perkin's *Works,* fol. 1616, vol. i. p. 11; where is a large
half sheet folded, containing, *A survey, or table, declaring the order
of the causes of salvation and damnation, &c.* the pedigree of damnation being distinguished by a broad black zig-zag line.

   [William Perkins (1558-1602). Brook says of him, that he used
to pronounce the word *damn* with so peculiar an emphasis "that it
left a doleful echo in the eares a long time after." His works were
frequently reprinted, and, according to Fuller, were translated into
Latin, French, Dutch, and Spanish.]

I appear'd before the archbishop,* 60
And all the high commission ;
 I gave him no grace,
 But told him to his face,
That he favour'd superstition.
  Boldly I preach, hate a cross, hate a surplice,
  Mitres, copes, and rochets : 66
  Come hear me pray nine times a day,
  And fill your heads with crotchets.

XIX.

THE LUNATIC LOVER,

MAD SONG THE THIRD,

S given from an old printed copy in the British Museum, compared with another in the Pepys collection; both in black letter.

[Black-letter copies of this ballad are to be found in the Bagford, Douce, and Roxburghe collections, as well as in the Pepys. The tune was a favourite one, and several other ballads were sung to it.]

RIM king of the ghosts, make haste,
  And bring hither all your train ;
  See how the pale moon does waste,
  And just now is in the wane.
Come, you night-hags, with all your charms, 5
  And revelling witches away,
And hug me close in your arms ;
  To you my respects I'll pay.

---

* Abp. Laud.

I'll court you, and think you fair,
    Since love does distract my brain :   10
I'll go, I'll wed the night-mare,
    And kiss her, and kiss her again :
But if she prove peevish and proud,
    Then, a pise on her love ! let her go ;
I'll seek me a winding shroud,   15
    And down to the shades below.

A lunacy sad I endure,
    Since reason departs away ;
I call to those hags for a cure
    As knowing not what I say.   20
The beauty, whom I do adore,
    Now slights me with scorn and disdain ;
I never shall see her more ;
    Ah ! how shall I bear my pain !

I ramble, and range about   25
    To find out my charming saint ;
While she at my grief does flout,
    And smiles at my loud complaint.
Distraction I see is my doom,
    Of this I am now too sure ;   3
A rival is got in my room,
    While torments I do endure.

Strange fancies do fill my head,
    While wandering in despair,
I am to the desarts lead,   35
    Expecting to find her there.
Methinks in a spangled cloud
    I see her enthroned on high ;
Then to her I crie aloud,
    And labour to reach the sky.   40

When thus I have raved awhile,
  And wearyed myself in vain,
I lye on the barren soil,
  And bitterly do complain.
Till slumber hath quieted me,   45
  In sorrow I sigh and weep;
The clouds are my canopy
  To cover me while I sleep.

I dream that my charming fair
  Is then in my rival's bed,
Whose tresses of golden hair   50
  Are on the fair pillow bespread.
Then this doth my passion inflame,
  I start, and no longer can lie:
Ah! Sylvia, art thou not to blame   55
  To ruin a lover? I cry.

Grim king of the ghosts, be true,
  And hurry me hence away,
My languishing life to you
  A tribute I freely pay.   60
To the elysian shades I post
  In hopes to be freed from care,
Where many a bleeding ghost
  Is hovering in the air.

XX.

THE LADY DISTRACTED WITH LOVE,

Mad Song the Fourth,

WAS originally sung in one of *Tom D'urfey's* comedies of *Don Quixote* in 1694 and 1696; and probably composed by himself. In the several stanzas, the author represents his pretty Mad-woman as 1. sullenly mad: 2. mirthfully mad: 3. melancholy mad: 4. fantastically mad: and 5. stark mad.   Both this, and Num. XXII. are printed from D'urfey's *Pills to purge Melancholy*, 1719, vol. i.

FROM rosie bowers, where sleeps the god
    of love,
    Hither ye little wanton cupids fly;
    Teach me in soft melodious strains to
    move
With tender passion my heart's darling joy:
Ah! let the soul of musick tune my voice,   5
To win dear Strephon, who my soul enjoys.

Or, if more influencing
    Is to be brisk and airy,
With a step and a bound,
With a frisk from the ground,   10
    I'll trip like any fairy.

As once on Ida dancing
    Were three celestial bodies:
With an air, and a face,
And a shape, and a grace,   15
    I'll charm, like beauty's goddess.

Ah! 'tis in vain! 'tis all, 'tis all in vain!
Death and despair must end the fatal pain:
Cold, cold despair, disguis'd like snow and rain,
Falls on my breast; bleak winds in tempests blow;
My veins all shiver, and my fingers glow: 21
My pulse beats a dead march for lost repose,
And to a solid lump of ice my poor fond heart is froze.

Or say, ye powers, my peace to crown,
Shall I thaw myself, and drown   25
  Among the foaming billows?
Increasing all with tears I shed,
  On beds of ooze, and crystal pillows,
Lay down, lay down my lovesick head?

No, no, I'll strait run mad, mad, mad,   30
  That soon my heart will warm;
When once the sense is fled, is fled,
  Love has no power to charm.
Wild thro' the woods I'll fly, I'll fly,
  Robes, locks——shall thus——be tore!   35
A thousand, thousand times I'll dye
Ere thus, thus, in vain,—ere thus in vain adore.

XXI.

THE DISTRACTED LOVER,

MAD SONG THE FIFTH,

WAS written by *Henry Carey*, a celebrated composer of
music at the beginning of this century, and author
of several little Theatrical Entertainments, which the
reader may find enumerated in the *Companion to the
Play-house*, &c. The sprightliness of this songster's fancy could
not preserve him from a very melancholy catastrophe, which was

effected by his own hand. In his *Poems*, 4to. Lond. 1729, may be
seen another Mad-Song of this author, beginning thus:

> "Gods! I can never this endure,
> Death alone must be my cure," &c.

GO to the Elysian shade,
    Where sorrow ne'er shall wound me;
Where nothing shall my rest invade,
    But joy shall still surround me.

I fly from Celia's cold disdain,   5
    From her disdain I fly;
She is the cause of all my pain,
    For her alone I die.

Her eyes are brighter than the mid-day sun,
When he but half his radiant course has run,   10
When his meridian glories gaily shine,
And gild all nature with a warmth divine.

    See yonder river's flowing tide,
        Which now so full appears;
    Those streams, that do so swiftly glide,   15
        Are nothing but my tears.

There I have wept till I could weep no more,
And curst mine eyes, when they have wept their
    store:
Then, like the clouds, that rob the azure main,
I've drain'd the flood to weep it back again.   20

    Pity my pains,
    Ye gentle swains!
Cover me with ice and snow,
I scorch, I burn, I flame, I glow!

Furies, tear me,   25
  Quickly bear me
To the dismal shades below!
  Where yelling, and howling
  And grumbling, and growling
Strike the ear with horrid woe.   30

  Hissing snakes,
  Fiery lakes
Would be a pleasure, and a cure:
  Not all the hells,
  Where Pluto dwells,   35
Can give such pain as I endure.

To some peaceful plain convey me,
On a mossey carpet lay me,
Fan me with ambrosial breeze,
Let me die, and so have ease!   40

XXII.

THE FRANTIC LADY,

Mad Song the Sixth.

THIS, like Num. XX., was originally sung in one of *D'urfey's* comedies of *Don Quixote*, (first acted about the year 1694) and was probably composed by that popular songster, who died Feb. 26, 1723.
  This is printed in the *Hive, a Collection of Songs*, 4 vols. 1721, 12mo. where may be found two or three other *Mad Songs* not admitted into these Volumes.

BURN, my brain consumes to ashes!
Each eye-ball too like lightning flashes!
Within my breast there glows a solid fire,
Which in a thousand ages can't expire!

Blow, blow, the winds' great ruler!   5
  Bring the Po, and the Ganges hither,
  'Tis sultry weather,
  Pour them all on my soul,
  It will hiss like a coal,
But be never the cooler.   10

'Twas pride hot as hell,
That first made me rebell,
From love's awful throne a curst angel I fell
  And mourn now my fate,
  Which myself did create: 15
Fool, fool, that consider'd not when I was well!

Adieu! ye vain transporting joys!
Off ye vain fantastic toys!
  That dress this face—this body—to allure!
  Bring me daggers, poison, fire!   20
  Since scorn is turn'd into desire.
All hell feels not the rage, which I, poor I, endure.

XXIII.

LILLI BURLERO.

THE following rhymes, slight and insignificant as they may now seem, had once a more powerful effect than either the Philippics of Demosthenes, or Cicero; and contributed not a little towards the great revolution in 1688. Let us hear a contemporary writer.

"A foolish ballad was made at that time, treating the Papists,

and chiefly the Irish, in a very ridiculous manner, which had a
burden said to be Irish words, *Lero, lero, liliburlero,* that made an
impression on the (king's) army, that cannot be imagined by those
that saw it not. The whole army, and at last the people, both in
city and country, were singing it perpetually. And perhaps never
had so slight a thing so great an effect."—*Burnet.*

It was written, or at least republished, on the earl of Tyrconnel's
going a second time to Ireland in October, 1688. Perhaps it is
unnecessary to mention, that General Richard Talbot, newly
created earl of Tyrconnel, had been nominated by K. James II.
to the lieutenancy of Ireland in 1686, on account of his being a
furious papist, who had recommended himself to his bigotted
master by his arbitrary treatment of the protestants in the preceding year, when only lieutenant general, and whose subsequent
conduct fully justified his expectations and their fears. The vio-
lences of his administration may be seen in any of the histories of
those times : particularly in bishop King's *State of the Protestants
in Ireland,* 1691, 4to.

This song is attributed to Lord *Wharton* in a small pamphlet,
intitled, *A true relation of the several facts and circumstances of the
intended riot and tumult on Q. Elizabeth's birth-day, &c.* 3d ed.
Lond. 1712, pr. 2*d.*—See p. 5, viz.—" A late Viceroy (of Ireland,)
who has so often boasted himself upon his talent for mischief.
invention, lying, and for making a certain *Lilliburlero Song;* with
which, if you will believe himself, he sung a deluded Prince out
of Three Kingdoms."

Lilliburlero and *Bullen-a-lah* are said to have been the words of
distinction used among the Irish Papists in their massacre of the
Protestants in 1641.

[To no song could be better attributed Fletcher of Saltoun's
dictum than to this poor specimen of verse, which caught the fancy
of the people and drove James from his throne. Macaulay wrote
of it as follows:—" From one end of England to the other all
classes were constantly singing this idle rhyme. It was especially
the delight of the English army. More than seventy years after the
Revolution, Sterne delineated with exquisite skill a veteran who
had fought at the Boyne and at Namur. One of the characteristics
of the good old soldier is his trick of whistling *Lilliburlero.*" The
air is attributed to Purcell, but it is supposed that he only arranged
an earlier tune. Hume thought that the popularity of the song
was rather due to the composer of the air than to the author of
the words.

Mr. Markland, in a note to Boswell's *Life of Johnson,* says, that
" according to Lord Dartmouth there was a particular expression
in it, which the king remembered that he had made use of to the

Earl of Dorset, from whence it was concluded that he was the author." Upon this Mr. Chappell remarks, 1. that "the Earl of Dorset laid no claim to it, and it is scarcely to be believed that the author of *To all you ladies now on land* could have penned such thorough doggrel." 2. That "the ballad contains no expression that the King would have used, which might not equally have been employed by any other person."* There can now be little doubt that the author was Thomas Marquis of Wharton, father of the mad Duke Philip of Wharton. He discerned the indications of the political horizon and espoused the winning side. He was well rewarded for his wisdom. Mr. S. Redmond (*Notes and Queries*, third series, viii. 13) writes that he has often heard the girls in the south and south-east of Ireland, while engaged in binding the corn into sheaves after the reapers, sing the following chorus, which always had reference to one of the gang who was not so quick at her work as the others, and who consequently was left behind :

> " Lully by lero,
> Lully by lero,
> Lully by lero,
> Help her along."]

O ! broder Teague, dost hear de decree ?
    Lilli burlero, bullen a-la.
Dat we shall have a new deputie,
    Lilli burlero burlen a-la.
Lero lero, lilli burlero, lero lero, bullen a-la,   5
    Lero lero, lilli burlero, lero lero, bullen a-la.

Ho ! by shaint Tyburn, it is de Talbote :
    Lilli, &c.
And he will cut de Englishmen's troate.
    Lilli, &c.   10

Dough by my shoul de English do praat,
    Lilli, &c.
De law's on dare side, and Creish knows what.
    Lilli, &c.

Ver. 7. Ho by my shoul, *al. ed.*
[* *Popular Music of the Olden Time*, vol. ii. p. 569.]

But if dispence do come from de pope,　　　15
　　Lilli, &c.
We'll hang Magna Charta, and dem in a rope.
　　Lilli, &c.

For de good Talbot is made a lord,
　　Lilli, &c.　　　　　　　　　　　　　20
And with brave lads is coming aboard :
　　Lilli, &c.

Who all in France have taken a sware,
　　Lilli, &c.
Dat dey will have no protestant heir.　　　25
　　Lilli, &c.

Ara ! but why does he stay behind ?
　　Lilli, &c.
Ho ! by my shoul 'tis a protestant wind.
　　Lilli, &c.　　　　　　　　　　　　　30

But see de Tyrconnel is now come ashore,
　　Lilli, &c.
And we shall have commissions gillore.
　　Lilli, &c.

And he dat will not go to de mass,　　　35
　　Lilli, &c.
Shall be turn out, and look like an ass.
　　Lilli, &c.

Now, now de hereticks all go down,
　　Lilli, &c.　　　　　　　　　　　　　40
By Chrish and shaint Patrick, de nation's our own.
　　Lilli, &c.

Dare was an old prophesy found in a bog,
　　Lilli, &c.
" Ireland shall be rul'd by an ass, and a dog."　　45
　　Lilli, &c.

Ver. 43. What follows is not in some copies.

And now dis prophesy is come to pass,
  Lilli, &c.
For Talbot's de dog, and JA**s is de ass.
  Lilli, &c.   50

XXIV.

THE BRAES OF YARROW,

IN IMITATION OF THE ANCIENT SCOTS MANNER,

AS written by William Hamilton, of Bangour, Esq; who died March 25, 1734, aged 50. It is printed from an elegant edition of his *Poems*, published at Edinburgh, 1760, 12mo. This song was written in imitation of an old Scottish ballad on a similar subject, with the same burden to each stanza.

[The beautiful river Yarrow has few rivals as an inspirer of song. These verses of Hamilton's are copied from the old ballad—*The Dowie Dens* (melancholy downs) *of Yarrow*, a collated version of which was first printed by Scott in his *Minstrelsy of the Scottish Border*. Scott was of opinion that with many readers the greatest recommendation of the old ballad will be that it suggested to Hamilton his modern one. We may say that the greatest recommendation of Hamilton's poem to us is the fact that it inspired Wordsworth to write his three lovely little poems, *Yarrow Unvisited, Visited*, and *Revisited*.

There are two old ballads which have been much mixed up by reciters, viz. *The Dowie Dens* and *Willie's drowned in Yarrow*. The Rev. John Logan's *Braes of Yarrow* is founded on the latter.

William Hamilton of Bangour was born in 1704 and died at Lyons in 1754, from which place his remains were brought to Scotland, and interred in Holyrood Abbey. He was a Jacobite, and after the battle of Culloden was forced to skulk about the Highlands in disguise until he was able to escape to France. He returned to Scotland after the country had quieted down in 1749.]

A.

USK[1] ye, busk ye, my bonny bonny bride,
　　Busk ye, busk ye, my winsome marrow,[2]
　Busk ye, busk ye, my bonny bonny bride,
　　And think nae mair on the Braes[3] of
　Yarrow.

B. Where gat ye that bonny bonny bride?　　　5
　　Where gat ye that winsome marrow?
A. I gat her where I dare na weil be seen,
　　Puing the birks[4] on the Braes of Yarrow.

　Weep not, weep not, my bonny bonny bride,
　　Weep not, weep not, my winsome marrow;　10
　Nor let thy heart lament to leive
　　Puing the birks on the Braes of Yarrow.

B. Why does she weep, thy bonny bonny bride?
　　Why does she weep thy winsome marrow?
　And why dare ye nae mair weil be seen　　15
　　Puing the birks on the Braes of Yarrow?

A. Lang maun she weep, lang maun she, maun she
　　　weep,
　　Lang maun she weep with dule and sorrow;
　And lang maun I nae mair weil be seen
　　Puing the birks on the Braes of Yarrow.　20

　For she has tint[5] her luver, luver dear,
　　Her luver dear, the cause of sorrow;
　And I hae slain the comliest swain
　　That eir pu'd birks on the Braes of Yarrow.

[[1] dress.　　　　[2] companion.　　　[3] hilly banks.
[4] pulling the birch trees.　　　[5] lost.]

Why rins thy stream, O Yarrow, Yarrow, reid ? 25
  Why on thy braes heard the voice of sorrow ?
And why yon melancholious weids
  Hung on the bonny birks of Yarrow ?

What's yonder floats on the rueful rueful flude ?
  What's yonder floats ? O dule and sorrow ! 30
O 'tis he the comely swain I slew
  Upon the duleful Braes of Yarrow.

Wash, O wash his wounds, his wounds in tears,
  His wounds in tears with dule and sorrow ;
And wrap his limbs in mourning weids,   35
  And lay him on the Braes of Yarrow.

Then build, then build, ye sisters, sisters sad,
  Ye sisters sad, his tomb with sorrow ;
And weep around in waeful wise
  His hapless fate on the Braes of Yarrow.   40

Curse ye, curse ye, his useless, useless shield,
  My arm that wrought the deed of sorrow,
The fatal spear that pierc'd his breast,
  His comely breast on the Braes of Yarrow.

Did I not warn thee, not to, not to luve ?   45
  And warn from fight ? but to my sorrow
Too rashly bauld a stronger arm
  Thou mett'st, and fell'st on the Braes of Yarrow.

Sweet smells the birk, green grows, green grows
      the grass,
  Yellow on Yarrow's bank the gowan,[1]   50
Fair hangs the apple frae the rock,
  Sweet the wave of Yarrow flowan.

[1 daisy.]

Flows Yarrow sweet? as sweet, as sweet flows
    Tweed,
  As green its grass, its gowan as yellow,
As sweet smells on its braes the birk,   55
  The apple frae its rock as mellow.

Fair was thy luve, fair fair indeed thy luve,
  In flow'ry bands thou didst him fetter;
Tho' he was fair, and weil beluv'd again
  Than me he never luv'd thee better.   60

Busk ye, then busk, my bonny bonny bride,
  Busk ye, busk ye, my winsome marrow,
Busk ye, and luve me on the banks of Tweed,
  And think nae mair on the Braes of Yarrow.

C. How can I busk a bonny bonny bride?   65
  How can I busk a winsome marrow?
How luve him upon the banks of Tweed,
  That slew my luve on the Braes of Yarrow?

O Yarrow fields, may never never rain,
  Nor dew thy tender blossoms cover,   70
For there was basely slain my luve,
  My luve, as he had not been a lover.

The boy put on his robes, his robes of green,
  His purple vest, 'twas my awn sewing:
Ah! wretched me! I little, little kenn'd   75
  He was in these to meet his ruin.

The boy took out his milk-white, milk-white steed,
  Unheedful of my dule and sorrow:
But ere the toofall[1] of the night
  He lay a corps on the Braes of Yarrow.   80

[1 twilight.]

Much I rejoyc'd that waeful waeful day;
 I sang, my voice the woods returning:
But lang ere night the spear was flown,
 That slew my luve, and left me mourning.

What can my barbarous barbarous father do,   85
 But with his cruel rage pursue me?
My luver's blood is on thy spear,
 How canst thou, barbarous man, then wooe me?

My happy sisters may be, may be proud
 With cruel, and ungentle scoffin',   90
May bid me seek on Yarrow's Braes
 My luver nailed in his coffin.

My brother Douglas may upbraid, upbraid,
 And strive with threatning words to muve me:
My luver's blood is on thy spear,   95
 How canst thou ever bid me luve thee?

Yes, yes, prepare the bed, the bed of luve,
 With bridal sheets my body cover,
Unbar, ye bridal maids, the door,
 Let in the expected husband lover.   100

But who the expected husband husband is?
 His hands, methinks, are bath'd in slaughter:
Ah me! what ghastly spectre's yon
 Comes in his pale shroud, bleeding after?

Pale as he is, here lay him, lay him down,   105
 O lay his cold head on my pillow;
Take aff, take aff these bridal weids,
 And crown my careful head with willow.

Pale tho' thou art, yet best, yet best beluv'd,
 O could my warmth to life restore thee!   110
Yet lye all night between my breists,
 No youth lay ever there before thee.

Pale, pale indeed, O luvely luvely youth,
  Forgive, forgive, so foul a slaughter,
And lye all night between my breists,   115
  No youth shall ever lye there after.

A. Return, return, O mournful, mournful bride,
    Return and dry thy useless sorrow :
  Thy luver heeds none of thy sighs,
    He lyes a corps in the Braes of Yarrow.   120

XXV.

ADMIRAL HOSIER'S GHOST

WAS a party song written by the ingenious author of
*Leonidas,** on the taking of Porto Bello from the Spaniards by Admiral Vernon, Nov. 22, 1739.—The case
of Hosier, which is here so pathetically represented,
was briefly this.   In April, 1726, that commander was sent with a
strong fleet into the Spanish West-Indies, to block up the galleons
in the ports of that country, or should they presume to come out,
to seize and carry them into England: he accordingly arrived at
the Bastimentos near Porto Bello, but being employed rather to
overawe than to attack the Spaniards, with whom it was probably
not our interest to go to war, he continued long inactive on that
station, to his own great regret.   He afterwards removed to Cartha-
gena, and remained cruizing in these seas, till far the greater part
of his men perished deplorably by the diseases of that unhealthy
climate.   This brave man, seeing his best officers and men thus
daily swept away, his ships exposed to inevitable destruction, and
himself made the sport of the enemy, is said to have died of a
broken heart.   Such is the account of Smollett, compared with
that of other less partial writers.

The following song is commonly accompanied with a Second
Part, or Answer, which being of inferior merit, and apparently
written by another hand, hath been rejected.

---

* An ingenious correspondent informs the Editor, that this
ballad hath been also attributed to the late Lord Bath.

[Dr. Rimbault (*Musical Illustrations*, p. 30) writes: "The earliest copy of the tune to this ballad is contained in the ballad opera of *Sylvia, or the Country Burial*, 1731. It may also be found in Walsh's *British Musical Miscellany*, vol. iv. and in other works of a similar description. The ballads of *Come and listen to my ditty* and *Cease, rude Boreas*, were sung to this tune, which appears to have been always a favourite for 'sea ditties.'"

In Hannah More's *Life* (vol. i. p. 405) is the following interesting note: "I was much amused with hearing old Leonidas Glover sing his own fine ballad of *Hosier's Ghost*, which was very affecting. He is past eighty." In the matter of the last item Mrs. More was wrong. Richard Glover was born in 1712, and died on Nov. 25, 1785.]

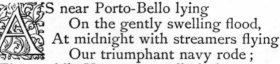

S near Porto-Bello lying
 On the gently swelling flood,
  At midnight with streamers flying
  Our triumphant navy rode ;
There while Vernon sate all-glorious   5
 From the Spaniards' late defeat :
And his crews, with shouts victorious,
 Drank success to England's fleet :

On a sudden shrilly sounding,
 Hideous yells and shrieks were heard ; 10
Then each heart with fear confounding,
 A sad troop of ghosts appear'd,
All in dreary hammocks shrouded,
 Which for winding-sheets they wore,
And with looks by sorrow clouded   15
 Frowning on that hostile shore.

On them gleam'd the moon's wan lustre,
 When the shade of Hosier brave
His pale bands was seen to muster
 Rising from their watry grave.   20

O'er the glimmering wave he hy'd him,
    Where the Burford* rear'd her sail,
With three thousand ghosts beside him,
    And in groans did Vernon hail.

Heed, oh heed our fatal story,   25
    I am Hosier's injur'd ghost,
You, who now have purchas'd glory,
    At this place where I was lost!
Tho' in Porto-Bello's ruin
    You now triumph free from fears,   30
When you think on our undoing,
    You will mix your joy with tears.

See these mournful spectres sweeping
    Ghastly o'er this hated wave,
Whose wan cheeks are stain'd with weeping; 35
    These were English captains brave.
Mark those numbers pale and horrid,
    Those were once my sailors bold:
Lo, each hangs his drooping forehead,
    While his dismal tale is told.   40

I, by twenty sail attended,
    Did this Spanish town affright;
Nothing then its wealth defended
    But my orders not to fight.
Oh! that in this rolling ocean   45
    I had cast them with disdain,
And obey'd my heart's warm motion
    To have quell'd the pride of Spain!

For resistance I could fear none,
    But with twenty ships had done   50
What thou, brave and happy Vernon,
    Hast atchiev'd with six alone.

---

* Admiral Vernon's ship.

Then the bastimentos never
　　Had our foul dishonour seen,
Nor the sea the sad receiver　　　　　　　55
　　Of this gallant train had been.

Thus, like thee, proud Spain dismaying,
　　And her galleons leading home,
Though condemn'd for disobeying,
　　I had met a traitor's doom,　　　　　60
To have fallen, my country crying
　　He has play'd an English part,
Had been better far than dying
　　Of a griev'd and broken heart.

Unrepining at thy glory,　　　　　　　65
　　Thy successful arms we hail;
But remember our sad story,
　　And let Hosier's wrongs prevail.
Sent in this foul clime to languish,
　　Think what thousands fell in vain,　70
Wasted with disease and anguish,
　　Not in glorious battle slain.

Hence with all my train attending
　　From their oozy tombs below,
Thro' the hoary foam ascending,　　　75
　　Here I feed my constant woe:
Here the bastimentos viewing,
　　We recal our shameful doom,
And our plaintive cries renewing,
　　Wander thro' the midnight gloom.　80

O'er these waves for ever mourning
　　Shall we roam depriv'd of rest,
If to Britain's shores returning
　　You neglect my just request;

After this proud foe subduing,   85
   When your patriot friends you see,
Think on vengeance for my ruin,
   And for England sham'd in me.

XXVI.

JEMMY DAWSON.

JAMES DAWSON was one of the Manchester rebels, who was hanged, drawn, and quartered, on Kennington-common, in the county of Surrey, July 30, 1746.— This ballad is founded on a remarkable fact, which was reported to have happened at his execution. It was written by the late *William Shenstone*, Esq; soon after the event, and has been printed amongst his posthumous works, 2 vols. 8vo. It is here given from a MS. which contained some small variations from that printed copy.

[Captain James Dawson was one of eight officers belonging to the Manchester regiment of Volunteers in the service of the young Chevalier, who were executed on Kennington Common.

   The following ballad is founded upon a narrative first published in a periodical entitled *The Parrot*, Saturday, 2d August, 1746, three days after the occurrence. In the *Whitehall Evening Post,* Aug. 7, 1746, the same story is told with the addition, that "upon enquiry every circumstance was literally true." Another ballad is said to have been written upon Dawson's fate, and sung about the streets. It is reprinted in the *European Magazine*, April, 1801, p. 248, and begins as follows:

      " Blow ye bleak winds around my head,
      Sooth my heart corroding care, &c."]

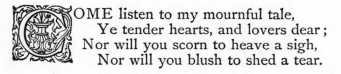

COME listen to my mournful tale,
   Ye tender hearts, and lovers dear;
Nor will you scorn to heave a sigh,
   Nor will you blush to shed a tear.

And thou, dear Kitty, peerless maid,   5
   Do thou a pensive ear incline;
For thou canst weep at every woe,
   And pity every plaint, but mine.

Young Dawson was a gallant youth,
   A brighter never trod the plain;   10
And well he lov'd one charming maid,
   And dearly was he lov'd again.

One tender maid she lov'd him dear,
   Of gentle blood the damsel came,
And faultless was her beauteous form,   15
   And spotless was her virgin fame.

But curse on party's hateful strife,
   That led the faithful youth astray
The day the rebel clans appear'd:
   O had he never seen that day!   20

Their colours and their sash he wore,
   And in the fatal dress was found;
And now he must that death endure,
   Which gives the brave the keenest wound.

How pale was then his true love's cheek,   25
   When Jemmy's sentence reach'd her ear!
For never yet did Alpine snows
   So pale, nor yet so chill appear.

With faltering voice she weeping said,
   Oh Dawson, monarch of my heart,   30
Think not thy death shall end our loves,
   For thou and I will never part.

Yet might sweet mercy find a place,
   And bring relief to Jemmy's woes,
O GEORGE, without a prayer for thee   35
   My orisons should never close.

The gracious prince that gives him life
  Would crown a never-dying flame,
And every tender babe I bore
  Should learn to lisp the giver's name.   40

But though, dear youth, thou should'st be dragg'd
  To yonder ignominious tree,
Thou shalt not want a faithful friend
  To share thy bitter fate with thee.

O then her mourning coach was call'd,   45
  The sledge mov'd slowly on before;
Tho' borne in a triumphal car,
  She had not lov'd her favourite more.

She followed him, prepar'd to view
  The terrible behests of law ;
And the last scene of Jemmy's woes
  With calm and stedfast eye she saw.

Distorted was that blooming face,
  Which she had fondly lov'd so long :
And stifled was that tuneful breath,   55
  Which in her praise had sweetly sung :

And sever'd was that beauteous neck,
  Round which her arms had fondly clos'd :
And mangled was that beauteous breast,
  On which her love-sick head repos'd :   60

And ravish'd was that constant heart,
  She did to every heart prefer ;
For tho' it could his king forget,
  'Twas true and loyal still to her.

Amid those unrelenting flames   65
  She bore this constant heart to see ;
But when 'twas moulder'd into dust,
  Now, now, she cried, I'll follow thee.

My death, my death alone can show
  The pure and lasting love I bore :   70
Accept, O heaven, of woes like ours,
  And let us, let us weep no more.

The dismal scene was o'er and past,
  The lover's mournful hearse retir'd ;
The maid drew back her languid head,   75
  And sighing forth his name, expir'd.

Tho' justice ever must prevail,
  The tear my Kitty sheds is due ;
For seldom shall she hear a tale
  So sad, so tender, and so true.   80

THE END OF THE THIRD BOOK.

APPENDIX.

APPENDIX.

ON THE ALLITERATIVE METRE, WITHOUT RHYME, IN PIERCE PLOWMAN'S VISIONS.

E learn from Wormius (*a*), that the ancient Islandic poets used a great variety of measures: he mentions 136 different kinds, without including rhyme, or a correspondence of final syllables, yet this was occasionally used, as appears from the Ode of Egil, which Wormius hath inserted in his book.

He hath analysed the structure of one of these kinds of verse, the harmony of which neither depended on the quantity of the syllables, like that of the ancient Greeks and Romans; nor on the rhymes at the end, as in modern poetry; but consisted altogether in alliteration, or a certain artful repetition of the sounds in the middle of the verses. This was adjusted according to certain rules of their prosody,

---

(*a*) *Literatura Runica.* Hafniæ, 1636, 4to.—1651, fol. The *Islandic* language is of the same origin as our *Anglo-Saxon*, being both dialects of the ancient *Gothic* or *Teutonic.* Vid. *Hickesii Præfat. in Grammat. Anglo-Saxon. & Moeso-Goth.* 4to. 1689.

one of which was, that every distich should contain at least three words beginning with the same letter or sound. Two of these correspondent sounds might be placed either in the first or second line of the distich, and one in the other : but all three were not regularly to be crowded into one line. This will be best understood by the following examples (*b*):

> " *M*eire og *M*inne
> *M*ogu heimdaller."

> " *G*ab *G*inunga
> Enn *G*ras huerge."

There were many other little niceties observed by the Islandic poets, who, as they retained their original language and peculiarities longer than the other nations of Gothic race, had time to cultivate their native poetry more, and to carry it to a higher pitch of refinement, than any of the rest.

Their brethren, the Anglo-Saxon poets, occasionally used the same kind of alliteration, and it is common to meet, in their writings, with similar examples of the foregoing rules. Take an instance or two in modern characters (*c*) :

> " *Sk*eop tha and *Sk*yrede
> *Sk*yppend ure."

> " *H*am and *H*eahsetl
> *H*eofena rikes."

I know not, however, that there is anywhere extant an entire Saxon poem all in this measure. But distichs of this sort perpetually occur in all their poems of any length.

Now if we examine the versification of Pierce Plowman's *Visions*, we shall find it constructed exactly by these rules ; and therefore each line, as printed, is in reality a distich of two verses, and will, I believe, be found distinguished as such, by some mark or other in all the ancient MSS. viz. :

(*b*) Vid. **Hickes** *Antiq. Literatur. Septentrional.* tom. i. p. 217.
(*c*) *Ibid.*

"In a *S*omer *S*eason, | when ' hot' (*d*) was the *S*unne,
I *Sh*ope me into *Sh*roubs, | as I a *Sh*epe were ;
In *H*abite as an *H*armet | un*H*oly of werkes,
*W*ent *W*yde in thys world | *W*onders to heare, &c."

So that the author of this poem will not be found to
have invented any new mode of versification, as
some have supposed, but only to have retained that
of the old Saxon and Gothic poets ; which was probably never wholly laid aside, but occasionally used
at different intervals : though the ravages of time will
not suffer us now to produce a regular series of poems
entirely written in it.

There are some readers whom it may gratify to
mention, that these *Visions of Pierce* (*i.e.* Peter) *the
Plowman*, are attributed to Robert Langland, a
secular priest, born at Mortimer's Cleobury in Shrop-
shire, and fellow of Oriel College in Oxford, who
flourished in the reigns of Edward III. and Richard
II., and published his poem a few years after 1350.
It consists of xx. *passus* or breaks (*e*), exhibiting
a series of visions which, he pretends, happened to
him on Malvern hills in Worcestershire. The author
excells in strong allegoric painting, and has with
great humour, spirit, and fancy, censured most of the
vices incident to the several professions of life; but
he particularly inveighs against the corruptions of
the clergy, and the absurdities of superstition. Of
this work I have now before me four different
editions in black-letter quarto. Three of them are
printed in 1550, "by Robert Crowley, dwelling in Elye

(*d*) So I would read with Mr. Warton, rather than either " soft,"
as in MS. or "set," as in PCC.

(*e*) The poem properly contains xxi. parts: the word *passus*,
adopted by the author, seems only to denote the break or division between two parts, though by the ignorance of the printer
applied to the parts themselves.   See vol. iii. pieface to ballad iii.
where *Passus* seems to signify *Pause*.

Rentes in Holburne." It is remarkable that two of these are mentioned in the title-page as both of the second impression, though they contain evident variations in every page (*f*). The other is said to be "newlye imprynted after the authors olde copy . . . . by Owen Rogers," Feb. 21, 1561.

As Langland was not the first, so neither was he the last that used this alliterative species of versification. To Rogers's edition of the *Visions* is subjoined a poem, which was probably writ in imitation of them, intitled *Pierce the Ploughman's Crede*. It begins thus:

> " *C*ros, and *C*urteis *C*hrist, this beginning spede
> For the *F*aders *F*rendshipe, that *F*ourmed heaven,
> And through the *Sp*ecial *Sp*irit, that *Sp*rong of hem tweyne,
> And al in one godhed endles dwelleth."

The author feigns himself ignorant of his Creed, to be instructed in which he applies to the four religious orders, viz., the gray friers of St. Francis, the black friers of St. Dominic, the Carmelites or white friers, and the Augustines. This affords him occasion to describe in very lively colours the sloth, ignorance, and immorality of those reverend drones. At length he meets with Pierce, a poor ploughman, who resolves his doubts, and instructs him in the principles of true religion. The author was evidently a follower of Wiccliff, whom he mentions (with honour) as no longer living (*g*). Now that reformer died in 1384. How long after his death this poem was written, does not appear.

(*f*) That which seems the first of the two, is thus distinguished in the title-page, "nowe the seconde tyme imprinted by Roberte Crowlye;" the other thus, "nowe the seconde time imprinted by Robert Crowley." In the former the folios are thus erroneously numbered 39, 39, 41, 63, 43, 42, 45, &c. The booksellers of those days did not ostentatiously affect to multiply editions.

(*g*) Signature T. ii.

In the Cotton library is a volume of ancient English poems (*h*), two of which are written in this alliterative metre, and have the division of the lines into distichs distinctly marked by a point, as is usual in old poetical MSS. That which stands first of the two (though perhaps the latest written) is entitled *The Sege of Ïerlam*, (*i.e.* Jerusalem), being an old fabulous legend composed by some monk, and stuffed with marvellous figments concerning the destruction of the holy city and temple. It begins thus :

> " In *T*yberius *T*yme . the *T*rewe emperour
> *S*yr *S*esar hymself . be*S*ted in Rome
> Whyll *P*ylat was *P*rovoste . under that *P*rynce ryche
> And *J*ewes *J*ustice also . of *J*udeas londe
> *H*erode under empere . as *H*erytage wolde
> *K*yng, &c."

The other is intitled *Chevalere Assigne* (or De Cigne), that is, *The Knight of the Swan*, being an ancient Romance, beginning thus :

> " All-*W*eldynge God . *W*hene it is his *W*ylle
> *W*ele he *W*ereth his *W*erke . *W*ith his owene honde
> For ofte *H*armes were *H*ente . that *H*elpe we ne my3te
> Nere the *H*y3nes of *H*ym . that lengeth in *H*evene
> For this, &c."

Among Mr. Garrick's collection of old plays (*i*) is a prose narrative of the adventures of this same Knight of the Swan, "newly translated out of Frenshe into Englyshe, at thinstigacion of the puyssaunt and illustryous prynce, lorde Edward duke of Buckynghame." This lord it seems had a peculiar interest in the book, for, in the preface, the translator tells us, that this "highe dygne and illustryous prynce my lorde Edwarde by the grace of god Duke of Buckyngham, erle of Hereforde, Stafforde, and Northampton, desyrynge cotydyally to encrease and

---

augment the name and fame of such as were relucent in vertuous feates and triumphaunt actes of chyvalry, and to encourage and styre every lusty and gentell herte by the exemplyficacyon of the same, havyng a goodli booke of the highe and miraculous histori of a famous and puyssaunt kynge, named Oryant, sometime reynynge in the parties of beyonde the sea, havynge to his wife a noble lady; of whome she conceyved sixe sonnes and a daughter, and chylded of them at one only time; at whose byrthe echone of them had a chayne of sylver at their neckes, the whiche were all tourned by the provydence of god into whyte swannes, save one, of the whiche this present hystory is compyled, named Helyas, the knight of the swanne, *of whome linially is dyscended my sayde lorde.*   The whiche ententifly to have the sayde hystory more amply and unyversally knowen in thys hys natif countrie, as it is in other, hath of hys hie bountie by some of his faithful and trusti servauntes cohorted mi mayster Wynkin de Worde(*k*) to put the said vertuous hystori in prynte . . . . at whose instigacion and stiring I (Roberte Copland) have me applied, moiening the helpe of god, to reduce and translate it into our maternal and vulgare english tonge after the capacitè and rudenesse of my weke entendement." A curious picture of the times! While in Italy literature and the fine arts were ready to burst forth with classical splendor under Leo X. the first peer of this realm was proud to derive his pedigree from a fabulous knight of the swan (*l*) !

(*k*) W. de Worde's edit. is in 1512. See Ames, p. 92. Mr. G.'s copy is " ¶ Imprinted at London by me Wylliam Copland."

(*l*) He is said in the story-book to be the grandfather of God-frey of Boulogne, through whom I suppose the duke made out his relation to him. This duke was beheaded May 17, 1521, 13 Hen. VIII.

To return to the metre of Pierce Plowman : In the folio MS. so often quoted in these volumes, are two poems written in that species of versification. One of these is an ancient allegorical poem intitled *Death and Life*, (in 2 fitts or parts, containing 458 distichs) which, for ought that appears, may have been written as early, if not before, the time of Langland. The first forty lines are broke as they should be into distichs, a distinction that is neglected in the remaining part of the transcript, in order, I suppose, to save room. It begins :

> " *Chr*ist *Chr*isten king,
>   that on the *Cr*osse tholed ;
> Hadd *Pa*ines and *Pa*ssyons
>   to defend our soules ;
> Give us *Gr*ace on the *Gr*ound
>   the *Gr*eatlye to serve,
> For that *R*oyall *R*ed blood
>   that *R*ann from thy side."

The subject of this piece is a vision, wherein the poet sees a contest for superiority between " our lady Dame Life," and the " ugly fiend Dame Death;" who with their several attributes and concomitants are personified in a fine vein of allegoric painting. Part of the description of Dame Life is :

> " Shee was *B*righter of her *B*lee,
>   then was the *B*right sonn :
> Her *R*udd *R*edder then the *R*ose,
>   that on the *R*ise hangeth :
> *M*eekely smiling with her *M*outh,
>   And *M*erry in her lookes ;
> Ever *L*aughing for *L*ove,
>   as shee *L*ike would.
> And as shee came by the *B*ankes,
>   the *B*oughes eche one
> They *L*owted to that *L*adye,
>   and *L*ayd forth their branches ;
> *B*lossomes, and *B*urgens
>   *B*reathed full sweete ;

> *F*lowers *F*lourished in the *F*rith,
>   where shee *F*orth stepped;
> And the *G*rasse, that was *G*ray,
>   *G*reened belive."

Death is afterwards sketched out with a no less bold and original pencil.

The other poem is that which is quoted in the 32nd page of this volume, and which was probably the last that was ever written in this kind of metre in its original simplicity unaccompanied with rhyme. It should have been observed above in page 32, that in this poem the lines are throughout divided into distichs, thus:

> " *G*rant *G*racious God,
>   *G*rant me this time," &c.

It is intitled *Scottish Feilde* (in 2 fitts, 420 distichs,) containing a very circumstantial narrative of the battle of Flodden, fought Sept. 9, 1513: at which the author seems to have been present from his speaking in the first person plural:

> " Then *we T*ild downe *our T*ents,
>   that *T*old were a thousand."

In the conclusion of the poem he gives this account of himself:

> " He was a *G*entleman by *J*esu,
>   that this *G*est (*m*) made:
> Which *S*ay but as he *S*ayd (*n*)
>   for *S*ooth and noe other.
> At *B*agily that *B*earne
>   his *B*iding place had;
> And his ancestors of old time
>   have yearded (*o*) theire longe,
> Before William *C*onquerour
>   this *C*untry did inhabitt.

(*m*) Jest, MS.
(*n*) Probably corrupted for—" *S*ays but as he *S*aw."
(*o*) Yearded, *i.e. buried, earthed*, earded. It is common to pro-

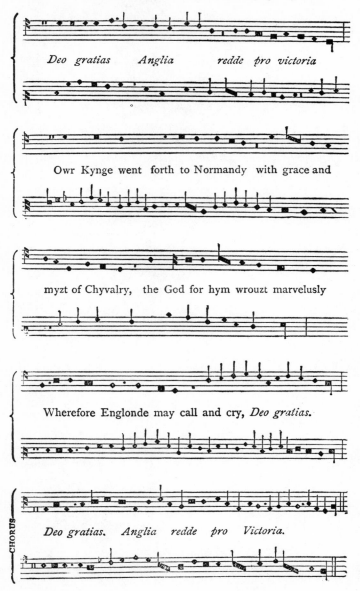

Deo gratias   Anglia   redde pro victoria

Owr Kynge went forth to Normandy with grace and

myzt of Chyvalry,   the God for hym wrouzt marvelusly

Wherefore Englonde may call and cry, *Deo gratias.*

Deo gratias.   Anglia   redde   pro   Victoria.

Jesus *B*ring ' them' (*p*) to *B*lisse,
that *B*rought us forth of *Bale*,
That hath *H*earkned me *H*eare
or *H*eard my *tale*."

The village of Bagily or Baguleigh is in Cheshire, and had belonged to the ancient family of Legh for two centuries before the battle of Flodden. Indeed that the author was of that county appears from other passages in the body of the poem, particularly from the pains he takes to wipe off a stain from the Cheshiremen, who it seems ran away in that battle, and from his encomiums on the Stanleys, earls of Derby, who usually headed that county. He laments the death of James Stanley, bishop of Ely, as what had recently happened when this poem was written; which serves to ascertain its date, for that prelate died March 22, 1514-5.

Thus have we traced the alliterative measure so low as the sixteenth century. It is remarkable that all such poets as used this kind of metre, retained along with it many peculiar Saxon idioms, particularly such as were appropriated to poetry: this deserves the attention of those who are desirous to recover the laws of the ancient Saxon poesy, usually given up as inexplicable: I am of opinion that they will find what they seek in the metre of Pierce Plowman (*q*).

About the beginning of the sixteenth century this kind of versification began to change its form: the author of *Scottish Field*, we see, concludes his poem with a couplet in rhyme: this was an innovation that did but prepare the way for the general admission of

nounce " Earth," in some parts of England " Yearth," particularly in the north.—Pitscottie speaking of James III. slain at Bannockbourn, says, " Nae man wot whar they *yearded* him."

(*p*) "us." MS. In the 2d line above, the MS. has " bidding."

(*q*) And in that of Robert of Gloucester. See the next note.

that more modish ornament; till at length the old uncouth verse of the ancient writers would no longer go down without it. Yet when rhyme began to be superadded, all the niceties of alliteration were at first retained along with it; and the song of *Little John Nobody* exhibits this union very clearly. By degrees the correspondence of final sounds engrossing the whole attention of the poet, and fully satisfying the reader, the internal imbellishment of alliteration was no longer studied, and thus was this kind of metre at length swallowed up and lost in our common burlesque Alexandrine, or Anapestic verse (*r*), now never used but in ballads and pieces of light humour, as in the song of *Conscience*, and in that well-known doggerel,

> " A cobler there was, and he lived in a stall."

But although this kind of measure hath with us oeen thus degraded, it still retains among the French

---

(*r*) Consisting of four Anapests (◡ ◡ -) in which the accent rests upon every third syllable. This kind of verse, which I also call the burlesque Alexandrine (to distinguish it from the other Alexandrines of eleven and fourteen syllables, the parents of our lyric measure: see examples, pp. 151, 152, &c.), was early applied by Robert of Gloucester to serious subjects. That writer's metre, like this of Langland's, is formed on the Saxon models (each verse of his containing a Saxon distich), only instead of the internal alliterations adopted by Langland, he rather chose final rhymes, as the French poets have done since. Take a specimen:

> " The Saxons tho in ther power, tho thii were so rive,
> Seve kingdoms made in Engelonde, and suthe but vive:
> The king of Northomberlond, and of Eastangle also,
> Of Kent, and of Westsex, and of the March, therto."

Robert of Gloucester wrote in the western dialect, and his language differs exceedingly from that of other contemporary writers, who resided in the metropolis, or in the midland counties. Had the Heptarchy continued, our English language would probably have been as much distinguished for its different dialects as the Greek; or at least as that of the several independent states of Italy.

its ancient dignity; their grand heroic verse of twelve
syllables(*s*) is the same genuine offspring of the old
alliterative metre of the ancient Gothic and Francic
poets, stript like our Anapestic of its alliteration, and
ornamented with rhyme : but with this difference, that
whereas this kind of verse hath been applied by us
only to light and trivial subjects, to which by its
quick and lively measure it seemed best adapted, our
poets have let it remain in a more lax unconfined
state(*t*), as a greater degree of severity and strictness
would have been inconsistent with the light and airy
subjects to which they have applied it. On the other
hand, the French having retained this verse as the
vehicle of their epic and tragic flights, in order to
give it a stateliness and dignity were obliged to confine it to more exact laws of scansion : they have
therefore limited it to the number of twelve syllables;
and by making the cæsura or pause as full and

(*s*) Or of thirteen syllables, in what they call a feminine verse.
It is remarkable that the French alone have retained this old Gothic
metre for their serious poems; while the English, Spaniards, &c.
have adopted the Italic verse of ten syllables, although the Spaniards, as well as we, anciently used a short-lined metre. I believe the success with which Petrarch, and perhaps one or two
others, first used the heroic verse of ten syllables in Italian poesy,
recommended it to the Spanish writers; as it also did to our
Chaucer, who first attempted it in English ; and to his successors
Lord Surrey, Sir Thomas Wyat, &c.; who afterwards improved it
and brought it to perfection. To Lord Surrey we also owe the first
introduction of blank verse in his versions of the second and
fourth Books of the *Æneid*, 1557, 4to.

(*t*) Thus our poets use this verse indifferently with twelve,
eleven, and even ten syllables. For though regularly it consists
of four Anapests (ᵕ ᵕ -) or twelve syllables, yet they frequently
retrench a syllable from the first or third Anapest; and sometimes
from both; as in these instances from *Prior*, and from the Song
of *Conscience*:

"Whŏ hăs eēr beĕn ăt Pārĭs, mŭst nēeds knŏw thĕ Grēve,
Thĕ fātăl rĕtrēat ŏf th' ŭnfŏrtŭnăte brāve.
Hĕ stēpt tŏ hĭm strāight, ănd dĭd hĭm rĕquīre."

distinct as possible, and by other severe restrictions, have given it all the solemnity of which it was capable. The harmony of both however depends so much on the same flow of cadence and disposal of the pause, that they appear plainly to be of the same original ; and every French heroic verse evidently consists of the ancient distich of their Francic ancestors : which, by the way, will account to us why this verse of the French so naturally resolves itself into two complete hemistics. And indeed by making the cæsura or pause always to rest on the last syllable of a word, and by making a kind of pause in the sense, the French poets do in effect reduce their hemistics to two distinct and independent verses : and some of their old poets have gone so far as to make the two hemistics rhyme to each other.(*u*)

After all, the old alliterative and anapestic metre of the English poets being chiefly used in a barbarous age, and in a rude unpolished language, abounds with verses defective in length, proportion, and harmony ; and therefore cannot enter into a comparison with the correct versification of the best modern French writers ; but making allowances for these defects, that sort of metre runs with a cadence so exactly resembling the French heroic Alexandrine, that I believe no peculiarities of their versification can be produced, which cannot be exactly matched in the alliterative metre. I shall give by way of example a few lines from the modern French poets accommodated with parallels from the ancient poem of *Life and Death ;* in these I shall denote the cæsura or pause by a perpendicular line, and the cadence by the marks of the Latin quantity.

(*u*) See instances in *L'Hist. de la Poesie Françoise, par Massieu,* &c. In the same book are also specimens of alliterative French verses.

Lĕ sŭccēs fŭt toŭjoūrs	*ŭn ĕnfānt dĕ l' ăudāce;*
All shăll drȳe wĭth thĕ dĭnts	thăt I dĕal wĭth mȳ hānds.
L'hŏmmĕ prūdĕnt vŏit trōp	*l'ĭllŭsĭŏn lĕ sūit,*
Yōndĕr dāmsĕl ĭs dēath	thăt drēssĕth hĕr tŏ smīte.
L'ĭntrĕpīdĕ vŏit mīeux	*ĕt lĕ fantōmĕ fŭit.* (*x*)
Whĕn shĕ dōlefŭllȳ sāw	hōw shĕ dāng dōwne hĭr fōlke.
Mĕme aŭx yeŭx dĕ l'injŭste	*ŭn injŭste ĕst hŏrrīblĕ.* (*y*)
Thĕn shĕ cāst ŭp ă crȳe	tŏ thĕ hīgh kĭng ŏf heāvĕn.
Dŭ mĕnsōngĕ toŭjoūrs	*lĕ vrāi dĕmēurĕ māitrĕ,*
Thŏu shălt bĭttĕrlyĕ bȳe	ŏr ēlse thĕ bōokĕ fāilĕth.
Poŭr părōitre hŏnnĕte hōmme	*ĕn ŭn mōt, ĭl făut l'ētre.*(*z*)
Thŭs I fāred thrōughe ă frȳthe	whĕre thĕ flōwĕrs wĕre mānȳe.

To conclude: the metre of Pierce Plowman's Visions has no kind of affinity with what is commonly called blank verse; yet has it a sort of harmony of its own, proceeding not so much from its alliteration, as from the artful disposal of its cadence, and the contrivance of its pause; so that when the ear is a little accustomed to it, it is by no means unpleasing; but claims all the merit of the French heroic numbers, only far less polished; being sweetened, instead of their final rhymes, with the internal recurrence of similar sounds.

(*x*) Catalina, A. 3.　　(*y*) Boileau Sat.　　(*z*) Boil. Sat. 11.

ADDITIONS TO THE ESSAY ON THE ALLITERATIVE METRE.

SINCE the foregoing essay was first printed, the Editor hath met with some additional examples of the old alliterative metre. The first is in MS. (*a*) which begins thus:

" *C*rist *C*rowned *K*yng, that on *C*ros didest,(*b*)
And art *C*omfort of all *C*are, thow(*c*) kind go out of *C*ours,
With thi *H*alwes in *H*even *H*eried mote thu be,
And thy *W*orshipful *W*erkes *W*orshiped evre,
That suche *S*ondry *S*ignes *S*hewest unto man,
In *D*remyng, in *D*recchyng,(*d*) and in *D*erke swevenes."

The Author from this proemium takes occasion to give an account of a dream that happened to himself: which he introduces with the following circumstances:

" *O*nes y me *O*rdayned, as y have *O*fte doon,
With *F*rendes, and *F*elawes, *F*rendemen, and other;
And *C*aught me in a *C*ompany on *C*orpus *C*hristi even,
*S*ix, other(*e*) *S*even myle, oute of *S*uthampton,
To take *M*elodye, and *M*irthes, among my *M*akes;
With *R*edyng of *R*omaunces, and *R*evelyng among,
The *D*ym of the *D*erknesse *D*rewe me into the west;
And be*G*on for to spryng in the *G*rey day.
Than *L*ift y up my *L*yddes, and *L*oked in the sky,
And *K*newe by the *K*ende *C*ours, hit clered in the est:
*B*lyve y *B*usked me down, and to *B*ed went,
For to *C*omforte my *K*ynde, and *C*acche a slepe."

He then describes his dream:

(*a*) In a small 4to. MS. containing thirty-eight leaves in private hands.

(*b*) Didst dye.　　(*c*) though.　　(*d*) being overpowered.
(*e*) *i. e.* either, or.

" Methought that y *H*oved on *H*igh on an *H*ill,
And loked *D*oun on a *D*ale *D*epest of othre ;
Ther y *S*awe in my *S*ighte a *S*elcouthe peple ;
The *M*ultitude was so *M*oche, it *M*ighte not be nombred :
Methoughte y herd a *C*rowned *K*yng, of his *C*omunes axe
A *S*oleyne(*f*) *S*ubsidie, to *S*usteyne his werres.

 *   *   *   *

With that a *C*lerk *K*neled adowne and *C*arped these wordes,
 *L*iege *L*ord, yif it you *L*ike to *L*isten a while,
*S*om *S*awes of *S*alomon y shall you shewe sone."

The writer then gives a solemn lecture to kings on the art of governing. From the demand of subsidies " to susteyne his werres," I am inclined to believe this poem composed in the reign of K. Henry V., as the MS. appears from a subsequent entry to have been written before the 9th of Henry VI. The whole poem contains but 146 lines.

The alliterative metre was no less popular among the old Scottish poets, than with their brethren on this side the Tweed. In Maitland's collection of ancient Scottish poems, MS. in the Pepysian library, is a very long poem in this species of versification, thus inscribed :

" *Heir* begins the Tretis of the Twa Marriit Wemen, and the Wedo,
   compylit be Maister *William Dunbar*.(*g*)
Upon the *M*idsummer evven *M*irriest of nichtis
I *M*uvit furth alane quhen as *M*idnight was past
Besyd ane *G*udlie *G*rene *G*arth,(*h*) full of *G*ay flouris
*H*egeit (*i*) of ane *H*uge *H*icht with *H*awthorne treeis
Quairon ane *B*ird on ane *B*ransche so *B*irst out hir notis
That nevir ane *B*lythfuller *B*ird was on the *B*euche(*k*) hard &c."

The Author pretends to overhear three gossips sitting in an arbour, and revealing all their secret

---

(*f*) solemn.
(*g*) Since the above was written, this poem hath been printed in *Ancient Scottish Poems, &c.* from the MS. Collections of Sir R. Maitland, of Lethington, knight, of London, 1786, 2 vols. 12mo. The two first lines are here corrected by that edition.
 (*h*) Garden. (*i*) Hedged. (*k*) Bough.

methods of alluring and governing the other sex ; it
is a severe and humorous satire on bad women, and
nothing inferior to Chaucer's Prologue to his *Wife of
Bath's Tale.* As Dunbar lived till about the middle of
the sixteenth century, this poem was probably composed after *Scottish Field* (described above in p. 384),
which is the latest specimen I have met with written in
England. This poem contains about five hundred
lines.

But the current use of the alliterative metre in
Scotland, appears more particularly from those popular vulgar prophecies, which are still printed for
the use of the lower people in Scotland, under the
names of Thomas the Rymer, Marvellous Merling,
&c. This collection seems to have been put together
after the accession of James I. to the crown of England, and most of the pieces in it are in the metre of
Pierce Plowman's Visions. The first of them begins
thus :

> " Merling sayes in his book, who will *R*ead *R*ight,
> Although his *S*ayings be uncouth, they *S*hall be true found.
> In the seventh chapter, read *W*hoso *W*ill,
> One thousand and more after Christ's birth, &c."

And the prophesie of Beid :

> " Betwixt the chief of *S*ummer and the *S*ad winter ;
> Before the *H*eat of summer *H*appen shall a war
> That *E*urop's lands *E*arnestly shall be wrought
> And *E*arnest *E*nvy shall last but a while, &c."

So again the prophesie of Berlington :

> " When the *R*uby is *R*aised, *R*est is there none,
> But much *R*ancour shall *R*ise in *R*iver and plain
> Much *S*orrow is *S*een through a *S*uth-hound
> That beares *H*ornes in his *H*ead like a wyld *H*art, &c."

In like metre is the prophesie of Waldhave :

> " Upon *L*owdon *L*aw alone as I *L*ay,
> *L*ooking to the *L*ennox, as me *L*ief thought,
> The first *M*orning of *M*ay, *M*edicine to seek
> For *M*alice and *M*elody that *M*oved me sore, &c."

And lastly, that intitled the prophesie of Gildas:

> " When holy kirk is *W*racked and *W*ill has no *W*it
> And *P*astors are *P*luckt, and *P*il'd without *P*ity
> When *I*dolatry *I*s *I*n *ens* and *re*
> And spiritual pastours are vexed away, &c."

It will be observed in the foregoing specimens, that the alliteration is extremely neglected, except in the third and fourth instances; although all the rest are written in imitation of the cadence used in this kind of metre. It may perhaps appear from an attentive perusal, that the poems ascribed to Berlington and Waldhave are more ancient than the others: indeed the first and fifth appear evidently to have been new modelled, if not intirely composed about the beginning of the last century, and are probably the latest attempts ever made in this species of verse.

In this and the foregoing essay are mentioned all the specimens I have met with of the alliterative metre without rhyme: but instances occur sometimes in old manuscripts, of poems written both with final rhymes and the internal cadence and alliterations of the metre of Pierce Plowman.

This Essay will receive illustration from another specimen in Warton's *History of English Poetry*, vol. i. p. 309, being the fragment of a MS. poem on the subject of *Alexander the Great*, in the Bodleian Library, which he supposes to be the same with No. 44 in the Ashmol. MSS. containing twenty-seven *passus*, and beginning thus:

> "Whener folk fastid [feasted, *qu.*] and fed,
>   fayne wolde thei her [*i. e.* hear]
> Some farand thing, &c."

It is well observed by Mr. Tyrwhitt on Chaucer's sneer at this old alliterative metre (vol. iii. p. 305), viz. :

" ———— I am a Sotherne [*i. e.* Southern] man,
I cannot geste, rom, ram, raf, by my letter,"

that the fondness for this species of versification, &c. was retained longest in the northern provinces : and that the author of *Pierce Plowman's Visions* is in the best MSS. called *William,* without any surname. See vol. iv. p. 74.

[The Rev. Walter W. Skeat, editor of *Piers Plowman,* for the Early English Text Society, has written *An Essay on Alliterative Poetry,* for Hales and Furnivall's edition of the Percy folio MS., which will be found in the third volume of that work (pp. xi.-xxxix.). He gives a list of all the poems he has met with that have been written as alliterative, yet without rhyme, since the Conquest, and ends his essay with the following note :—" The reader must be warned against three extraordinary mis-statements in this (Percy's) essay, following close upon one another near the end of it. These are (1) that Robert of Gloucester wrote in anapæstic verse, whereas he wrote in the long Alexandrine verse, containing (when perfect) six *Returns;* (2) that the French alone have retained this old Gothic metre [the twelve-syllabled Alexandrine] for their serious poems, whereas we may be sure that Michael Drayton, the author of the Polyolbion, meant his poem seriously; and (3) that the cadence of *Piers Plowman* 'so exactly resembles the French Alexandrine, that I believe no peculiarities of their versification can be produced which cannot be exactly matched in the alliterative metre.' This is indeed a curious craze, for the alliterative metre is founded on *Dominants,* the Alexandrine on *Returns.* Percy gives some examples, and the metre which he selects for numbering is the *French* one, as the reader may easily judge for himself when he finds that the line

"Lĕ sŭccēs fŭt toŭjoūrs | ŭn ĕnfānt dĕ l'aŭdāce "

is marked by him as it is marked here, and is supposed to consist of *four Anapæsts!* Yet one more blunder to be laid at the door of the 'Anapæsts!' Would that we were well rid of them, and that the 'longs' and 'shorts' were buried beside them."]

INDEX OF BALLADS AND POEMS IN
THE SECOND VOLUME.

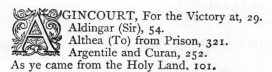

END OF VOLUME THE SECOND.

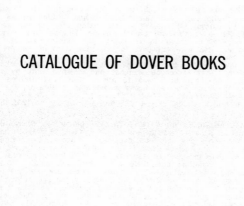

CATALOGUE OF DOVER BOOKS

Art, History of Art, Antiques, Graphic Arts, Handcrafts

ART STUDENTS' ANATOMY, E. J. Farris. Outstanding art anatomy that uses chiefly living objects for its illustrations. 71 photos of undraped men, women, children are accompanied by carefully labeled matching sketches to illustrate the skeletal system, articulations and movements, bony landmarks, the muscular system, skin, fasciae, fat, etc. 9 x-ray photos show movement of joints. Undraped models are shown in such actions as serving in tennis, drawing a bow in archery, playing football, dancing, preparing to spring and to dive. Also discussed and illustrated are proportions, age and sex differences, the anatomy of the smile, etc. 8 plates by the great early 18th century anatomic illustrator Siegfried Albinus are also included. Glossary. 158 figures, 7 in color. x + 159pp. 5⅝ x 8⅜. T744 Paperbound **$1.50**

AN ATLAS OF ANATOMY FOR ARTISTS, F Schider. A new 3rd edition of this standard text enlarged by 52 new illustrations of hands, anatomical studies by Cloquet, and expressive life studies of the body by Barcsay. 189 clear, detailed plates offer you precise information of impeccable accuracy. 29 plates show all aspects of the skeleton, with closeups of special areas, while 54 full-page plates, mostly in two colors, give human musculature as seen from four different points of view, with cutaways for important portions of the body. 14 full-page plates provide photographs of hand forms, eyelids, female breasts, and indicate the location of muscles upon models. 59 additional plates show how great artists of the past utilized human anatomy. They reproduce sketches and finished work by such artists as Michelangelo, Leonardo da Vinci, Goya, and 15 others. This is a lifetime reference work which will be one of the most important books in any artist's library. "The standard reference tool," AMERICAN LIBRARY ASSOCIATION. "Excellent," AMERICAN ARTIST. Third enlarged edition. 189 plates, 647 illustrations. xxvi + 192pp. 7⅞ x 10⅝. T241 Clothbound **$6.00**

AN ATLAS OF ANIMAL ANATOMY FOR ARTISTS, W. Ellenberger, H. Baum, H. Dittrich. The largest, richest animal anatomy for artists available in English. 99 detailed anatomical plates of such animals as the horse, dog, cat, lion, deer, seal, kangaroo, flying squirrel, cow, bull, goat, monkey, hare, and bat. Surface features are clearly indicated, while progressive beneath-the-skin pictures show musculature, tendons, and bone structure. Rest and action are exhibited in terms of musculature and skeletal structure and detailed cross-sections are given for heads and important features. The animals chosen are representative of specific families so that a study of these anatomies will provide knowledge of hundreds of related species. "Highly recommended as one of the very few books on the subject worthy of being used as an authoritative guide," DESIGN. "Gives a fundamental knowledge," AMERICAN ARTIST. Second revised, enlarged edition with new plates from Cuvier, Stubbs, etc. 288 illustrations. 153pp. 11⅜ x 9. T82 Clothbound **$6.00**

THE HUMAN FIGURE IN MOTION, Eadweard Muybridge. The largest selection in print of Muybridge's famous high-speed action photos of the human figure in motion. 4789 photographs illustrate 162 different actions: men, women, children—mostly undraped—are shown walking, running, carrying various objects, sitting, lying down, climbing, throwing, arising, and performing over 150 other actions. Some actions are shown in as many as 150 photographs each. All in all there are more than 500 action strips in this enormous volume, series shots taken at shutter speeds of as high as 1/6000th of a second! These are not posed shots, but true stopped motion. They show bone and muscle in situations that the human eye is not fast enough to capture. Earlier, smaller editions of these prints have brought $40 and more on the out-of-print market. "A must for artists," ART IN FOCUS. "An unparalleled dictionary of action for all artists," AMERICAN ARTIST. 390 full-page plates, with 4789 photographs. Printed on heavy glossy stock. Reinforced binding with headbands. xxi + 390pp. 7⅞ x 10⅝. T204 Clothbound **$10.00**

ANIMALS IN MOTION, Eadweard Muybridge. This is the largest collection of animal action photos in print. 34 different animals (horses, mules, oxen, goats, camels, pigs, cats, guanacos, lions, gnus, deer, monkeys, eagles—and 21 others) in 132 characteristic actions. The horse alone is shown in more than 40 different actions. All 3919 photographs are taken in series at speeds up to 1/6000th of a second. The secrets of leg motion, spinal patterns, head movements, strains and contortions shown nowhere else are captured. You will see exactly how a lion sets his foot down; how an elephant's knees are like a human's—and how they differ; the position of a kangaroo's legs in mid-leap; how an ostrich's head bobs; details of the flight of birds—and thousands of facets of motion only the fastest cameras can catch. Photographed from domestic animals and animals in the Philadelphia zoo, it contains neither semiposed artificial shots nor distorted telephoto shots taken under adverse conditions. Artists, biologists, decorators, cartoonists, will find this book indispensable for understanding animals in motion. "A really marvelous series of plates," NATURE (London). "The dry plate's most spectacular early use was by Eadweard Muybridge," LIFE. 3919 photographs; 380 full pages of plates. 440pp. Printed on heavy glossy paper. Deluxe binding with headbands. 7⅞ x 10⅝. T203 Clothbound **$10.00**

CATALOGUE OF DOVER BOOKS

DESIGN MOTIFS OF ANCIENT MEXICO, J. Enciso. This unique collection of pre-Columbian stamps for textiles and pottery contains 766 superb designs from Aztec, Olmec, Totonac, Maya, and Toltec origins. Plumed serpents, calendrical elements, wind gods, animals, flowers, demons, dancers, monsters, abstract ornament, and other designs. More than 90% of these illustrations are completely unobtainable elsewhere. Use this work to bring new barbaric beauty into your crafts or drawing. Originally $17.50. Printed in three colors. 766 illustrations, thousands of motifs. 192pp. 7⅞ x 10¾.
T84 Paperbound **$1.85**

DECORATIVE ART OF THE SOUTHWEST INDIANS, D. S. Sides. A magnificent album of authentic designs (both pre- and post-Conquest) from the pottery, textiles, and basketry of the Navaho, Hopi, Mohave, Santo Domingo, and over 20 other Southwestern groups. Designs include birds, clouds, butterflies, quadrupeds, geometric forms, etc. A valuable book for folklorists, and a treasury for artists, designers, advertisers, and craftsmen, who may use without payment or permission any of the vigorous, colorful, and strongly rhythmic designs. Aesthetic and archeological notes. 50 plates. Bibliography of over 50 items. xviii + 101pp. 5⅝ x 8⅜.
T139 Paperbound **$1.00**

PAINTING IN THE FAR EAST, Laurence Binyon. Excellent introduction by one of greatest authorities on subject studies 1500 years of oriental art (China, Japan; also Tibet, Persia), over 250 painters. Examines works, schools, influence of Wu Tao-tzu, Kanaoka, Toba Sojo, Masanobu, Okio, etc.; early traditions; Kamakura epoch; the Great Decorators; T'ang Dynasty; Matabei, beginnings of genre; Japanese woodcut, color print; much more, all chronological, in cultural context. 42 photos. Bibliography. 317pp. 6 x 9¼.
T520 Paperbound **$2.25**

ON THE LAWS OF JAPANESE PAINTING, H. Bowie. This unusual book, based on 9 years of profound study-experience in the Late Kano art of Japan, remains the most authentic guide in English to the spirit and technique of Japanese painting. A wealth of interesting and useful data on control of the brush; practise exercises; manufacture of ink, brushes, colors; the use of various lines and dots to express moods. It is the best possible substitute for a series of lessons from a great oriental master. 66 plates with 220 illustrations. Index. xv + 177pp. 6⅛ x 9¼.
T30 Paperbound **$2.00**

THE MATERIALS AND TECHNIQUES OF MEDIEVAL PAINTING, D. V. Thompson. Based on years of study of medieval manuscripts and laboratory analysis of medieval paintings, this book discusses carriers and grounds, binding media, pigments, metals used in painting, etc. Considers relative merits of painting al fresco and al secco, the procession of coloring materials, burnishing, and many other matters. Preface by Bernard Berenson. Index. 239pp. 5⅜ x 8.
T327 Paperbound **$1.85**

THE CRAFTSMAN'S HANDBOOK, Cennino Cennini. This is considered the finest English translation of IL LIBRO DELL' ARTE, a 15th century Florentine introduction to art technique. It is both fascinating reading and a wonderful mirror of another culture for artists, art students, historians, social scientists, or anyone interested in details of life some 500 years ago. While it is not an exact recipe book, it gives directions for such matters as tinting papers, gilding stone, preparation of various hues of black, and many other useful but nearly forgotten facets of the painter's art. As a human document reflecting the ideas of a practising medieval artist it is particularly important. 4 illustrations. xxvii + 142pp. D. V. Thompson translator. 6⅛ x 9¼.
T54 Paperbound **$1.35**

VASARI ON TECHNIQUE, G. Vasari. Pupil of Michelangelo and outstanding biographer of the Renaissance artists, Vasari also wrote this priceless treatise on the technical methods of the painters, architects, and sculptors of his day. This is the only English translation of this practical, informative, and highly readable work. Scholars, artists, and general readers will welcome these authentic discussions of marble statues, bronze casting, fresco painting, oil painting, engraving, stained glass, rustic fountains and grottoes, etc. Introduction and notes by G. B. Brown. Index. 18 plates, 11 figures. xxiv + 328pp. 5⅜ x 8.
T717 Paperbound **$2.25**

METHODS AND MATERIALS OF PAINTING OF THE GREAT SCHOOLS AND MASTERS, C. L. Eastlake. A vast, complete, and authentic reconstruction of the secret techniques of the masters of painting, collected from hundreds of forgotten manuscripts by the eminent President of the British Royal Academy: Greek, Roman, and medieval techniques; fresco and tempera; varnishes and encaustics; the secrets of Leonardo, Van Eyck, Raphael, and many others. Art historians, students, teachers, critics, and laymen will gain new insights into the creation of the great masterpieces; while artists and craftsmen will have a treasury of valuable techniques. Index. Two volume set. Total of 1025pp. 5⅜ x 8.
T718 Paperbound **$2.25**
T719 Paperbound **$2.25**
The set **$4.50**

BYZANTINE ART AND ARCHAEOLOGY, O. M. Dalton. Still the most thorough work in English— both in breadth and in depth—on the astounding multiplicity of Byzantine art forms throughout Europe, North Africa, and Western Asia from the 4th to the 15th century. Analyzes hundreds of individual pieces from over 160 public and private museums, libraries, and collections all over the world. Full treatment of Byzantine sculpture, painting, mosaic, jewelry, textiles, etc., including historical development, symbolism, and aesthetics. Chapters on iconography and ornament. Indispensable for study of Christian symbolism and medieval art. 457 illustrations, many full-page. Bibliography of over 2500 references. 4 Indexes. xx + 727pp. 6⅛ x 9¼.
T776 Clothbound **$8.50**

Language Books and Records

GERMAN: HOW TO SPEAK AND WRITE IT. AN INFORMAL CONVERSATIONAL METHOD FOR SELF STUDY, Joseph Rosenberg. Eminently useful for self study because of concentration on elementary stages of learning. Also provides teachers with remarkable variety of aids: 28 full- and double-page sketches with pertinent items numbered and identified in German and English; German proverbs, jokes; grammar, idiom studies; extensive practice exercises. The most interesting introduction to German available, full of amusing illustrations, photographs of cities and landmarks in German-speaking cities, cultural information subtly woven into conversational material. Includes summary of grammar, guide to letter writing, study guide to German literature by Dr. Richard Friedenthal. Index. 400 illustrations. 384pp. 5⅜ x 8½.
T271 Paperbound **$2.00**

FRENCH: HOW TO SPEAK AND WRITE IT. AN INFORMAL CONVERSATIONAL METHOD FOR SELF STUDY, Joseph Lemaitre. Even the absolute beginner can acquire a solid foundation for further study from this delightful elementary course. Photographs, sketches and drawings, sparkling colloquial conversations on a wide variety of topics (including French culture and custom), French sayings and quips, are some of aids used to demonstrate rather than merely describe the language. Thorough yet surprisingly entertaining approach, excellent for teaching and for self study. Comprehensive analysis of pronunciation, practice exercises and appendices of verb tables, additional vocabulary, other useful material. Index. Appendix. 400 illustrations. 416pp. 5⅜ x 8½.
T268 Paperbound **$2.00**

DICTIONARY OF SPOKEN SPANISH, Spanish-English, English-Spanish. Compiled from spoken Spanish, emphasizing idiom and colloquial usage in both Castilian and Latin-American. More than 16,000 entries containing over 25,000 idioms—the largest list of idiomatic constructions ever published. Complete sentences given, indexed under single words—language in immediately useable form, for travellers, businessmen, students, etc. 25 page introduction provides rapid survey of sounds, grammar, syntax, with full consideration of irregular verbs. Especially apt in modern treatment of phrases and structure. 17 page glossary gives translations of geographical names, money values, numbers, national holidays, important street signs, useful expressions of high frequency, plus unique 7 page glossary of Spanish and Spanish-American foods and dishes. Originally published as War Department Technical Manual TM 30-900. iv + 513pp. 5⅜ x 8.
T495 Paperbound **$1.75**

SPEAK MY LANGUAGE: SPANISH FOR YOUNG BEGINNERS, M. Ahlman, Z. Gilbert. Records provide one of the best, and most entertaining, methods of introducing a foreign language to children. Within the framework of a train trip from Portugal to Spain, an English-speaking child is introduced to Spanish by a native companion. (Adapted from a successful radio program of the N. Y. State Educational Department.) Though a continuous story, there are a dozen specific categories of expressions, including greetings, numbers, time, weather, food, clothes, family members, etc. Drill is combined with poetry and contextual use. Authentic background music is heard. An accompanying book enables a reader to follow the records, and includes a vocabulary of over 350 recorded expressions. Two 10″ 33⅓ records, total of 40 minutes. Book. 40 illustrations. 69pp. 5¼ x 10½.
T890 The set **$4.95**

AN ENGLISH-FRENCH-GERMAN-SPANISH WORD FREQUENCY DICTIONARY, H. S. Eaton. An indispensable language study aid, this is a semantic frequency list of the 6000 most frequently used words in 4 languages—24,000 words in all. The lists, based on concepts rather than words alone, and containing all modern, exact, and idiomatic vocabulary, are arranged side by side to form a unique 4-language dictionary. A simple key indicates the importance of the individual words within each language. Over 200 pages of separate indexes for each language enable you to locate individual words at a glance. Will help language teachers and students, authors of textbooks, grammars, and language tests to compare concepts in the various languages and to concentrate on basic vocabulary, avoiding uncommon and obsolete words. 2 Appendixes. xxi + 441pp. 6½ x 9¼.
T738 Paperbound **$2.45**

NEW RUSSIAN-ENGLISH AND ENGLISH-RUSSIAN DICTIONARY, M. A. O'Brien. Over 70,000 entries in the new orthography! Many idiomatic uses and colloquialisms which form the basis of actual speech. Irregular verbs, perfective and imperfective aspects, regular and irregular sound changes, and other features. One of the few dictionaries where accent changes within the conjugation of verbs and the declension of nouns are fully indicated. "One of the best," Prof. E. J. Simmons, Cornell. First names, geographical terms, bibliography, etc. 738pp. 4½ x 6¼.
T208 Paperbound **$2.00**

96 MOST USEFUL PHRASES FOR TOURISTS AND STUDENTS in English, French, Spanish, German, Italian. A handy folder you'll want to carry with you. How to say "Excuse me," "How much is it?", "Write it down, please," etc., in four foreign languages. Copies limited, no more than 1 to a customer.
FREE

Say It language phrase books

These handy phrase books (128 to 196 pages each) make grammatical drills unnecessary for an elementary knowledge of a spoken foreign language. Covering most matters of travel and everyday life each volume contains:

Over 1000 phrases and sentences in immediately useful forms — foreign language plus English.

Modern usage designed for Americans. Specific phrases like, "Give me small change," and "Please call a taxi."

Simplified phonetic transcription you will be able to read at sight.

The only completely indexed phrase books on the market.

Covers scores of important situations: — Greetings, restaurants, sightseeing, useful expressions, etc.

These books are prepared by native linguists who are professors at Columbia, N.Y.U., Fordham and other great universities. Use them independently or with any other book or record course. They provide a supplementary living element that most other courses lack. Individual volumes in:

Russian 75¢	Italian 75¢	Spanish 75¢	German 75¢
Hebrew 75¢	Danish 75¢	Japanese 75¢	Swedish 75¢
Dutch 75¢	Esperanto 75¢	Modern Greek 75¢	Portuguese 75¢
Norwegian 75¢	Polish 75¢	French 75¢	Yiddish 75¢
Turkish 75¢		English for German-speaking people 75¢	
English for Italian-speaking people 75¢		English for Spanish-speaking people 75¢	

Large clear type. 128-196 pages each. 3½ x 5¼. Sturdy paper binding.

Listen and Learn language records

LISTEN & LEARN is the only language record course designed especially to meet your travel and everyday needs. It is available in separate sets for FRENCH, SPANISH, GERMAN, JAPANESE, RUSSIAN, MODERN GREEK, PORTUGUESE, ITALIAN and HEBREW, and each set contains three 33⅓ rpm long-playing records—1½ hours of recorded speech by eminent native speakers who are professors at Columbia, New York University, Queens College.

Check the following special features found only in LISTEN & LEARN:

- **Dual-language recording. 812 selected phrases and sentences, over 3200 words,** spoken first in English, then in their foreign language equivalents. A suitable pause follows each foreign phrase, allowing you time to repeat the expression. You learn by unconscious assimilation.

- **128 to 206-page manual** contains everything on the records, plus a simple phonetic pronunciation guide.

- **Indexed for convenience. The only set on the market** that is completely indexed. No more puzzling over where to find the phrase you need. Just look in the rear of the manual.

- **Practical.** No time wasted on material you can find in any grammar. LISTEN & LEARN covers central core material with phrase approach. Ideal for the person with limited learning time.

- **Living, modern expressions,** not found in other courses. Hygienic products, modern equipment, shopping—expressions used every day, like "nylon" and "air-conditioned."

- **Limited objective.** Everything you learn, no matter where you stop, is immediately useful. You have to finish other courses, wade through grammar and vocabulary drill, before they help you.

- **High-fidelity recording.** LISTEN & LEARN records equal in clarity and surface-silence any record on the market costing up to $6.

"Excellent . . . the spoken records . . . impress me as being among the very best on the market," **Prof. Mario Pei,** Dept. of Romance Languages, Columbia University. "Inexpensive and well-done . . . it would make an ideal present," CHICAGO SUNDAY TRIBUNE. "More genuinely helpful than anything of its kind which I have previously encountered," **Sidney Clark,** well-known author of "ALL THE BEST" travel books.

UNCONDITIONAL GUARANTEE. Try LISTEN & LEARN, then return it within 10 days for full refund if you are not satisfied.

Each set contains three twelve-inch 33⅓ records, manual, and album.

SPANISH	the set $5.95	GERMAN	the set $5.95
FRENCH	the set $5.95	ITALIAN	the set $5.95
RUSSIAN	the set $5.95	JAPANESE	the set $5.95
PORTUGUESE	the set $5.95	MODERN GREEK	the set $5.95
MODERN HEBREW	the set $5.95		

Trubner Colloquial Manuals

These unusual books are members of the famous Trubner series of colloquial manuals. They have been written to provide adults with a sound colloquial knowledge of a foreign language, and are suited for either class use or self-study. Each book is a complete course in itself, with progressive, easy to follow lessons. Phonetics, grammar, and syntax are covered, while hundreds of phrases and idioms, reading texts, exercises, and vocabulary are included. These books are unusual in being neither skimpy nor overdetailed in grammatical matters, and in presenting up-to-date, colloquial, and practical phrase material. Bilingual presentation is stressed, to make thorough self-study easier for the reader.

COLLOQUIAL HINDUSTANI, A. H. Harley, formerly Nizam's Reader in Urdu, U. of London. 30 pages on phonetics and scripts (devanagari & Arabic-Persian) are followed by 29 lessons, including material on English and Arabic-Persian influences. Key to all exercises. Vocabulary. 5 x 7½. 147pp. **Clothbound $1.75**

COLLOQUIAL PERSIAN, L. P. Elwell-Sutton. Best introduction to modern Persian, with 90 page grammatical section followed by conversations, 35-page vocabulary. 139pp. **Clothbound $1.75**

COLLOQUIAL ARABIC, DeLacy O'Leary. Foremost Islamic scholar covers language of Egypt, Syria, Palestine, & Northern Arabia. Extremely clear coverage of complex Arabic verbs & noun plurals; also cultural aspects of language. Vocabulary. xviii + 192pp. 5 x 7½. **Clothbound $2.50**

COLLOQUIAL GERMAN, P. F. Doring. Intensive thorough coverage of grammar in easily-followed form. Excellent for brush-up, with hundreds of colloquial phrases. 34 pages of bilingual texts. 224pp. 5 x 7½. **Clothbound $1.75**

COLLOQUIAL SPANISH, W. R. Patterson. Castilian grammar and colloquial language, loaded with bilingual phrases and colloquialisms. Excellent for review or self-study. 164pp. 5 x 7½. **Clothbound $1.75**

COLLOQUIAL FRENCH, W. R. Patterson. 16th revision of this extremely popular manual. Grammar explained with model clarity, and hundreds of useful expressions and phrases; exercises, reading texts, etc. Appendixes of new and useful words and phrases. 223pp. 5 x 7½. **Clothbound $1.75**

COLLOQUIAL CZECH, J. Schwarz, former headmaster of Lingua Institute, Prague. Full easily followed coverage of grammar, hundreds of immediately useable phrases, texts. Perhaps the best Czech grammar in print. "An absolutely successful textbook," JOURNAL OF CZECHO-SLOVAK FORCES IN GREAT BRITAIN. 252pp. 5 x 7½. **Clothbound $3.00**

COLLOQUIAL RUMANIAN, G. Nandris, Professor of University of London. Extremely thorough coverage of phonetics, grammar, syntax; also included 70-page reader, and 70-page vocabulary. Probably the best grammar for this increasingly important language. 340pp. 5 x 7½. **Clothbound $2.50**

COLLOQUIAL ITALIAN, A. L. Hayward. Excellent self-study course in grammar, vocabulary, idioms, and reading. Easy progressive lessons will give a good working knowledge of Italian in the shortest possible time. 5 x 7½. **Clothbound $1.75**

COLLOQUIAL TURKISH, Yusuf Mardin. Very clear, thorough introduction to leading cultural and economic language of Near East. Begins with pronunciation and statement of vowel harmony, then 36 lessons present grammar, graded vocabulary, useful phrases, dialogues, reading, exercises. Key to exercises at rear. Turkish-English vocabulary. All in Roman alphabet. x + 288pp. 4¾ x 7¼. **Clothbound $4.00**

DUTCH-ENGLISH AND ENGLISH-DUTCH DICTIONARY, F. G. Renier. For travel, literary, scientific or business Dutch, you will find this the most convenient, practical and comprehensive dictionary on the market. More than 60,000 entries, shades of meaning, colloquialisms, idioms, compounds and technical terms. Dutch and English strong and irregular verbs. This is the only dictionary in its size and price range that indicates the gender of nouns. New orthography. xvii + 571pp. 5½ x 6¼. **T224 Clothbound $2.75**

LEARN DUTCH, F. G. Renier. This book is the most satisfactory and most easily used grammar of modern Dutch. The student is gradually led from simple lessons in pronunciation, through translation from and into Dutch, and finally to a mastery of spoken and written Dutch. Grammatical principles are clearly explained while a useful, practical vocabulary is introduced in easy exercises and readings. It is used and recommended by the Fulbright Committee in the Netherlands. Phonetic appendices. Over 1200 exercises; Dutch-English, English-Dutch vocabularies. 181pp. 4¼ x 7¼. **T441 Clothbound $2.25**

CATALOGUE OF DOVER BOOKS

INVITATION TO GERMAN POETRY record. Spoken by Lotte Lenya. Edited by Gustave Mathieu, Guy Stern. 42 poems of Walther von der Vogelweide, Goethe, Hölderlin, Heine, Hofmannsthal, George, Werfel, Brecht, other great poets from 13th to middle of 20th century, spoken with superb artistry. Use this set to improve your diction, build vocabulary, improve aural comprehension, learn German literary history, as well as for sheer delight in listening. 165-page book contains full German text of each poem; English translations; biographical, critical information on each poet; textual information; portraits of each poet, many never before available in this country. 1 12" 33⅓ record; 165-page book; album. **The set $4.95**

ESSENTIALS OF RUSSIAN record, A von Gronicka, H. Bates-Yakobson. 50 minutes of spoken Russian based on leading grammar will improve comprehension, pronunciation, increase vocabulary painlessly. Complete aural review of phonetics, phonemics—words contrasted to highlight sound differences. Wide range of material: talk between family members, friends, sightseeing; adaptation of Tolstoy's "The Shark;" history of Academy of Sciences; proverbs, epigrams; Pushkin, Lermontov, Fet, Blok, Maikov poems. Conversation passages spoken twice, fast and slow, let you anticipate answers, hear all sounds but understand normal speed. 12" 33⅓ record, album sleeve. 44-page manual with entire record text. Translation on facing pages, phonetic instructions. **The set $4.95**

Note: For students wishing to use a grammar as well, set is available with grammar-text on which record is based, Gronicka and Bates-Yakobson's "Essentials of Russian" (400pp., 6 x 9, clothbound; Prentice Hall), an excellent, standard text used in scores of colleges, institutions. Augmented set: book, record, manual, sleeve **$10.70**

DICTIONARY OF SPOKEN RUSSIAN, English-Russian, Russian-English. Based on phrases and complete sentences, rather than isolated words; recognized as one of the best methods of learning the idiomatic speech of a country. Over 11,500 entries, indexed by single words, with more than 32,000 English and Russian sentences and phrases, in immediately useable form. Probably the largest list ever published. Shows accent changes in conjugation and declension; irregular forms listed in both alphabetical place and under main form of word. 15,000 word introduction covering Russian sounds, writing, grammar, syntax. 15-page appendix of geographical names, money, important signs, given names, foods, special Soviet terms, etc. Travellers, businessmen, students, government employees have found this their best source for Russian expressions. Originally published as War Department Technical Manual TM 30-944. iv + 573pp. 5⅝ x 8⅜. T496 Paperbound **$3.00**

THE GIFT OF LANGUAGE, M. Schlauch. Formerly titled THE GIFT OF TONGUES, this is a middle-level survey that avoids both superficiality and pedantry. It covers such topics as linguistic families, word histories, grammatical processes in such foreign languages as Aztec, Ewe, and Bantu, semantics, language taboos, and dozens of other fascinating and important topics. Especially interesting is an analysis of the word-coinings of Joyce, Cummings, Stein and others in terms of linguistics. 232 bibliographic notes. Index. viii + 342pp. 5⅜ x 8. T243 Paperbound **$1.95**

Prices subject to change without notice.

Dover publishes books on art, music, philosophy, literature, languages, history, social sciences, psychology, handcrafts, orientalia, puzzles and entertainments, chess, pets and gardens, books explaining science, intermediate and higher mathematics, mathematical physics, engineering, biological sciences, earth sciences, classics of science, etc. Write to:

Dept. catrr.
Dover Publications, Inc.
180 Varick Street, N.Y. 14, N.Y.